Lecture Notes in Computer Science 7889

Commenced Publication in 1973
Founding and Former Series Editors:
Gerhard Goos, Juris Hartmanis, and Jai

Vassilis Tsaoussidis   Andreas J. Kassler
Yevgeni Koucheryavy   Abdelhamid Mellouk (Eds.)

Wired/Wireless Internet Communication

11th International Conference, WWIC 2013
St. Petersburg, Russia, June 5-7, 2013
Proceedings

 Springer

Volume Editors

Vassilis Tsaoussidis
Democritus University of Thrace, 67100 Xanthi, Greece
E-mail: vtsaousi@ee.duth.gr

Andreas J. Kassler
Karlstad University, 651 88 Karlstad, Sweden
E-mail: andreas.kassler@kau.se

Yevgeni Koucheryavy
Tampere University of Technology, 33720 Tampere, Finland
E-mail: yk@cs.tut.fi

Abdelhamid Mellouk
University of Paris-Est Créteil VdM (UPEC) - LiSSi, 94400 Vitry-sur-Seine, France
E-mail: mellouk@u-pec.fr

ISSN 0302-9743   e-ISSN 1611-3349
ISBN 978-3-642-38400-4   e-ISBN 978-3-642-38401-1
DOI 10.1007/978-3-642-38401-1
Springer Heidelberg Dordrecht London New York

Library of Congress Control Number: 2013937753

CR Subject Classification (1998): C.2, K.6.5, H.4, D.4, D.2

LNCS Sublibrary:
SL 5 – Computer Communication Networks and Telecommunications

Typesetting: Camera-ready by author, data conversion by Scientific Publishing Services, Chennai, India

Printed on acid-free paper

Springer is part of Springer Science+Business Media (www.springer.com)

Preface

We welcome you to the proceedings of the 11th WWIC (International Conference on Wired/Wireless Internet Communications) conference held in St. Petersburg, Russia, during June 5–7, 2013. The 11th WWIC technical program addressed various aspects of next-generation wired and wireless networks. Based on interesting submissions, we selected a program covering a diverse set of topics presenting new and innovative developments. In particular, issues of MAC layer and scheduling were dealt with, as well as different aspects of mobility and security. It is also worth mentioning the emphasis on wireless networks, including, but not limited to, cellular networks, wireless local area networks, cognitive networks, and sensor networks. We wish to thank the Technical Program Committee members of both conferences and associated reviewers for their hard work and important contribution to the conference. This year the conferences were organized in cooperation with St. Petersburg State University of Telecommunications (Russia), Tampere University of Technology (Finland), the FRUCT Program, and Popov Society. The support of these organizations is gratefully acknowledged. Finally, we wish to thank many people who contributed to the organization. In particular, Olga Galinina and Roman Florea (TUT, Finland) carried a substantial load of the submission and review work, website maintaining, and did an excellent job on the compilation of camera-ready papers and interaction with Springer. We believe that the 11th WWIC conference provided an interesting and up-to-date scientific program. We hope that participants enjoyed the technical and social conference program, the Russian hospitality, and the beautiful city of St. Petersburg.

April 2013

Vassilis Tsaoussidis
Andreas Kassler
Yevgeni Koucheryavy
Abdelhamid Mellouk

Organization

General Co-chairs

Yevgeni Koucheryavy   Tampere University of Technology, Finland
Abdelhamid Mellouk   University of Paris-Est, France

TPC Chair

Andreas J. Kassler   Karlstad University, Sweden

Steering Committee

Torsten Braun   University of Bern, Switzerland
Georg Carle   TU München, Germany
Geert Heijenk   University of Twente, The Netherlands
Yevgeni Koucheryavy   Tampere University of Technology, Finland
Peter Langendörfer   IHP Microelectronics, Germany
Ibrahim Matta   Boston University, USA
Vassilis Tsaoussidis   Democritus University of Thrace, Greece

Technical Program Committee

Ozgur Akan   Koc University, Turkey
Khalid Al-Begain   University of Glamorgan, UK
Onur Altintas   Toyota InfoTechnology Center, Japan
Fernando Boavida   University of Coimbra, Portugal
Torsten Braun   University of Bern, Switzerland
Wojciech Burakowski   Warsaw University of Technology, Poland
Scott Burleigh   Jet Propulsion Laboratory, California Institute of Technology, USA
Maria Calderon   Universidad Carlos III de Madrid, Spain
Georg Carle   Technische Universität München, Germany
Paulo Carvalho   University of Minho, Portugal
Nirbhay Chaubey   Institute of Science and Technology for Advanced Studies and Research, India
Arsenia Chorti   Princeton University, USA
Stylianos Dimitriou   Democritus University of Thrace, Greece
Ognjen Dobrijevic   University of Zagreb, Croatia
Jarmo Harju   Tampere University of Technology, Finland
Sonia Heemstra de Groot   Delft Technical University, The Netherlands
Geert Heijenk   University of Twente, The Netherlands

Table of Contents

Sensor Networks

Services

Wireless

Performance Analysis
of Uplink Coordinated Multi-Point Reception
in Heterogeneous LTE Deployment

Olga Galinina[1], Alexey Anisimov[2], Sergey Andreev[1],
and Yevgeni Koucheryavy[1]

[1] Tampere University of Technology, Finland
{olga.galinina,sergey.andreev}@tut.fi, yk@cs.tut.fi
[2] Nokia Siemens Networks, MBB LTE, Russia
alexey.anisimov@nsn.com

Abstract. In this work, we study a heterogeneous 3GPP LTE network where macro base station deployment is coupled with underlay low power (pico) nodes to augment system capacity. However, at the cell edges, a macro-associated user may still suffer from poor performance due to low uplink channel quality. This is when the neighboring low power nodes can help by independently trying to receive data packets from the macro user and share the result with the base station if successful. Known as coordinated multi-point (CoMP) reception, this scheme is expected to dramatically improve uplink cell-edge performance. To predict the actual gains, we conduct our analysis of a typical CoMP setup for dynamic traffic load and depending on the user proximity to the serving base station.

1 Introduction and Background

Recent advances in wireless communications introduce fundamental changes to mobile Internet access, as well as challenge the researchers with increasingly demanding problems. As long as the proportion of mobile traffic is expected to grow [1], the currently deployed cellular technologies are very likely to face dramatic overloads resulting in shortage of available capacity and general degradation of the user service experience. Reacting to this pressing demand, the fourth generation (4G) broadband communication standard [2] offers decisive improvements to the levels of achievable spectral and energy efficiency as well as quality of service. However, user performance may still remain unsatisfactory at the cell edges, where the connection to the serving base station is weak and the transmission is further limited by interference from the neighboring cells.

Conventionally, user service uniformity has been achieved with appropriate network planning, when specific frequency reuse patterns were employed to combat the inter-cell interference. This, however, often resulted in low spatial reuse factors and poor resource utilization [3]. A more advanced solution may be to enable collaborative transmission or reception by multiple network entities. Such approach

V. Tsaoussidis et al. (Eds.): WWIC 2013, LNCS 7889, pp. 1–14, 2013.

is expected to naturally leverage the diversity gains between geographically separated points. In 3GPP Long Term Evolution (LTE) cellular technology, this technique is known as Coordinated Multi-Point (CoMP) and is believed to boost the system performance dramatically, especially at the edges of a cell.

The performance of CoMP in both uplink (UL) and downlink (DL) of conventional macro deployment has been thoroughly studied in the literature. Noteworthy, UL CoMP schemes tend to receive more research attention as they have less impact on the LTE specification [4]. Therefore, already in [5] the cell-edge benefits promised by UL CoMP have been quantified with system-level simulations. Whereas the first evaluation attempts focused on static full-buffer environments, more recent works [6], [7] employ dynamic processes and rigorously analyze the network design aspects of CoMP in terms of the required density of the serving base stations. In particular, the research in [6] suggests the use of *selection combining* CoMP scheme, when upon a reception failure the serving base station chooses the decoding outcome with the highest channel quality among the available alternative receivers of a particular data packet. Since only successful outcomes are exchanged, this approach is attractive due to moderate amounts of data transferred between the collaborating points.

Whereas much work has been dedicated to evaluating UL CoMP in the neighborhood of (macro) base stations of the same type and power class, the selection combining technique is expected to yield even higher gains across heterogeneous deployments. Heterogeneous networks are characterized by a mixture of macro base stations and low power (pico) nodes, which may generate excessive inter-cell interference. As interference coordination in such harsh environments can be complex, UL CoMP may prove to be very useful in the metropolitan areas with dense network deployment [8].

Offering a general classification of CoMP techniques, the work in [4] suggests an important use case when a macro-cell collaborates with several low power receive points within its coverage to better serve UL traffic by a macro user. By concentrating on its design principles and choices, the research in [8] also confirms that UL CoMP may render user experience more uniform in a similar heterogeneous scenario. Moreover, the outdoor measurements reported in [3] showcase the attractiveness of CoMP-based approaches while at the same time indicating several technical challenges, such as the need for high-capacity and low-latency interface (backhaul connection) between the serving points.

In particular, the performance of selection combining technique in a heterogeneous deployment has been investigated by [9] and [10] with full-buffer system-level simulations to exploit the pico-node proximity to the macro-associated users. Further, [11] considers a similar CoMP setup and takes advantage of the asymmetry between the UL and the DL with appropriate cooperation-aware power control to mitigate the near-far effect. Complementing prior simulation data, [12] reports field trial results of selection combining CoMP in dense heterogeneous networks to leverage the macro diversity gain around the cell edge.

By taking the idea of UL/DL asymmetry of CoMP further on, it is also possible to tailor the conventional handover procedures specifically to heterogeneous networks. With a suitable scheduling discipline, macro-cell traffic may be dynamically offloaded onto small cells [13] to provide seamless handover-like user experience. More broadly, handover procedure in cellular networks is an important aspect and may actually be improved by properly accounting for CoMP [14]. Last but not least, energy efficiency is becoming increasingly important for small-scale battery-powered mobile devices. Consequently, catering for the best trade-off between spectral- and energy-efficiency (such as bits-per-Joule capacity) is a crucial and timely problem [15]. The related analysis implies that UL CoMP results in higher cell-edge energy efficiency than a non-cooperative system. Finally, the practical aspects of DL CoMP design, including the impact of imperfect backhaul connections, have recently been addressed in [16].

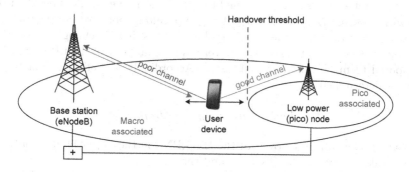

Fig. 1. Selection combining UL CoMP in a heterogeneous LTE network

Summarizing, the various aspects of the UL CoMP operation have indeed been addressed by the existing work, but the majority of the findings are disjoint due to the difference in adopted system models, assumptions, and methodologies. Furthermore, most papers evaluate CoMP performance with simulation, while analytical attempts are singular and only loosely connected with respective simulation assumptions. Therefore, we are motivated to propose a comprehensive CoMP-centric evaluation methodology by coupling both analytical and simulation components. While remaining simple, our closed-form analysis captures many important CoMP features, such as heterogeneous environment, user mobility, impact of power control and handover decisions, energy efficiency, as well as imperfect UL channel to the serving base station (see Figure 1). In particular, we evaluate the selection combining UL CoMP scheme, where the cooperating low power nodes are independently trying to receive data packets from a macro user and share their successful outcomes with the serving base station.

The rest of this text is organized as follows. Section 2 details our system model and the main assumptions. In Section 3, we introduce our analytical approach to calculate the key performance metrics, such as data packet service time (9), mean packet delay (14), packet drop probability (15), and the corresponding energy consumption (19). Section 4 contains some important numerical results, while Section 5 concludes the paper.

2 System Model

In this section, we summarize the assumptions of our system model. We consider a heterogeneous 3GPP LTE deployment consisting of one macro base station (BS) and $N - 1$ neighboring low power nodes (LPNs). The user equipment (UE) is assumed to be constantly associated with the macro BS. Technically, it measures the quality of the DL signal from the serving base station and sets its transmit power as given by e.g. [9]:

$$P_{TX} = \min\{P_{max}, P_{TX,0} + 10\log_{10} N_r + \alpha L\}, \tag{1}$$

where P_{max} is the maximum transmit power, $P_{TX,0}$ is the target receive power, N_r is the number of resources assigned to the UE, L is the pathloss between the UE and its serving BS, and $0 \le \alpha \le 1$ is the pathloss compensation factor.

It is also assumed that the user is mobile, that is, it may change its location with respect to the serving BS. Whenever approaching any of the LPNs, the UE is supposed to make a handover decision. Accordingly, the effective macro-cell border is determined as:

$$\Phi_{BS} - L_{BS} = \Phi_{LPN} - L_{LPN}, \tag{2}$$

where $\Phi_{[\cdot]}$ is the transmit power of the BS/LPN (on the logarithmic scale), $L_{[\cdot]}$ is the pathloss between the BS/LPN and the UE.

Hence, we are interested in the UE performance at the macro cell-edges and before the macro-associated user has actually made its LPN handover decision. In these areas, the user channel quality to the BS is typically poor (see Figure 1). We thus analyze the benefits of UL CoMP selection combining scheme when the UE data packets are independently received by the proximal LPNs. All the collaborating LPNs are synchronized and connected to the macro BS via a high-capacity and low-latency interface (assumed to be instantaneous and error-free without the loss of generality), so that the successful packet reception outcomes by the LPNs can be immediately shared with the BS.

Further, we consider a Single-Carrier Frequency Division Multiple Access (SC-FDMA) system with Multi-level Quadrature Amplitude Modulation (M-QAM) in the presence of Additive White Gaussian Noise (AWGN). In the UL of every subframe, a certain number of resource blocks is provided for the target user by the BS where the user may transmit its equal-size packets.

The numbers of new data packets arriving at the UE during the consecutive subframes are i.i.d. random variables. For simplicity of further analysis, we assume Poisson arrival flow. Hence, the UE generates new data packets with the average arrival rate of λ packets per slot.

We further assume that the UE is equipped with K independent (virtual) buffers according to the LTE specification [2]. Upon its arrival at the UE, a packet is being placed into one of the K buffers with the constant probability $q = 1/K$. The data packets in a particular buffer i may only be attempted for transmission (served) in every ith subframe (slot) and the transmission of every

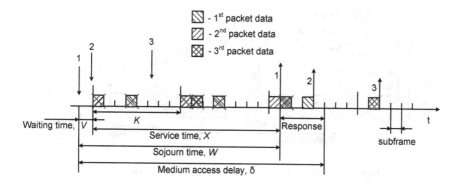

Fig. 2. Example time diagram of UL CoMP

packet takes exactly one slot (see Figure 2). All the buffers are assumed to have unlimited size.

A data packet may be received by the macro BS or an LPN with some constant probability. This probability depends on the UL Signal-to-Noise Ratio (SNR) and thus varies for different receive points. A data packet transmission is considered successful if the BS or at least one of the LPNs receives this packet. The chance of success therefore depends on the corresponding events at BS/LPNs.

Following Hybrid Automatic Repeat Request (HARQ) procedure, the BS forwards the per-packet positive (ACK) and negative (NACK) acknowledgments to the user after the fixed delay of τ subframes. In case of failure, the UE may retransmit its packet after exactly K subframes. The maximum number of allowed transmission attempts per packet equals n_{max}. If the last transmission attempt has been unsuccessful, the packet is dropped (discarded) by the user.

As we are also interested in the user energy consumption, we differentiate between the following UE power states (see Figure 3):

- Idle state. In this state, the UE's buffer is empty and the minimum power P_0 is consumed.
- Active state. The device is active and has at least one packet in any of the buffers. However, it does not transmit in the current subframe and the power P_1 is spent.
- Transmit (Tx) state. The device is transmitting its data with the power of $P_2 = P_{TX}$ as defined by (1). In this state, the maximum power $P_1 + P_2$ is consumed.

In what follows, we concentrate on the analytical modeling of the above system in order to investigate its primary performance metrics, such as packet success and drop probabilities, energy efficiency, and the expected packet delay.

3   Performance Evaluation

Given a particular BS/LPN deployment (e.g., by [17]), the system parameters of interest are primarily determined by the probability of successful data packet

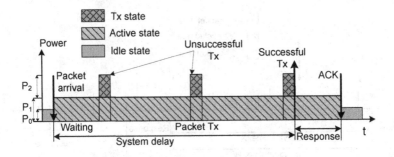

Fig. 3. Example UE power consumption diagram

transmission. With UL CoMP based on selection combining, this probability depends on respective individual probabilities to receive this data packet at the macro BS or a particular LPN. Below we detail our approach to the calculation of the sought probability basing on the UL SNR values at the receiving points.

3.1 Probability of Success

The Case of One Receiver. Consider the system with a single receiver (i.e., macro BS) of UE data. The corresponding value of Bit Error Rate (BER) can be determined from the UL SNR value, which depends on the transmit power and radio conditions at the BS. We employ the approximation from [18] for uncoded M-QAM and replace the Q-function by elementary functions, which makes our interpretation more tractable analytically.

Hence, for a particular UE-BS distance, the actual modulation order in M-QAM may vary to mimic the process of user rate adaptation. Assuming an ideal coherent phase detection in the AWGN channel n, the value of BER is well approximated by (see [18]):

$$p_n = \frac{4}{\log_2 M} Q\left(\sqrt{\frac{3\gamma_n}{M-1}}\right),$$
(3)

where γ_n is the SNR in the channel n, $Q(x) = \frac{1}{\sqrt{2\pi}} \int_x^\infty e^{-\frac{1}{2}t^2} dt = 1 - \Phi(x)$, $\Phi(x)$ is an error function which is the integral of the standard normal distribution [19].

For the sake of analytical tractability, we propose to modify the above approximation by using solely elementary functions. We note that $Q(x) = \frac{1}{2}\mathrm{erfc}\left(\frac{1}{\sqrt{2}x}\right)$, $x \geq 0$. Here, $\mathrm{erfc} = 1 - \mathrm{erf}$ is the complementary error function and erf is the error function. Further, we borrow the approximation for the error function from [20]:

$$\mathrm{erf}(x) \approx \mathrm{sgn}(x)\sqrt{1 - \exp\left(-x^2 \frac{4/\pi + ax^2}{1 + ax^2}\right)}.$$
(4)

where $a = \frac{8(\pi-3)}{3\pi(4-\pi)} \approx 0.14$.

Eliminating the unnecessary components by simple transformation, we arrive at the following:

$$\text{erf}(x) \approx \text{sgn}(x)\sqrt{1 - \exp\left(-\frac{x^2}{2}\right)}. \tag{5}$$

Finally, in Figure 4 we compare our proposed BER approximation against its alternatives from [18] (based on Q-function and other elementary functions) and intend to use it in what follows.

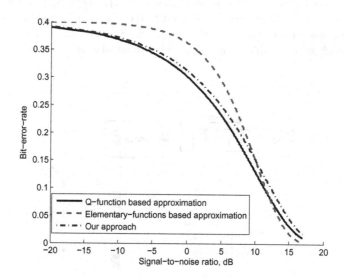

Fig. 4. Example BER approximation for 32-QAM

Therefore, the probability of successful packet reception at the BS follows as:

$$p_n = \frac{2}{\log_2(M)}\left[1 - (1 - e^{-\frac{3\gamma_n}{2(M-1)}})^{0.5}\right]. \tag{6}$$

The Case of Multiple Receivers. Consider the system with several receivers (i.e., macro BS and LPNs) of UE data. The total probability of successful reception by at least one receiving point can be easily calculated accounting for the independence of individual success events with the probabilities p_n, $n = \overline{1, N}$:

$$p = Pr\{\text{at least one receiver succeeds}\} =$$

$$= \prod_{n=1}^{N} p_n - \sum_{i=1}^{N} \prod_{n=1,n\neq i}^{N} p_n + \sum_{i=1}^{N}\sum_{j=1}^{N} \prod_{n=1,n\neq i,j}^{N} p_n + \dots - (-1)^N \sum_{i=1}^{N} p_n. \tag{7}$$

Hence, we derive an expression for the packet success probability p, agnostic to a particular BS/LPN deployment, which scales with the actual number of neighboring LPNs. We proceed further with our queuing model.

3.2 Proposed Queuing Model

We note that for the adopted system model (see Section 2), all K virtual buffers are served independently. Therefore, we decouple system operation into K independent First-Come-First-Served (FCFS) queues. The arrival process at a particular queue i is the result of splitting (thinning) the initial Poisson process. Hence, it also constitutes a Poisson process with the arrival rate of $\lambda_i = \lambda/K$.

Consequently, we formulate an M/G/1 model (see Figure 5), i.e. consider a stochastic process $N_i(t)$ on the state space $\{0, 1, 2, ...\}$, where $N_i(t)$ is the number of packets in the queue i at the end of a subframe. Arrivals happen according to a Poisson process with the arrival rate $\lambda_i = \lambda/K$. Service times are i.i.d. random variables which will be addressed below. The queue size is unbounded.

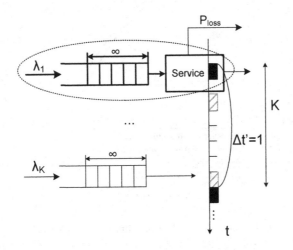

Fig. 5. Aggregated queuing system

We denote the random variable representing the packet service time as X_i, which is the time interval between the first attempt to serve this packet and the packet departure time (success or drop). Further, the total time interval between the arrival of a packet and the time its service begins is denoted as $W_i = V_i + X_i$, where V_i is the waiting time in the queue. Importantly, V_i includes (i) the time of waiting between the arrival and the moment when the queue i obtains opportunity to be served ($V_i^{(1)}$) and (ii) waiting time as long as the preceding packets in the queue i are being served ($V_i^{(2)}$).

Finally, we denote the queue load as $\rho_i = \lambda_i E[X_i]$ and assume that $\rho_i < 1$, so that the steady-state distribution exists. Below, we concentrate on the expected time $E[W_i]$ that a packet spends in our system. For the sake of simplicity, we scale our system up and aggregate K subframes into one time unit $\Delta t' = 1$ to calculate some auxiliary variables with respect to the aggregate time.

3.3   Service Time Distribution and Packet Drop Probability

The random variable representing service time X_i is distributed according to the truncated geometric distribution:

$$\Pr\{X_i = 1\} = p,$$

$$\Pr\{X_i = 2\} = p(1-p), ...,$$

$$\Pr\{X_i = n_{\max}\} = p(1-p)^{n_{\max}-1} + (1-p)^{n_{\max}},$$

where p is the (integral) probability of successful packet transmission, i.e. when at least one receiver acquires the packet, see (7). We note that here we have already taken into account the effect of time aggregation.

The expected service time is defined as:

$$E[X_i] = \sum_{i=1}^{\infty} i \Pr\{X = i\} = \sum_{i=1}^{n_{max}} i p(1-p)^{i-1} + n_{\max}(1-p)^{n_{\max}}.$$

Therefore, the expectation $E[X_i]$ may readily be calculated as:

$$E[X_i] = \frac{1}{p}\left[1 - (1-p)^{n_{\max}}(n_{\max}p + 1)\right] + n_{\max}(1-p)^{n_{\max}}. \tag{8}$$

Due to the fact that the queues are identical and independent, the expected service time $E[X] = E[X_i] + \tau$ can also be derived in terms of the original system time as:

$$E[X] = \frac{K}{p}\left[1 - (1-p)^{n_{\max}}(n_{\max}p + 1) + n_{\max}(1-p)^{n_{\max}}\right] - (K-1) + \tau, \tag{9}$$

where τ is the additional time of waiting for the BS response.

For our further calculations, we need to obtain the respective coefficient of variation, which is defined as the ratio between the standard deviation and the mean. Substituting expressions (8) and (11), we derive the sought formula as:

$$c_i = \frac{\sqrt{D[X_i]}}{E[X_i]} = \frac{\sqrt{E[X_i^2] - (E[X_i^2])^2}}{E[X_i]}, \tag{10}$$

where $E[X_i^2]$ is the second moment of the random variable X_i calculated as:

$$E[X_i^2] = \sum_{i=1}^{\infty} i^2 \Pr\{X = i\} = \sum_{i=1}^{n_{max}} i^2 p(1-p)^{i-1} + n_{\max}^2(1-p)^{n_{\max}}.$$

By the same calculations as above, it can be easily established that:

$$E[X_i^2] = \frac{1}{p}\left[1 - (1-p)^{n_{\max}}(n_{\max}p + 1)\right] + n_{\max}^2(1-p)^{n_{\max}}. \tag{11}$$

3.4   System Delay

The packet delay component of while the preceding packets in a particular queue i are being served (that is, waiting time in our M/G/1 system) can be given by the Pollaczek-Khinchine formula [21] as follows:

$$V_i^{(2)} = \frac{\rho_i E[X_i]\left(1 + c_i^2\right)}{2(1 - \rho_i)},\tag{12}$$

where c_i and $E[X_i]$ are given above, and $\rho_i = \lambda_i E[X_i]$ is the load of the queue i.

When a packet arrives, it can join the queue which is the next one to be served (with the probability q), as well as any other queue uniformly. Hence, the period of waiting between the arrival and the moment when the queue i obtains opportunity to be served is:

$$V_i^{(1)} = q\left((K - 1) + (K - 2) + ... + (0)\right) = \frac{K(K - 1)}{2K} = \frac{K - 1}{2}.\tag{13}$$

Then, the total data packet delay δ in terms of the original system time may be given as the sum of the sojourn time W and the feedback time τ:

$$\delta = E[W_i] + \tau = E[V_i^{(1)}] + E[V_i^{(1)}] + E[X_i] + \tau =$$

$$= \frac{K - 1}{2} + \frac{\rho E[X_i]\left(1 + c_i^2\right)}{2(1 - \rho)} + KE[X_i] - (K - 1) + \tau,\tag{14}$$

where $E[X_i]$ and c_i are given by expressions (9) and (10) respectively, while $\rho = K\lambda_i E[X_i] = \lambda E[X_i]$ is the system load and $E[X_i]$ is given by (8).

From the distribution of the service time, we derive the packet drop probability as the probability that a packet exhausts the maximum number of transmission attempts and would be discarded by the user:

$$P_{loss} = \Pr\{\text{packet is dropped} \mid \text{packet has been attempted}\} = (1 - p)^{n_{max}}.\tag{15}$$

3.5   User Energy Efficiency

The user energy consumption per subframe may be established as the sum of the fractions of time spent in every UE power state weighted by the actual power consumption in the respective state. We note that with respect to the original system time, the proportion of time that the UE spends in the transmit state exactly equals the system load [21]:

$$q_2 = \lambda E[X_i].\tag{16}$$

Some additional energy expenditures come from the fact that the UE has to wait for the BS response/feedback for τ subframes after its successful transmission. We note that if the system is empty, that is, all the queues have no packets at the same subframe, then the UE would spend the idle power. However, due to the period τ of waiting after the successful transmission, the UE has to change its idle power level to active. The expected number of subframes per packet, when the UE thus spends P_1 instead of P_0 may be obtained as:

$$E[\tau_0] = \sum_{i=1}^{\tau-1} i p_0^i (1 - p_0) + \tau p_0^\tau = \left[\frac{p_0}{1 - p_0} \left(1 - \tau p_0^{\tau-1} + \tau p_0^\tau - p_0^\tau \right) + \tau p_0^\tau \right],$$

where $p_0 = (1 - \rho_i)^K$ is the probability that all the queues are empty at the same time and the individual queue load is given by:

$$\rho_i = \rho \left[1 - \lambda_i a \left(\frac{a(1 - (K-2)a^{K-3} + (K-3)a^{K-2})}{1-a} + (K-1)a^{K-1} - 1 \right) \right], \quad (17)$$

where $a = e^{-\lambda_i}$. Hence, the proportion of the idle subframes, which have switched to the active subframes, can be calculated as:

$$q_{0 \to 1} = \lambda \left[\frac{p_0}{1 - p_0} \left(1 - \tau p_0^{\tau-1} + \tau p_0^\tau - p_0^\tau \right) + \tau p_0^\tau \right]. \quad (18)$$

Further, we evaluate the remaining time fractions that the user spends in other states:

$$q_0 = p_0 - \lambda \left[\frac{p_0}{1 - p_0} \left(1 - \tau p_0^{\tau-1} + \tau p_0^\tau - p_0^\tau \right) + \tau p_0^\tau \right],$$

where p_0 is the probability that all the queues are empty. Obviously,

$$q_1 = 1 - \left[(1 - \rho_i)^K + \rho \right] + \lambda \left[\frac{p_0}{1 - p_0} \left(1 - \tau p_0^{\tau-1} + \tau p_0^\tau - p_0^\tau \right) + \tau p_0^\tau \right].$$

Accounting for the parameters q_0, q_1, q_2, we may obtain the exact value of the mean user energy expenditure as:

$$\epsilon = P_0 q_0 + P_1 q_1 + (P_2 + P_1) q_2 =$$

$$= P_0 p_0 + P_1 [1 - p_0 - \rho] + (P_2 + P_1) \lambda E[X_i] + (P_1 - P_0) q_{0 \to 1}, \quad (19)$$

where $p_0 = (1 - \rho_i)^K$, and $q_{0 \to 1}$ and $E[X_i]$ are given by expressions (18) and (8) respectively. Finally, the mean user energy efficiency, which is defined as the effective stable arrival rate λ normalized by the corresponding energy consumption ϵ, follows from:

$$\phi = \frac{\lambda}{\epsilon}. \quad (20)$$

4   Numerical Results

In this section, we validate our analytical model with some simulation results. As the baseline case, we consider one LPN and a single UE moving between the macro BS and this LPN (see Figure 1). Note that the proposed approach can technically be applied to an arbitrary LPN deployment, as only the packet success probability is affected. Table 1 summarizes the main system parameters.

In Figure 6, energy efficiency as a function of the distance between the macro BS and the LPN is given. The UE cell-edge mobility is limited by the handover

Table 1. Primary system parameters

Notation	Parameter description	Value
–	Inter-cell distance	500 m [9]
Δt	Subframe size	1 ms
λ	Mean arrival rate of packets at the UE	0.5
N	Number of CoMP points per cell	2
$P_{\max}$	Maximum UE transmit power	23 dBm
$P_{Tx,0}$	Target transmit power	-82 dBm [9]
α	Pathloss compensation factor	0.8 [9]
Φ_{BS}	Macro BS transmit power	46 dBm [9]
Φ_{LPN}	LPN transmit power	30 dBm [9]
P_1	UE active power	100 mW
P_0	UE idle power	10 mW
K	Number of buffers at the UE	8
τ	BS response/feedback time	4 ms
$n_{\max}$	Max. number of packet transmissions	4
D	Distance between macro BS and LPN	250 m
N_0	Thermal noise power	-103 dB

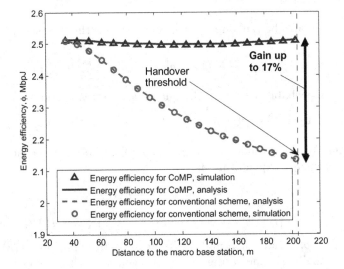

Fig. 6. User energy efficiency w.r.t. the distance between macro BS and LPN

threshold as defined in Section 2. Two alternatives are compared for the user in the UL: (i) its transmission to the serving macro BS exclusively (red curves) and (ii) improved macro given by CoMP selection combining scheme (blue curves). As expected, UL CoMP demonstrates consistent energy gains, which increase as long as the UE is moving toward the cell-edge. Hence, we conclude that already with one LPN the system may recover up to 17% of user energy efficiency.

We also investigate the behavior of user data packet delay. Figure 7 demonstrates the mean UE delay again depending on the distance between the macro BS and the LPN. Clearly, the use of UL CoMP enables significant delay reductions which become more pronounced at the edge of the cell. This is due to the improved values of packet success probability.

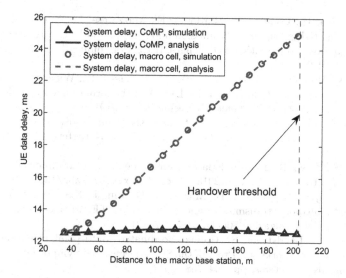

Fig. 7. User data packet delay w.r.t. the distance between macro BS and LPN

5   Conclusion

In this paper, we consider a heterogeneous 3GPP LTE deployment where neighboring LPNs may assist the macro-associated UE by independently receiving its UL data packets and forwarding the successful outcomes to the serving BS. Such CoMP scheme is known as selection combining and is believed to considerably improve user cell-edge performance. With our evaluation methodology, we combine analysis and simulations to account for the UE mobility, power control, and dynamic traffic load. We confirm that the expected energy efficiency and packet delay gains remain significant and consistent even for the low number of available LPNs.

Acknowledgments. This work is supported by Graduate School in Electronics, Telecommunications and Automation (GETA) as well as Internet of Things program of Tivit, funded by Tekes.

References

1. Cisco. Cisco Visual Networking Index: Global Mobile Data Traffic Forecast Update, 2011-2016 (February 2012)
2. 3GPP LTE Release 10 & beyond (LTE-Advanced)
3. Irmer, R., Droste, H., Marsch, P., Grieger, M., Fettweis, G., Brueck, S., Mayer, H.-P., Thiele, L., Jungnickel, V.: Coordinated multipoint: Concepts, performance, and field trial results. IEEE Communications Magazine 49(2), 102–111 (2011)

4. Lee, D., Seo, H., Clerckx, B., Hardouin, E., Mazzarese, D., Nagata, S., Sayana, K.: Coordinated multipoint transmission and reception in LTE-Advanced: Deployment scenarios and operational challenges. IEEE Communications Magazine 50(2), 148–155 (2012)

5. Zheng, N., Boussif, M., Rosa, C., Kovacs, I., Pedersen, K., Wigard, J., Mogensen, P.: Uplink coordinated multi-point for LTE-A in the form of macro-scopic combining. In: Proc. of the IEEE Vehicular Technology (2010)

6. Choi, K., Kim, D.: Outage probability analysis of macro-diversity combining in Poisson field of access points. IEEE Communications Letters 16(8), 1208–1211 (2012)

7. Banani, S., Adve, R.: Required Base Station Density in Coordinated Multi-Point Uplink with Rate Constraints (2013), http://arxiv.org/abs/1302.1592

8. Lee, J., Kim, Y., Lee, H., Ng, B., Mazzarese, D., Liu, J., Xiao, W., Zhou, Y.: Coordinated multipoint transmission and reception in LTE-Advanced systems. IEEE Communications Magazine 50(11), 44–50 (2012)

9. Falconetti, L., Landstrom, S.: Uplink coordinated multi-point reception in LTE heterogeneous networks. In: Proc. of the 8th International Symposium on Wireless Communication Systems, pp. 764–768 (2011)

10. Huiyu, Y., Naizheng, Z., Yuyu, Y., Skov, P.: Performance evaluation of coordinated multipoint reception in CRAN under LTE-Advanced uplink. In: Proc. of the 7th International ICST Conference on Communications and Networking in China, pp. 778–783 (2012)

11. Zhang, J., Soldati, P., Liang, Y., Zhang, L., Chen, K.: Pathloss determination of uplink power control for UL CoMP in heterogeneous network. In: Proc. of the International Workshop on Cloud Base-Station and Large-Scale Cooperative Communications, pp. 250–254 (2012)

12. Simonsson, A., Andersson, T.: LTE uplink CoMP trial in a HetNet deployment. In: Proc. of the IEEE Vehicular Technology Conference (2012)

13. Mazzarese, D., Zhou, Y., Ren, X., Sun, J., Xia, L., Zhang, J.: An efficient feedback and scheduling scheme for cooperative multiple-point transmission in heterogeneous networks. In: Proc. of the 23rd Annual IEEE International Symposium on Personal, Indoor and Mobile Radio Communications, pp. 112–117 (2012)

14. Lin, C.-C., Sandrasegaran, K., Zhu, X., Xu, Z.: Limited CoMP handover algorithm for LTE-Advanced. Journal of Engineering 2013, 1–9 (2013)

15. Onireti, O., Heliot, F., Imran, M.: On the energy efficiency-spectral efficiency trade-off in the uplink of CoMP system. IEEE Transactions on Wireless Communications 11(2), 556–561 (2012)

16. Yang, C., Han, S., Hou, X., Molisch, A.: How do we design CoMP to achieve its promised potential? IEEE Wireless Communications 20(1), 67–74 (2013)

17. 3GPP TR 36.819. Coordinated multi-point operation for LTE physical layer aspects (Release 11) (December 2011)

18. Goldsmith, A.: Wireless Communications. Cambridge University Press (2005)

19. Feller, W.: An introduction to probability theory and its applications, vol. 1. Wiley, New York (1968)

20. Winitzki, S.: A handy approximation for the error function and its inverse (2008)

21. Kleinrock, L.: Queueing Systems, vol. 1. Wiley Interscience, New York (1975)

Additive-Increase Multiplicative-Decrease MAC Protocol with Multi-Packet Reception

Ke Li[1], Majid Ghanbarinejad[2], Ioanis Nikolaidis[1], and Christian.Schlegel[3]

[1] Department of Computing Science, University of Alberta,
Edmonton, Alberta, Canada, T6G 2R3
{kli4,nikolaidis}@ualberta.ca

[2] Department of Electrical and Computer Engineering, University of Alberta,
Edmonton, Alberta, Canada, T6G 2R3
madjid@ualberta.ca

[3] Department of Electrical and Computer Engineering, Dalhousie University,
Halifax, Nova Scotia, Canada, B3H 4R2
christian.schlegel@dal.ca

Abstract. A distributed medium-access control (MAC) protocol for the time-slotted channel with multi-packet reception (MPR) capability is proposed. In contrast to the commonly assumed collision channel, in the MPR channel with channel capacity K, it is possible to decode up to K packets whose transmissions overlap in time. In order to exploit the MPR capability, the additive-increase multiplicative-decrease MAC (AIMD-MAC) protocol is designed to adaptively adjust the access probabilities of the independent nodes based on their local transmission histories. The examined performance metrics for evaluating this protocol include aggregate throughput, average packet delay and system fairness. Extensive simulations show that the performance of AIMD-MAC is superior to that of S-Aloha* under light traffic loads and achieves the optimum level after the system is saturated. With a suitable parameter set, AIMD-MAC can be adequately applied in a dynamic wireless environment.

Keywords: Medium-access control (MAC), multi-packet reception (MPR), additive-increase multiplicative-decrease (AIMD), congestion control.

1 Introduction

Ad hoc networks have become increasingly important in wireless communications. The self-organized network can be used in conference, disaster recovery, surveillance and distributed computing to connect wireless devices such as laptops, smart phones or application-oriented wireless sensors. One of the main characteristics of ad hoc networks is infrastructure-less which makes distributed algorithms for routing, scheduling and medium access particularly interesting.

In wireless systems, the primary channel model applied nowadays for medium-access control (MAC) protocol designs is the *collision* channel model. A well known example is IEEE 802.11 [20], based on which many modified protocols

V. Tsaoussidis et al. (Eds.): WWIC 2013, LNCS 7889, pp. 15–28, 2013.

were proposed either to improve the performance or to fulfill different application requirements [10, 15, 22, 24]. In collision channels, a packet can be considered received successfully only if no other transmission occurs in the same slot. However, this principle does not hold with sophisticated signal processing techniques, such as code-division multiple-access (CDMA), multiple-antenna arrays and space-time coding, which make it possible to process more than one packet simultaneously [19].

The capability to decode several packets concurrently is known as the multi-packet reception (MPR) capability. We apply the K-MPR model to describe a wireless channel in which the advanced receiver can decode up to K signals simultaneously. If the number of current transmissions exceeds K, which is called an interference outage, all packets will be destroyed. This K-MPR model has been widely applied in protocol designs and theoretical analyses [3, 6, 8, 23].

This paper is organized as follows. Section 2 reviews the related literature. Section 3 presents the system model of the communication network. In Section 4, we propose the AIMD-MAC protocol. The simulation examples are presented in Section 5, where the throughput and the delay performances of AIMD-MAC are compared to that of S-Aloha* and the fairness index is measured by a max-min criterion. Section 6 contains the conclusion.

2   Related Work

Slotted Aloha (S-Aloha) applies a "free-for-all" strategy and is unstable for the K-MPR channel for any finite K [7]. The instability of S-Aloha is caused by uncontrolled transmission attempts which can be organized by adjusting the access probability (ACP) for the packet ready to transmit. If the optimum ACP for achieving the maximum aggregate throughput is known *a priori* and applied by all accessing nodes, the access scheme is denoted by *S-Aloha**.

Ghez *et al.* [7] introduced the MPR matrix to describe MPR channels where the probability of a successful signal decoding is determined by the number of concurrent transmissions. This matrix model has been used in [3, 18, 21, 25] to design MAC protocols taking into account MPR. Chan *et al.* [3] proposed a cross-layer designed CSMA for the K-MPR channel model, assuming that a node can precisely estimate the number of simultaneous transmissions by sensing the energy of the carrier. In a more recent work by Ghanbarinejad *et al.* [6], an announcement channel is applied to exchange transmission information between users, based on which users can estimate future transmission attempts in the neighborhood. Multiqueue service room (MQSR) by Zhao *et al.* [25] is a centralized protocol in which a central station grants channel accesses to a set of users to maximize the throughput while satisfying the delay requirements of the nodes. Celik *et al.* [2] proposed the generic distributed probabilistic (GDP) protocol where nodes are divided into two categories: after success (AS) and after failure (AF). Each category applies a different transmission probability (p_{as} or p_{af}) to achieve the maximum overall throughput. GDP was designed for the system with saturated nodes and did not provide a method to find p_{as} or p_{af} in different scenarios.

The widely studied additive-increase multiplicative-decrease (AIMD) algorithm is a feedback control algorithm which is used in the transport layer (TCP) for congestion avoidance [13]. The seminal work by Chui and Jain [4] shows that the AIMD algorithm is able to converge to an efficient and fair state disregarding the initial window size (or access rate). AIMD has attracted enormous research attention and has been considered for MAC in recent research. Heusse *et al.* [9] adopted AIMD approach and counted the number of successive idle slots between two transmission attempts to adjust the size of the contention window (CW). Hu *et al.* [12] applied a similar approach and proposed MAC contention control (MCC). Instead of adjusting the size of CW, MCC monitors the number of successive collisions or idle slots to update the packet dequeueing rate, following the AIMD strategy. These methods require that all the users are in the sensing range of each other to decide if the channel is idle; otherwise RTS/CTS-like control messages are needed to coordinate the users.

Despite recent interest in MAC with MPR capability, little research has considered applying the AIMD algorithm to tackle this problem. Centralized protocols can achieve higher throughput than S-Aloha* (*e.g.*, [25]), however, fully distributed schemes are needed for ad hoc networks. [3, 6] require nodes to obtain state information of its neighborhood, either by sensing the carrier or using an announcement channel to communicate. [2] proposed a distributed approach but did not provide a method to find the desired transmission rates. We propose the AIMD-MAC protocol for K-MPR channels to achieve the same performance as S-Aloha*. The main properties of AIMD-MAC include: 1) It is a distributed protocol and a node does not need to know the status of its neighbors; 2) It can be applied in dynamic systems where the number of users and channel capacity are not constant; 3) We propose a threshold-free approach to perform the AIMD algorithm, which is controlled by the *success ratio* and the *utilization ratio*; 4) AIMD-MAC is superior to S-Aloha* in non-saturated state and achieves the optimum performance after the system is saturated.

3   System Model

The system model (Fig.1) consists of two components, the independent nodes and the shared channel. For our analysis we assume the view point of a single receiver within the range of M independent nodes.

We consider a buffered S-Aloha system where M independent nodes access the common channel. Data is transmitted in packets of equal (unit) size. The slot time is defined as the transmission time for a single packet. Each node is equipped with an unlimited queue to store backlog packets. Nodes apply the FCFS queueing service discipline. The packet at the head of the queue is transmitted in the next slot, t, with probability $p_m(t)$. A failed (collided) packet remains at the head of the queue until it is successfully transmitted. We assume that a 1-bit feedback from the receiver is immediately available at the end of each transmission. This feedback model has been used frequently in literature [3, 5, 16, 17].

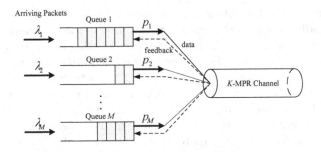

Fig. 1. System Model

4 The Additive-Increase Multiplicative-Decrease MAC (AIMD-MAC) protocol for K-MPR Channel

The AIMD-MAC protocol is a distributed algorithm designed for independent nodes accessing the common K-MPR channel. To demonstrate AIMD-MAC's performance, we compare it against the benchmark, S-Aloha*.

4.1 S-Aloha*

Let us categorize the communication networks into two classes: *specified* and *unspecified* systems. A network system that fulfills the following three requirements is a *specified* system: 1) The number of nodes M is constant and known *a priori*; 2) Nodes are always active (a node with a packet ready to transmit is an active node); 3) The channel capacity K is also constant and known beforehand. If the system fails to satisfy any of the three requirements, then we call it an *unspecified* system. For a *specified* system where $p_m(t) = p$, for all m and t, Ghanbarinejad *et al.* [6] presented Eq. 1 to compute the expected aggregate throughput

$$R(p, M, K) = \sum_{n=1}^{K} n \binom{M}{n} p^n (1 - p)^{M-n} \tag{1}$$

and defined the optimum access probability as

$$p^* = \underset{0 \le p \le 1}{\arg \max}\, R(p, M, K). \tag{2}$$

Hence, the optimum aggregate throughput can be expressed as

$$R^* = R(p^*, M, K). \tag{3}$$

In S-Aloha*, every node applies p^* for packet transmissions. $[0, R^*]$ is the *stability region* (Fig.2) of S-Aloha* because, as long as the aggregate load is limited to the bound ($\lambda \le R^*$), the queue growth is bounded. Fig.2 shows the aggregate

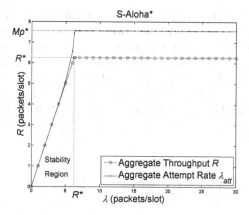

Fig. 2. Simulation Results of the Aggregate Throughput of S-Aloha* where $M = 30$, $K = 10$, $p^* = 0.25$ and $R^* = 6.3$

throughput in a scenario with $M = 30$, $K = 10$ and a Poisson arrival process with aggregate mean arrival rate λ. In this case, it can be computed numerically that $p^* = 0.25$ and $R^* = 6.3$. With S-Aloha*, $R = \lambda$ within the stability region ($\lambda \in [0, R^*]$) and $R = R^*$ beyond the stability region ($\lambda > R^*$). Because of transmission collisions, the aggregate attempt rate λ_{att} is slightly greater than R and is equal to Mp^* after the system is saturated since there are M active users transmit with the ACP equal to p^*.

However, S-Aloha* can only be applied in a *specified* system since it requires p^* before the node enters the network. After a new node enters the system, all nodes which are already in the system have to update their ACPs with a new p^* because the number of accessing nodes M is changed. If any node fails to invoke the updating, the system will crash since the aggregate demand exceeds the channel capacity. If any node leaves the system, such updating failure will result in a waste of channel resources. Furthermore, there is no closed formula to compute p^* even in a *specified* system. Collectively, it is more interesting if we can design a protocol to achieve the same performance as S-Aloha* and nodes can adaptively adjust their ACPs in a constantly changing wireless network.

4.2 The AIMD-MAC Protocol

The AIMD-MAC protocol consists of two steps: updating the transmission history and adjusting the ACP. The basic idea is that, without the knowledge of the number of active nodes and the channel capacity, each node collects its local transmission history as reference to estimate the most recent channel quality ("collision level"). Based on the collected information, each single node can independently and dynamically set a suitable ACP such that the number of concurrent transmissions approaches but does not exceed the channel capacity.

As this is a probabilistic approach, it is important to gather enough of the recent transmission histories before updating ACP values. Hence, instead of updating ACP at every slot, the AIMD-MAC protocol performs these two steps periodically. The updating period is specified by a preset parameter *updating window* (UW), denoted by τ, (Fig.3). The AIMD-MAC algorithm is performed at the first slot of every UW, starting from the time when a node enters the system. The UW should be long enough to collect sufficient information for determining the new ACP but not too long, because it can negatively impact the latency.

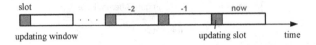

Fig. 3. The Updating Window

In this subsection we describe the operation of a single node and to enhance clarity, we have dropped the subscript m identifying the node. The transmission history records the most recent local transmission information and consists of two components, the *success ratio* s (Eq. 4) and the *utilization ratio* u (Eq. 5). n_{suc} is the number of successful transmissions and n_{att} is the number of attempted transmissions. i ($i = -1, -2$) is the index for the UW relative to the current UW (Fig.3). Because the ACP is constant during one UW, we use the superscript (*e.g.*, $p^{(i)}$) to denote parameters for different UWs.

$$s^{(i)} = \begin{cases} \frac{n_{suc}^{(i)}}{n_{att}^{(i)}}, & n_{att}^{(i)} \neq 0 \\ -1, & n_{att}^{(i)} = 0 \end{cases} \qquad (4)$$

$$u^{(i)} = \min(\frac{n_{att}^{(i)}}{p^{(i)}\tau}, 1.0) \qquad (5)$$

4.2.1   Success Ratio (s)

s is the proportion of successful transmissions for one UW and characterizes the recent channel conditions, hence, it is natural to consider s as the index of the channel quality and adjust ACPs accordingly.

Chiu and Jain's seminal work [4] explains that the AIMD algorithm converges to efficiency in the setting where the central station monitors the system and sends a unique command to users to inform them whether they should increase or decrease their transmission rates. The users need to accurately follow the instruction otherwise the system efficiency will be impaired. In AIMD-MAC, since central control does not exist and nodes adjust the ACPs according to independent channel estimates, it is important that all nodes achieve an agreement on the channel quality so that when the channel is overloaded (under loaded) all the nodes will decrease (increase) their ACPs. However, it is not trivial to find a unique success ratio threshold for the nodes to make such a decision.

Because the transmissions are random events controlled by the ACP and the queue occupancy, each node has a slightly different value of s even for the same UW. If a uniform threshold of success ratio is applied, the comparison of s and the threshold will produce different results at different nodes, which implies that some nodes will increase the ACPs while others will decrease them regardless of the channel state. This inconsistency will negatively affect the efficiency. We propose a threshold-free method to avoid this biased channel estimation.

Although a general threshold for s does not exist, there exists a certain level of consistency to how the relation of two successive success ratios (essentially, the slope of the success ratio $vs.$ UW "function") reveals the shared channel condition. An improved channel condition results in an increase in success ratios for all nodes ($s_m^{(i)} < s_m^{(i+1)}, \forall m$), while a compromised channel condition leads to a decrease in all success ratios ($s_m^{(i)} > s_m^{(i+1)}, \forall m$). This observation inspired the idea to compare $s^{(-1)}$ and $s^{(-2)}$ (*i.e.*, the two most recent success ratios as in Fig.3) at each single node to determine the channel condition trend so that nodes will perform uniform ACP adjustments. The following three rules explain the new approach:

Case I: Increase ACP: if $s^{(-2)} < s^{(-1)}$ ($s^{(-1)} \neq -1$), the channel quality improved from (-2)–th to (-1)–th UW;

Case II: Decrease ACP: if $s^{(-2)} > s^{(-1)}$ ($s^{(-1)} \neq -1$), the channel quality decreased from (-2)–th to (-1)–th UW;

Case III: Maintain ACP: if $s^{(-1)} = -1$, the channel condition is unknown.

This is a novel approach to get a relatively consistent ACP adjustments for all nodes without the need of the central control [4] or the optimum level (threshold) [9, 12].

4.2.2 Utilization Ratio (u)

While the employment of success ratio makes AIMD-MAC converge to efficiency, utilization ratio is applied to further reduce collisions when the system is not saturated.

With light traffic loads, it is possible that a node applies an ACP greater than necessary because nodes keep increasing the ACP when the channel condition is good disregarding the arrival rate. Formally, it can be expressed as $p^{(i)}\tau > n_{att}^{(i)}$ which means that the number of designed transmission slots is greater than the number of attempted slots. When the nodes with unnecessary large ACP has an abrupt increase in the traffic load (*e.g.*, bursty traffic), the channel will not be able to accommodate the sudden increase of traffic and will be jammed. This collision will be resolved by ACP adjustments eventually but it will increase the average packet delay. The average packet delay could be an order of magnitude larger if the unnecessary high ACP is not taken care of.

A simple method to solve this problem is to add one more condition for a node to increase the ACP: a node can only increase the ACP in Case I when the utilization ratio is equal to one ($u = 1$). u is the ratio between the number of attempted slots and designed slots (Eq. 5). When $u = 1$ it means that the node has used up the designed transmission slots and will not dramatically increase the traffic even with bursty traffic.

4.2.3 AIMD

The combined information from s and u enables the node to dynamically adjust the ACP to approach the optimum performance for an *unspecified* system. Fig.4 presents the pseudo code description of the AIMD-MAC protocol. This protocol is configured by three parameters including the UW (τ), the increase term (α) (also the minimum ACP applied by any node in the system) and the decrease factor (β). Lines 1-4 update the transmission history and lines 5-12 adjust the ACP periodically.

```
AIMD-MAC  (τ, α, β)
1    s^(-2) ← s^(-1)
2    u^(-2) ← u^(-1)
3    s^(-1) ← (n_att^(-1) ≠ 0? n_suc^(-1)/n_att^(-1) : -1)
4    u^(-1) ← MIN(n_att^(-1)/(p^(-1)τ), 1)
5    if s^(-1) = 0 then
6           p ← MAX(p^(-1) × 0.5, α)
7    elseif s^(-1) > 0 then
8           if s^(-1) ≥ s^(-2) then
9                  if u^(-1) = 1 then
10                        p ← MIN(p^(-1) + α, 1.0)
11          else
12                  p ← MAX(p^(-1) × β, α)
13   p^(-1) ← p
14   return p
```

Fig. 4. AIMD-MAC Protocol

Additive Increase: The ACP updating operation proceeds when $s^{(-1)} \geq 0$. A negative s (as defined in Eq. 4) represents an unknown channel condition and AIMD-MAC does not change ACP in this case (Case III). Line 7 indicates a positive success ratio and line 8 conditions on a channel improvement trend (Case I). Line 9 further signals that this node has to increase ACP because it has used up its designed slots for the last UW. The ACP linearly increases (line 10) for perfect resource utilization ($u = 1$).

Multiplicative Decrease: If $s^{(-1)} = 0$ (line 5), then all packet transmissions failed during the (-1)–th UW. This condition suggests a serious collision level and a slow recovery will negatively affect packet delay. In order to quickly decrease the ACP, β is assigned to be 0.5 and the ACP is halved. If $s^{(-1)}$ is positive but the channel condition worsens (Case II) (line 11: $s^{(-1)} < s^{(-2)}$), then the ACP is reduced less aggressively, by multiplying it by β which is a fraction greater than 0.5 but less than one.

5   Simulations

The AIMD-MAC protocol was simulated in various settings, including synchronous/asynchronous UWs, homogeneous/heterogeneous systems. To show the performance of the AIMD-MAC under different traffic loads, we apply both a Poisson arrival process and a bursty traffic model in the simulations.

5.1   Simulation Scenarios

5.1.1   Systems with Synchronous and Asynchronous UWs

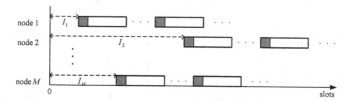

Fig. 5. The Asynchronous UW

In this subsection, we discuss the synchronism of the UWs. The time slots are synchronous at all times. For the purpose of extensive simulations, we specify a system as synchronous when the UWs from all nodes start at the same slot such that the ACP updating procedures proceed simultaneously. A more general circumstance is when nodes enter the system at different time slots where the UWs may be staggered (Fig.5). We model the asynchronous environment by specifying node m's starting time I_m as a discrete random variable uniformly distributed over the slot interval $[0, I_{MAX}]$.

5.1.2   Homogeneous and Heterogeneous Systems

Both homogeneous and heterogeneous systems are modeled. For the homogeneous environment, $\lambda_m = \lambda/M, m = 1, 2, ..., M$; for the heterogeneous environment, λ_m is uniformly distributed in the interval $[0, 2\frac{\lambda}{M}]$.

5.1.3   Poisson and Binary Source Traffic Models

Traffic loads with different statistical characteristics are examined. In the Poisson model, the packet inter-arrival times at node m are exponentially distributed with mean arrival rate λ_m. In the binary source model (Fig.6) [11], a node (source) is in one of two states at each slot: *On* or *Off*. The initial state of a node is decided randomly. The state transition probability from On to Off and from Off to On is p_{10} and p_{01}, respectively. With probability $1 - p_{10}$ or $1 - p_{01}$, a node stays in the On or Off state. If node m is in the On state, packets arrive at the node following a Poisson process with parameter λ'_m (Eq. 6); otherwise, this

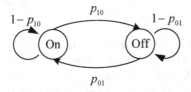

Fig. 6. The Binary Source Model

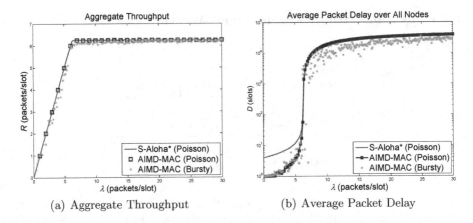

(a) Aggregate Throughput   (b) Average Packet Delay

Fig. 7. The Aggregate Throughput and Average Packet Delay where $M = 30$, $K = 10$, $\tau = 10$, $\alpha = 0.025$, $\beta = 0.9$ and $I_{MAX} = 10000$

node is idle. With the On-state arrival rate λ'_m, the mean arrival rate of node m is λ_m. This is applied to have a controllable aggregate load λ for convenient comparison.

$$\lambda'_m = \begin{cases} \lambda_m \times \frac{p_{10}+p_{01}}{p_{01}}, & \text{if } m \text{ is in On state} \\ 0, & \text{if } m \text{ is in Off state} \end{cases} \quad (6)$$

5.2   Simulation Results

Intuitively, to avoid oscillations of the ACP, the increase amount α and decrease amount $1 - \beta$ should be relatively small fractions. We present a network system example with $M = 30$, $K = 10$, $\tau = 10$, $\alpha = 0.025$, $\beta = 0.9$ and $I_{MAX} = 10000$. Nodes enter the system with $p_m = 1$, $\forall\, m$. Two network scenarios are considered, the homogeneous synchronous system with Poisson arrival traffic and a heterogeneous asynchronous system with bursty traffic, noted as "Poisson" and "Bursty" in Fig.7, respectively. Each experiment ran for 100,000 slots. The 99% CI error bars are sufficiently small and are not shown.

- **Aggregate Throughput** R: The total number of successful packet transmissions per slot over all nodes;
- **Packet Delay** D: The difference in time slots between the arrival and departure of the same packet.
- **Fairness** F: Fairness is evaluated by Jain's fairness index (Eq. 7) [14] based on the max-min fairness criterion [1].

$$F = \frac{(\sum_{m=1}^{M} x_m)^2}{M \times \sum_{m=1}^{M} x_m^2} \tag{7}$$

where $x_m = \frac{R_m}{O_m}$. R_m is the per node throughput of node m and O_m is the fair share defined by the max-min fairness criterion.

Fig.7(a) shows an exact match of the aggregate throughput between AIMD-MAC and S-Aloha*. Even in the heterogeneous system with bursty traffic, AIMD-MAC can achieve the optimum result. Fig.7(b) displays the average packet delay on a log scale. Before the system is saturated ($\lambda < 6.3$), the delay of AIMD-MAC is much lower than that of S-Aloha*. Under light traffic when the queue is empty, packets are delivered right after their arrivals because nodes can employ an ACP as high as 1 in AIMD-MAC. S-Aloha* does not perform immediate transmissions because p^* is less than one for all arrival rates. As λ increases, the proportion of empty nodes decreases. AIMD-MAC and S-Aloha* show the same average packet delay after the system is saturated. The fairness index is equal to one in both scenarios and the plots are omitted here.

5.3 Updating Window

The UW decides the frequency to reassess the channel collision condition and adjust the ACP. In this section, we examine how various UWs affect the system performance. Since the homogeneous synchronous systems with Poisson arrivals have relatively flat traffic compared to the heterogeneous asynchronous systems with bursty traffic, it can be expected that the UW will more dramatically affect the system performance in the latter scenario. To investigate the impact from UWs, we study the heterogeneous scenario where $M = 30$, $K = 10$, $\alpha = 0.025$, $\beta = 0.9$ and $I_{MAX} = 10000$.

Fig.8 demonstrates the aggregate throughput (Fig.8(a)) and the average packet delay (Fig.8(b)) when the UW varies from 1 to 500. Fig.8(b) confirms our speculation in Section 4.2 that the average delay is closely related to the length of the UW. Before λ reaches the stability limit (around 6.3), the packet delay increases with the value of the UW. When the UW is equal to 1, the system shows the shortest average delay while the longest delay appears when the UW is 500. Frequent channel assessments help users to react in time by adjusting the ACP to a proper value. After the system is saturated, the delay is dominated by the queue length and the impact of UWs is negligible.

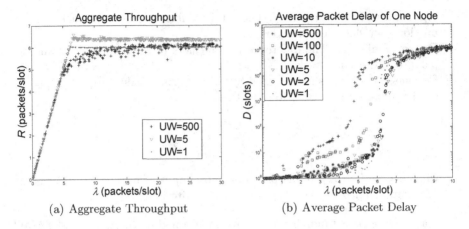

(a) Aggregate Throughput   (b) Average Packet Delay

Fig. 8. AIMD-MAC Performance with Different UWs when $M = 30$, $K = 10$, $\alpha = 0.025$, $\beta = 0.9$ and $I_{MAX} = 10000$

However, a shorter UW is not necessarily better. A tradeoff between throughput and delay is noticed in Fig.8. When the UW is 1, the system suffers slight throughput degradation (Fig.8(a)). Indeed, the optimum throughput is achieved when the UW is 5. As we mentioned earlier (Section 4.2), the UW needs to be long enough for users to collect sufficient data to estimate the channel quality. If it is too short, e.g., one slot, ACPs will continually oscillate around the optimum value which will negatively affect the throughput; while if it is too long, nodes will not be able to update ACPs timely which will also result in a performance degradation.

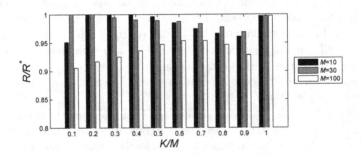

Fig. 9. The Performance Ratios for Different Scenarios when $M = 10, 30, 100$, $K = 1, ..., M$, $\alpha = 0.025$ $\beta = 0.9$ and $\tau = 10$

However, different lengths of UWs do not have a significant impact on max-min fairness. The simulation results show perfect fairness (i.e., $F = 1$) for the UWs in Fig.8 and the plot is omitted.

The increase term (α) and decrease factor (β) also impact the system performance. Preliminary studies show that increase/decrease amount should be relatively small to avoid ACPs fluctuating with large amplitudes, which means that both α and $1 - \beta$ should be small fractions. However, if they are too small, it will take a long time for a disturbed system to converge to the desired level. More detailed analysis of all the three parameters will be presented in our future work.

Fig.9 confirms that a suitable set of parameters can be applied to various scenarios. We investigated homogeneous synchronous systems with different number of nodes and various channel capacities. For each case, the aggregate throughput of AIMD-MAC (R) is compared with that of S-ALOHA* (R^*) when the system is saturated. The performance ratios R/R^* are plotted in Fig.9 with the channel capacity K normalized by the number of nodes M. The 99% error bars are smaller than the plotting symbols and are not shown. The performance ratios are greater than 0.9 in all the scenarios, which suggests that AIMD-MAC can efficiently exploit the MPR capability in dynamic wireless environments.

6   Conclusions

This paper proposed the AIMD-MAC protocol for multiple packet reception channels. It regulates the access probability of each node locally and periodically based on the transmission history. Simulation results suggest that its performance is superior to S-Aloha* under light traffic loads and achieves the optimum performance after the system is saturated. With a suitable of parameter set, the AIMD-MAC protocol can be adequately applied in a distributed and dynamic wireless environment.

References

1. Bertsekas, D., Gallager, R.: Data networks, 2nd edn. Prentice-Hall, Inc., Upper Saddle River (1992)
2. Celik, G.D., Zussman, G., Khan, W.F., Modiano, E.: Mac for networks with multipacket reception capability and spatially distributed nodes. Mobile Computing 9(2), 226–240 (2010)
3. Chan, D.S., Berger, T.: Performance and cross-layer design of csma for wireless networks with multipacket reception. In: Proc. IEEE Asilomar, vol. 2, pp. 1917–1921 (November 2004)
4. Chiu, D., Jain, R.: Analysis of the increase and decrease algorithms for congestion avoidance in computer networks. Comput. Netw. ISDN Syst. (June 1989)
5. Cleary, A.C., Paterakis, M.: An investigation of reservation random access algorithms for voice-data integration in microcellular wireless environments. In: IEEE Globecom (November 1994)
6. Ghanbarinejad, M., Schlegel, C., Gburzynski, P.: Adaptive probabilistic medium access in mpr-capable ad-hoc wireless networks. In: Proc. of the IEEE Global Telecommunication Conference, Honolulu, Hawaii, USA (2009)

7. Ghez, S., Verdu, S., Schwartz, S.C.: Stability properties of slotted aloha with multi-packet reception capability. IEEE Transactions on Automatic Control 33, 640–649 (1988)
8. Guo, M., Wang, X., Wu, M.: On the capacity of k-mpr wireless networks. Wireless Communications 8(7), 3878–3886 (2009)
9. Heusse, M., Rousseau, F., Guillier, R., Duda, A.: Idle sense: an optimal access method for high throughput and fairness in rate diverse wireless lans. In: ACM SIGCOMM (2005)
10. Holland, G., Vaidya, N., Bahl, P.: A rate-adaptive mac protocol for multi-hop wireless networks. Mobile Computing and Networking (2001)
11. Hou, T.-C., Lucantoni, D.M.: Buffer sizing for synchronous self-routing broadband packet switches with bursty traffic. International Journal of Digital and Analog Cabled Communication 2(1), 253–260 (1989)
12. Hu, C., Hou, J.C.: A novel approach to contention control in ieee 802.11e-operated wlans. In: IEEE INFOCOM, pp. 1190–1198 (May 2007)
13. Jacobson, V.: Congestion avoidance and control. In: SIGCOMM, Stanford, California, USA, pp. 314–329 (1988)
14. Jain, R., Chiu, D., Hawe, W.: A quantitative measure of fairness and discrimination for resource allocation in shared computer systems. Computing Research Repository, cs.NI/9809 (1998)
15. Jung, E., Vaidya, N.: A power control mac protocol for ad hoc networks. Wireless Networks 11, 55–66 (2005)
16. Kwack, S., Seo, H., Lee, B.: Suitability-based subcarrier allocation for multicast services employing layered video coding in wireless ofdm systems. In: Vehicular Technology Conference, pp. 1752–1756 (October 2007)
17. Lous, N.J.C., Bours, P.A.H., van Tilborg, H.C.A.: On maximum likelihood soft-decision decoding of binary linear codes. IEEE Transactions on Information Theory 39(1), 197–203 (1993)
18. Mergen, G., Tong, L.: Receiver controlled medium access in multihop ad hoc networks with multipacket reception. In: Military Communications Conference, vol. 2, pp. 1014–1018 (2001)
19. Schlegel, C., Grant, A.: Coordinated multiuser communications. Springer (2006)
20. LAN/MAN standards Committee, et al.: Information Technology – Telecommunications and Information Exchange Between Systems – Local and Metropolitan Area Networks – Specific Requirements: Part 11: Wireless LAN Medium Access Control (MAC) and Physical Layer (PHY) Specifications. IEEE Std. IEEE (1997)
21. Tong, L., Zhao, Q., Mergen, G.: Multipacket reception in random access wireless networks: from signal processing to optimal medium access control. IEEE Communications Magazine 39(11), 108–112 (2001)
22. Van Dam, T., Langendoen, K.: An adaptive energy-efficient mac protocol for wireless sensor networks. In: Proceedings of the 1st International Conference on Embedded Networked Sensor Systems, SenSys 2003, Los Angeles, California, USA, pp. 171–180 (2003)
23. Weber, S.P., Andrews, J.G., Yang, X., de Veciana, G.: Transmission capacity of wireless ad hoc networks with successive interference cancellation. IEEE Transactions on Information Theory 53(8), 2799–2814 (2007)
24. Ye, W., Heidemann, J., Estrin, D.: An energy-efficient mac protocol for wireless sensor networks. In: Proceedings of the IEEE Infocom, pp. 1567–1576 (June 2002)
25. Zhao, Q., Tong, L.: A multiqueue service room mac protocol for wireless networks with multipacket reception. IEEE/ACM Trans. Networking 11, 125–137 (2003)

Evaluating Battery Models
in Wireless Sensor Networks

Christian Rohner[1], Laura Marie Feeney[2], and Per Gunningberg[1]

[1] Uppsala University
{christian.rohner,perg}@it.uu.se
[2] Swedish Institute of Computer Science
lmfeeney@sics.se

Abstract. Recent measurements highlight the importance of battery-aware evaluation of energy efficiency in wireless sensor networks. However, existing battery models been not investigated in the context of the low duty cycle, short duration loads that are typical of sensor networks. We evaluate three battery models with regard to their applicability in the WSN context. Our evaluation focuses on how the models reflect two key battery discharge behaviors, the rate capacity effect and charge recovery. We find that the models handle the former better than the latter and are more sensitive to a load's peak current than to its timing.

1 Introduction

Many energy efficient wireless sensor network (WSN) protocols emphasize minimizing and coordinating the duty cycles of various hardware components. Other WSN applications do load balancing to maintain sensor coverage with a minimum number of active devices. The energy efficiency of these systems is typically evaluated based on measurements or estimates of the total charge (*current × time*) consumed by a device.

However, it is well-known that the available battery capacity is affected by the timing and intensity of the load being applied. Recent measurement results [1] highlight the need for battery-aware methods in evaluating energy efficiency and device lifetime in WSN's. For example, such methods are important for studying load scheduling for battery efficient WSN applications and protocols. If a device has to perform several operations, should it do them consecutively (maximizing the rest time) or separate them (minimizing the load duration)? Similarly, if several devices are sharing responsibility for sensor coverage of an area, what is the optimal length for each device's coverage period?

The practical challenges inherent in directly measuring a battery over its full lifetime suggest that battery modeling will be an essential complement to measurement experiments for battery-aware evaluation in WSN. Moreover, because of complex cross layer interactions, it will be important to incorporate battery models into system and protocol-level simulators operating at network scale.

Battery modeling, especially for Li-ion batteries, is an active research topic. However, there has been very little work studying the effectiveness of existing

V. Tsaoussidis et al. (Eds.): WWIC 2013, LNCS 7889, pp. 29–42, 2013.

battery models for WSN applications, with small, non-rechargeable batteries, low duty cycles and short load durations. In this paper, we investigate three existing battery modeling techniques with regard to their applicability to evaluating WSN protocols and systems: BatteryDesignStudio [2], a commercial electrochemical simulator; KiBaM [3], an analytic model based on a kinetic abstraction; and a hybrid battery model [4] which combines KiBaM with an electrical circuit abstraction.

We focus on how various models reflect two battery discharge behaviors that are particularly important for load scheduling: the rate capacity effect and charge recovery. Our contribution is primarily in the qualitative evaluation of the ability of these models to capture these effects. Our work is unique with regard to evaluating these models in the context of WSN typical loads and in highlighting the potential value of battery-aware energy evaluation to the WSN community.

The outline of this paper is as follows. We first provide some background on battery essentials, illustrated with some of our experimental measurement results on the CR2032 Li-coin cell ($LiMnO_2$) that we use as reference battery for our work. We then describe some background and related work in battery modeling. The core sections of the paper present the three battery modeling tools and evaluate the results we obtained using each. Finally, we conclude that the models are more sensitive to peak current than timing, and that they lack an effective mechanism to track energy efficiency.

2   Background and Experimental Data

This section provides background about batteries and presents measurement data that demonstrate some of the complex behaviors that motivate our work. We also introduce the load patterns used in both the measurements and battery modeling to study the rate capacity effect and charge recovery effects.

2.1   Electrochemical Preliminaries

A battery is a complex electrochemical system: The intensity and timing characteristics of the load affect the amount of charge that can be extracted before the cut-off voltage is reached. Two key battery discharge behaviors are the rate capacity effect and charge recovery: The former refers to the fact that a lower discharge rate (i.e. current) is more efficient than a higher one; more charge can be extracted from the battery before reaching a given cut-off voltage. The latter refers to the fact that an intermittent discharge is more efficient than a continuous one. Because of these effects, different battery loads that use the same total charge do not result in the same device lifetime.

Figure 1 is an oscilloscope trace of the output voltage of a 3V CR2032 battery under load. When a 300Ω ($\sim$10mA) load is applied, the output voltage initially drops sharply (V_{load}), then continues to drop more slowly (V_{min}). When the load is removed, the reverse happens ($V_{recover}$). The voltage $V_{recover}$ approximates the open circuit voltage V_{oc} after a sufficiently long recovery period

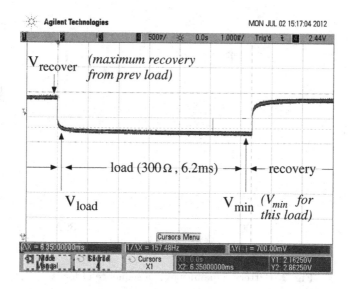

Fig. 1. Battery dynamics during a load

(hours). The details of the battery's voltage response depend on the size and duration of the load and the length of the recovery period (i.e. on the rate capacity and charge recovery effects).

The voltage response also depends on the battery state of charge (SOC). Figure 2 shows how the voltage response to a combination of periodic loads changes over the life of the battery. In this trace, the battery is repeatedly discharged with 1mA continuous load for 11h and allowed to rest for 8.5h. A 22mA pulse load is applied for 10 seconds followed by a rest interval of 30 minutes at the beginning of each load interval. The shape of the voltage response is similar to that in Figure 1. The rate capacity effect is seen in the difference between the battery response to the 1mA and 22mA loads. The voltage response also changes over the lifetime of the battery; the voltage drop becomes both larger and steeper and the recovery slower. Eventually, the battery's output voltage in response to load becomes too low to operate the device correctly; this cut-off value is device dependent. The battery efficiency therefore corresponds to the amount of charge (i.e. useful work) that can be extracted before the cut-off voltage is reached.

2.2 Experimental Results

Although these and other battery effects have been extensively studied for many kinds of high-end batteries, the results are very specific to a particular battery chemistry and structure. There is very little data about the discharge behavior of the cheap, non-rechargeable batteries, low duty cycles, short load durations, and relatively high loads typical of WSN's.

In reality, WSN's exhibit activity patterns that are a combination of periodic and non-periodic events, each with a distinct signature. For example, transmitting

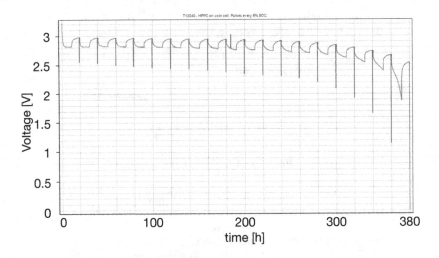

Fig. 2. Battery dynamics over a sequence of loads

a frame involves a sequence of transitions between backoff, listening, and transmitting states. However, it is impractical to control wireless contention and collisions well enough to ensure identical behavior for all frames over a long-term experiment. We therefore work with simple periodic loads, which allow us to isolate key effects and can also act as building blocks for modeling more complex loads.

The load parameters that we use in this paper are shown in Table 1 and are intended to reflect a range of plausible values, without being tied to any specific hardware or protocol. The load values are typical of low bit-rate transceivers such as the RFM TR1001[5]. The load durations are also consistent with low bit-rate frame reception and shorter wakeup/listen durations, while the periods are typical of MAC wakeup schedules. We also include a higher 25mA load, which is typical of sensor operation.

These loads allow us to make comparisons along several axes. For example, CI.3 and I.6 have the same duty cycle and load (i.e. the same time-average current), but I.6 has a longer period. Comparing these allows us to see how absolute load and rest times impact the recovery effect. Similarly, we can compare CI.3 and CI.9, which have the same period and time-average current, but CI.9 has a higher load and smaller duty-cycle. Comparing these allows us to observe the rate-capacity effect, where there is some tradeoff between brief, intense loads and longer duration loads with lower intensity.

We recently built a battery testbed [6] and used it to measure Panasonic CR2023 Li-coin cell batteries. Our automated testbed allows us to apply periodic resistive loads to sets of batteries in a controlled fashion and see how the voltage response evolves over time. Our results [1] are one of the first battery measurement studies that focuses on WSN scenarios.

Table 1. Battery loads used in this paper

name	note	load	duration	period	duty cycle	avg. current
CI.3	low current short period	750Ω (~4mA)	15 ms	200 ms	7.5%	300 μA
I.6	low current long period	750Ω (~4mA)	**150 ms**	**2.0 s**	7.5%	300 μA
CI.9	high current short period	120Ω (~**25mA**)	2.4 ms	200 ms	1.2%	300 μA

Figure 3 shows results of discharging batteries according to the three load patterns listed in Table 1. The voltage under load (V_{min}) is shown for each load pattern, the open circuit voltage (V_{oc}, approximated by $V_{recover}$) is shown for CI.3. For load patterns with similar time-averaged energy consumption, the variation in available capacity is around 10-15%, depending on cut-off voltage. The results confirm the importance of battery-aware evaluation and suggest that a shorter load duration is more battery efficient.

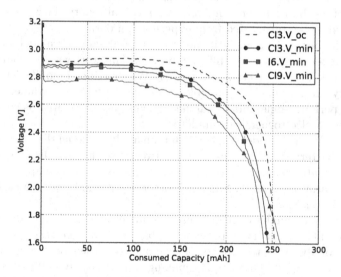

Fig. 3. Experimental data from our battery testbed. The mA-h that can be taken from the battery (at a given voltage) depends on the load pattern. CI9 has a slightly shorter load duration (mean current 262μA) due to a limitation in the testbed.

3   Battery Modeling and Related Work

Battery modeling and simulation is a very active topic [7]. As we have noted earlier, this work is mostly in the context of high-end Li-ion batteries, such as those used in electric vehicles. We roughly divide battery simulation into two categories: Electrochemical simulations model the physical processes in the battery, while analytic simulations use simpler abstractions to represent the battery's response to load.

Electrochemical simulation directly models the physical processes in the battery, based on its detailed chemical and structural properties. Although such models are considered "gold-standard", they have some disadvantages: They have a large number of highly detailed parameters describing the battery chemistry and physical structure. A simulation model is defined not just for a given battery chemistry or type of battery; its parameters are manufacturer-specific. These simulators are also very computationally intensive and their mathematical structure can be difficult to integrate with common discrete-event WSN simulators.

Analytic models replace complex physical models with much simpler representations of battery response to load. These are based on non-electrochemical abstractions, such as electrical circuits, kinetics, diffusion and stochastic processes. These abstractions are therefore more generic and more tractable than models of physical processes, but they present some non-trivial challenges in parameterization. Unlike physical parameters such as electrolyte concentration or surface area that are well-defined properties of a particular battery, abstract parameters such as diffusion constants have no physical reality. These parameters therefore need to be constructed from experimental data.

Perhaps the best known analytic model is the Rakhamatov model [8], which models the battery response as a diffusion process. This work was directed toward the rechargeable Li-ion battery found in early Wi-fi equipped mobile devices. Its short battery lifetime made it possible to define a practical parameterization process and perform some limited validation experiments, as well as simulation using Dualfoil[9] electrochemical simulator.

The Kinetic Battery Model (KiBaM) [3] is an analytic model that uses kinetics to model the battery state in terms of flow between two charge wells, representing bound and available charge. It has been shown that KiBaM is an approximation of the Rakhmatov model [10]. Section 5 describes KiBaM and our experience using KiBaM in detail.

Another class of analytic models uses as an electrical circuit abstraction. Electrical circuit models [11] represent the battery's voltage response using a combination of RC circuit elements. The model can then be evaluated using conventional circuit simulation tools, making it particularly suitable for combining with hardware simulation of the WSN device itself. Section 6 describes our experience with a hybrid model [4] that combines an electrical circuit model with KiBaM.

More recently, a stochastic battery model was proposed in [12]. Although the work was intended for WSN environments, the batteries studied in this work were rechargeable NiMH batteries. The measurement studies used for both parameterization and evaluation of the model had high duty cycles of 40-90%. By contrast, our work uses duty cycles that are more realistic for WSNs.

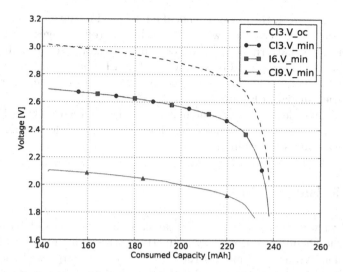

Fig. 4. Battery discharge curve for the electrochemical model in BatteryDesignStudio (note that the x-axis begins with the battery partially drained). Loads CI.3 and I.6 (both 4mA) have the same discharge curve.

In addition to our work on models, there have been some measurement studies of CR2354 Li-coin cells [13,14]. Both of these studies used much higher loads than typical WSNs, with duty cycles ranging from 25-100%. Their results showed the impact of rate capacity and charge recovery effects on available capacity. Compared to a straightforward calculation of energy consumption as *current × time*, the available capacity was seen to differ by as much as a factor of four.

4   Electrochemical Model

Models for $LiMnO_2$ cells have recently been added to a well-known commercial electrochemical simulator, BatteryDesignStudio [2,15]. We configured our experiments in BatteryDesignStudio using its builtin model of a CR2032 coin-cell battery manufactured by Varta. This battery is similar to the Panasonic CR2032 batteries used in our experiments, but has a slightly larger nominal capacity (240mA-h vs 225mA-h). The simulator was configured to model the periodic load patterns from the experiments described in Table 1.

Due to the computational complexity of the simulation and large number of load events in our experiments (experiment CI.3 has a 200ms period, or more than 20M loads over 1200 hours), the runtime of the simulation turns out to be close to real-time (i.e., ~50 days). To speed up the simulation, we configured the simulator to drain 60% of the battery capacity with a small continuous load of 0.2mA during a time period equivalent to 30 days and then apply the periodic load pattern for the remaining time. Our rationale is that our earlier experiments indicate that the battery response is approximately constant during the first 60% of its lifetime.

As shown in Figure 4, the electrochemical model used in BatteryDesignStudio captures the rate capacity effect, with CI9 reaching cutoff voltages much earlier than the other load patterns. On the other hand, the model seems to be insensitive to scaling the time period of a cycle (CI.3 and I.6 have the same results). Interestingly, the voltage levels are in general lower than in our measurements on real batteries shown in Figure 3.

As noted above, electrochemical models are computationally expensive. The computations run between two days and four weeks each, depending on the number of load events to be simulated.

5 Kinetic Battery Model

An established way to model the nonlinear capacity dynamics of batteries is to describe the chemical processes by a kinetic process. The analytical Kinetic Battery Model (KiBaM) [3] models the battery as two charge wells, with the charge distributed between the two wells with a capacity ratio c ($0 < c < 1$), as shown in Figure 5. The *available charge well* supplies charge directly to the load and the *bound charge well* supplies charge to the available charge well through a valve. The rate at which charge flows from the bound to the available charge well depends on the valve, characterized by the diffusion parameter k (($0 < k < 1$)), and the difference between the charge level in each of the two wells, h_1 and h_2. The total charge in the available well and the bound well are $y_1 = ch_1$ and $y_2 = (1 - c)h_2$, respectively. The state of charge of the battery is represented by h_1, and the battery is fully discharged when h_1 becomes zero. That is, the battery can be fully discharged, even if there is (bound) charge remaining.

Intuitively, we see that if the battery is discharged at a higher current, the available charge well is emptied more quickly than it would be if the battery were discharged at a lower current. This reflects the rate capacity effect. At rest, charge flows from the bound charge well to the available charge well until equilibrium $h_1 = h_2$ is reached. Replenishing the available charge well in this way reflects the charge recovery effect.

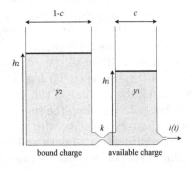

Fig. 5. Kinetic Battery Model

Following notation in [3], the kinetic process is expressed as:

$$\begin{cases} \frac{y_1(t)}{dt} = -i(t) + k[h_2(t) - h_1(t)] \\ \frac{dy_2(t)}{dt} = -k[h_2(t) - h_1(t)] \end{cases} \tag{1}$$

For a constant discharge current of $i(t) = I$, the differential equations (1) can be solved as:

$$\begin{cases} y_1(t) = y_{1,0}e^{-k'(t-t_0)} + \frac{(y_0 k' c - I)(1 - e^{-k'(t-t_0)})}{k'} - \frac{Ic(k'(t-t_0) - 1 + e^{-k'(t-t_0)})}{k'} \\ \\ y_2(t) = y_{2,0}e^{-k'(t-t_0)} + y_0(1-c)(1 - e^{-k'(t-t_0)}) \\ \qquad\qquad - \frac{I(1-c)(k'(t-t_0) - 1 + e^{-k'(t-t_0)})}{k'} \end{cases} \tag{2}$$

where $k' = \frac{k}{c(1-c)}$, and $y_0 = y_{1,0} + y_{2,0}$ the charge of the battery at time t_0.
The unavailable charge $u(t)$ of the battery can thus be expressed as:

$$u(t) = (1 - c)[h_1(t) - h_2(t)]. \tag{3}$$

The available charge can be described as $y_0 - \int i(t)dt - u(t)$.

The paramterization of the KiBaM model is based on the assumption that the delivered capacity under very small current loads corresponds to the initial charge y_0. Conversely, a large constant discharge drains the available charge well with only little charge replenished from the bound charge well ($y_{1,0}$), letting us compute the ratio $c = y_{1,0}/y_0$. The value of k' is determined such that the unavailable charge agrees with experimental results from constant discharge when the cutoff voltage of 2.0V is reached. Since $u(0)$ is zero at the beginning of the experiment and t_{co} is known, k' can be extracted. From our experimental measurements with small (1mA) and large (25mA) constant discharge we concluded $y_0 = 0.243Ah$ and $y_{1,0} = 0.028Ah$, respectively, resulting in to the parameters $c = 0.115$ and $k' = 0.266 \cdot 10^{-3}$.

We modeled our periodic load patterns assuming piecewise constant loads of $I > 0$ followed by rest intervals with $I = 0$, and iterated them over Equation (2) to compute the available charge after every cycle. Because KiBaM models available charge rather than output voltage, we use it to compute the lifetime t^* of the battery, at which the simulation reaches $h_1(t^*) = y_1(t^*)/c = 0$. This computation takes only minutes on an ordinary PC.

In practice, KiBaM captures the rate capacity and charge recovery effects to some extent, with higher sensitivity to charge recovery than rate capacity. However, the differences hardly have an impact on the expected lifetime of a battery in the chosen parameter space. The battery lifetimes for our load patterns were all in the range $2887069s \pm 9s$ ($\approx 800h$). This lifetime is shorter than that seen in the experiments (835-1083h for 2.0V cut-of voltage) and in the electrochemical model and furthermore shows no significant difference between load patterns.

The reason why the small differences per load do not sum up to a more significant difference over the large number of load cycles is because the amount of unavailable charge converges to the same value for all load patterns already after a few hours of operation. Loads applied after this convergence do not add to a difference between the patterns.

Moreover, the assumption of piecewise constant discharge is not fully accurate. As seen in Figure 1, the voltage level, and thus the charge drawn is not constant over the duration of a load. The higher the load, and the lower the state of charge, the larger the difference between V_{load} and V_{min}. Such behavior will make a difference for the rate capacity effect and can, for example, be captured with equivalent circuit models as shown in the next section.

6   Hybrid Battery Model

An electrical circuit model has two components: The Thevenin component is a sequence of RC circuits that models the transient response to load. The SoC component models the non-linear variation in battery's open circuit voltage as a function of the state of charge. This can be done within the circuit model by including an active element such as a current-controlled voltage source or it can be computed using some other method. The hybrid electrical circuit model described in [4] uses KiBaM to track the state of charge, as shown in Figure 6.

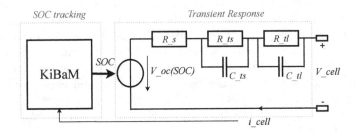

Fig. 6. Hybrid Battery Model

The RC circuits define the transient response to load changes. The circuit parameters define both the cell voltage V_{cell}, and the transient response given by the time constants $\tau_s = R_{ts}C_{ts}$ and $\tau_l = R_{tl}C_{tl}$, which represent the short- and long-term responses, respectively. The larger the time constants, the slower the response.

The cell voltage V_{cell} can be calculated as:

$$V_{cell}(t) = V_{oc}(SOC) - i_{cell}(t) \cdot R_s - V_{transient}(t) \tag{4}$$

For a period in which the battery cell is first discharged with a constant current $i_{cell}(t) = I$ for time t_d, and then rests (i.e., $i_{cell}(t) = 0$), the transient voltage $V_{transient}(t) = V_{ts}(t) + V_{tl}(t)$ is

$$V_{ts}(t) = \begin{cases} R_{ts}I(1 - e^{-t/\tau_s}) & t < t_d \\ V_{ts}(t_d)e^{-(t-t_d)/\tau_s} & t > t_d \end{cases} \qquad V_{tl}(t) = \begin{cases} R_{tl}I(1 - e^{-t/\tau_l}) & t < t_d \\ V_{tl}(t_d)e^{-(t-t_d)/\tau_l} & t > t_d \end{cases} \quad (5)$$

Both the circuit parameters and the open circuit voltage V_{oc} depend on the state of charge. Empirical measurements suggest the behavior described in equations 6 and 7, following the notation in [4]:

$$V_{oc}(SOC) = a_0 \cdot e^{-a_1 SOC} + a_2 + a_3 SOC - a_4 SOC^2 + a_5 SOC^3 \qquad (6)$$

$$\begin{cases} R_s(SOC) = b_0 \cdot e^{-b_1 SOC} + b_2 + b_3 SOC - b_4 SOC^2 + b_5 SOC^3 \\ R_{ts}(SOC) = c_0 \cdot e^{-c_1 SOC} + c_2 \\ C_{ts}(SOC) = d_0 \cdot e^{-d_1 SOC} + d_2 \\ R_{tl}(SOC) = e_0 \cdot e^{-e_1 SOC} + e_2 \\ C_{tl}(SOC) = f_0 \cdot e^{-f_1 SOC} + f_2 \end{cases} \qquad (7)$$

The negative exponential behavior of the circuit parameters reflects the increasing internal resistance (R_s) and slower reactive behavior (RC components) of the battery with decreasing SOC.

The model parameters are battery and temperature dependent and have to be determined experimentally. Our procedure is based on the one used in [4], where the parameterization is derived from the battery's recovery from a pulse load, as measured at various states of charge.

To do these measurements, we use the load pattern described in Figure 2. The battery is discharged with 1mA continuous load for 11h, then allowed to rest for 8.5h. This load slowly discharges 5% of the battery capacity, minimizing the impact of rate capacity effect, and the rest period allows for charge recovery. A 22mA pulse load (close to the maximum rated load for the CR2032 battery) then is applied for 10s and removed. The immediate voltage increase when the load is removed gives the internal resistance, while $V_{oc}(SOC)$ is estimated using exponential curve fitting on the voltage recovery curve. This also allows us to determine the two transient time constants τ_s and τ_l at the specific SOC.

At the end of this procedure, the circuit parameters at the different SOC levels are least square error fitted by Equations 6 and 7 to estimate the model parameters. Table 2 summarizes the model parameters obtained for the Panasonic CR2032 cell at room temperature.

We applied the battery loads defined in Table 1 to the hybrid battery model to evaluate its ability to capture the rate capacity and charge recovery effects. The simulation runtime is around one hour on a PC, using high time resolution to capture the load pattern. The results shown in Figure 7 indicate that the hybrid model captures the rate capacity effect (CI3 vs CI9), which is visible in the voltage level and in the shape of the curve at low SOC. The higher peak current load in CI9 causes the voltage to be lower than in CI3 in the beginning of the experiment and CI3 does not drop equally distinctly at the end. However, like the electrochemical model, the hybrid battery model cannot distinguish between two battery loads with the same peak current load and duty cycle (CI3 and I6).

Table 2. Battery model parameters for the Panasonic CR2032 derived from the battery's recovery from 10s pulses load at 22mA (c.f., Figure 2). These values are used in Equations (6) and (7).

$a_0 = 1.31$	$a_1 = 0.050$	$a_2 = 1.20$
$a_3 = 2.01$	$a_4 = 2.85$	$a_5 = 1.40$
$b_0 = 76.4$	$b_1 = 11.8$	$b_2 = 22.9$
$b_3 = -14.0$	$b_4 = -17.4$	$b_5 = -15.3$
$c_0 = 37.2$	$c_1 = 16.9$	$c_2 = 3.06$
$d_0 = -0.468$	$d_1 = 5.33$	$d_2 = 0.370$
$e_0 = 21.2$	$e_1 = 12.2$	$e_2 = 3.06$
$f_0 = -5.43$	$f_1 = 4.58$	$f_2 = 5.00$

The time constants of the transient response are on the order of 1s and 15s, which is significantly longer than the load duration (2-150ms), so they have have little impact.

Further investigation is needed to understand the sensitivity of model parameters on the current and timing. Results from Chen, et al. [11] show that the parameters of NiMH batteries strongly depend on current, while parameters of polymer Li-ion batteries don't. From our measurements on the CR2032, we have indications that the parameters indeed are sensitive to current, with the time constants getting larger (and thus less relevant for WSN) for lower currents.

Looking at the consumed capacity, the hybrid battery model does not favor any of the battery loads. This observation is expected as all the loads have the same time-average current driving the SOC tracking based on KiBaM. However,

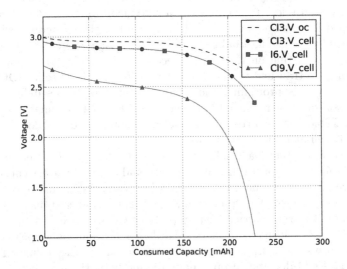

Fig. 7. Results from the Hybrid Battery Model. Loads CI.3 and I.6 (both 4mA) have the same discharge curve.

the result differs from our observations in the experiments and electrochemical model where the rate capacity effect has an impact on the consumed capacity.

7   Conclusions and Future Work

In this paper, we present measurement data motivating battery-aware evaluation of energy efficiency in WSN protocols and applications. However, this functionality is not currently provided by existing tools for evaluating WSN performance, nor have existing battery models been investigated in the WSN context, which is characterized by low duty cycles and short duration loads.

We have evaluated three well-known battery models using a parameterization based on the CR2032 Li-coin cell battery and three test loads with load values typical of WSN applications. Both BatteryDesignStudio's electrochemical model and the hybrid KiBaM-electrical circuit model capture the rate capacity effect. However, neither of these models seems to capture the effect of load timing, at least for the short load durations and recovery times used in our tests. KiBaM, which is the simplest of the three models, does not show any significant difference in battery lifetime among the three test loads.

The electrochemical model, which is the most complex and computationally expensive of the three models, is sensitive to the rate capacity effect, but not sensitive to timing aspects. The hybrid model behaves similarly, but cannot differentiate energy efficiency (i.e., consumed capacity) of the load patterns.

Because this work opens an area that has not been widely considered in the WSN community, there are many opportunities for future work. Most important is developing better understanding of the models' limitations with respect to modeling timing aspects. Further studies of the parameterization and its sensitivity analysis are also needed.

In the longer term, incorporating battery modeling into existing simulation and modeling tools presents a number of interesting challenges. We expect that the availability of tools for battery aware evaluation of WSN applications and systems will also enable new approaches in both software and hardware design.

Acknowledgements. This work was partly carried out within the Uppsala VINN Excellence Center for Wireless Sensor Networks WISENET, partly supported by VINNOVA, the Swedish Governmental Agency for Innovation Systems.

References

1. Feeney, L.M., Andersson, L., Lindgren, A., Starborg, S., Ahlberg Tidblad, A.: Poster abstract: Using batteries wisely. In: ACM Conf. on Embedded Networked Sensor Systems, Sensys (2012)
2. Battery Design LLC: Battery design studio, http://www.batsdesign.com
3. Manwell, J., McGowan, J.: Lead acid battery storage model for hybrid energy system. Solar Energy 50(5) (1993)

4. Kim, T., Qiao, W.: A hybrid battery model capable of capturing dynamic circuit characteristics and nonlinear capacity effects. IEEE Transactions on Energy Conversion 26(4) (2011)

5. RF Monolithics, Inc.: TR1001, http://www.rfm.com

6. Feeney, L.M., Andersson, L., Lindgren, A., Starborg, S., Ahlberg Tidblad, A.: Poster: A testbed for measuring battery discharge behavior. In: 7th ACM Int'l Workshop on Wireless Network Testbeds, Experimental Evaluation & Characterization, WiNTECH (2012)

7. Rao, R., Vrudhula, S., Rakhmatov, D.: Battery modeling for energy aware system design. IEEE Computer 36(12) (2003)

8. Rakhmatov, D.: Battery voltage modeling for portable systems. ACM Trans. on Design Automation of Electronic Systems (TODAES) 14(2) (2009)

9. Fuller, T.F., Doyle, M., Newman, J.: Simulation and optimization of the dual lithium ion insertion cell. Journal of the Electrochemical Society 141(1) (1994)

10. Jongerden, M.R., Haverkort, B.R.: Which battery model to use? IET Software 3(6) (2009)

11. Chen, M., Rincon-Mora, G.: Accurate electrical battery model capable of predicting runtime and iv performance. IEEE Transactions on Energy Conversion 21(2) (2006)

12. Chau, C., Qin, F., Sayed, S., Wahab, M., Yang, Y.: Harnessing battery recovery effect in wireless sensor networks: Experiments and analysis. IEEE Journal on Selected Areas in Communications 28(7) (2010)

13. Park, C., Lahiri, K., Raghunathan, A.: Battery discharge characteristics of wireless sensor nodes: An experimental analysis. In: IEEE Conf. on Sensor and Ad-hoc Communications and Networks, SECON (2005)

14. Park, S., Savvides, A., Srivastava, M.B.: Battery capacity measurement and analysis using lithium coin cell battery. In: Int'l Symp. on Low Power Electronics & Design, ISLPED (2001)

15. Yeduvaka, G., Spotnitz, R., Gering, K.: Macro-homogenous modeling of commercial, primary Li/MnO2 coin cells. ECS (Electrochemical Society) Trans. 19(16) (2009)

Service Creation and Self-management Mechanisms for Mobile Cloud Computing

Tatiana Aubonnet[1,2] and Noëmie Simoni[2]

[1] CNAM, CEDRIC, 292 rue Saint Martin, 75003, Paris
[2] Télécom Paristech, 46, rue Barrault, 75634, Paris Cedex 13
{tatiana.aubonnet,noemie.simoni}@telecom-paristech.fr

Abstract. Today, service providers need to develop competitive applications for a quick time-to-market to attract and retain end users. To facilitate the task of developers, we introduce a reference Service Creation Environment based on service component and self-management mechanisms. This environment uses a fairly high integration level using meta-modeling techniques and exchange formats: Meta-Object Facility (MOF), Extensible Markup Language (XML), OVF ++ (Open Virtualization Format). Our approach allows developers to design the basic service components based on Quality of Service (QoS), to build the service by composition, and to manage a mobile session by ubiquitous services and the Virtual Service Community.

Keywords: service components, ubiquitous services, self-management.

1 Introduction

Today, the Next Generation Networks (NGN) [3], [14] are considered to be a "user-centric" approach in the economic and technological world. Thanks to this new concept, the user can use any access to services and any terminal. However, with this freedom of access guaranteed by NGN, we have new challenges like the demand for quickly delivering new applications. Service providers need to develop competitive applications for a quick time-to-market to attract and retain end users.

Mobile Cloud Computing (MCC) is introduced as an integration of cloud computing into the mobile environment. Mobile Cloud Computing [1] brings new types of services and facilities for mobile users to take full advantage of cloud computing. It is important for the service provider to fulfill mobile users' expectations by monitoring their preferences and providing appropriate services to each user.

With each evolution, the new actors are trying to facilitate implementation. Thus, the key concepts such as (1) OSA (Open Service Architecture) PARLAY APIs, (2) enabled services in IP Multimedia Subsystem (IMS), (3) Service Creation Environment (SCE), and Service Logic Execution Environment (SLEE) in Intelligent Networks, (4) Web Services APIs, (5) and infrastructure APIs for Cloud Computing are proposed.

V. Tsaoussidis et al. (Eds.): WWIC 2013, LNCS 7889, pp. 43–55, 2013.

But important concepts are not taken into account in these environments such as *QoS* and *continuity of service* in a mobile context.

Can we solve or at least help to solve these concepts through a service creation platform? Our motivation is based on offering the maximum number of elements through this platform. This means that we must answer the following questions: What can we offer in term of construction *(by construction)*? What are the conditions to achieve maximum agility and flexibility?

In this paper, we present a software development environment for a Service Composition and Self-Management creation in Service-Oriented Architecture (SOA) context. We discuss fundamental concepts of the service creation platform and detail its main architectural components in order to have a reference framework.

The Service Components proposed are like actual automata that are accessible after any event, because, the properties of these services are not only those of SOA, namely: reusable, interoperable and autonomous, but also mutualizable, stateless, ubiquitous and self-managed. This architecture ensures cloud users a composition of Mobile Cloud Services in a seamless and dynamic way. A fairly high integration level has been reached using meta-modeling techniques (OMG standard MOF, XML, OVF++). We recommend taking the Service Components in the Referential of Service Creation Environment.

This paper is organized as follows. The related works for service creation is described in Section 2. Section 3 is devoted to our propositions for Workbench Architecture modules of the Service Creation Environment (Service Components, Links and Referential) for MCC including service component definition, Service Composition and piloting. Our propositions for Self-Management Mechanisms are presented in Section 4. Finally, in Section 5, we exhibit the advantages of our approach in a Mobile Cloud Computing use case.

2   Related Works

Works interests in the service creation field are the existing platforms in the Intelligent Network, Web Services, active networks and also Mobile Cloud Services gateway.

The Intelligent Network introduced two concepts: Service Creation Environment (SCE) [5] and a Service Logic Execution Environment (SLEE). These two concepts have been introduced with Intelligent Networks to ease and speed up the development and deployment of services [2]. An SCE is generally a graphical user-interface for developing services using predefined components, also called building blocks. A SLEE is the environment in which the services are actually executed.

This approach has been a precursor in separating the service components and of execution logic (enchainment).

Industry shows interest in Web Services due to their potential in facilitating seamless business-to-business or enterprise application integration [11], [13]. The contributions of Web Service creation are: improving the semantics of creation and collaboration services, introducing Web Services APIs and the decentralized vision for *the composition of services (choreography)*.

The active network context enables customers to install and run their own customized services on a provider's network; a framework for service creation and management for active networks in telecom environments is defined in [4]. A key problem in this context is how on the one hand, a customer, who wants to run its service on the network, and on the other hand, the provider, who owns the network, interacts for the purpose of service installation and management. This problem has been addressed by introducing a service application based on Service Components and by network *virtualization* [7].

The paradigms of Service-Oriented Architecture, user mobile centric and Cloud Computing provide service-orientation for both software and the infrastructure services. In particular, the mobile cloud computing environment distributes and allocates IT resources according to an user's request, so there should be a study on technology that manages these resources and deals with effectively. C. Chapman and al. [6] discusses the implications of the on-demand cloud provisioning and architectural definition of distributed applications deployed in the cloud. It underlines especially that such an architecture has to be dynamically configured at runtime. It proposes language elements for describing software architectures, requirements towards the execution platforms, architectural constraints (e.g. concerning placement and collocation) and rules relating to applications elasticity. Concerning the requirements for the underlying IaaS platforms, both approaches are based on OVF (Open Virtualization Format) formalism.

We note that for the mobile context there is a missing feature, the continuity of service. Our motivation is to design, self managed components, reacting throughout the life cycle and during run time to trigger the load balancing based on user localization. That is why we integrate two new aspects and we present our two proposals: a service creation environment with the QoS (non-functional aspects of the service) integration and Self-Management Mechanisms to satisfy the continuity of service in MCC.

3   First Proposal: A Service Creation Environment

In this section, we present our propositions for a Service Creation Environment. The SCE showed in this paper can reside in the PaaS for Mobile Cloud Computing. Each component of the SCE consists of a consistent functionality the developer can manipulate for its creation of services. The Service Creation Environment is given in Figure 1. The architecture is based on a double separation: on one side the separation between *Service Components* and *Links*, and on the other side the separation between *Modeling* and *Piloting* (see Figure 1). SCE eases designing and provides a guide for each stage of development. The Service Components and Links are accessible through *Referentials* that are exported in the OpenCloudware Self-Service Portal. The Referential modules constitute a space for knowledge sharing on the basis of a common representation and they are built on standards allowing model storing, reuse and activation. In the context of the SCE workbench, the developer draws on the referential for services and links suited to their needs and defines the sequence and control desired.

For MCC, we can find for example a set of basic services such as Location Basic Service, Geographic-Location Basic Service, Presence Basic Service, etc. Location Basic Service (LBS) takes out the logic address (SIP URI) of a resource from the knowledge database. Geographic-Location Basic Service (Geo-LBS) takes out the geographical position (longitude, latitude) of a resource from the knowledge database. Presence Basic Service (PBS) takes out the state of the Resource from the knowledge database. It allows us to know if a resource is "Available", "Can be activated" or "Enabled". But we can also find component security service (authentication, authorization) or management services.

The role of Referential is to assure consistent communication between modeling and piloting tools during the service creation process. The interface between the Modeling, Piloting and the Referential is assured by an exchange of models based on the OVF++/XML standards.

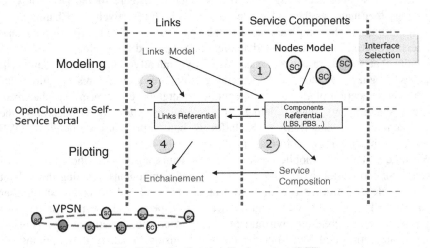

Fig. 1. Service Creation Environment (SCE)

This architecture also illustrates the separation between static (*Service Component and Link Component*) and dynamic (*Piloting*) aspects. This separation gave us a greater independence (static and dynamic) and consequently betters opportunities to evolve, as well as a more effective communication.

Compared to the SIB (Service Independent Block) approach [2], Service Component Architecture (SCA) is considered as a promising technique for service building. The main advantages of our approach are modeling the overall behavior of the system, and flexibility: our Service Components based on QoS are independent, modular, reusable and interoperable like the SOA components, but in more they are autonomous, stateless, ubiquitous and self-managed. These components form the basis for the definition of a Service Element Library called Components Referential in OpenCloudware Self-Service Portal.

The last important input for SCE is the "NLN" model (Node, Link, Network) [8], which provides an abstract image of the global system. Indeed, we divide the system into four decision views (visibility level): User, Service, Transport Network and Equipment. Each level consists of abstract nodes and links forming a subsystem called abstract network.

In this article the SCE is focalized by "Service Level" in where the nodes are the *Service Component (SC) and Links* (service interactions) and the *whole forming a Virtual Private Network Service (VPSN)*. In this section, the question is: how to define a service creation platform allowing the introduction of self-management. To reply, we present:

- Service Component (Section 3.1).
- Service Composition (Section 3.2).
- Piloting (Section 3.3)
- E2E Process (Section 3.4) (life cycle: think, build, run.)

3.1   Service Component

Service Component Properties

All the services are built according to SOA principles to allow the design of new services via a composition of service elements, a loose coupling between them and an exchange standard by standard interface. We present the set of important Properties to respect and follow in any design and deployment of SOA architecture.

Reuse: consists in designing services to make them more reusable. Reusing the same service in various business processes allows to reduce the development effort to meet new business needs.

Loose coupling: it is to limit the dependencies between services. It ensures agility that allows an SOA solution to adapt to changes in the IT world efficiently. Usually, these changes are due to external needs in the IT environment and therefore are difficult to be planned in advance. For this reason, loosely coupled relationships become an essential property for SOA. It is carried out by using the service contract, which allows the services to interact according to predefined parameters, and to share some knowledge while remaining independent from one another.

Stateless: it represents a service that does not keep state information and does not handle it. If a service maintains a state in the long-term, it will thus lose its property of loose coupling, its availability for other queries, as well as its potential to scalability. To do this, the services must be designed in a stateless way even if it means delegating state management to someone else. For a service to be stateless, its operations need to be designed to make stateless treatments, i.e. the treatment of an operation should not rely on information received during a previous invocation. It should be noted that the more intelligent the messages exchanged are, the more the services will stateless.

But specially, in addition to these SOA Properties, we introduce the *mutualization property* of the Service Component. It is designed to offer the same treatment to multiple users. This requires all component operations to be executed for all requesters. It is the contrary of the object, because the user can execute a selected method. This property will enable Ubiquitous Services Components to by make.

Among properties, we also introduce the four QoS criteria types: availability, reliability, delay, and capacity describe below in the Management Interface.

Service Component Interfaces

The Service Component is illustrated in Figure 2 with three Interfaces: Usage, Control, and Management.

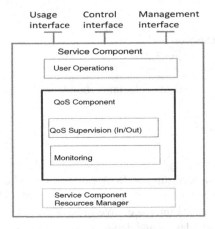

Fig. 2. Service Component

The *Usage Interface* is used to enable a basic service.

The *Control Interface* is used to reserve resources.

The *Management Interface* is represented by a QoS management interface integrated into each component composite. We use the same modeling to which we add the following models: *QoS generic model* and *interaction model*. The QoS model is generic and represents the behavior.

Four criteria have been proposed to describe a behavior:

(1) *Availability*: accessibility rate of the Service Component (accessibility rate).
(2) *Reliability*: running without alteration of information (error rate).
(3) *Delay*: time for request processing (response time).
(4) *Capacity*: maximum load of the Service Component (processing capacity).

Unlike some contexts, where just the throughput criterium as in UMTS is considered, or two criteria (throughput and fault tolerance) in the G1010, we found that these four criteria were necessary to describe the behavior of any function. We can say that these are sufficient because these criteria are independent of context. Indeed, they meet the following *transparencies*. The first is temporal and spatial transparency, i.e. to process and to transfer the information every time it is produced by the user (availability). The second is semantic transparency, i.e. the processing and the transfer is made without changing its content (reliability). The third is transparency in the distance, i.e. to process and transfer without changing the temporal relationship to the information generated (delay). Finally, transparency to the source, i.e. treat and transfer the information generated instantly (capacity).

These criteria are evaluated by Key Performance Indicators (KPI) which are measurable parameters. A KPI is a metric capturing some aspects of the performance of one or more resources which is measured either directly, or could be defined in hierarchies. An example of KPI for the delay criteria is defining access time < 2s.

The interaction model specifies the autonomous degree of the distributed components, roles. The different roles are: *passive, active, reactive, proactive.* The developer of the service creation platform chooses to activate one of the roles. A reactive and proactive component describes the interaction behavior of an active component in which the object, which is highly-autonomous, does not simply act in response to its environment stimulus (changes). The proactive component can be used to maintain the QoS dynamically.

Figure 2 shows a service component where all interfaces are enabled. We obtain a composite component incorporating a QoS component and a control component. You can also associate a monitoring component. It is an autonomous Service Component (SC independent) satisfying stateless, and self-management, because it supervises the compliance of the delivered QoS. The OpenCloudware project adopted a Service Component approach based on QoS [9].

Remark : Link Component

In accordance with the <Node, Link, Network> abstract model, we see that the service is a resource composed of nodes (Service Components) and Links (network link, interconnection) of the same visibility level. We have assigned links to different network protocols (HTTP, SIP). The QoS Link will be integrated in the template OVF/XML.

3.2   Service Composition

In the Referential of the OpenCloudware Self-Service Portal (Figure 1) we have the service components. These are basic services.

To build the VPSN that will meet the customer request, we must identify and then select the right *VPSN nodes* (SC) - regarding their processing functionality and QoS- and establish the right *VPSN links* - regarding their communication capabilities and QoS that connect the selected nodes. Identifying the required VPSN nodes means to find which nodes are necessary to carry out the VPSN processing and thus the customer requested service functionalities. This is done thanks to service profiles that are created for each offered service by the service supplier. Among the identified nodes, we have to choose which one can carry out the requested behavior. This service node selection must be carried out in parallel with the link establishment to connect the selected nodes.

The VPSN uses the logic (the sequence) that specifies how the selected nodes must be connected according to the semantic of the requested service. The link establishment is thus carried out according to the VPSN logic.

The concept of "everything is a service" or "X-as-a-Service" allows the composition of a mobile application in the Cloud (Figure 3). The MCC application is composed by Service Components, for example SC1, SC2, SC3, SC4, SC5 *{security as a service authentication, security as a service authorization, service logic builder as a service, mobility as a service, and charging as a service, etc}.* But also, this application is composed by meta-services for example MSC1 *{monitoring as a service},* see Figure 3.

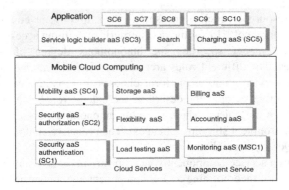

Fig. 3. Service Composition

The meta-services are the supervision services used for the management of each service component. These services manage the end-to-end application. Virtual resources will have a provisioning and will be instantiated.

3.3   Piloting: Event Driven Approach

As we have seen, the Virtual Private Service Network represents the selection of the services components and their sequencing. The link represents the interactions between services at the logical level. The entities of this level provide an application service. The VPSN is created at the time when the developer connects to the platform. When the developer connects, the platform knows the commercial offers it has subscribed to. These commercial offers are available in Referentials. A component of the platform, the "translator", knows the mapping between offers and the Services Components that provide this offer. The VPSN is created when all of SC corresponding to the commercial offers of the developer have been attached to the VPSN.

In our proposition, we favor an event-based approach. Our QoS management architecture is associated with a computing model that analyzes the QoS-based event and consequently adapts the VPSN configuration. Its QoS-component detects a QoS degradation and notifies the cloud management system. This latter monitors the event.

In order to support our event-driven approach, we create an Events Manager on the platform. The latter receives the notification (QoS degradation event) and matches this event to a specific action.

More precisely, the developer has at his disposal a decision table where for each event he indicates the next SC. The SC may be an application component or management component. Normally, a management action is a notification sent inside the service platform to a management service that is already subscribed to this type of events. In our example, a specific manager is subscribed to QoS degradation event. Hence, the Events Manager sends to the right manager, the right notification, to inform it that he is now able to start its control action and management process on the service layer. For the QoS degradation, the VSC service (that is explained later) is invoked.

For the mobility we have "spatial mobility event".

To illustrate the QoS integration in Service Creation Environment, in the following section we describe an E2E Process of the life cycle.

3.4   End to End Process

We propose to take into account the four processes of the life cycle: design, (THINK), Deployment (BUILD), Provisioning, and Operating (RUN), see Figure 4.

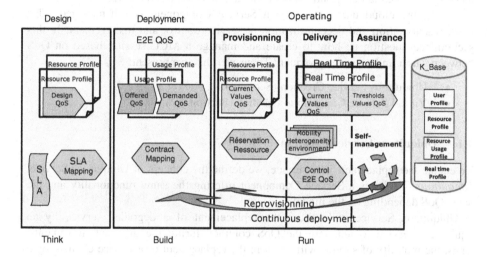

Fig. 4. End to End Process

The QoS component managed the behavior of the Service Component. Figure 4 shows the functions that it performs at each life cycle phase. The information is contained in appropriate profiles that are located in the referential.

In the *design phase* the QoS is evaluated as a design value in the service profile (instance of "Resource Profile").

In the *deployment phase* we can install the component in the right place by comparing the values that we find in the profile called "Usage Profile": the QoS offered and QoS requested.

In the *provisioning phase*, the QoS component is evaluated according to resource availability, to determine whether answer the query with the required QoS.

In the *operating phase*, the QoS component monitors continuously the availability of the Service Component resources. If the availability of the resources does not fulfill the QoS, then the QoS component emits an event of "out_contract" type. It uses its Management Interface. This event is received by the Event Manager of *MCC session* which will then seek SC replacement by Ubiquitous Services.

In the following section we propose Self-Management, i.e., Self-Management by the Ubiquitous Services compatible with the objectives in the Mobile Cloud Computing, and Virtual Service Community creation.

4　Second Proposal: Self-management Mechanisms

We introduce *Self-Management Mechanisms*. The management of the QoS is possible thanks to reactive and proactive role of the Service Component.

In our research, we rely on the objectives of the OpenCloudware project which will incorporate: (1) the components of modeling (THINK), (2) the development and production of applications (BUILD), (3) a PaaS platform compatible with multi-IaaS (RUN) for deployment, orchestration, performance testing, and self-management, (4) and the provisioning of virtualized multi-tier applications of type JavaEE.

During the cloud user session each Service Component is self-managed. This ensures automation and decentralization of service control and management. In this section, the question is: how to create and manage a MCC session based on QoS between a user and a service provider? To answer this, we present:

- Ubiquitous Service Creation (Section 4.1).
- Virtual Service Community Creation (Section 4.2)

4.1　Ubiquitous Service Creation

To enable the replacement of a service, we define the concept of Ubiquitous Service. *Ubiquitous Service* is a Service Component offering the same functionality and the same QoS depending on the model.

Ubiquitous Service will ensure the replacement of a degraded service by an equivalent service to maintain the QoS contract during the different movements. Thus, the mobility of service will result in the replacement of a service element by a Ubiquitous Service element. This replacement is done without breaking session thanks to the concept of VSC. The Virtual Service Community (VSC) contains a set of ubiquitous SCs (section 4.2).

4.2　Virtual Service Community Creation

To guarantee a continuous end-user's session, the Service Creation Platform proposes to regroup elements into Virtual Service Communities in order to have a dynamic E2E mobility management solution. This concept is also called the Community of Interest (CoI) concept. Each CoI defines a group of elements that share a common interest. Community members are self-managed and can exchange information with each other in pursuit of shared goals.

When deploying a new service in the supplier platforms, the Virtual Service Community management provides the service called *VSC Creation*. VSC Profile is included in the referential on the platform. This VSC Profile contains the following attributes: Service ID, Functionality, QoS criteria, Provider ID, SIP URI, Longitude, and Latitude, but also other attributes.

For each deployment, there is a search for the existence of the appropriate VSC. When found, this new component is attached to the VSC. Thus the VSC will contain all components functionally equivalent and with the same QOS.

However, due to mobility, some components used in the end user's session may not continue to fulfill their SLA or end-to-end user QoS requirements. To solve these mobility problems, according to the VSC concept, a ubiquitous counterpart that respects these requirements (a member of the same VSC) is dynamically found to replace the current component. As a result, this ubiquitous solution that is based on gathering QoS and functionality equivalent elements into communities guarantees all mobility cases by maintaining end-to-end sessions and their E2E QoS.

5   Use Case Service Creation and MCC Session Self-management

Today, the cloud users have become nomadic and expect to access their services without any temporal, geographical, technical or economic constraints (Figure 5). The developer defines the components they will need with their QoS requirements.

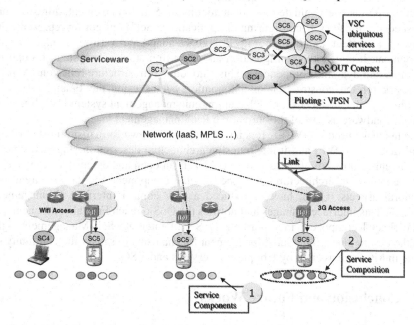

Fig. 5. Mobile Cloud Computing Use Case

Thanks to Service Creation Platform the developer will be able to in design phase (THINK):

- (1) Select the Service Components (SC) in the Referential (if they exist, otherwise it will create them), see Figure 5.
- (2) Define the service composition.
- (3) Select link, see Figure 6.
- (4) Define the service logic since the control is done on the basis of its VPSN.

In case the developer would also like to implement self-management, in the deployment phase (BUILD) he will be able select Ubiquitous Services (SC5, see Figure 5), and create the VSC.

```
<!—Network as a Service (NaaS) constraint element definitions -->
<xs:element name="appE2EDelay" type="tns:linkSetVmSetConstraint"
                   QoS requested=" currentvalue " QoS offered=" thresholdvalue " />
<xs:element name="appE2EAvaibility" type="tns:linkSetVmSetConstraint"
                   QoS requested=" currentvalue " QoS offered=" thresholdvalue " />
<xs:element name="appE2EReliability" type="tns:linkSetVmSetConstraint"
                   QoS requested=" currentvalue " QoS offered=" thresholdvalue " />
<xs:element name="appE2ECapacity" type="tns:linkSetVmSetResourceConstraint"
                   QoS requested=" currentvalue " QoS offered=" thresholdvalue " />
```

Fig. 6. OVF network link

During the operating phase (RUN), depending on the mobility, the system provides the services requested by maintaining QoS and service continuity according to these rules. As a result, VPSN and VSC establish a dynamic session that best suits the users' preferences and their QoS requirements.

Our proposals are evaluated on an autonomous Self-Management infrastructure and especially for the self-configuring of applications. Self-configuring represents the ability of a system to configure itself and to adapt the various changes in its environment. It allows the configuration and reconfiguration of a system through its autonomic and dynamic components. This autonomic infrastructure relies on JADE, a framework for the construction of autonomic systems using the Fractal reflective component model, and TUNe, a global autonomic management system [12]. It is used in OpenCloudware as part of the autonomic PaaS management layer.

The language used is OVF++. It is based on a well known formalism for describing virtual machines (OVF) and it integrates an architecture description language Fractal ADL (Architecture Definition Language). ADL is an open and extensible language to define component architectures for the Fractal component model. To treat the behavioral aspects (QoS), have introduced a new control interface (Management Interface). This interface manages and notifies the QoS of each Fractal component.

The Fractal component incorporating QoS will integrate Self-Management right from the design phase. The Self-Management Mechanisms to satisfy the continuity of service in MCC are assured by Ubiquitous Services and VSC.

6   Conclusion and Future Works

We have presented an innovative approach to domain engineering based on Service Components and Self-Management Mechanisms. This approach has been assessed and refined based on our experience in the Service Creation Environment. Our SCE adopted a Service Composition approach. Thus, the Service Components proposed have the properties recommended by SOA, namely: reusable, interoperable and autonomous, enhanced by the following properties: *mutualizable, stateless, ubiquitous and self-managed.* The Fractal *Service Component is based on a QoS* applicable in all phases of the life cycle. This architecture ensures cloud users have a composition of mobile cloud services in a seamless and dynamic way.

We have proposed the dynamic composition of the user session and a Self-Management by the Ubiquitous Services and VSC. This flexible way to create a service is essential if operators wish to by competitive.

Our future works will be the integration of our *Self-Management approach* in the PaaS platform of the OpenCloudware project.

Acknowledgments. This work is supported by the OpenCloudware project. OpenCloudware is funded by the French FSN (Fond national pour la Société Numérique), and is supported by Pôles Minalogic, Systematic and SCS.

References

1. ABI Research. Research report on Entreprise Mobile Cloud Computing: cloud Services, mobile devices, and the IT supply chain analysis (2009),
   http://www.abiresearch.com/research/1004608
2. ITU-T recommendation Y.2001: general overview of NGN. Y-Series recommendations: global information infrastructure, internet protocol aspects and next-generation networks, next generation networks - frameworks and functional architecture models (December 2004)
3. Mikoczy, E., Kotuliak, I., Deventer, O.V.: Evolution of the Converged NGN Service Platforms Towards Future Networks. Future Internet Journal 3(1) (March 2011)
4. Brunner, M.: Service Management in a Telecom Environment based on Active Network Technology. Ph.D. thesis No. 13433, Swiss Federal Institute of Technology Zurich (ETH Zurich), Switzerland (2000)
5. Aubonnet, T., Simoni, N.: PILOTE: A Service Creation Environment in Next Generation Network. In: Proceedings of the IEEE Intelligent Network Workshop, IN 2001, Boston, USA, Mai 6-9, pp. 36–40 (2001)
6. Chapman, C., Emmerich, W., Marquez, F.G., Clayman, S., Galis, A.: Software architecture definition for on-demand cloud provisioning. In: Hariri, S., Keahey, K. (eds.) HPDC, pp. 61–72. ACM (2010)
7. Distefano, S., Puliafito, A., Rak, M., Venticinque, S., Villano, U., Cuomo, A., Di Modica, G., Tomarchio, O.: QoS management in Cloud@Home infrastructures. In: Proc. of CyberC, Beijing, China, pp. 190–197 (October 2011)
8. Simoni, N., Xiong, X., Yin, C.: Virtual Community for the Dynamic Management of NGN Mobility. In: Proceedings of the Fifth International Conference on Autonomic and Autonomous Systems, ICAS 2009, Valencia, April 20-25, 2009, pp. 82–87 (2009)
9. Opencloudware project (2011-2014), http://www.opencloudware.org/
10. Modica, G.D.: Resource and Service Discovery in SOAs: A P2P Oriented Semantic Approach. International Journal of Applied Mathematics and Computer Science 21(2), 285–294 (2011)
11. Zhang, X., Yin, Y., Zhang, M., Zhang, B.: A Composite Web services Discovery Technique Based on Community Mining. In: Proc. IEEE Asia-Pacific Service Computing Conference (APSCC 2009), Singapore, December 7-11, pp. 445–450 (2009)
12. Bouchenak, S., Boyer, F., Hagimont, D., Krakowiak, S., Mos, A., De Palma, N., Quema, V., Stefani, J.-B.: Architecture-based autonomous repair management: An application to J2EE clusters. In: Proceedings of the IEEE Reliable Distributed Systems (2005)
13. Guinard, D., Trifa, V., Karnouskos, S., Spiess, P., Savio, D.: Interacting with the SOA-based Internet of Things: Discovery, Query, Selection, and On-Demand Provisioning of Web Services. IEEE Transactions on Services Computing 3(3), 223–235 (2010)
14. Mikoczy, E., Kotuliak, I., Deventer, O.V.: Evolution of the Converged NGN Service Platforms Towards Future Networks. Future Internet Journal 3(1), 67–86 (2011)

Modelling Mobility Based on Human Behaviour in Disaster Areas

Luís Conceição and Marilia Curado

Dept. Informatics Engineering, Centre for Informatics and Systems,
University of Coimbra
{lamc,marilia}@dei.uc.pt

Abstract. Mobility models are used to mimic the realistic movement of entities. Mobility models for wireless networks feature different objectives and characteristics, most based on random behaviour. However, random based mobility models, e.g. Random Waypoint (RWP), are often not suitable to represent the reality of node mobility, particularly in disaster areas where the search time for victims is a critical factor. Moreover, the studied mobility models for disaster environments are either random based or not suitable for such scenarios. This work proposes a new mobility model based on Human Behaviour for Disaster Areas (HBDA) to properly evaluate the performance of mobile wireless networks in disaster environments. HBDA is designed to cover as much area as possible, regarding search time as an important factor. This work evaluates HBDA concerning movement and link performances. Results show that HBDA provides an even distribution of nodes, a high coverage area and an efficient routing performance.

Keywords: Mobile Wireless Networks, Mobility Model, Disaster Scenarios.

1 Introduction

Post-disaster scenarios are typically considered to exist in deserts, forests or heavily damaged urban areas, often lacking operational network infrastructures. The establishment of a temporary communication system is crucial for the assistance of victims. Mobile wireless networks are often the only capable technology to answer to this type of demands. The evaluation of the network performance for such situations in a real world scenario is, in most cases infeasible, since the cost of the repeatability of the disaster scenario would be very high and extremely difficult to reproduce. Thus, simulation evaluation is the only feasible tool to study the behaviour and performance of mobile wireless networks in post-disaster environments. The results of a simulated performance evaluation strongly depend on the used mobility models. Since in post-disaster environments most nodes are mobile, the used mobility model has a crucial impact on the results. Despite of this fact, most performance evaluations existent in literature are simply based on random

V. Tsaoussidis et al. (Eds.): WWIC 2013, LNCS 7889, pp. 56–69, 2013.

mobility models. This work proposes a new mobility model based on Human Behaviour for Disaster Areas (HBDA). This model attempts to reproduce the human behaviour in search for victim operations.

The remaining of this document is organized as follows. Section 2 discusses the related work, covering some of the most significant mobility models in literature. Section 3 describes the HBDA mobility model. Section 4 performs a performance evaluation of HBDA, compared to the most common used mobility model: the Random Waypoint (RWP). Finally, Section 5 concludes this work and discusses future steps.

2   Related Work

Mobility models can be segmented according to node dependencies. Currently in literature there are two types of mobility models, namely *Entity Mobility Models* and *Group Mobility Models*. Entity Mobility models represent mobile nodes whose movements are independent of each other, whereas Group Mobility Models represent mobile nodes that have spatial dependencies, where the movement of a node influences the movement of at least one node around it. Regardless of their type, mobility models can be characterized according to their attributes, as shown in Table 1.

Table 1. Mobility Model Attributes

Attribute	Description
Random based	Node movement relies mainly in random decisions
Geographic restrictions	Nodes are restricted to a sub-area within the scenario
Target Area	Nodes have the objective of reaching a pre-determined point or area
Temporal dependencies	The node movement is influenced by its past movement
Constant velocity	Node velocities can not be modified during execution
Nodes join/leave	Leaving and joining the scenario is supported
Obstacles	The mobility model has obstacle avoidance mechanisms

2.1   Entity Mobility Models

In this subsection several proposed entity mobility models are discussed. The Random Waypoint Mobility Model is the most common and used by researchers, thus its discussion is performed in more depth than the remaining.

The **Random Waypoint (RWP)** mobility model was first introduced in [1]. The RWM model is based on pause times between changes of direction and/or speed. Initially, nodes are placed within the scenario area in a random fashion. After deployment, nodes do not have any attachments or restrictions towards remaining nodes. Each node begins by staying in a location for a period of time. When this time expires, it travels in a random direction with a random speed $[Vmin, Vmax]$, whereas $Vmin$ and $Vmax$ are the minimum and maximum velocity of the node, respectively. After reaching a waypoint (a decision position), the node waits another constant period of time and repeats the previous procedure until it reaches another waypoint. This process is repeated endlessly until the execution is over. Due to its simplicity, the RWP is a widely used model in research and it is the foundation for many recent mobility models. However, it does not represent realistic movements [2], and its use should only be considered for general purpose scenarios.

One important problem of the RWP model is the uneven distribution of nodes. Several publications (e.g. [3]) have shown that, over execution time, nodes tend to accumulate in the middle of the simulation scenario. To overcome this issue, a variation of the RWP, called **Random Waypoint with Attraction Points (RWAP)** is proposed in [4]. This model generates more realistic non-equally distributed mobility. However, the probability of a node visiting an attraction point is larger than the random choice of other points, resulting in a larger concentration of nodes in the attraction points.

The **Mobility (ClusM) Model** [5] is very similar to the RWAP model, using RWP with attraction points to disaster areas. The main difference is that the attraction to the disaster area depends on concentration of nodes nearby. In other words, nodes are have a lower probability of moving towards attraction areas where there is already a high density of nodes. Thus, in a scenario with multiple disaster areas (in this case, used as attraction points), nodes tend to be evenly distributed across those areas.

2.2   Group Mobility Models

The previous subsection presented the mobility models whose nodes actions are completely independent of each other. However, there are situations where nodes must mutually coordinate to achieve a certain objective, such as search and rescue operations. In order to model cooperative situations, a group mobility model is required. The Reference Point Group Mobility (RPGM) [6] can be considered a reference model, as there are many improvements of it in literature.

The **Reference Point Group Mobility (RPGM)** [6] allows the random motion of a group and also enables the individual motion of a node within its group. Every group has a logical centre, which controls the mobility parameters, such as motion behaviour, location, speed and direction of the entire group. Furthermore, every group is confined to a well defined geographical scope, from where its nodes can not exit. Therefore, all nodes have spatial dependencies defined by the logical centre. Sánchez et al. proposed three variations of the RPGM model in order to cover distinct objectives, namely the Column Mobility Model (CM), the Nomadic Community Mobility Model (NCM) and the Pursue Mobility Model (PM) [7]. The **Column Mobility Model (CM)** can be used for searching purposes. A group of mobile nodes moves in a line formation (or column) towards a random direction. Each node is tied to a reference point and each reference point is followed by another, i.e. each reference point depends on another until the head of the column is reached. Within groups, each node can move randomly around its reference point, however not exceeding a pre-configured maximum distance. The CM Model can be useful for searching purposes, whereas several groups/columns move in distinct directions and nodes move randomly inside each column. This mobility model can be obtained using a variation of the RPGM model implementation. The **Nomadic Community Mobility Model (NCM)** is also a variation of the RPGM model. The community (or group) is defined as several nodes following only one reference point. A random direction and speed of the reference point is calculated. The group of nodes follows the reference point and can also move randomly around it, once more not exceeding a pre-configured maximum distance. The **Pursue Mobility Model (PM)** attempts to imitate the tracking of a certain target. A group of nodes follows one particular node, adjusting their speed and direction according to the target. Within the group, nodes can move randomly but can not exceed a pre-configured distance from each other. For example, to better illustrate, this model could represent a group of police officers attempting to catch an individual. Again, this mobility model can be obtained using a modified version of the RPGM model.

The authors in [8] designed a mobility model for disaster scenarios, namely **Disaster Area (DA)**. The work studied the displacement of civil protection forces in real life and developed a corresponding model. The simulation area is divided according to several categories (e.g. incident site, casualties treatment area, transport zone, hospital zone). Technically, the disaster area scenario consists of several sub-areas with different configurations. Each sub-area uses a visibility graph to avoid obstacles. Each node is manually assigned to one sub-area and it is not allowed to exit unless it belongs to the transport zone sub-area. In the transport zone sub-area, nodes are allowed to leave and join, in order to represent the transportation of injured patients to the hospital. Despite the effort of mimicking a real scenario, the mobility model is still quite unrealistic as movement of rescue agents is based on the Random Waypoint (RWP) mobility model, particularly in the disaster site sub-area, where agents are performing search-for-victim operations.

Authors in [9] also proposed a **Composite Mobility (CoM)** model for disaster scenarios. It is a combination of several existing models to better represent human mobility in disaster areas. For group mobility the original RPGM model is used, however for better realism the RWP is replaced by the Levy-Walk model, proposed in [10]. The CoM model also concerns obstacle avoidance based on a modified Voronoï diagram. Thus, this model is based on a well known geographic map and is driven by a specific target, using the Dijkstra algorithm to calculate the shortest path between two points. However, in a disaster scenario it is very difficult to accurately obtain the current map, whereas its infrastructures may be modified or non existent. Therefore, following a known map of the area could not be sufficient to successfully perform search and rescue operations.

2.3 Summary of Mobility Models

This section studied some of the most relevant mobility models in literature, presented in table 2. The Entity Mobility Models do not establish any relationship between nodes, thus not being suitable to represent movements in disaster scenarios due to the lack of group coordination. On the other hand, the Group

Table 2. Studied Mobility Models and their Attributes

Models	Random based	Geographic Restrictions	Temporal dependencies	Target Area	Constant velocity	Nodes join/leave	Obstacles
RWP[1]	✔				+		
RWAP[4]	✔			✔			
ClusM[5]	✔			+			
RPGM[6]				+		+	
CM[7]				+		+	
NCM[7]				+		+	
PM[7]							
DA[8]		✔	✔	✔		✔	✔
CoM[9]		✔		✔			✔

[1]**Note:** ✔represents explicitly supported and +represents not originally supported but can be modified to support

Mobility Models provide node coordination. The RPGM model is widely used in literature and many proposals derive from it, due to its configuration versatility.

There are also a few Group Entity Models designed specifically for disaster environments. The DA mobility model is not mainly based in random movements, since it implements specific movements between the sub-areas of the scenario. However, within each sub-area the RWP model is used, ultimately resulting in the disaster sub-area being explored by the RWP. The CoM model uses the Levy-Walk model instead. Nonetheless, a map of the post-disaster area must be known in advance, which in most situations very difficult to obtain. Thus, to the best of our knowledge, there is no mobility model that is both not random based in disaster area exploration and Thus, to the best of our knowledge, there is no mobility model that provides blind (post-disaster area is unknown) exploration with non random major decisions.

3   Modelling Mobility Based on Human Behaviour in Disaster Areas

In order to obtain accurate evaluation results in mobile wireless networks it is necessary to use a mobility model that is capable of reproducing as much as possible a real scenario. This work is focused on post-disaster areas whereas the typical mobility pattern is based in search for victim (SFV) operations. As previously studied, most of simulation evaluations are based on the Random Waypoint (RWP) model, which often does not represent the reality of node movements. Furthermore, the studied mobility models for disaster areas are random based, such as Disater Area (DA), which also uses the RWP inside each sub-area. Thus, it becomes necessary to develop a new model, not random based, capable of representing node movements in such scenarios.

This work proposes a new mobility model based on Human Behaviour for Disaster Areas (HBDA), aiming to mimic real node movements in search operations in order to properly evaluate the network performance.

3.1   Mobility Description

Regarding human behaviour, when a group of people is performing search operations, each person tends to physically separate from one another, in order to scout unexplored areas. On the other hand, each person typically maintains a line of sight (or in-range communicable) to at least one other person in order to be able to announce a possible victim discovery. The group of people start the area exploration from an initial position and step-by-step, each individual makes his way to a Target Position, constantly maintaining a light of sigh to another (*maximum distance*) and, at the same time, not becoming too close (*minimum distance*). This method of search seamlessly forces individuals to evenly spread across the scenario in order to cover as much area as possible.

To maintain a compromise between the minimum distance and maximum distance to neighbour nodes, the HBDA model uses a system based on force vectors. To better illustrate this process, Figure 1 shows an example of the resultant force vector for three neighbour nodes.

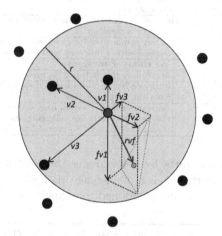

Fig. 1. Example of a Resultant Vorce Vector rfv

A node considers that another node is its neighbour if the distance is less than the maximum distance, represented in the Figure as r. During exploration, each node adjusts its position in order to become separated from its closest neighbours. To achieve this, first it is calculated a vector from the node position (represented in the middle) to each neighbour position ($v1$, $v2$ and $v3$). Afterwards, a force vector is calculated for each neighbour vector ($fv1$, $fv2$ and $fv3$). The force vectors always have the opposite direction of the neighbour vectors and their length is provided by the subtraction of the maximum distance (r) by the length of the neighbour vectors. This method allows closer neighbour nodes to have an higher opposite direction force. Finally, the sum of the force vector is computed, resulting in a single force vector (rfv).

Upon the arrival to the Target position, a new Target is determined for all nodes, which immediately start moving towards it. This process is repeated until the end of execution. The new Target is determined based on the previous by the inversion of the x or y positions, e.g. assuming a previous Target $PT(x,y)$, the new Target will be located in $NT(-x,y)$ or $NT(x,-y)$. The decision of inverting x or y is random with 50% of probability for each.

3.2   Algorithm Description

For a better comprehension of the HBDA model, this subsection discusses the main procedures of the algorithm. Table 3 describes the model of the system, including the parameters and functions used in the algorithm.

Table 3. HBDA Parameters and Functions

Parameters	
x and y	current position of a node (x,y)
$targetX$ and $targetY$	current position of the Target in the form $(targetX, targetY)$
$MinVelocity$ and $MaxVelocity$	minimum and maximum velocities of nodes
$MinDistance$ and $MaxDistance$	minimum and maximum distances that nodes separate from each other
$MinTravelTime$ and $MaxTravelTime$	minimum and maximum amount of time that a node travels towards a position
Rnd	object responsible for random generations. This object is initialized with a different seed for each execution
Auxiliary Functions	
$distance(n1, n2)$	determines the distance (in meters) between nodes $n1$ and $n2$
$getInRangeNodes(x,y)$	returns a list of nodes which distance less than $MaxDistance$ from the (x,y) position
$generateUnitVectors()$	generates a new random unit vector. This method is used in the network start up, allowing the nodes to distance from themselves in order to proceed to their objective.

The HBDA algorithm starts by determining the next node movement (Algorithm 1). In this function, a list of in-range nodes is obtained in order to determine if the node is optimal positioned towards its neighbours.

Algorithm 1. Determining next move - **determineNextMove()**

```
# {Obtain in-range neighbours}
optimalDistance ← true
inRangeNodes[] ← getInRangeNodes(x, y)
for i = 0 to length(inRangeNodes) do
    if distance(this, inRangeNodes[i]) < MinDistance then
        optimalDistance ← false
        break
    end if
end for

# {Determine if node is well positioned}
if optimalDistance and length(inRangeNodes) > 0 then
    followTarget()
else
    adjustPosition()
end if
```

A node is considered to be optimal positioned when its distance to all neighbours is comprehended between $MinDistance$ and $MaxDistance$. When a node is in optimal position, it follows the Target, otherwise it has to adjust its position. Regardless of the decision, the node will calculate a trajectory from its current position towards a new location, spending a certain amount of time, between $MinTravelTime$ to $MaxTravelTime$ to traverse it.

Algorithm 2. Following Target Position - **followTarget()**

\# {Determine vector to target from current position}
$vectorX \leftarrow (targetX - x)$
$vectorY \leftarrow (targetY - y)$

\# {Calc velocity between MinVelocity and MaxVelocity}
$velocity \leftarrow MinVelocity + (Rnd.NextDouble() \times MaxVelocity - MinVelocity)$
\# {Calc travel time between MinTravelTime and MaxTravelTime}
$travelTime \leftarrow MinTravelTime + (Rnd.NextInt() \times MaxTravelTime - MinTravelTime)$

\# {Normalize vectors}
$distanceToTarget \leftarrow \sqrt{(vectorX^2 + vectorY^2)}$
$unitVectorX \leftarrow vectorX/distanceToTarget$
$unitVectorY \leftarrow vectorY/distanceToTarget$

\# {Calc new positions}
$x \leftarrow x + (unitVectorX \times velocity \times travelTime)$
$y \leftarrow y + (unitVectorY \times velocity \times travelTime)$

Upon reaching its new location, and upon that time expires, a new node movement determination is performed. This process is repeated until the end of execution.

The Following Target procedure (Algorithm 2) will calculate a trajectory based on a vector from the current node location towards the target. It begins by determining the vector from the current node position (x, y). Afterwards a velocity between $MinVelocity$ and $MaxVelocity$ is randomly generated. Finally, based on the generated velocity and travel time, the unit vector is calculated and a new vector towards the next position is computed.

When nodes are not in optimal position they are required to adjust it (Algorithm 3). The adjustment towards an optimal position is based on force vectors, as previously described in subsection 3.1. This procedure starts by analysing if the current unit vectors are null, i.e. none have been previously generated. This only occurs in the network start up. Since all nodes start from the same position, new random unit vectors are generated allowing the nodes to spread apart.

For the remaining cases, a list of the in-range neighbours is obtained and a force vector is determined, based on the distances to neighbours. The resultant force vector is then normalized and a vector towards the next position is computed based on a randomly generated velocity between $MinVelocity$ and $MaxVelocity$. To be noted that this procedure always expends one second,

---

Algorithm 3. Adjusting To Optimal Position - **adjustPosition()**

\# {If unit vectors are null, generate new (Startup)}
if $unitVectorX = 0$**and**$unitVectorY = 0$ **then**
    $generateUnitVectors()$
else
    \# {Obtain in-range neighbours}
    $inRangeNodes[] \leftarrow getInRangeNodes(x, y)$
    $vectorX \leftarrow 0$
    $vectorY \leftarrow 0$
    for $i = 0$ to $length(inRangeNodes)$ **do**
        \# {Obtain vector for each neighbour}
        $nX \leftarrow inRangeNodes[i].getX()$
        $nY \leftarrow inRangeNodes[i].getY()$
        $distance(this, inRangeNodes[i])$
        $nVectorX \leftarrow (x - nX)/distance$
        $nVectorY \leftarrow (y - nY)/distance$
        \# {Add neighbour vector to overall force vector, based on distance}
        $distance \leftarrow MaxDistance - distance$
        $vectorX \leftarrow vectorX + (nVectorX \times distance)$
        $vectorY \leftarrow vectorY + (nVectorY \times distance)$
    end for
    \# {Normalize vectors}
    $distanceToTarget \leftarrow \sqrt{(vectorX^2 + vectorY^2)}$
    $unitVectorX \leftarrow vectorX/distanceToTarget$
    $unitVectorY \leftarrow vectorY/distanceToTarget$
end if
\# {Calc velocity between MinVelocity and MaxVelocity}
$velocity \leftarrow MinVelocity + (Rnd.NextDouble() \times MaxVelocity - MinVelocity)$
\# {Calc new positions}
$x \leftarrow x + (unitVectorX \times velocity)$
$y \leftarrow y + (unitVectorY \times velocity)$

---

disregarding both $MinTravelTime$ and $MaxTravelTime$. Nonetheless, the position adjustment can be called consecutively.

4   Evaluation and Results

In this section, an evaluation study of the HBDA model performance is conducted. The main objective of this evaluation is to assess the movement and performance differences between RWP and HBDA mobility models.

4.1   Environment and Parameters

The scenario and parameter variations utilized to evaluate HBDA were selected carefully, in the attempt of representing, as much as possible, realistic disaster environments. In this specification the evaluation parameters were divided in four groups (Table 4). The General Parameters and Traffic Generation Parameters are common to the HBDA and RWP models. The RWP Parameters and

HBDA Parameters are specific to the RWP and HBDA models, respectively. The conducted simulations were performed using the OPNET Modeler [11]. Network sizes were varied between 25 and 100 nodes in order to assess the scalability of routing for the different models. In this evaluation it has been decided that a proactive routing protocol should be used in order to evaluate the impact of constant path establishment. The Optimized Link State Routing protocol (OLSR) [12] was utilized for this purpose.

Table 4. Simulation Parameters

General Parameters	
Simulator	OPNET Modeler 17.1
Simulation duration time (s)	900
Transmission range (m)	150
Network size (number of nodes)	25; 50; 75; 100
Area Size (m^2)	500 × 500
WLAN IEEE Standard	802.11g (54 Mbps)
Routing Protocol	OLSR
Mobility Model	HBDA; RWP
Traffic Generation Parameters (Per Node)	
Start-Stop Time (s)	50-End of Execution
Traffic pattern	Constant Bit Rate (CBR)
Transport Protocol	User Datagram Protocol (UDP)
Packet generation rate (s)	4
Packet Size (bits)	4096
Destination Node	Random
RWP Parameters	
Min-Max node speed (m/s)	1-5
Pause time (s)	None
HBDA Parameters	
Min-Max node speed (m/s)	1-5
Min-Max Distance Threshold (m)	50-100
Min-Max Travel Time	1-10

The metrics used to evaluate HBDA are divided in two categories, Mobility-based and Link-based. The Mobility-based metrics attempt to assess the movement characteristics produced by the mobility model. The Link-based metrics evaluate the network performance. The Mobility-based metrics are defined as follows.

- *Density Distribution of Nodes* - to study the distribution of nodes, the scenario area is divided in 25 × 25 sub-areas. At each second, the amount of nodes is measured inside each sub-area, in order to study the distribution of nodes during execution time.
- *Node Degree* - represents the amount of in-range nodes per node. In this evaluation, a node is considered to be in-range to another if they distance no more than 100 meters. Typically, a low mean node degree represents a low density network with poor connectivity. On the other hand, a high mean node degree symbolizes a high density network with potential for high connectivity.
- *Area Coverage* - represents the cumulative amount of covered area during execution time. For evaluation and comparison purposes, it has been considered that each node is able to cover 5 meters around it. Thus, a radius of 5 meters along the trajectory of each node is considered covered.

The Link-based metrics are defined as follows.

- *Topology Changes* - measures the amount of topology changes of the OLSR protocol. This metric assesses the performance of the routing protocol. Since each topology change leads to a route table recalculation, a big amount represents a poor performance efficiency.
- *Throughput* - represents the average rate at which data packets are successfully delivered from one node to another. This metric can be defined by Equation 1.

$$Throughput = \frac{Number\ Delivered\ Packets \times Packet\ Size(bits)}{Simulation\ Duration\ Time(s)} \tag{1}$$

4.2 Mobility-Based Results

As previously stated, this evaluation studies the movement characteristics of the mobility model.

Density Distribution of Nodes. Figure 2 shows the average density distribution of nodes for all network sizes, represented in two dimensions, i.e. across the x axis. This measurement is the result of 500 executions with different seeds, in order to produce a precise and even representation of the distribution.

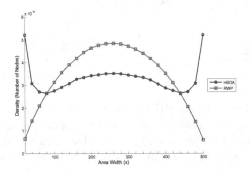

Fig. 2. Density Distribution of Nodes

As shown in the chart, the RWP model tends to concentrate nodes in the center of the scenario, producing an unbalanced distribution. This centralized distribution is characteristic of RWP and has already been demonstrated in several papers [9][2]. In contrast, the HBDA model tends to distribute its nodes more evenly across the scenario. However, it also shows a considerable density of nodes in the edges of the scenario. This fact only occurs because the start position of nodes is always located in the edges of the scenario.

Node Degree. Figure 3 shows the average node degree for the different network sizes. The HBDA model presents a consistent node degree, i.e. it increases slightly along the network size. On the other hand, RWP presents a small node degree for the 25 node network and rapidly increases with network size, overcoming the HBDA model. This occurs due to the unbalanced distribution of nodes in RWP. For the 25 node network, the node density is low, and since most nodes keep losing connectivity due to its random mobility, the mean node degree is low. For the 100 node network, the mean node degree is remarkably high, mostly due to the high density of nodes but also due to the its unbalanced distribution.

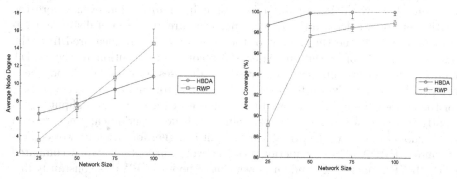

Fig. 3. Average Node Degree

Fig. 4. Average Area Coverage

Area Coverage. Figure 4 shows the average area coverage for different network sizes. Clearly, the HBDA model covers significantly more area when compared to RWP, reaching 100% coverage for the 100 node network. Despite of the superior coverage of the HBDA model, it has higher deviations from its mean, when compared to the RWP, particularly in smaller networks.

4.3 Link-Based Results

The Link-based evaluation covers the evaluation of network performance. This evaluation mainly assesses the routing efficiency for the different scenarios.

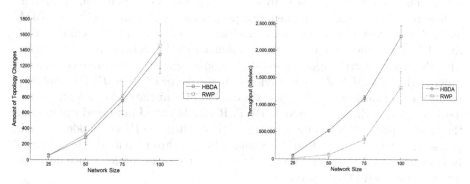

Fig. 5. Average Topology Changes

Fig. 6. Average Throughput

Topology Changes. Figure 5 depicts the average amount of topology changes for the different network sizes. As shown, the number of topology changes grow significantly with the network size, particularly for networks larger than 50 nodes. This means that the OLSR protocol is performing a high amount of route recalculations, potentially having a big overhead.

Throughput. Concerning that in the HBDA model nodes start from the same position, they would be capable of transmitting information even before the routing protocol calculate the paths, since they are at 1-Hop of distance. Considering this fact, the throughput of the network was only measured from the first 120 seconds of execution. After 120 seconds of execution in the HBDA model, it has been empirically observed, in all cases, that nodes already been completely spread. Figure 6 shows the average throughput over network size, for the entire network. As depicted in the figure, the average throughput significantly increases for larger networks. Since each node periodically generates a fixed amount of traffic, the overall throughput is higher for larger networks. Furthermore, HBDA offers a superior mean network throughput, when compared to the RWP model. The random movement of nodes in RWP is constantly disrupting node connections, resulting in a higher packet loss.

To be noted that the measured throughput complies both generated traffic and routing control traffic. Therefore, by the analysis of the chart, it can be observed that the mean throughput increases almost exponentially for larger networks. Despite the fact that more nodes are transmitting in larger networks, the amount of generated traffic per node is always the same. Regarding this fact, the mean throughput should grow proportionally to the network size. However, the chart confirms that the control traffic of the routing protocol strongly increases for networks larger than 75 nodes.

5   Conclusion and Future Work

In this work, a study of the existent mobility models was conducted and a new mobility model for disaster areas was proposed. The simulation evaluation demonstrated significant movement and performance differences between HBDA and RWP models. Concerning mobility-based evaluation, results demonstrated that HBDA provides better node distribution across the scenario area, in contrast with the RWP centralization of nodes. The node degree is also more consistent, proving that the HBDA connectivity is more balanced. The HBDA mobility model also performs a better area coverage, however at the cost of a higher standard deviation, when compared to RWP. Regarding the Link-based evaluation, the routing protocol generally is more efficient when the HBDA model is used, providing a lower End-to-End delay and a higher throughput. However, it can be concluded that the routing algorithm has a significant performance decrease for networks larger than 50 nodes.

Summarizing, the proposed mobility model provides a more real simulation possibility for disaster scenarios, instead of random based movement decisions. The future of this work concerns the scalability of the network. In order to enable the simulation of more than 100 nodes it is necessary to create a network hierarchy, allowing the routing protocol to scale. Thus, the next steps of this work will contemplate the integration of a clustering algorithm for mobile wireless networks, providing an hierarchical structure for the routing protocol.

Acknowledgments. This work was supported by a PhD Scholarship (SFRH / BD / 81829 / 2011) from the Portuguese National Foundation for Science and Technology (FCT) and by the project MORFEU (PTDC / EEA-CRO / 108348 / 2008). The authors would like to thank the OPNET University Program for the licenses provided for the OPNET Modeler Wireless Suite R.

References

1. Johnson, D., Maltz, D.: Dynamic source routing in ad hoc wireless networks. In: Mobile Computing (1996), `http://www.springerlink.com/index/QG8843V474571123.pdf`
2. Kumar, S., Sharma, S.C., Suman, B.: Mobility Metrics Based Classification & Analysis of Mobility Model for Tactical Network. International Journal of Next-Generation Networks 2(3), 39–51 (2010), `http://www.airccse.org/journal/ijngn/papers/0910ijngn05.pdf`
3. Bettstetter, C., Resta, G., Santi, P.: The Node Distribution of the Random Waypoint Mobility Model for Wireless Ad Hoc Networks 2(3), 257–269 (2003)
4. Bettstetter, C., Wagner, C.: The spatial node distribution of the random waypoint mobility model. In: German Workshop on Mobile Ad Hoc ... (2002), `http://citeseerx.ist.psu.edu/viewdoc/download?doi=10.1.1.93.1351&rep=rep1&type=pdf`
5. Lim, S., Yu, C., Das, C.: Clustered Mobility Model for Scale-Free Wireless Networks. In: Proceedings of the 2006 31st IEEE Conference on Local Computer Networks, pp. 231–238 (November 2006), `http://ieeexplore.ieee.org/lpdocs/epic03/wrapper.htm?arnumber=4116552`
6. Hong, X., Gerla, M.: A group mobility model for ad hoc wireless networks (1999), `http://citeseerx.ist.psu.edu/viewdoc/summary?doi=10.1.1.138.971`
7. Sanchéz, M.: Mobility models @ONLINE, `http://www.disca.upv.es/misan/mobmodel.htm` (page last accessed in December 30, 2012)
8. Aschenbruck, N., Gerhards-Padilla, E., Gerharz, M., Frank, M., Martini, P.: Modelling mobility in disaster area scenarios. In: Proceedings of the 10th ACM Symposium on Modeling, Analysis, and Simulation of Wireless and Mobile Systems - MSWiM 2007, p. 4 (2007), `http://portal.acm.org/citation.cfm?doid=1298126.1298131`
9. Pomportes, S., Tomasik, J., Vèque, V.: A Composite Mobility Model for Ad Hoc Networks in Disaster Areas 1(1), 62–68 (2011)
10. Rhee, I., Shin, M., Hong, S., Lee, K., Chong, S.: On the Levy-Walk Nature of Human Mobility. In: 2008 IEEE INFOCOM - The 27th Conference on Computer Communications, pp. 924–932 (April 2008), `http://ieeexplore.ieee.org/lpdocs/epic03/wrapper.htm?arnumber=4509740`
11. OPNET, Opnet simulator (1986), `http://www.opnet.com/`
12. Jacquet, P., Mhlethaler, P., Clausen, T., Laouiti, A., Qayyum, A., Viennot, L.: Optimized link state routing protocol for ad hoc networks, pp. 62–68 (2001)

Robust Association for Multi-radio Devices under Coverage of Multiple Networks

Enrica Zola[1], Peter Dely[2], Andreas J. Kassler[2], and Francisco Barcelo-Arroyo[1]

[1] Telematics Engineering Dept., Universitat Politècnica de Catalunya (UPC),
Barcelona, Spain
{enrica,barcelo}@entel.upc.edu
[2] Computer Science Dept., Karlstad University, Karlstad, Sweden
{peter.dely,andreas.kassler}@kau.se

Abstract. Many devices are nowadays equipped with multiple wireless network interfaces such as GSM, HSPA+ and WLAN. This requires a mechanism for identifying which access network to use at a given time so to provide best user experience. Such decision is typically made using past information available at the user (e.g. history of signal strength measurements), or using a prediction of the future status of the parameters of interest. The key problem is that the parameter estimation is difficult and that the predictions may be inaccurate. In this paper, we develop a mathematical model for the access network selection problem, which is solved using robust optimization techniques. The objective is to maximize the download rate the user can achieve during a certain period in the future. The model provides guidelines for selecting the access network which guarantees, within a given probability bound, a minimum download rate for a given rate uncertainty.

Keywords: Access network selection, Uncertain rates, Robust optimization.

1 Introduction

Nowadays, mobile terminals such as smartphones or tablets are equipped with several Network Interface Cards (NICs), thus allowing the user to connect to different wireless Access Networks (AN) including GSM, HSPA+, LTE or 802.11. This requires a mechanism to select the best access network providing the best quality of experience. Such network selection problem is challenging as it involves multiple variables and decision criteria, including user preferences, movement patterns, battery status, network load or cost. What makes this problem challenging is that information that guides this decision making is mostly inaccurate and typically reflects past, not current or future network states. For example, if one wants to decide which AN to select based on available bandwidth estimates, such estimates mostly are not reflecting the true available capacity due to limitations in the mechanisms to obtain such estimates.

An interesting approach to solve the AN selection problem is to define a mathematical model which guides such selection process. Such model uses multiple

V. Tsaoussidis et al. (Eds.): WWIC 2013, LNCS 7889, pp. 70–82, 2013.

variables as input such as available bandwidth estimates or rate profiles and tries to select the AN which provides the optimum solution in terms of e.g. throughput, reliability or battery power. In order to solve such a model, mechanisms need to be applied that deal with uncertain data. A common approach is to define a so-called worst-case scenario and obtain a solution that is widely deemed to be too conservative for practical implementations [13]. The key problem is the impact of the amount of uncertainty on the solution. For example, if one assumes a too small variability, only the expected rate is considered when selecting the best radio access network, thus providing a solution which is not robust to possible larger rate variations in the future. This may lead to sub-optimal performance. In contrast, by taking into account the possible total uncertainty in the rates, the solution will be too conservative, thus selecting a radio access network with the highest minimum rate. A robust solution lies in between these two extreme cases. We are interested in finding a robust solution that can guarantee a given minimum rate with a given probability, thus selecting the AN that guarantees the selected performance, despite the uncertain future.

"Robust optimization" refers to the optimization for a set of input parameter matrices, instead of one fixed system matrix, as typical for deterministic optimization problems. Such concept has been applied by developing e.g. a self-optimization algorithm for handover (HO) parameters [12]. The key feature of the proposed algorithm is the mobility robustness, which means that the HO performance is robust against the change in user mobility. In [16], robust optimization models are applied in energy limited wireless sensor networks so to e.g. minimize the energy consumed, maximize the data extracted, and maximize the network lifetime. In [7], it has been applied to solve the problem of power control in mobile ad hoc wireless networks. The authors seek a solution set that trades off the dual objectives of achieving optimality (i.e., minimize the aggregate power employed by the transmitters) and maintaining feasibility (i.e., the received signal must exceed the threshold required for successful reception). The "cost of uncertainty" is measured by the total additional power required when all channel states are known. The authors in [6] introduce a new mixed integer linear optimization problem that provides the best association scheme for mobile users in a wireless local area network (WLAN) scenario with multiple access points (APs). However, they do not deal with multiple ANs.

In this paper, we develop a mathematical model that helps a user to select the best AN under uncertain parameters. We assume that the user aims to download data during a given period of time. We model the problem that a user wants to select the AN that guarantees the highest bit rate during the entire connection. The challenge is that rate profiles for the different ANs are uncertain and may vary in the future. We use ROME [8] to solve our robust optimization problem. We introduce a parameter that enables a trade-off between the uncertainty to be taken into account during the optimization. This allows us to select between an AN that provides a conservative but not optimal decision or a more risky strategy. To the best of our knowledge, this paper is the first one that deals with robust optimization for the selection of the best available AN given variability in the rate profiles.

The remainder of this paper is organized as follows. In Section 2, we describe our model for access network selection based on robust optimization. In Section 3, the estimated rate profiles used to feed the optimization model are presented for the two technologies under study (i.e. 3G and WLAN). Section 4 presents and interprets our results. Finally, section 5 concludes the paper.

2   Network Model

2.1   Motivating Example

Consider a user who wants to download some video with his smartphone while he is in a cafeteria. Furthermore, consider that he is under coverage of both WLAN and 3G networks. Which technology should the user select in order to be sure (i.e., 90%) of achieving at least a given bit rate (minimum guaranteed rate) along the duration of the connection?

In order to answer this question, one needs to consider the uncertainty in the download rate estimation. Often, WLANs provide a higher average download rate than 3G networks. However, the variation of download rates in WLANs is also higher, because of the smaller communication distances, which lead to a stronger dependency of the download rate on user mobility. In contrast, the download rate in 3G networks is typically more stable. Usually, it is not possible to precisely predict the achievable download rate for a given AN. However, based on historic information one can extract statistics about the achievable rates, such as the minimum, the maximum and the average achievable rate. This information can then be used to guide the AN selection.

2.2   A Robust Model for AN Selection

We formulate the problem of selecting the best AN under rate uncertainty as a robust binary optimization problem. This problem can be modelled as a variant of the robust portfolio optimization problem introduced in [3], in which one picks stocks with uncertain return with the objective to maximize the return of the overall stock portfolio.

In our case we want to select *one* AN a, given a set of available ANs A, all with uncertain download rates. We assume that the time is divided into slots of equal, but arbitrary length (e.g. 1 second slots). We further assume, that at time $t = 1$, the user wants to select one network and to use it for a period of t_{max} slots. We consider a one-shot optimization, i.e. a user selects the AN at $t = 1$ and stays connected during the whole connection period.

With $r_a(t)$ we denote a random variable specifying the download rate via AN a in slot t. We describe r by the 3-tuple $\left[\bar{r}_a(t), r_a^{max}(t), r_a^{min}(t)\right]$, where $\bar{r}_a(t)$ denotes the mean download rate via AN a during slot t, and $r_a^{max}(t)$ and $r_a^{min}(t)$ describe the maximum positive and negative deviation from the mean. We refer to this 3-tuple also as *estimated rate profile*.

Moreover, we introduce the binary variable x_a, which is 1 if the user selects AN a and 0 otherwise. One can thus compute the optimal AN by maximizing

$$\sum_{a \in A} \sum_{t=1}^{t_{max}} r_a(t)x_a \tag{1}$$

subject to

$$\sum_{a \in A} x_a = 1 \tag{2}$$

$$\left\| -\mathbf{r}^{min} - \mathbf{r}^{max} \right\|_1 \leq \Gamma t_{max} \tag{3}$$

Eq. 2 states that a user can only use one AN during his download. Eq. 3 specifies that the average negative deviation must not exceed Γ, which is a parameter to control the maximum allowed deviation of the input parameters. $\|.\|_1$ is the Manhattan norm. Due to eq. 3, the posed optimization problem cannot be solved right away with a commercial solver such as ILOG CPLEX [10]. However, [3] shows how to transform the problem into a common integer optimization problem, for which efficient algorithms exist.

The process of transforming the problem can be automated with ROME [8], an algebraic modelling toolbox for modelling robust OPs. ROME's core functionality involves translating modelling code, input by the user, into an internal structure in ROME, which is then marshalled into a solver specific input format for solving (e.g., ILOG CPLEX [10]). We have solved the following numerical examples of the problem with ROME and CPLEX.

3   Estimated Rate Profiles

Our model requires estimation of application-level download rates for each technology, which we derive in this section for the different ANs considered.

3.1   Estimated Rate Profiles for 3G

Estimated rate profiles for the 3G network are taken from [14], where the authors tested the performance of four US national wireless carriers (AT&T, Sprint, T-Mobile, and Verizon) at various locations. Different cities were chosen based on varying population densities, physical topography, and cellular environments. Measurements were performed at ten locations (e.g., five indoor and five outdoor) in each of 13 cities in the USA. Four phones from different brands were used for the test (refer to [14] for more details). On each phone, a test application measured the download rate at each test location by sending data to and from a server on one coast, and then to and from a server on the opposite coast. Finally, results were averaged.

For this study, we selected San Francisco and AT&T as operator. We only consider data from the 5 indoor sites as the scenario in the following simulations

Table 1. Application-level rates for 3G (from [14])

Expected rate $(\bar{r}_{3G}(t))$	3.36 Mbps
Deviations (min, max)	(-1.46, +0.74) Mbps

is based on indoor wireless usage. Table 3.1 shows the estimated rate profile used in this study for 3G. The expected rate is the download speed in [14] averaged over the 5 indoor sites. Minimum and maximum deviations are obtained from the minimum and maximum download speeds of the 5 sites, respectively. For simplicity, as 3G covers larger areas with respect to WLAN, in this study we assume that the 3G download rate is independent on the position of the user; that is, while the user is moving, the average and minimum and maximum deviations do not vary over time (i.e., $r_{3G}(t)$ is constant for any t).

3.2   Estimated Rate Profiles for WLAN

In order to derive rate profiles for WLAN, we assume that users are mobile and roam around within the coverage area of an AP. Because of varying Signal to Noise Ratio (SNR), rates change as WLAN adapts its modulation and coding scheme accordingly. In this paper, we assume that a user moves within the coverage of an AP according to the Random Waypoint mobility model (RWP) [19]. Although it may generate unrealistic movements, the RWP mobility model is the most used in simulation studies of wireless technologies [5, 11, 15, 17] due to its simplicity and well-known behavior. We remark, that our modelling approach is independent of the underlying movement pattern.

We place an AP in the center of a circular area of radius 300 m and we assume that a user moves according to the RWP with a speed that is uniformly distributed among 0.7 and 2.0 m/s (i.e., pedestrian movement). We can thus derive the coverage area and the maximum distance for achieving a given bitrate (related to the SNR [2]). For simplicity, in this study we assume the log-distance path loss model and ideal channel conditions (no fading, shadowing or other source of interference). As a result, different rings can be drawn around the AP; in each ring, the user can achieve a given physical bit rate. We assume that, when walking outside the 6 Mbps ring, the user cannot longer be associated to the AP (i.e., the only available network is 3G). We use Matlab to simulate the movements of the user and to evaluate the expected rates after a given period of time. Eight different initial conditions have been considered; for each, the user is randomly placed inside one of the rings (i.e., 54, 48, 36, 24, 18, 12, 9, and 6) at the beginning of the simulation. We will refer to each initial condition as IniRing 54, IniRing 48, etc. For each IniRing, a maximum time interval is provided for the user to move. The complete description and analysis of how these rate profiles have been generated can be found in [18].

If the user has to share the resources with other users inside the AP coverage area, the effective rate each user gets will decrease. We assume 3 other users are currently associated with the AP using 54 Mbps (interference scenario). If the

Table 2. Application-level rates for the single user and for the interference scenarios (3 other users are associated to the AP at 54Mbps). The probability of transmission when the user is in one of the eight IniRings is also displayed.

PHY rate [Mbps]	54	48	36	24	18	12	9	6
App-level rate [Mbps] [1]	22.25	21.12	18.00	14.30	11.72	8.68	6.90	4.89
Prob. of transmission	0.25	0.27	0.33	0.43	0.50	0.60	0.68	0.75
App. rate [Mbps] (interf. scen.)	5.56	5.70	5.94	6.15	5.86	5.21	4.69	3.67

user also connects to the AP, in total four users have to share the resources. Assuming that collision and/or idle periods are negligible, one can roughly estimate that each user will be able to access the medium a fourth of the time. As a result, each user will continuously download at a fourth of the achieved bit rate. Based on the IEEE 802.11g standard and the corresponding overheads, we computed the expected application-level bit rate. Table 2 shows these rates both for the case when only one user is associated to the AP (single user scenario, [1]) and for the interference scenario (fourth row). The latter are obtained multiplying the former by the probability of transmission (third row). For more external IniRings (i.e., lower physical bit rate), the probability of transmitting increases due to the performance anomaly effect [9] (i.e., a slower user occupies the channel for longer time than a user transmitting at higher data rate). Similarly, the application-level rate for the interference scenario also increases except for the most outer rings.

Figure 1 shows the expected application-level rate for each IniRing in the interference scenario. For clearness, minimum and maximum deviations are not displayed. The expected rate refers to the application level rate the user can achieve after a given amount of time. The average rate during a given time interval can be obtained by averaging the corresponding expected rates. So, for example, the expected rate for IniRing 54 after the first 10 seconds ($\bar{r}_{WLAN}(10)$) is 5.36 Mbps, while the user can download data at an average rate of 5.47 during the first 10 seconds. For the most internal rings (i.e., IniRing 54 and 48), the rate decreases as the time interval increases. For the most external rings (i.e., IniRing 12, 9 and 6), the expected rate increases as the time increases, since the user tends to move towards more internal rings (i.e., achieving higher rates). Even for long time intervals, the expected rate is always greater than zero due to the capture effect of the RWP mobility model, for which the user concentrates its movements in the center of the simulation area [4], thus reducing the probability of exiting the coverage of the AP and never come back.

4   Results

Given the uncertain estimated rate profiles, the objective is to decide whether to associate to WLAN or 3G, provided that we want to guarantee that the user can download at a minimum rate during all the time needed for the download.

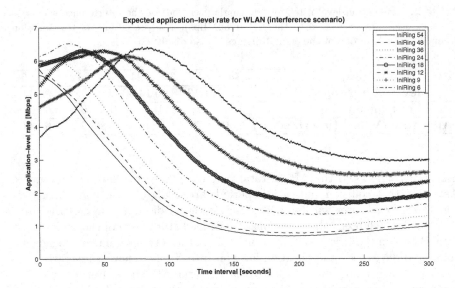

Fig. 1. Expected download rate (application-level) for each IniRing in the interference scenario

This minimum rate can be guaranteed with a given probability. This optimization problem provides a solution which is robust with respect to a certain amount of variability (Γ) in the expected rate.

4.1   Impact of Γ on Robust Association

In this section, the impact of Γ over the robust optimization is analyzed. The robust association is provided for the eight initial locations (IniRings). For each IniRing, different maximum downloading times (t_{max}) are considered. The downloading time depends on the length of the file and on the bit rate achieved during the download.

Figure 2 displays the average and the minimum guaranteed rate for a given Γ for different t_{max} for IniRing 54. The average rate is the expected rate shown in Section 3 averaged over t_{max} (i.e., the expected rate for 3G is constant, so it is the average rate). In contrast, the minimum guaranteed rate represents the minimum rate that the robust association will guarantee with a given probability along t_{max}, which can vary with Γ. First, consider the case in which Γ is zero. As shown in Figure 2, the minimum guaranteed rate equals the average rate (i.e., 5.11 Mbps for t_{max} 30 s, 4.40 Mbps for t_{max} 60 s, 3.36 for $t_{max} \geq 120$ s). As long as we want to provide a solution for longer periods in the future (i.e., $t_{max} \geq 120$s), the best strategy is to use 3G, while the best association for $t_{max} \leq 60$s is with WLAN. Setting Γ to zero is equivalent to selecting the technology with the best expected rate regardless of their variability.

When increasing the allowed variability Γ (i.e., we want a solution that is more robust to uncertain rates), the average rates remain constant unless a change in

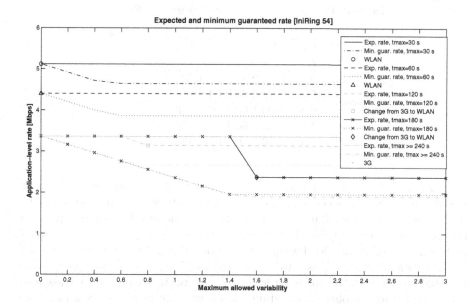

Fig. 2. Expected and minimum guaranteed rate for different download times (t_{max}) and for IniRing 54

the association is required (from 3G to WLAN or viceversa), thus matching the average expected rate over t_{max} for that technology. In contrast, the minimum guaranteed rates decrease as Γ increases until a point at which they stabilize. This equals the average minimum rate over t_{max} (i.e., for 3G it is 1.9 Mbps for any t_{max}, while for WLAN it is: 4.64 Mbps for t_{max} 30 s, 3.86 Mbps for t_{max} 60 s, 2.66 for t_{max} 120 s, 1.88 Mbps for $t_{max} \geq$ 240s). Consequently, for $t_{max} \leq$ 60 s, the best association is always with WLAN, while for $t_{max} \geq$ 240s it is always with 3G. For t_{max} 120 s and t_{max} 180 s, we can observe that if we take into account a small amount of variability in the rate (i.e., $\Gamma \leq$ 0.8 and 1.6, respectively), the robust association is with 3G, provided that the average rate for 3G is 3.36 Mbps, while for WLAN it is 3.14 Mbps for t_{max} 120 s and 1.96 Mbps for t_{max} 180 s. For higher values of Γ, the best association is with WLAN because, unless it has a lower average, it guarantees a higher minimum rate (2.66 Mbps vs. 1.90 Mbps). Depending on the time needed for downloading the video, the user should connect to one or the other technology, accordingly. In Section 4.2, we will provide a deeper insight into this aspect.

Table 3 provides the probability for which the minimum rate is guaranteed for IniRing 54. This value is obtained by dividing the average minimum rate for the worst case by the minimum guaranteed rate for a given t_{max}. Whenever Γ is zero, the probability for the minimum guaranteed rate is always lower than one, since the robust association is provided without taking into account uncertainties at all. As t_{max} increases, the probability that the minimum rate

Table 3. Percentage of guaranteed rate for IniRing 54

t_{max} Γ	30	60	120	$\geq$180
0	0.91	0.88	0.56	0.56
0.4	0.98	0.96	0.64	0.64
0.8	1.00	1.00	1.00	0.74
1.2	1.00	1.00	1.00	0.88
$\geq$1.6	1.00	1.00	1.00	1.00

is guaranteed decreases; that is, the dangers of "not worrying enough" about uncertainty grows. As a certain amount of uncertainty is taken into account, the probability increases until it stabilizes to one (i.e., the solution is the same as in the worst-case scenario). For short download times (i.e., $t_{max} = 30$s), the robust association could be provided without taking into account uncertainties (i.e., the risk is very low). Even if Γ is zero, the rate of 5.11 Mbps can be guaranteed with a probability of 0.91. Of course, for longer periods of time it is better to take into account a certain amount of uncertain rates if we want to guarantee an average minimum download rate with a given probability.

Similarly, the other seven IniRings have been considered and similar results are obtained, which are not shown here for space constraints.

4.2   Maximum Download Time for Robust Association in WLAN

Section 4.1 showed that the percentage for guaranteeing a minimum download rate varies depending on the maximum time in the future for which the optimal solution is needed. In this section we aim at finding the maximum download time t_{max} for which the WLAN network guarantees a robust association and a minimum rate. Recall that guaranteeing the minimum download rate with probability one is the same as considering the worst-case scenario.

Figure 3 shows the minimum rate guaranteed with probability 0.90. The rates tend to decrease over time (i.e., maximum time for which the optimization is made). For the outer IniRings (i.e., 12 and 6), we can observe an initial increase in the minimum guaranteed rate (i.e., $t_{max} \leq 120$ s). This is because the user can move towards inner rings where data rate is higher. For more internal rings (i.e., IniRing 54 to 36), at some point (marked with a circle in the figure) the robust association changes from WLAN to 3G (i.e., at time 180 s, 190 s and 230 s for IniRings 54, 48 and 36, respectively). This is because the user may move towards outer rings where data rate is lower. Notice that after this point the data rate is constant because the minimum rate for 3G does not change over time. For all the other rings, the robust association is always with WLAN regardless of the time needed for downloading. We can also observe that at certain t_{max} the minimum guaranteed rate decreases abruptly (i.e., at t_{max} 30 s and 100 s for

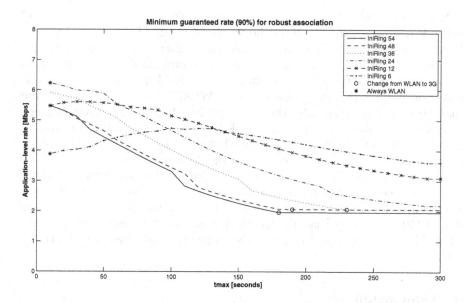

Fig. 3. Minimum guaranteed rate (probability=0.9) for robust association over time for each WLAN ring. The maximum t_{max} for which WLAN should be selected is displayed.

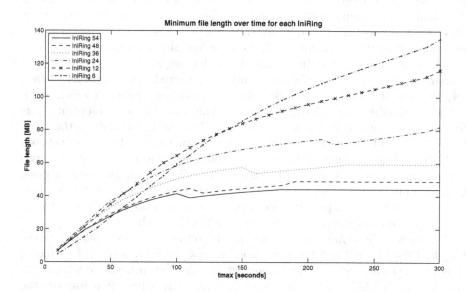

Fig. 4. Minimum file length that can be downloaded over time (guaranteed with probability 0.9) if associated with the WLAN and for each IniRing

IniRing 54, at t_{max} 110 s for IniRing 48, at t_{max} 150 for IniRing 36, and at t_{max} 50 and 210 for IniRing 24). Finally, for a maximum downloading time of 180 s, the user can always connect to the WLAN, disregardless of its initial position.

It would be interesting to provide the user with a decision strategy (which network to connect to) based on the length of the file he aims to download. Previous results on the minimum download rate guaranteed along a time interval can be easily related to the bits that can be downloaded during that period of time. Figure 4 displays the minimum guaranteed length of file that can be downloaded when the user is associated to WLAN. For time intervals shorter than 60 s, IniRing 6 provides the minimum length. For time intervals longer than 60 s, the minimum length is provided by IniRing 54. In this scenario, for file lengths of up to 44 MB, the user can select the WLAN regardless of its initial position. For longer files of up to 135 MB, the decision will depend on where the user is initially located. We can also observe that for the most internal IniRings (54 to 24), the minimum file length does not always increase along with t_{max}. For example, for IniRing 54, the minimum file length that the user can download during 110 s is shorter than the length that can be downloaded during 100 s. This is due to the abrupt decrease in the minimum guaranteed rate observed in Figure 3.

5   Conclusions

In this work, we have applied the concept of robust optimization techniques to guide the user in selecting the best radio access network in a multi-radio device. This is difficult because estimated rate profiles for the available networks are uncertain and may vary in the future. The objective was to maximize the download rate during the entire download. We show here that the amount of tolerated variability in the estimated rate profiles has a clear impact on the results. In case a small amount is taken into account, only the expected rate is considered when selecting the best radio access network, thus providing a solution which is not robust to possible variations in the future. This may lead to sub-optimal performance. In contrast, by taking into account the total uncertainty in the rates, the solution will be too conservative, thus selecting the radio access network with the highest minimum rate. A robust solution lies in between of these two extreme cases. We have shown that the robust solution can guarantee a given minimum rate with a given probability, thus selecting the access network which guarantees the selected performance, regardless of the uncertain future. To the best of our knowledge, our work represents a novelty in this field.

Results on which radio access network to select have been related to the length of the file that can be downloaded with a given probability. Our model thus provides the user with an important criterion when deciding whether to associate to WLAN or 3G. This work presents thus a first step towards the application of robust optimization methods for selecting a proper radio access network. In the future, we aim to improve our approach in several aspect, e.g., considering more realistic rate profiles for WLAN, multi-APs scenario, or taking into account handover cost.

Acknowledgments. This research was supported by the Spanish Government and ERDF through CICYT projects TEC2009-08198. The authors would like to thank the COST Action IC0906 for supporting a Short Term Scientific Mission and thus fostering collaboration between the two departments.

References

[1] Anonymous: Sewcut (2012), `http://seronline.de/sewcut/` (last accessed on February 2013)

[2] Aruba Networks: Retail Wireless Networks Validated Reference Design (2008), `http://es.scribd.com/doc/50478528/117/Converting-SNR-to-Data-Rate` (last accessed on February 2013)

[3] Bertsimas, D., Sim, M.: The Price of Robustness. Operations Research 52(1), 35–53 (2004)

[4] Bettstetter, C., Resta, G., Santi, P.: The Node Distribution of the Random Waypoint Mobility Model for Wireless Ad Hoc Networks. IEEE Transactions on Mobile Computing 2(3), 257–269 (2003)

[5] Camp, T., Boleng, J., Davies, V.: A Survey of Mobility Models for Ad Hoc Network Research. Wireless Communications and Mobile Computing (WCMC): Special Issue on Mobile Ad Hoc Networking - Research, Trends and Applications 2, 483–502 (2002)

[6] Dely, P., Kassler, A., Bayer, N., Einsiedler, H.J., Peylo, C.: Optimization of WLAN Associations Considering Handover Costs. EURASIP J. Wireless Comm. and Networking 2012, 255 (2012)

[7] Fridman, A., Grote, R., Weber, S., Dandekar, K., Kam, M.: Robust Optimal Power Control for Ad Hoc Networks. In: 2006 40th Annual Conference on Information Sciences and Systems, pp. 729–733 (March 2006)

[8] Goh, J., Sim, M.: Robust Optimization Made Easy with ROME. Operations Research 59(4), 973–985 (2011)

[9] Heusse, M., Rousseau, F., Berger-Sabbatel, G., Duda, A.: Performance Anomaly of 802.11b. In: INFOCOM 2003. Twenty-Second Annual Joint Conference of the IEEE Computer and Communications, March 30-April 3, vol. 2, pp. 836–843. IEEE Societies (2003)

[10] IBM: IBM ILOG CPLEX Optimization Studio (2011), `http://www-01.ibm.com/software/integration/optimization/cplex-optimization-studio/` (last accessed on February 2013)

[11] Kim, T.H., Yang, Q., Lee, J.H., Park, S.G., Shin, Y.S.: A Mobility Management Technique with Simple Handover Prediction for 3G LTE Systems. In: 2007 IEEE 66th Vehicular Technology Conference, VTC 2007 Fall, September 30-October 3, pp. 259–263 (2007)

[12] Kitagawa, K., Komine, T., Yamamoto, T., Konishi, S.: A Handover Optimization Algorithm with Mobility Robustness for LTE Systems. In: 2011 IEEE 22nd International Symposium on Personal Indoor and Mobile Radio Communications (PIMRC), pp. 1647–1651 (September 2011)

[13] Soyster, A.L.: Convex Programming with Set-Inclusive Constraints and Applications to Inexact Linear Programming. Operations Research 21(5), 1154–1157 (1973)

[14] Sullivan, M.: 3G/4G Performance Map: Data Speeds for AT&T, Sprint, T-Mobile, and Verizon (2012), http://www.pcworld.com/article/255068/ 3g_4g_performance_map_speeds_from_everywhere_we_tested.html (last accessed on February 2013)

[15] Xiang, H., Liu, J., Kuang, J.: Minimum Node Degree and Connectivity of Two-dimensional MANETs under Random Waypoint Mobility Model. In: 2010 IEEE 10th International Conference on Computer and Information Technology (CIT), June 29-July 1, pp. 2800–2805 (2010)

[16] Ye, W., Ordonez, F.: Robust Optimization Models for Energy-Limited Wireless Sensor Networks under Distance Uncertainty. IEEE Transactions on Wireless Communications 7(6), 2161–2169 (2008)

[17] Zola, E., Barcelo-Arroyo, F.: Impact of Mobility Models on the Cell Residence Time in WLAN Networks. In: Proceedings of the IEEE 32nd International Conference on Sarnoff Symposium, SARNOFF 2009, pp. 1–5. IEEE Press, Princeton (2009)

[18] Zola, E., Barcelo-Arroyo, F., Kassler, A., Dely, P.: Expected Bit Rate for Terminals Moving According to the Random Waypoint Model in a WLAN Cell. To Appear in 6th Joint IFIP Wireless and Mobile Networking Conference (WMNC). IEEE, Dubai (2013)

[19] Zola, E., Barcelo-Arroyo, F., Martin-Escalona, I.: Forecasting the Next Handoff for Users Moving with the Random Waypoint Mobility Model. EURASIP J. Wireless Comm. and Networking 2013, 16 (2013)

Phase Planning for Overall Copper-Fiber Switch-Over

Jose M. Gutierrez, Michael Jensen, Morten Henius, and Jens Myrup Pedersen

Department of Electronic Systems, Network and Security Section
Aalborg University, Denmark
Fredriks Bajers vej 7, 9220 Aalborg O, Denmark
{jgl,mj,mha,jens}@es.aau.dk

Abstract. This paper introduces a phase planning concept to the imminent copper-fiber switch-over action. Traditional copper loops are to be replaced by modern fiber lines in order to keep up with the current evolution of data communications. This work proposes two novel approaches of how to schedule this transition by systematically selecting the most attractive areas, in terms of economic efficiency, to be upgraded first. These are alternatively based on 1) distance to the access point and 2)population density, and the overall plan is divided into three phases. In both cases the final network solution is the same, but the different prioritization on what areas to upgrade first implies a different distribution of the investment over the deployment period. Two case studies using real geographical data in Denmark show these differences, and the results suggest that planning the phases based on population density is more favourable in terms of economic efficiency.

Keywords: Optical Access, Copper-Fiber Switch-over, Phase Planning.

1 Introduction

Copper infrastructure represents around 70% of the broadband access in Europe [1], and carriers are still making obtain a good profit. However, the copper lines are becoming obsolete due to their datarate transmission capabilities, specially in a mid and long range it is not possible to fulfil the demands of new services and applications. For example, a household 3000 m away from the access point can only access a DSL connection with a theoretical maximum data rate of approximately 5 mbs downstream.

Therefore, these carriers owning the copper access need to progressively start substituting the old copper cables by optical fiber lines at a global scale, not only to keep being competitive in the market but it will also facilitate a faster development of the society [2].

For example, current and near future services, such a high definition telepresence (i.e. remote doctor consultancy) cannot be supported by most DSL customers due to the high upload speed requirements (5 Mbs) [3]. However, it is

V. Tsaoussidis et al. (Eds.): WWIC 2013, LNCS 7889, pp. 83–94, 2013.
© Springer-Verlag Berlin Heidelberg 2013

proven that telehealth services may decrease mortality [4], or increase the effectiveness of treatments [5], among other benefits. A global copper-fiber transition will allow for these services to reach the majority of the population.

Moreover, the switch-over will also contribute to succeed in the 2020 EU Digital Agenda objective of providing access of 30 mbs to 100% of the households [6] and 50% of them subscribing to at least a 100 mbs connection. In this way, carriers and European authorities can work together towards similar goals and complement each other.

This transition is a long and complex process due to the size of the project, thousands of households to be connected over a number of years, and the prioritization of which areas should be upgraded first. Thus, this transition process should be conveniently scheduled in order to perform it in an organized and efficient way. Unfortunately, this problem has not been covered in depth, and no solid initiatives have been proposed yet to perform this prioritization to the best of our knowledge.

Hence, this paper presents for the first time two systematic approaches for scheduling the deployment plan for copper-fiber transition in broadband access. Basically, the idea is to prioritize the connection of areas where the the most profit can be achieved in relation to invested money in deploying the fiber. In this way, the investment at an early phase of the deployment can be efficiently distributed in the sense of payback period.

The proposal is to divide the transition plan into phases, but always seen from a global perspective. The planning for 100% coverage is calculated, and then divided in three phases for its realization. The two criteria proposed for this division are based on the distance from the households to the access point and population density. The three phases are considered based on coverage information (percentage of households) of three types of areas: Urban, Sub-Urban, and Rural, defined in [7] by the European Bank of Investment.

Therefore, the main contribution of this work is the proposal, illustration, and comparison of these two novel prioritization schemes for a global copper-fiber switch-over plan. It is important to note that the overall network solution is the same regardless of the scheduling criteria, the difference being on which areas are selected to be upgraded first.

Two real geographical scenarios in Denmark are used in order to evaluate the economic efficiency of the two selected criteria. More concretely, the relation between the household coverage in the phases and its associated capital expenditure (CapEx) anticipates which of the options is more attractive to be adopted by carriers when proceeding to upgrade their copper access. These scenarios consist of real location of households, roads, accesses points and their predefined coverage area by a Danish carrier.

The rest of the document is as follows: Section 2 summarizes important concepts and studies in relation to this work. Section 3 describes the methodology followed to carry out the related experiments and analyses. Section 4 presents the case studies, approach comparison, and results. Finally, Section 5 highlights the most relevant conclusions of this research.

2   Background

This section covers important concepts and definitions in relation to the topic of this study, as well as the relevant related work and references.

2.1   Concepts and Definitions

- *Phase planning*: The deployment of the fiber lines takes a long time (years) mainly due to trenching tasks. This action can be strategically planned in phases to define which parts of the network have priority according to the deployment timetable. Usually, the most profitable areas are prioritized by carriers trying to maximize, to some extent, the profit while still deploying the rest of the network.
- *Single trenching*: The plan is always considered to have a final goal of global coverage. Thus, the proposed method ensures that each road required for laying down the fiber is only opened once, in order to avoid extra necessary expenses due to inaccurate planning. This concept is explained in more detail in Section 3.
- *Access Point, AP*: It is referred to the transition point in the copper infrastructure where it is connected to the fiber distribution network.
- *Network Termination, NT*: It referred to the all the points which the fibre will ultimately reach. These could be household, apartment buildings, industry, etc....
- *Geographical Information System (GIS)*: Data regarding the exact location of *NTs*, *AP*, and roads is used in order to carry out the experiments.
- *Brownfield scenario*: The problem to be solved is based on an already existing infrastructure, the *APs* are given and their location is fixed.
- *Economic efficiency*: In this paper it is referred to the relation between CapEx and potential payback period in a given phase.

2.2   Related Work

Fiber access planning methods have been treated in the existing literature from many different perspectives. In terms of deployment methods, examples of relevant work are: Introduction to a systematic approach for fiber access planning based on GIS data [8], proposal of a method to evaluate the feasibility of network designs and deployment strategies [9], or even fiber installation techniques in [10]. Also, in connection with economic parameters, some representative studies are: Study of market challenges and opportunities for high speed broadband in [11], survey of FTTH business models and profitability in [12], or FTTH roll-out cost estimations [13].

However, none of these studies considered deployment of fiber access networks as a task that requires specific planning and scheduling in time. This lack allow us to propose a systematic method to prioritize and schedule for a global copper-fiber switch-over at an entity level (individual household level).

2.3   European Demographic Statistic

The division in phases symbolically follows the coverage statics of Europe in [7] regarding the three types of area considered: Urban, Sub-urban, and Rural. These values are taken as a guideline to carry out the experiments in Section 4, and obtain numerical results. These coverage values are 51 % of the total households for urban areas, 30 % for sub-urban areas, and 19 % for rural areas, and each type of area corresponds to a different phase. As an initial step, the values are taken as constant thresholds to differentiate the phases, but these can be varied in future experiments, in order to investigate their sensibility over parameters such as CapEx or payback period. In addition, other selection criteria or division reference can be taken into account in future further research.

3   Methodology

This section explains in detail the methodology followed in this study. Assumptions, models, planning procedures, and phase division are presented below.

3.1   Assumptions

- The road network is used to model the fiber lines geographical installation.
  - Each NT is connected to the AP using the shortest road path. $Dist$ is the distance between a NT to its associated AP.
  - Each NT is associated to a population density value Pop_d.
  - Point-to-point infrastructure: A dedicated fiber is installed per NT to the AP.
  - Capital Expenditure, CapEx: It is referred to the cost of building the network.
  - The cost model used to calculate the CapEx only considers the passive infrastructure. Trenches, fiber, and tubes are the three types of expenses considered.
  - The trenching price is considered to cover all the digging expenses. The average trenching price per meter used in the case studies is 30 €.
  - The tube price is considered to cover all the expenses related to materials, installation, and extra equipment in connection with the ducts used to place the fiber in. The given average price per meter of tube is 3 €.
  - In a similar way, the fiber price is considered to cover all the expenses related to its purchase, installation, and required extra equipment. A price of 0.05 € per meter of fiber is assumed.
  - The values for all prices above are given symbolically.
  - Cost model: The used cost model is defined as Eq. (1), C_{nt} being the total cost of deploying the network or CapEx, and C_{tr}^i, C_f^i, and C_t^i the cost of trenching, fiber, and tubes in phase i respectively.

$$C_{nt} = \sum_{i=1}^{3} C_{tr}^i + C_f^i + C_t^i \tag{1}$$

- One tube is installed per road segment used, per phase, and with a maximum capacity of 1000 NTs. In this sense, for example a road segment used to lay down fiber for 500 NTs in each of the three phases will be provided with three tubes. Then, the required fiber is blown accordingly and at the time it is required for each of the phases. This concept can be mathematically described as Eq. (2), $T_s(i)$ being the tubes required to be installed in segment s at phase i, and T_s^j the tubes necessary to blow the fiber in phase j. Phase i should be the first to require a tube in segment s.

$$T_s(i) = \sum_{j=i}^{3} T_s^j \tag{2}$$

- Payback period: This parameter represents the time it would take to pay off the deployment investment based on the profit generated by the customers. Symbolically, a penetration rate of 50 % and monthly average connection price per customer of 20 € are assumed, in order to obtain numerical results in the case studies.

3.2 Procedure

Global Solution

Firstly, the global fiber access switch-over solution is calculated (coverage of 100 % of the households). Real geographical coordinates for APs, NTs, and roads are given as input for planning of the network. The resulting plan describes the exact traces of the lines connecting all the NTs to the AP, the roads these follow, and the amount of fiber and tube required. Then, the CapEx related to this global solution is calculated based on the cost model and assumptions described above.

Phase Division

Secondly, the global solution is divided into three phases, grouping the NTs to be connected based alternatively on 1) population density and 2) distance to AP.

One important remark in the proposed method is that each road segment is dug only once. This implies that when fiber is required to be deploy at a road segment, all the required tubes for 100% coverage are also installed. In this way, only the fiber installed at later phases has to be blown, without reopening the trenches.

As mentioned in Section 2, the division of the phases is based on given NT coverage values for each phase. Then, the NTs are selected for each phase, based on the two criteria of population density or distance to AP. As an illustrative example, the coverage in Phase 1 is 51 % of the households, if the density criterion is applied, 51 % of the NTs with the highest population density value (Pop_d) are selected to be connected. If selection is based on distance to the AP, then 51 % of the closest NTs to the AP (shortest $Dist$) are chosen to be connected.

This priority selection leads to equal coverage, as a hard input to the problem, but different required investment at each phase. Implicitly, it can be derived that equal investment will lead to a difference in coverage at early phases.

Economic Analysis

The following step is to calculate the CapEx associated to each phase and selection criterion. In addition, the payback period in each of the cases is calculated and used as a reference to compare the different solutions. It is assumed that the active equipment is the same when comparing these solutions over the same scenario, same coverage, and same phase. Thus, the difference relays on the passive equipment, and the PP^j (cumulative payback period in Phase j) can be simplified as Eq. (3) to compare equivalent solutions. C_{nt}^i is the cost of deploying the network in Phase i, $\#NT^i$ number of NTs connected in Phase i, P_r customer penetration rate, and $Cust_€$ the average monthly revenue per customer.

$$PP^j = \frac{\sum_{i=1}^{j} C_{nt}^i}{\sum_{i=1}^{j} \#NT^i \cdot P_r \cdot 12 \cdot Cust_€} \quad \text{[years]} \tag{3}$$

4   Case Study

This section describe the experiments carried, in order to test the proposed phase division models, and the results obtained.

4.1   The Scenarios

Two scenarios are used in this case study. Basically, each of these consists of a set of NTs to connect to a given fixed AP and its predefined coverage area by a Danish carrier.

Table 1 presents the information about the NTs for both scenarios, and Figs. 1(a) and 2(a) illustrate the geographical location of the NTs (crosses), AP (black square), and roads (lines).

Table 1. NT Coverage by Case and Phase

Case	Phase 1	Phase 2	Phase 3	Total
A	726	424	266	1416
B	966	568	359	1893

4.2   Results

Tables 2 and 3 show the planning numeral results for each case and selection criteria. These include fiber, tubes, and trenches length in km and CapEx millions

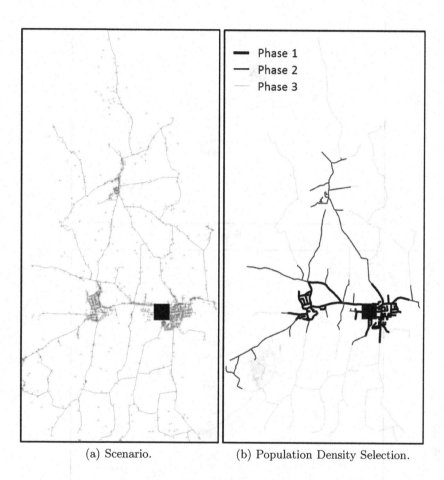

(a) Scenario.   (b) Population Density Selection.

Fig. 1. Case A

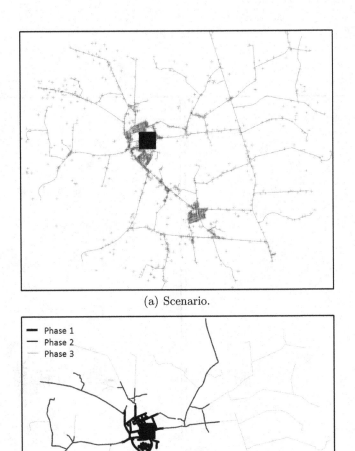

(a) Scenario.

(b) Population Density Selection.

Fig. 2. Case B

of €. It can noticed that there is a difference in CapEx between the density and distance based approaches for the same scenario. This difference is due the tube installation criterion (by number of NTs and stage), implying different amount of tube required by each approach. However, the deviation on the total CapEx is not very significant ($< 0,5\%$)[1], and therefore the solutions are considered to be equivalent in terms of total CapEx. Figs. 1(b) and 2(b) show the planning and scheduling solutions based on population density, as illustrative examples.

Table 2. Planning Results Case A. CapEx in millions of €, rest in km.

Dens.	Phase 1	Phase 2	Phase 3	Total	Dist.	Phase 1	Phase 2	Phase 3	Total
Fiber	830,8	1363,8	1127,1	3323,7	Fiber	688,2	1244,5	1391,0	3323,7
Tubes	29,7	64,9	22,9	117,5	Tubes	45,1	48,9	20,3	114,3
Tren.	15,3	37,5	22,9	75,7	Tren.	22,2	33,2	20,3	75,7
CapEx	0,59	1,39	0,81	2,79	CapEx	0,83	1,20	0,74	2,78

Table 3. Planning Results Case B. CapEx in millions of €, rest in km.

Dens.	Phase 1	Phase 2	Phase 3	Total	Dist.	Phase 1	Phase 2	Phase 3	Total
Fiber	1230,4	1631,5	1558,5	4420,4	Fiber	899,7	1797,0	1723,7	4420,4
Tubes	37,4	57,8	41,9	137,1	Tubes	51,4	50,9	39,3	141,6
Tren.	19,0	32,5	41,9	93,4	Tren.	24,9	29,2	39,3	93,4
CapEx	0,74	1,23	1,46	3,43	CapEx	0,95	1,12	1,38	3,45

Regardless of the phase and scenario, trenching is the most expensive task when deploying these networks. It represents between 76-86 % of the total CapEx, depending on the phase, scenario, and selection criterion. In addition, the tube costs represent between 8-16 %, and the fiber cost between 4-8 % of the total CapEx. These small fluctuations indicate a consistent pattern in relation to the investment distribution by deployment task/component.

Fig. 3 illustrates the difference in the cumulative CapEx between the two selection criteria over the two scenarios. The results for both regions indicate that to prioritize the connection of households based on population density implies lower investment at early phases than based on distance. The concept can be summarized in the following statement: *Equal number of NTs connected implies lower cumulative CapEx for Phases 1 and 2 when applying the population density*

---

[1] More CapEx significant digits are required to obtain this value in Case B. Density based CapEx=3,434 and distance based CapEx=3,448.

based approach. Consequently, since the total cumulative CapEx is considered the to be the same for both selection criteria, the investment in Phase 3 must be higher for the density based approach.

Fig. 4 shows the cumulative payback period for the two selection criteria and regions. In both cases, the payback period for Phase 1 is lower, and the same for the complete coverage. To recover the investment at early phases may be convenient for carrier as a business strategy. In this way, a lower investment is required in order to connect the first customers, leaving a higher investment for when early customers are already generating revenue.

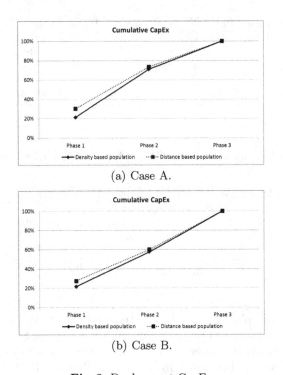

(a) Case A.

(b) Case B.

Fig. 3. Deployment CapEx

The most relevant results to be highlighted are the difference in CapEx and payback period after Phase 1 for both scenarios. Basing the prioritization on population density implies significantly lower CapEx requiring less time to payback the investment than basing it on distance to the access point (29% lower in Case A and 22% lower in Case B).

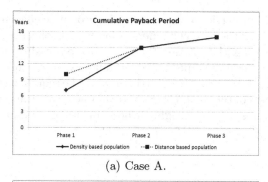

(a) Case A.

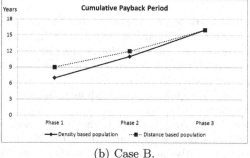

(b) Case B.

Fig. 4. Payback Period

5   Conclusion

Copper-fiber switch-over actions are, or will be in a near future, required by every traditional copper carrier in the world to keep up with technological demands and customers expectations. However, the deployment of such networks has never been treated from a planning and scheduling perspective.

This paper presents an analysis of how to schedule a switch-over plan with a 100% household coverage as a framework. The decision of which households have priority in time for obtaining a fiber connection has an effect on the deployment investment (CapEx) and payback period distributions.

This work proposes to divide the fiber deployment plan into three phases using two different selection criteria, based on 1) population density and 2) distance to the access point. Consequently, the covered household by an access point are selected at an individual entity level into one of three deployment phases. These selection techniques are evaluated over two real geographical scenarios in Denmark. The results indicate that the overall switch-over plan over the same region, results in similar CapEx and payback period regardless of the prioritization used. However, the distribution in time varies substantially.

The connection selection based on population implies lower CapEx are early phases than based on distance and covering the same number costumers, specially for Phase 1 where 51% of the household are covered. Thus, this approach may be interesting for carrier in terms of initial economic efficiency. In this way, the cost of connecting the first customers is lower and collecting revenue with a lower associated CapEx than basing the prioritization on distance.

In addition to these two presented techniques, new and more complex approached may be tested in order to further reduce the required investment to deploy the early phases of the plan. Examples could be prioritization based on variable penetration rates by area/neighbourhood or other relevant socio-economic factors.

References

1. European commission statistics, http://epp.eurostat.ec.europa.eu
2. A framework for evaluating the value of next generation broadband: A report for the broadband stakeholder group. Plum Consulting (June 2008)
3. Ezell, S.J., Atkinson, R.D., Castro, D., Ou, G.: The need for speed: The importance of next-generation broadband networks (2009)
4. Whole system demonstrator programme: Headline findings. Department of Health, UK, Gateway reference 16972 (2011)
5. Berkley, R., Bauer, S., Rowland, C.: How telehealth can increase the effectiveness of chronic heart failure management. Nurs. Times 106(26), 14–15
6. 2011 telecommunication market and regulatory developments. European Comission Scoreboard 2012 (June 2012)
7. Hätönen, J.: The economic impact of fixed and mobile high-speed networks. EIB Papers 7/2011, European Investment Bank, Economics Department (December 2011)
8. Riaz, M., Pedersen, J., Madsen, O.: A Method for Automated Planning of FTTH Access Network Infrastructures (2005)
9. Conner, M.E., Hanlon, P.K.: Ftth design metrics for greenfield deployments. In: Optical Fiber Communication Conference and Exposition and the National Fiber Optic Engineers Conference, p. NWD2. Optical Society of America (2006)
10. Flecker, B., Gebhart, M., Leitgeb, E., Muhammad, S.S., Chlestil, C.: Results of attenuation-measurements for optical wireless channels under dense fog conditions regarding different wavelengths. In: Proceedings in IWCS 2006 (2006)
11. Shinohara, H.: Broadband access in Japan: rapidly growing ftth market. IEEE Communications Magazine 43, 72–78 (2005)
12. Verbrugge, S., Casier, K., Lannoo, B., Machuca, C., Monath, T., Kind, M., Forzati, M.: Research approach towards the profitability of future ftth business models. In: Future Network Mobile Summit (FutureNetw), pp. 1–10 (June 2011)
13. Casier, K., Verbrugge, S., Meersman, R., Colle, D., Pickavet, M., Demeester, P.: A clear and balanced view on ftth deployment costs. Journal of the Institute of Telecommunications Professionals 2(3), 27–30 (2008)

Design and Implementation
of HDFS over Infiniband with RDMA

Dong Buyun, Fang Pei, Fu Xiao*, Luo Bin, and Zhao Zhihong

Software Institute
Nanjing University
Nanjing, China
dbybyron@gmail.com, fangpei@yahoo.cn,
{fx,luobin,zhaozh}@software.nju.edu.cn

Abstract. Nowadays more and more data have been generated every day in some enterprises such as facebook and google. These data need to be collected and analyzed in time. So the speed of transmitting data must be very high and the latency must be very low. Hadoop is applied in these enterprises and they use several data centers to store and process these data. But if the amount of data is growing fast or we will use only one data center then the bandwidth of the Ethernet Hadoop Distributed File System (HDFS) using cannot meet the need. The bandwidth of the Ethernet is going to become the performance bottleneck of HDFS. In order to solve this problem we will introduce a relatively new switched fabric communication link——Infiniband in this paper. Based on Infiniband we have designed a new communication mechanism of HDFS and implemented it by modifying the code of HDFS. We use remote direct memory access (RDMA) to send and receive data rather than socket. The new HDFS will not use original stream mode to transmit data. Instead it will dynamically expand buffer and use changeable threshold. In this way the new HDFS will make CPU idle and improve performance. Unlike IPoIB which only uses Infiniband hardware device, our optimized HDFS is not only based on Infiniband hardware but also changes the code of HDFS to use RDMA. Our HDFS uses socket to transmit control message and RDMA to transmit data to make full use of the bandwidth of Infiniband. So applying the Infiniband with RDMA network bandwidth has not been the performance bottleneck of HDFS any more. According to the experiment results we have found that the network bandwidth of HDFS over Infiniband is 60 percent higher than the Ethernet and our optimized HDFS has much better performance than the HDFS over the Ethernet. On the other hand, the performance of our HDFS is also higher than the one which only use IPoIB.

Keywords: Infiniband, RDMA, DFS, Network bandwidth.

---

* Corresponding author.

V. Tsaoussidis et al. (Eds.): WWIC 2013, LNCS 7889, pp. 95–114, 2013.
© Springer-Verlag Berlin Heidelberg 2013

1   Introduction

As technology has been developed fast in recent years, more and more data has been generated especially in enterprises. So the systems of enterprise require much higher processing performance. Since the requirement of high performance for the systems in enterprise, the distributed system has become one of the best architecture for processing a great deal of data. Generally in an enterprise cluster there are a distributed system and a distributed file system. The distributed system manages the whole system and the distributed file system is used to store and process large amounts of data. Using distributed system and file system can obviously improve the performance of whole system. The factors of influencing the performance of processing data of distributed file system are the I/O of hard disk, memory copying, network connection and transmission. Nowadays, the I/O of hard disk can be solved by RAID. In Hadoop Distributed File System (HDFS) hard disk is always be RAID0 and distributed. So even if the I/O of one disk is low, all disks together are high enough. However, the network distributed file system using is always the Ethernet. Although the speed of the Ethernet has been increased to 10Gbps, the bandwidth is still not enough for transmitting huge data and has gradually become the main obstacle to improve the performance of distributed file system. The main reason for relatively low bandwidth is that the transport mechanism of the Ethernet is socket which has some problems that lead to the existing socket-based network becoming a bottleneck. Socket-based communication mechanism requires CPU intervention, so the CPU time slice results in the high delay of the transmission. Furthermore, the socket-based communication mechanism requires memory copying. CPU firstly needs to get the data from the memory and put it to the buffer. Then the data can be sent by NIC. In the receiver, CPU again gets the data from the buffer and puts it to the memory. So the process costs lots of time. During the process of socket-based transmission the status of data needs to be changed many times. When the data is ready to be sent, the sender needs to convert the status of data from kernel mode to user mode. When the data is received, the receiver needs to reconvert it. Therefore, several status transitions also lead to time consuming, and thus greatly degrade the performance of the distributed file system.

In order to solve the problem of low bandwidth, we have used a relatively new network media—-Infiniband [1,2,3] and remote direct memory access (RDMA) mechanism to modify HDFS. Infiniband is mainly used in enterprise data centers and high-performance computing. It is different from the Ethernet because of its transport mechanism. Infiniband is based on remote direct memory access (RDMA) protocol. RDMA is similar to DMA and the only difference between them is that RDMA can directly access the memory of remote host. Since RDMA-based operations can directly access the remote host's address space, the time of data copying from memory to buffer is eliminated and the whole transmission process only needs a little CPU intervention. So it can improve network bandwidth and the performance of the whole system. The characteristics of Infiniband and RDMA brings new opportunities to the distributed file system because nowadays all the things in distributed file system are based on socket and the Ethernet. We can change the implementation of communication mechanism of distributed file system.

In this paper we mainly describe how to use Infiniband with RDMA to optimize the performance of HDFS. We have replaced the hardware and software of original HDFS with the ones for Infiniband. We have designed a new transport mechanism that works over Infiniband instead of the Ethernet. In order to implement the new transport mechanism we have modified the source code of HDFS and changed the transport mechanism from socket-based to RDMA-based. Using the verbs defined by Infiniband we can implement RDMA-based read and write operations. To evaluate the performance of our optimized HDFS, we have designed the experiments and compared the transferring rate among Infiniband, IPoIB and the Ethernet. We have found that our optimized HDFS have enhanced nearly 0.5Gbps transferring rate. So obviously HDFS over Infiniband with RDMA has a much higher performance than HDFS over socket. In recent years, there are many kinds of methods to optimize the performance of HDFS. But most of them are modifying the performance of MapReduce. In [20] they also use Infiniband to optimize HDFS but they only used the Infiniband hardware device and did not change any code of HDFS. In other words they use IPoIB not RDMA to change HDFS. But in this paper we not only use Infiniband hardware but also use RDMA by modifying the code of HDFS and changing the transport mechanism to optimize HDFS.

The structure of this paper is like this: in section 2 we will introduce the basic concept of HDFS. In section 3 we will describe some relate works on HDFS optimization. In section 4 we will specially explain the Infiniband and RDMA. Then we will show the design and implementation of our methods of optimizing HDFS in section 5. In section 6 we will give our experiment results and analysis. In section 7 we will summarize our work and show the future of our work.

2   Hadoop Distributed File System

Hadoop Distributed File System (HDFS) is the component of Hadoop as a distributed file system [4]. HDFS is meant for processing large amounts of data in the enterprise to improve the process performance of applications.

Figure 1 shows the structure of HDFS. HDFS has master-slave architecture. It consists of a name node and many data nodes. Name node is the key node of HDFS which manages the meta data of the distributed file system, the configuration of the system and the whole process of accessing a file as a main server. Data node, as the name suggests, is the server of storing data of the distributed file system.

When transferring data in HDFS, name node firstly checks the existence of the file. If the file exists, name node will find data nodes to transfer data according to the meta data. HDFS uses socket-based transmission mechanism. So during the transmission process operation system always joins, results in consuming the process capacity of operation system and decreasing the transmission performance of HDFS.

Nowadays, in most enterprises HDFS they are using is based on the Ethernet. So it brings the problem of network performance bottleneck. The Ethernet uses socket to transmit data and socket needs more CPU intervention and has lower speed than RDMA we will discussed later. So our work is meant to solve the performance problem of HDFS by replacing socket with RDMA.

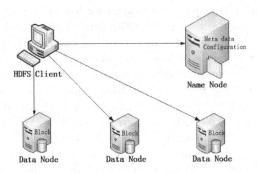

Fig. 1. HDFS

3   Related Work

For Hadoop and HDFS there are three kinds of optimizing method today including optimizing from applications, optimizing from configuration and optimizing from system implementation. For the terms of applications, the optimizing method is decided by the specific requirement. This method is difficult because it requires long-term experience and accumulation. In [5] it introduced the optimization of HBase. HBase is a big data database based on HDFS. Its optimization method depends on the application requirement. For example, it mentioned the circumstance that needs to be considered such as the ratio of read and write and the size and time of data storing. For the terms of configuration, parameters need to be adjusted according to the level of the hardware of the clusters and specific application requirement. In [5] it also introduced the optimization method of HDFS to optimize HBase. HBase is based on HDFS so the performance of HBase also depends on HDFS. The chosen of data node is considered. For example it mentioned the size of checksum. Through configuring the size of checksum CPU cost can be decreased. Therefore, through configuration it also can improve performance of HDFS and HBase. For the terms of system implementation the method is difficult but the effect is good. In [6,7,8,9] there are kinds of method to optimize MapReduce performance in order to improve the performance of HDFS. To optimize MapReduce means to modify the implementation of the map function and reduce function.

Our optimizing method in this paper belongs to system implementation. It is similar to the methods for optimizing MapReduce. They modify the implementation of map and reduce function to improve the performance of MapReduce while ours modify the transmission mechanism of HDFS in order to run HDFS over Infiniband with RDMA like other applications mentioned in such as MPICH2 [10], MPI [11] and PVFS [12]. In [20] it mentioned that HDFS can use Infiniband to optimize performance. Out work is based on it. In [20] they did not make full use of Infiniband. They changed the hardware to Infiniband hardware and did not modify anything about HDFS or any applications. So they used IPoIB which is a convenient way to optimize HDFS. Although the performance has improved, it still has many things to do becasuse IPoIB is not the best way to use Infiniband. We use RDMA instead of IPoIB to use Infiniband and make the performance improved a lot. Our work can essentially improve the performance much and is suitable for enterprise clusters because it not only improve the bandwidth but also solve the bottleneck problem. Section 5 will introduce this kind of method specifically.

4   Infiniband and RDMA

A. Overview of Infiniband

Infiniband architecture defines a kind of storage area network (SAN) that processes the connection between nodes. It provides a communication management framework of computer communication and I/O. In Infiniband network, request nodes and processing nodes are both connected by Infiniband medium and transfer data through channel adapters. Channel Adapters are the hardware devices of connecting two nodes that exist at both ends of the Infiniband medium [13]. There is a program of direct memory access (DMA) in channel adapters. So using this program Infiniband can transfer data based on RDMA. There are two kinds of channel adapters—host channel adapter (HCA) and target channel adapter (TCA). HCA is generally in the processing node. Generally, applying Infiniband to a system the network structure is shown in Figure 2. Host nodes and Target nodes are connected by Infiniband fabric in a system. They communicate with each other through HCAs and TCAs. In Infiniband Fabric there are some Infiniband-switches and Infiniband-routes. Since every node has a channel adapter it can communicate with a remote node by using DMA through Infiniband fabric.

Infiniband is different from the OSI model of the Ethernet. It provides a very simple messaging service for applications. The messaging service contains a communication stack like OSI. Channel adapters provide interfaces that belong to transport layer for users. Transport layer uses a model based on queue pair (QP), as illustrated in Figure 3. QPs are the structure that RDMA-based messaging service uses. One QP includes two queues: a sending queue and a receiving queue. Each queue is the node of the channel. The sending queue is responsible for sending data and the receiving queue is responsible for receiving data to the destination. When an application is going to send a message it will send a request of message sending to a queue. This request is called work request (WR), as illustrated in Figure 4. WR represents the workload of the application. Infiniband will put work request into send or receive queue by verbs. When

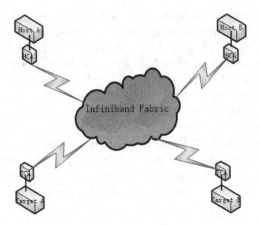

Fig. 2. Network Structure of Infiniband

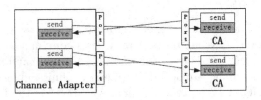

Fig. 3. Queue Pairs

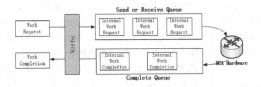

Fig. 4. Work Request Processing

completing, Infiniband will report the finishing message to the computer through complete queue (CQ). So the work request essentially describes the work that an application needs to do.

Then Infiniband defines the concept of a verb [14,15]. The word verb was chosen since a verb describes action, and this is exactly how an application requests action from the messaging service; it uses a verb. The set of verbs, taken together, are simply a semantic description of the methods the application uses to request service from the RDMA messaging service. For example, Post Send Request is a commonly used verb to request transmission of a message to another application. The verbs are fully defined by the Infiniband specification, and they are the basis for specifying the APIs that an application uses. But the

InfiniBand Architecture specification does not define the actual APIs; that is left to other organizations such as the Open Fabrics Alliance, which provides a complete set of open source APIs and software which implements the verbs and works seamlessly with the InfiniBand hardware.

B. Infiniband Architecture

Infiniband Architecture (IBA) is actually the portion of Virtual Interface Architecture (VIA). Its concept is based on VIA. VIA is a zero-copy network abstract model in the user layer that provides standard interface for high performance network technology [16]. VIA makes applications skip kernel management to manage communication and transmit data by creating a virtual interface by themselves. In other words, VIA changes the original communication mechanism—putting data into pre-allocated buffer firstly and then copying it to the destination. So by this way VIA can directly access data and reduce the time of copying greatly. VIA is a data transmission standard that defines the kernel by-pass way of using RDMA essentially. Therefore, it is the basis of Infiniband Architecture.

Specifically IBA provides a messaging service mentioned above for applications to transfer data. In fact it creates a private protected channel between virtual address spaces of two non-connected nodes. The IBA includes software transport interface layer, transport layer, network layer, link layer and physical layer. RDMA Message Transport service consists of software transport interface layer and transport layer. These five layers compose Infiniband messaging service, as shown in Figure 5.

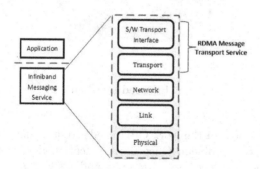

Fig. 5. Infiniband Architecture

The software transport interface layer contains QP that is the structure RDMA Message Transport service uses and accesses. Software transport interface layer mainly defines all the methods and communication mechanism that application needs to use RDMA Message Transport service, such as the method for creating a channel between applications. Implementation of software transport interface layer includes all APIs and libraries of creating, controlling and using QPs to transmit messages.

Under the software transport interface layer is a complete network stack that all the traditional network have, including Infiniband transport layer, network layer, link layer and physical layer. The transport layer provides the reliability of the transportation for Infiniband, like TCP in the IP network. Network layer is similar to the same one in traditional network. It encapsulates IP packet and routes it to the interface layer. Link layer and physical layer include cables and switches special for Infiniband. Although this network stack looks like the general network stack, it has a feature which makes it become a high-performance network. It provides a number of services to make mutual data transmission between virtual memory of applications very simple, even if these applications are very far away and are not on the same computer.

C. Remote Direct Memory Access

Remote direct memory access, namely RDMA, means one node can directly send data to the given memory address of remote computer without the help of CPU. Since typical TCP/IP network stack gives CPU too much work, CPU time consumes a lot. The paper written by IBM has mentioned the CPU load distribution in Figure 6.

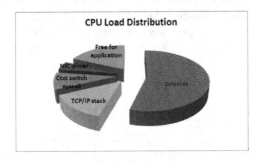

Fig. 6. CPU Load Distribution

We can see that most of the work CPU needs to do is data copying. RDMA is meant to solve this problem. Once communication does not need the help of CPU, CPU does not need to copy data and CPU can do its jobs. Then performance can be improved a lot.

The work mode of RDMA is shown in Figure 7. Firstly, in host A CPU programs NIC and tells NIC the source address of data, the destination address of data in host B and the length of data. NIC contains RDMA engine so it can transfer data by itself. NIC gets data from Buffer1 according to the source address and then sends it to the NIC in host B. Finally NIC in host B receives the data and the destination address. Then it puts the data to the destination memory address. When the transmission is done NIC notifies the CPU. So during the transmission CPU only tells NIC to transfer data when the transmission is started. While the NIC is transferring data CPU can do its jobs and wait to

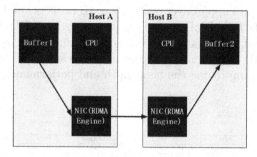

Fig. 7. RDMA work mode

be notified by NIC. This work mode makes sure that RDMA has little CPU intervention.

5 Optimizing HDFS over Infiniband

For applying HDFS over Infiniband, a new protocol called IPoIB can use Infiniband while not modifying anything. IPoIB as the bridge of IP and IB makes applications run IP over Infiniband [17]. It only needs to convert IP packets to IB packets. By this way HDFS not only improves its performance but also makes little effort. Since the characteristics of not modifying the source code of original system, high bandwidth and low latency, IPoIB has started to be applied in the fields like high performance computing, enterprise data center and cloud computing.

IPoIB gives us a new idea of improving network performance of HDFS over Infiniband. But in essential the transmission mechanism of IPoIB and the Ethernet are similar. They both use socket-based operations to transmit data. Therefore, if we use RDMA-based operations instead of the low-bandwidth socket-based ones to optimize HDFS by modifying the source code of HDFS then the bandwidth and performance would be further improved.

A. The Way of using IPoIB

As the network bandwidth becomes the bottleneck of HDFS, we thought of a high-performance network technology——Infiniband. We changed the network of distributed file system from the Ethernet to the Infiniband. Then distributed file system transmitted data by using the protocols of the Infiniband Architecture. At first we used a very convenient way to apply Infiniband, named IPoIB. IPoIB architecture is shown in Figure 8. We can see that IPoIB is between TCP/IP and Link layer which means for existing applications they can still use TCP/IP and socket-based transmission mechanism. IPoIB layer is responsible for converting. So IPoIB not only can make HDFS use Infiniband, but do not modify the original program as well [18]. So it costs a small price but gets a good result. HDFS over IPoIB only needs IPoIB hardware devices. Then IPoIB will automatically convert IP packets and upper layer protocols to IB packets and lower IB address. For the terms of HDFS, IPoIB is only a layer interface. HDFS does not care about how to use Infiniband and only needs to transmit data by original socket-based operations. IPoIB will automatically make socket-based methods run over Infiniband, thereby improving the bandwidth and performance.

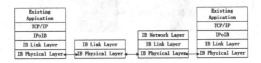

Fig. 8. IPoIB Architecture

When we use the optimized HDFS over IPoIB to store and process data, the performance of HDFS has improved a lot. This shows that increasing network bandwidth is significant for the performance of HDFS. However, we also find that although IPoIB enhances the bandwidth and the performance of HDFS, the bandwidth still has nearly 60 percent gap comparing to the theoretical value Infiniband official provided. After analyzing the essential of IPoIB, we find that since we do not make any changes to the original HDFS, address resolution, packets encapsulation and conversion consume a lot of time, resulting in the gap of network bandwidth. In fact, applications do not have to make any changes, which means that applications are still based on socket to transmit data essentially. IPoIB only servers as a bridge between socket and Infiniband. Therefore, although IPoIB improves the performance of HDFS, there is still a large space of improvement for HDFS. Then how can we avoid the address and message conversion to reduce time-consuming? Only by modifying the source code of HDFS to change original communication mechanism of HDFS can we improve the performance further. To a certain extent, establishing RDMA connection and using RDMA data transmission can be considered as truly using Infiniband.

B. The way of using RDMA

In order to avoid the time cost of conversion of protocols and packets over IPoIB, we need to change the original transmission mechanism of HDFS by modifying its source code. We use RDMA-based operations to transmit data right now. Figure 9 below is the flow chart of RDMA-based transmission:

The upper part of Figure 9 shows the flow of sender: The sender firstly puts the data needed to be sent into memory buffer users allocate. In other words HDFS puts the data into its own memory area that applications can use by JNI invoking. Then HDFS copies the sending data into the system management memory area. The system management memory area is the registered memory by RDMA. Only in this registered memory area can data be sent by RDMA. At last the sender sends the data through NIC and Infiniband hardware devices.

The lower part of Figure 9 shows the flow of receiver: The receiver firstly receives the data through NIC and Infiniband hardware devices. Then HDFS puts

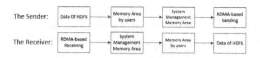

Fig. 9. The flow of RDMA-based transmission

the data into registered memory area by RDMA, namely system management memory area. Likewise HDFS again copies the data from the registered memory area to user-allocated memory area HDFS owns. Lastly the data is copied into the destination.

Above is the brief introduction to the flow of RDMA-based transmission in HDFS. Next we will specifically show how to use RDMA. The communication of HDFS in the enterprise cluster is actually the communication between datanodes. So we have designed the control flow of RDMA in the datanodes specially and modified HDFS source code. Here is the pseudocode of RDMA in datanodes in Figure 10.

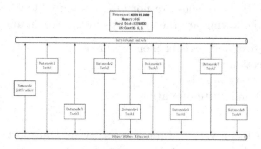

Fig. 10. Topology

```
GET DATANODE NEEDS :
    CASE SERVER :
        setup tcp and rdma mem region
        get data and length
        tcp listen
        exchange connection data
        start transmit
    CASE CLIENT :
        setup tcp connection
        if ok
            setup rdma mem region
            exchange connection data
            start transmit
            store data to jni caller
        end if
        if ng
            return exit code
```

end if
CASE DOWN
   check send and receive queue
   if ok
     release all alocated mem
   else
     wait and continue to check
   end if

At first we get datanodes' requirement. According to the needs if the datanode serves as server then it will set up TCP connection and RDMA memory region. The server needs to get data and length to exchange connection data and start to transmit. If the datanode serve as client then it will set up TCP connection and wait for OK. If the connection is OK, it does the things as the server and then stores the data to JNI caller. If the connection is not OK, it exits. If the datanode is down or the cluster is down for some reason then it will check the send and receive queues firstly. If the queues are OK, the system will release all allocated memory. If the queues are not OK, system will wait and continue to check the queues. Following are the key steps in the design above [19]:

   a. Initialize context and register memory area
   b. Set up connection
   c. Exchange memory area key
   d. Perform read and write operation
   e. Disconnect

Each step is defined as a verb in Infiniband software transport interface.

Step one is initializing context and registering memory area. At first HDFS needs to initialize resources and create resources. Resources creation means to get the devices' information including IB devices' names, the devices that are going to communicate and the handlers of the devices. Then HDFS needs to register memory area. This means HDFS asks for a memory protection area that is used to communicate. The requested memory protection area cannot be released until communication is finished. Complete queue (CQ) is created at that time and its size is one because only one work request (WR) exists. Then HDFS will allocate memory area to store data and then create the key structure QP of RDMA.

Step two is creating connection. Creating connection means creating TCP connection. Once the sender and the receiver have TCP connection, they can use it to send some key information to create QP and set up RDMA connection.

Step three is exchanging memory area key. The sender and the receiver use memory area key to create QP. So for creating QP at first HDFS needs to exchange some basic information including remote address, remote memory key, remote QP number and remote id of registered memory protection area. When the local computer saves the remote information it can start to initialize QP. Then the receiver gets ready to receive messages. During the receiving process the receiver firstly changes the status of QP to ready to receive (RTR). When the status is RTR the receiver sends a ready to use (RTU) message to the sender. When the sender receives the RTU message it knows that RDMA-based connection is created and starts to transmit data. So the sender changes its QP status to ready to send (RTS). In order to guarantee the reliable of QP connection and Infiniband transmission, after creating QP connection, HDFS needs a synchronize test. The sender and the receiver both send a testing char to make sure that QPs of the sender and the receiver are connected in order to prevent message discarding.

Step four is performing read and write operations. Since QPs of the sender and the receiver are connected, HDFS can start to transmit a large amount of data. With the help of APIs of the verbs, we can invoke *ibv_post_send/receive* [7,19] method to send and receive data. By this way two computers can use RDMA-based operations to communicate with each other. *Post_send* and *Post_receive* are the verbs that software transport interface defines.

Above is the complete flow of RDMA-based transmission. Through the five steps the sender and the receiver can transmit data to each other. So to optimize HDFS we only need modify the source code of HDFS to change original socket-based mechanism to RDMA-based mechanism. By this way HDFS runs over Infiniband with RDMA completely and avoids the time cost of address and packets conversion. Therefore, HDFS fully uses Infiniband network bandwidth and improves the performance a lot.

6 Performance Evaluation

A. Experiment setup

Our experimental test bed consists of a cluster system of computers with XEON E5 2680 processor. Each computer has 64G memory and can use both SSD and HDD. The cluster is connected by 56Gbps FDR RDMA interfaces of Infiniband. We use CentOS 6.3 operating system. Following is the topology of our experiment. There are one namenode and eight datanodes. The JobTracker is used to manage the tasks and the task node is responsible to do the task. Each node in this topology has the configuration mentioned above. All the datanodes are connected by the Infiniband switch and the Ethernet.

B. Design and Execution

Our experiment is based on Hadoop and HDFS. In order to prove the improvement of our HDFS, we run the original and optimized HDFS to read and write data. Through comparing the results of reading and writing operations and CPU utilization we analyzed and got a conclusion.

When we start to do the experiment, at first we should check all the index of the servers, such as hardware I/O and network bandwidth. This is important because we should make sure that any server runs rightly. If one of the servers is abnormal, the result can be very strange. In our experiment we check the I/O performance of sequential reading, sequential writing, randomly reading and randomly writing by FIO which is the tool of checking I/O of hardware. In order to optimize the performance we chose SSD. We use single SSD and the size of a block is 128K. Through testing the speed of sequential writing is 300MB/s and the speed of randomly writing is 250MB/s. The speed of sequential reading is 300MB/s and the speed of randomly reading is 100MB/s as follows. We find that these values are normal so we can start to run the test cases.

Table 1. I/O speed of SSD

	Speed (MB/s)
Sequential Writing	300
Randomly Writing	250
Sequential Reading	300
Randomly Reading	100

Before running our test cases we have another important thing to do. We should find the configuration parameters of HDFS and MapReduce that affect the result of our modification greatly. Through our test we found the parameters of HDFS in table 2 and MapReduce in table 3 are critical.

In table 2 we listed the parameters of HDFS we need to pay attention. Dfs.packet.size is the size of data transmitted based on socket each time. Dfs.local.dir and dfs.system.dir configure the storage directory of system and local data. These two directories can affect the performance because when we configure several storage directories for one parameter system can parallelizing write data which improves hard disk I/O. So we configure the parameters value all the disk to increase hard disk I/O. We set the parameters value as follows:

Table 2. The parameters of HDFS

Parameters	Value
dfs.packet.size	64K
dfs.local.dir	All the disk
dfs.system.dir	All the disk

In table 3 we listed the parameters of MapReduce we need to pay attention. The parameter of mapred.reduce.slowstart.completed.maps controls the time of slow start. The default value is 5% because when 5% map tasks are finished the reduce process is scheduled to start. Since network bandwidth is high, the speed of mapping is much lower than the speed of copying in reducing task. So we changed 5% to 20% to let mapping task run for a long time. The parameters of mapred.tasktracker.map.tasks.maximum and mapred.tasktracker.reduce.tasks.maximum control the maximum number of map or reduce tasks that will be run simultaneously by a task tracker. So we should balance the maximum number of map and reduce because if we set large maximum number of map such as 64 then reduce task will be very slow. The parameters of total concurrent map tasks and reduce tasks control the concurrent map and reduce tasks. We set these parameters' value as follows:

Table 3. The parameters of MapReduce

Parameters	Value
mapred.reduce.slowstart.completed.maps	20%
mapred.tasktracker.reduce.tasks.maximum	16
mapred.tasktracker.map.tasks.maximum	20
total concurrent reduce tasks	128 (16*8)
total concurrent map tasks	160 (20*8)

After configuring the key parameters we can start HDFS and run the test cases. Our servers use CentOS 6.3 operating system. In our experiment we firstly configured the local domain name resolve in the directory of /etc/hosts, the NIC in the directory of /etc/sysconfig/network-script/ifcfg-eth0, the number of .txt files opened at the same time in the directory of /etc/security/limits.conf and the network name in the directory of /etc/network. Then we configured the core, mapred-site.xml, hdfs-site.xml. When all the parameters are configured we can execute the commands as follows to read or write data.

/hadoop namenode Cformat
./start-dfs.sh
./hadoop dfsadmin -report
./hadoop fs CcopyFromLocal /

During running the test cases we need to remember this point that we should clear the memory after finishing one test case each time. If we do not clear the memory, the result of next test case will be incorrect because the system will get data from the memory firstly.

C. Results and Evaluation

1)The read and write performance of HDFS: According to the parameters and configurations we run the test. We used our optimized HDFS to transfer data. Figure 12 shows the contrast of the speed of write operation in HDFS based on socket, HDFS over IPoIB and optimized HDFS over Infiniband with RDMA. Figure 13 shows the contrast of the speed of read operation in HDFS based on socket, HDFS over IPoIB and optimized HDFS over Infiniband with RDMA. We have referenced the data used in [20]. The abscissa represents the whole size of all the transferring files and the ordinate indicates the transmission rate (Gbps).

Comparing the speed of write operation it is clear that the gap of the performance of write operation in HDFS based on socket and HDFS over Infiniband is very large. The speed of our optimized RDMA-based HDFS is higher than that of HDFS over IPoIB. According to the experiment result, the speed of writing in our own optimized RDMA-based HDFS is nearly 50 percent higher than IPoIB. On the other hand, with the increasing size of transferring files, HDFS based on socket and HDFS over Infiniband become increasingly evident in the speed gap. So using optimized RDMA-based HDFS over Infiniband in the fields that need to transfer large amounts of data like enterprise data centers, high performance computing will bring significant performance gains.

We also tested the performance of read operation. We found that the gap of the performance of read operation in HDFS based on socket and HDFS over Infiniband is also very large. But unlike the write operation the performance of HDFS over IPoIB and our RDMA-based HDFS is almost the same. Our optimized RDMA-based HDFS does not improve a lot.

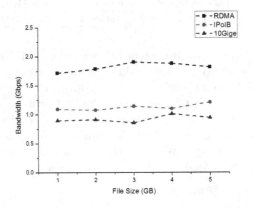

Fig. 11. The comparison of writing

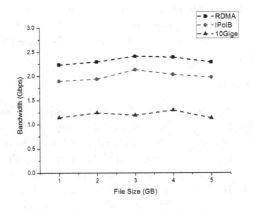

Fig. 12. The comparison of reading

2) The CPU utilization of HDFS: The experiment above gave us the comparison of read and write operations among RDMA, IPoIB and The Ethernet of 10Gb. Then we found that HDFS with RDMA has a very high bandwidth in both read and write operations. We have known that Infiniband with RDMA has not only a very high bandwidth but also little CPU intervention. Less CPU intervention means higher process performance.

Figure 13 shows the CPU intervention of RDMA, IPoIB and The Ethernet of 10Gb. The abscissa represents the size of the transferring files and the ordinate indicates the CPU intervention.

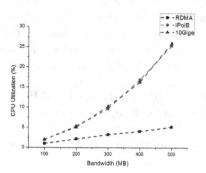

Fig. 13. CPU Utilization

According the result of the experiment we have found that RDMA has less CPU intervention than IPoIB and The Ethernet of 10Gb and the CPU intervention of IPoIB and the Ethernet of 10Gb are almost the same. When the bandwidth is 500MB, RDMA only has 5% CPU utilization but IPoIB and the Ethernet of 10Gb have more than 25% CPU utilization. And as the bandwidth grows, the gap between RDMA and the Ethernet of 10Gb or IPoIB is larger. So we have found that HDFS with RDMA can have a higher process performance than HDFS with IPoIB and the Ethernet because in HDFS with RDMA CPU can do more jobs while transmitting data.

3) Evaluation: According to the results got from the experiments above we can conclude that Infiniband with RDMA has a higher bandwidth and less CPU intervention than IPoIB mentioned in [20] and the Ethernet. Since RDMA can make one node directly access memory data and send data to another node, CPU can do its jobs. While the Ethernet based on socket needs a lot of help of CPU to data copying, status conversion and so on. So in HDFS with RDMA CPU can do much more jobs than the one based on socket which means HDFS with RDMA has a higher CPU process performance than HDFS with IPoIB and the Ethernet.

From the comparison of write operation we can see that HDFS over Infiniband has much higher performance than HDFS based on socket. No matter IPoIB or RDMA we use HDFS has a very high performance. Therefore, for write operation over IPoIB mentioned in [20], although the performance has improved a lot, the conversion of protocols and packets consumes most of its time, so using the optimized RDMA-based HDFS will make HDFS improve the performance to the highest.

From the comparison of read operation we have found a strange thing that HDFS over IPoIB mentioned in [20] had nearly the same performance as our optimized RDMA-based HDFS. So what's exactly the reason for causing our optimized HDFS not enhancing the speed of read operation? After deliberation, we have found that the read operation reads and stores data serially. So although our optimized RDMA-based HDFS has advantage in network bandwidth, the speed has to slow down because of storing serially to wait for queue. To get the highest HDFS performance, we have changed the way of reading and storing, from the original serial to parallel. Through the same test, the experiment results are shown in Figure 16. The results show that as the size of the reading files increasing, the speed of read operation of our optimized RDMA-based HDFS improves more.

Therefore, we can see our optimized RDMA-based HDFS has greatly improved the performance of the read and write operations and we have better performance than the original HDFS and the one mentioned in [20]. In our optimized HDFS network bandwidth is no longer the performance bottleneck of HDFS.

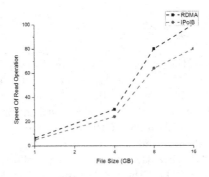

Fig. 14. The comparison of reading after optimizing

7   Conclusions and Future Work

In this paper we have described the work mechanism of Infiniband and RDMA and used Infiniband and RDMA to optimize HDFS. At first we found that the bandwidth of network is the performance bottleneck of HDFS. Then we used IPoIB to optimize HDFS. We found that the performance improved a lot through testing. But we also found that there was still a big gap with the theoretical value Infiniband official provided because of the time consuming of converting data status and data packet. So we have designed and implemented a new HDFS over Infiniband based on RDMA. Although HDFS over IPoIB does not need to modify any code, time consuming is the cost. Using Infiniband based on RDMA, we modified HDFS source code to make operations based on RDMA not socket. We used verbs provided by Infiniband to program for implementing RDMA-based read and write operations between two computers. We did the experiments to compare the performance of HDFS based on socket, HDFS over IPoIB and our optimized HDFS. The experiment result has shown that Infiniband can indeed significantly enhance the performance of HDFS especially when transmitting large amounts of data. At the same time, we also have proved that our new HDFS has a better performance than HDFS over IPoIB. In our optimized HDFS bandwidth is no longer the bottleneck. So the conclusion is that HDFS running over Infiniband with RDMA is one of the most effective methods to optimize HDFS performance.

The idea of using Infiniband with RDMA instead of the Ethernet can give us a new way to solve the problem of large amounts of data. In the future enterprise like facebook, google has to face more and more data in one day. And to transmit and process data need a very high network bandwidth. Using Infiniband with RDMA instead of the Ethernet may be a good choice.

With the technology of CPU and hardware developing, more and more data will be generated in enterprise clusters and enterprise data center. So this means in these fields which process large amounts of data such as data center and high-performance computing (HPI) we will require high performance for HDFS. In other words, Infiniband will have a bright future in enterprise-level distributed file system.

In our paper, we have supposed only two computers in the point-to-point test of HDFS over Infiniband and our optimized HDFS are worked under single-user and single-tasking. In the future, we will apply our optimized HDFS in the enterprise clusters to practice. At the same time we will let out optimized HDFS work under multi-user and multi-tasking scenarios in the future.

Acknowledgment. We would like to thank Fang Pei for his support and collaboration. Especially Fu Xiao, Luo Bin and Zhao Zhihong gave us impressive intuitions to initiate this work.

This work is supported by the National Natural Science Foundation of China (61100198/F0207) and National 973 Project(2010CB327903).

References

[1] Deshmukh, V.D.: InfiniBand: A New Era in Networking. In: National Conference on Innovative Paradigms in Engineering & Technology, NCIPET (2012)
[2] Infiniband Trade Association, http://www.Infinibandta.org
[3] Infiniband Trade Association. Socket Direct ProtocolSpecification V1.0 (2002)
[4] Apache Hadoop Project, http://hadoop.apache.org/
[5] Deng, M.: Performance Analysis of HBase Considering Scenarios. Programmer Magazine, 100 pages (August 2012)
[6] Wang, Y., Que, X., et al.: Hadoop Acceleration Through Network Levitated Merge. In: Proceedings of the 2010 International Conference on Supercomputing, Seattle, WA, USA, pp. 57–66 (November 2011)
[7] Seo, S., Jang, I., et al.: HPMR: Prefetching and pre-shuffling in shared MapReduce computation environment. In: IEEE Cluster Conference, pp. 1–8 (August 2009)
[8] Zaharia, M., Konwinski, A., et al.: Improving mapreduce performance in heterogeneous environments. Technical Report UCB/EECS-2008-99, EECS Department, University of California, Berkeley (August 2008)

[9] Mao, Y., Morris, R., et al.: Optimizing mapreduce for multicore architectures. Technical Report MIT-CSAIL-TR-2010-020, MIT (May 2010)

[10] Liu, J., Jiang, W., et al.: Design and Implementation of MPICH2 over InfiniBand with RDMA Support. In: Proceedings of the 18th International Parallel and Distributed Processing Symposium, IPDPS 2004 (2004)

[11] Liu, J., Wu, J., et al.: High Performance RDMA-Based MPI Implementation over InfiniBand. International Journal of Parallel Programming 32(3) (June 2004)

[12] Wu, J., Wyckoff, P., et al.: PVFS over InfiniBand: Design and Performance Evaluation. In: Proc. International Conference on Parallel Processing (2003)

[13] Mellanox Technologies, Mellanox InfiniBand InfiniHost MT23108 Adapters (July 2002), http://www.mellanox.com

[14] Open Fabrics Alliance, http://www.openfabrics.org/

[15] RDMA Read and Write with IB Verbs,
http://thegeekinthecorner.wordpress.com/

[16] Dunning, D., Regnier, G., et al.: The Virtual Interface Architecture. IEEE Micro 18(2), 66–76 (1998)

[17] Liu, A., Qian, D., et al.: IPoIB Architecture and its Application. Computer Science (September 2003)

[18] Transmission of IP over InfiniBand (IPoIB),
http://www.hjp.at/doc/rfc/rfc4391.html

[19] Hilland, J., Culley, P., et al.: draft-hilland-iwarp-verbs-v1.0, RDMA Protocol Verbs Specification, Version 1.0 (April 2003)

[20] Sur, S., Wang, H., et al.: Can High-Performance Interconnects Benefit Hadoop Distributed File System? In: Workshop on Micro Architectural Support for Virtualization, Data Center Computing, and Clouds (MASVDC). Held in Conjunction with MICRO (December 2010)

How Paradoxical Is the "Paradox of Side Payments"? Notes from a Network Interconnection Perspective[*]

Peter Reichl[1,3], Patrick Zwickl[2], Christian Löw[2],
and Patrick Maillé[1]

[1] Télécom Bretagne Rennes
2, Rue de la Châtaigneraie, F-35510 Cesson-Sévigné, France
{peter.reichl,patrick.maille}@telecom-bretagne.eu
[2] FTW Telecommunications Research Center Vienna
Donau-City-Straße 1, A-1220 Vienna, Austria
{zwickl,christian.loew}@ftw.at
[3] Universite Europeenne de Bretagne
5, Boulevard Laënnec, F-35000 Rennes, France

Abstract. The world of content provisioning over IP-based networks is currently undergoing a significant change, as Content Providers (CPs) have started to connect directly to Network Service Providers (NSPs) or even operate networks on their own. The resulting novel network architectures pose several fundamental economical challenges, for instance with respect to incentives for traditional network operators to offer Internet access to large Over-The-Top (OTT) providers. In this paper, we discuss these challenges from a techno-economic perspective, with an emphasis on new business and charging models. We focus on the so-called "Paradox of Side Payments", an important property for charging frameworks enabling more sophisticated cooperation with OTTs. After briefly revisiting the paradox itself, we critically discuss its underlying assumptions. Based on a numerical analysis, we point out limitations of the model, including aspects of applicability for commercial scenarios and future business models. A summary of the main results concludes the paper.

1 Introduction

The networking business is currently undergoing a series of significant changes. Despite of rising network traffic volumes, revenues are stagnating or even falling. Novel interconnection scenarios, where for instance Over-The-Top (OTT) providers directly interconnect with Network Service Providers (NSPs) or even operate their own network,

[*] The research leading to these results has received funding from the European Community's Seventh Framework Programme (FP7/2007-2013) under grant agreement n° 248567 for the ETICS project. Further information is available at www.ict-etics.eu. Additional support from the Austrian government and the City of Vienna in the context of the COMET program as well as from the EU Marie Curie program in the framework of the RBUCE WEST International Research Chair on "Network-based Information and Communication Ecosystems (NICE)" is gratefully acknowledged. The authors would like to thank their colleagues from the ARC MENEUR project for helpful discussions.

V. Tsaoussidis et al. (Eds.): WWIC 2013, LNCS 7889, pp. 115–128, 2013.
© Springer-Verlag Berlin Heidelberg 2013

may (besides of technical issues) also pose challenges for the establishment of sustainable business agreements and the understanding of monetary flows, e.g., for converging networks which enable in-house caching or similar other paradigms of increasing relevance.

In this generally difficult situation, the disagreement on the fairness of profiting from the Internet is substantially growing, e.g., Telefonica[1] and other NSPs publicly claim an inherent need for NSPs to charge OTT providers, i.e., to demand side payments from OTTs to NSPs, in order to obtain their "legitimate" share of revenues allowing them a.o. sufficient investment into their future infrastructure. This seems partly turning into practice recently, as shown with the example of France[2]. While the validity of such statements may be discussed, the very vital research field of Network Neutrality has reached the society's center of attention[3], see, e.g., [1]. Interventions in traffic handling or charging may be regarded as threatening violation of free speech – e.g., see the legal discussion of content neutrality in [2] – or as impairment of the Internet's openness. However, apart from the political dimension of Net Neutrality, it is also interesting to discuss the economic relevance of side payments first.

This path has been followed by Altman and al. [3] and Caron et al. [4] within their deep analysis of application neutrality of networks, focussing on such side payments between CPs and NSPs, leading to an interesting result: contrary to the intuitive assumption that side payments could be an appropriate solution to this problem, the authors claim to have identified a paradox rendering the reception of side payments unbeneficial in terms of overall revenue. This might provide a severe limitation for evolving on today's Internet business models; hence such conclusions on side payments may highly impact the nature of converging networks and require more attention. On the other hand, there are alternative models with partially conflicting results (e.g., [5]), and it seems there does not yet exist a clear view on this matter. Moreover, the topicality of the research question on side payments is also backed by qualitative attempts for arguing new charging principles for tomorrow's Internet, e.g., [6].

In this context, the main contributions of this paper are threefold: after a quick review of the basic model due to Altman et al. [3] (Section 2), we (a) provide a critical discussion of fundamental assumptions and limitations of this model from the perspective of network interconnection services (Section 3). Based on that, we (b) present numerical results for the case of competing oligopolistic providers, and finally we (c) investigate an alternative approach for the price-driven distribution of customers amongst competing providers (Section 4). The paper concludes with a summary and outlook on future work.

---

[1] http://www.eitb.com/en/news/detail/350113/spanish-telefonica-charge-google-yahoo-bing/, last accessed: Feb 12, 2013.

[2] *Orange and Google agreeing on terms:*
http://www.forbes.com/sites/ewanspence/2013/01/20/why-oranges-dominance-in-africa-forced-google-to-pay-for-traffic-over-their-mobile-network/, last accessed: Feb 12, 2013.

[3] *New York Times topic on Net Neutrality:* http://topics.nytimes.com/topics/reference/timestopics/subjects/n/net_neutrality/index.html, last accessed: Feb 12, 2013.

2   Revisiting the Paradox of Side Payments

This section briefly revisits the main ideas presented by [4], before we analyse various aspects and underlying assumptions from the perspective of converging interconnect networks.

Basically, Caron et al. construct a sophisticated mathematical model incorporating a series of market challenges on which game-theoretic phenomena are discussed. Explicitly, a neutral model (side payments p_s between providers are zero) variant with several competing providers is compared to a non-neutral alternative for typical consumption of an Internet service, e.g., a video stream. For the present analysis, the non-neutral case is of special importance, while the competitive nature of the model is more elaborated later on. Subsequently, the key aspects of this model are briefly revisited. Suppose the demand depends on the prices charged both by NSPs and CPs and is expressed relative to the maximum achievable demand D_{max},

$$D(p_i^N, p_j^C) = D_{max} - d^N p_i^N - d^C p_j^C \quad , \tag{1}$$

where price p_i^N is the price NSP i charges to the end customer, and p_j^C relates to the price Content Provider (CP) j charges, while d^N and d^C describe corresponding weights. Hence, the overall demand is influenced by the prices of both providers. Moreover, for simplicity we assume for now $d^N = d^C =: d$ and define p_{max} as

$$p_{max} := \frac{D_{max}}{d} \geq p_i^N + p_j^C \quad . \tag{2}$$

To complete the model, σ_i^N is defined to be the percentage of all users which have a contract with NSP i, and σ_j^C to be the percentage of all users which have a contract with CP j. Note that [4] understands these parameters in terms of customer stickiness to a provider as follows:

$$\sigma_i^N := \frac{1/p_i^N}{\sum_{k=1}^n 1/p_k^N} \tag{3}$$

for the case of NSPs (a similar definition is provided also for CPs). This interpretation will be critically reviewed later.

Non-neutral revenues for both types of providers are constructed as follows, where the price p_s represents the universal side payment from CP to NSP (i.e., independent of i and j; also unlike [4] where side payments in both directions have been considered):

$$U_i^N := \sum_{j=1}^m \sigma_i^N \sigma_j^C D(p_i^N, p_j^C)(p_i^N + p_s) = \sigma_i^N D(p_i^N, \bar{p}^C)(p_i^N + p_s), i = 1 \ldots n \tag{4}$$

$$U_j^C := \sum_{i=1}^n \sigma_i^N \sigma_j^C D(p_i^N, p_j^C)(p_j^C - p_s) = \sigma_j^C D(\bar{p}^N, p_j^C)(p_j^C - p_s), j = 1 \ldots m \tag{5}$$

where $\bar{p}^N$ and $\bar{p}^C$ refer to the respective harmonic means of NSP or CP prices, resp.

According to [4], it is assumed that p_s is provided by a regulator in lieu of being accessible to market forces. Moreover, only the overall volume of p_s is considered, not its partition between the individual paying and/or receiving providers (we will discuss these assumptions later). Whenever p_s is positive, the side payment is paid from the CP to the NSP side (and vice versa). Note that the model does not differentiate between quality levels or product types, and assumes the demand for an NSP service is directly comparable (and equally measurable) to the consumption of CP services.

The basic model is solved in [4] using the SAGE tool. As a result, generally two internal Nash Equilibrium Points NEP_1 and NEP_2 and potentially a series of external (boundary) NEPs (NEP_B) are identified, with a couple of interesting properties:

- NEP_1 and NEP_2 are internal NEPs where the derivatives of all revenue functions as described in equations (4) and (5) disappear, while NEP_B is a boundary NEP (with potentially non-zero derivatives).
- NEP_1 is equivalent to the non-discriminatory case ($p_s = 0$).
- NEP_2 does not exist whenever $p_s = 0$. If existing, it is an unstable saddle point equilibrium.
- NEP_B like all boundary cases implies that the price for one player is 0, i.e., a market exit would be realistic.
- Based on a theorem proven in [3], side payments have to be small ($|p_s| < 4.64\%$ of p_{max}) in order to guarantee the existence of an interior NEP (otherwise either CPs or NSPs or both will opt out).
- NSP revenues are higher at NEP_2 than at NEP_B
- At each interior NEP the player receiving side payments has a lower revenue than the player sending them. This is termed the "paradox of side payment".

While the second part of [4] provides a usage-based sensitivity analysis in the context of an application neutrality model, this discussion is out of scope for the present paper. Instead, in the next section we provide a critical discussion of several fundamental aspects of the model, before we turn to our own numerical analysis.

3   Critical Discussion of the Model

We will start our critical inspection with an investigation on underlying assumptions:

Homogeneity. The network services provided by competing players are regarded to be equal in product and quality, e.g., Best-Effort Internet connection between two fixed destination pairs. Based on topological constraints this may not hold for each end-to-end connection, while services provided by content providers or protocol providers may often be regarded to be comparable in this context.

Value Network Aspects. The definition of value flows and dependencies may strongly affect the bargaining powers, i.e., *Value Network* dependency factors [7], of players in the game. Facing the demand of QoS differentiated interconnection services, end users may be limited to a few NSPs, while having the opportunity to choose from a set of CPs' services, though the opposite constellation may result from highly comparable best effort Internet services (i.e., a lemon market [8] with many network service offers, but limited quality expectations by users). This in turn renders the presented conclusions subject to fully balanced bargaining powers across different player types, i.e., also implying identical numbers of players.

Moreover, there may be concerns that e.g., due to different market phases, the demand curves for service types may non-linearly differ in their characteristics, i.e., different willingness-to-pay for service types. As such, the *aggregate demand curve* may be seen as oversimplification required for algebraic solvability.

Resulting from the *two-sided nature* of the sketched market, it may be realistic to claim that the fungibility of traded services may be limited. It may even be claimed that the demand for CPs' and NSPs' services is difficult to express through a single demand metric, i.e., a *symmetry* of demand and revenue equations. Thus, rather the compatibility of consumptions of appropriate bundles of both service types may be required. By the introduction of side payments ($p_s > 0$) this symmetry is resolved. As stated in the paper, this may not be realistic in practice though.

Markets. Through establishing the side condition $p_i^N, p_j^C > 0$ (non-zero prices for NSP and CP service) a mechanism for *market exit* is neglected, while, due to the focus on one aggregate provider, market entrance may not be captured sufficiently. In this paper, we specifically focus on 2×2 player games rather than the 1×1 case. Early *market phases* for new services may however yield $1 \times N$ constellations, where e.g. a single type of network service may only be provided by a single NSP.

Regulation. As already mentioned, [3] and [4] assume that side payments have to be subject to regulation, as otherwise the market side which is in control would tend to gain advantages. From our perspective, this is not necessarily the case, and one could equally set up a two-stage game where in the first stage, the sign (i.e., direction) and value of side payments is determined before optimizing prices per provider in the second stage. However, by naively searching for pure NEs on the basis of obtained equilibria in the price-centric stage, no NE can be found (confirming the claim raised by Caron et al. and Altman et al.), as it is the dominant strategy for the NSP to opt for receiving higher side payments, while the CPs of course wants to stay on the lower side of the payments spectrum. Nevertheless, this game may resemble coordination games like the well studied "battle of the sexes" where mixed NEs may be formed or correlated equilibria may be set up, i.e., implying the intervention of a regulating authority.

User Modelling. Usually, *customer loyalty* or *churn*, respectively, refers to the end user's (un-)intentional degradation of monetary disadvantage/dissatisfaction over non-rational customer relationship effects, where a more attractive offer (e.g., opting out) is superimposed and/or sugarcoated by positive past experiences. Despite [3] using the concept of stickiness σ as equivalent to loyalty, indeed it rather serves as non-historic parameter for indicating *market shares* of the overall demand. With respect to the above argumentation on Value Network effects, a consistent loyalty factor across different player types would be useful. Moreover, the model also neglects CPs' and NSP's competition for a share of the user's contingent by presuming *usage exclusivity*.

Model Clarifications. Finally, a careful review of the original model presented by [3] and [4] reveals also some open mathematical issues. First of all, equation (1) formulates a demand function which is valid for customers using services from NSP i and CP j. This reflects the fact that users fundamentally rely on having a parallel relationship with one NSP and one CP, but does not model the hierarchical dependencies between NSPs and CPs/OTTs in more detail. Moreover, it is not clear whether this demand function is consistent with the later concept of σ_i^N and σ_j^C as indicators for the market shares of the different providers. A second aspect concerns the degree of provider competition. [3] and [4] somehow (but not very precisely) assume that NSP prices and CP prices, respectively, are identical in a first order approximation, which in a sense contradicts the assumption of competition between individual NSPs or individual CPs. Moreover, in the course of their mathematical argumentation, eventually the authors deal with harmonic means of NSP and CP prices only, and thus the analysed games could be interpreted as games between aggregated providers, omitting further competition aspects.

Based on this discussion and complementing the mathematical analysis, in the following section we provide a comprehensive analysis of the situation *from a numerical point of view*. Indeed, our results indicate that paradoxical effects resulting from side payments do exist, however they require a rather careful description of the underlying scenario which turns out to be a non-trivial task and much more sophisticated than suggested by Altman et al. and Caron et al.

4   Numerical Analysis

While the paradoxical results described in [4] and [3] have mainly been achieved by an analytical model of the game played by the NSPs and/or CPs, we provide a numerical analysis of the claimed paradox. To this end, based on Matlab we have built a dedicated numerical model which allows to directly determine the Nash Equilibria Points with feasible computational efficiency.

4.1   Basic Model

Taking one representative player and assuming everybody to act rationally in a more or less identical manner based on defined rules, we simplify the equation (4) to an aggregate player utility (w.l.o.g. representing an NSP),

$$U^N := D(\bar{p}^N, \bar{p}^C)(\bar{p}^N + p_s) \quad , \tag{6}$$

in the first stage. Correspondingly, the utility for the CP is formulated by

$$U^C := D(\bar{p}^N, \bar{p}^C)(\bar{p}^C - p_s) \quad . \tag{7}$$

Accordingly, a two aggregate player (1 NSP, 1 CP) game is constructed. There, we are looking for matching best responses for each price value of the other player in a given interval – e.g., (0,1] or [0,1]. Through the identification of equilibria between best responses[4], pure Nash Equilibria (NEs) are obtained for each side payment level

---

[4] No differences have been observed testing several different degrees of rounding the utilities of players combined with suitable step sizes, thus exact best response matches have been used.

(corresponding to [3], we have used the same interval as for the prices of NSPs and CPs). Thus, in the optimal case, for each considered side payment level one or more NEs are identified, stored and depicted. Please take note that for this case the question of end user stickiness/loyalty expressed through σ can be neglected as there is no competition between NSPs and/or CPs, resp.

We observe that in this game with only one aggregated NSP and one aggregated CP, the side payments paradox cannot be reproduced. Nonetheless, the curves largely correspond to the expected bidding behaviours of both players: the revenues are fraternally shared by both types of players, which implies that side payments are compensated by the receiving player (i.e., the price p_1 by the NSP is decreased by the same amount). However, when the price p_1 approaches zero, the rising side payments cannot be compensated anymore (see Figure 1(a)). At this point, the utility of the CP suddenly decreases, while the NSP first profits from higher side payments. Finally, both utilities expeditiously converge to zero (see Figure 1(b)).

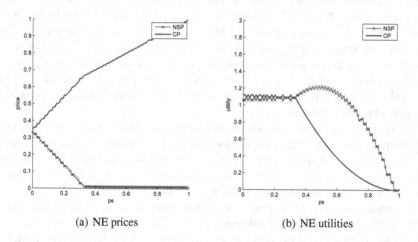

(a) NE prices   (b) NE utilities

Fig. 1. Base case: Equilibrium prices and utilities of the NSP and the CP for all side payments p_s

Hence, receiving side payments is beneficial or at least neutral for the receiving player, which implies that a paradox cannot be confirmed for aggregate players. Most notably, this result seems to be in line with those obtained by Altman et al. and Caron et al. for a neutral scenario without side payment discrimination.

4.2 NSP and CP Competition

Having dealt with the neutral case so far, we now extend our model towards oligopolistic competition between several NSPs and/or CPs which is reflected by the customer distribution functions σ^N and σ^C, resp. Specifically, in this subsection we employ the original definitions of these functions according to [4], cf. equation (3).

For our numerical approach, the difficulty arises which input data may be used for competing players for each player type, i.e., NSPs and CPs. To simplify the scenario, we consider competition between two NSPs and two CPs. W.l.o.g. we consider NSP 1 (and CP 1, resp.) to be "representative" and rational players charging prices p_1^N and p_1^C, resp. Both NSP 1 and CP 1 face one competitor each which may or may not charge different prices p_2^N and p_2^C, resp. Moreover, define $\beta^N := p_2^N/p_1^N$ and $\beta^C := p_2^C/p_1^C$. Then, we consider for both NSPs and CPs three cases each:

- **Low cost competitor** whose price is 25% below the price of the representative player (i.e., $\beta = 0.75$)
- **Neutral competitor** who charges the same price as the representative player (i.e., $\beta = 1.00$)
- **Premium price competitor** whose price is 25% above the price of the representative player (i.e., $\beta = 1.25$)

Hence, in total nine relevant cases result with equilibria as depicted in Figure 2. Note that for each figure, β^N and β^C indicate the relative price level between the NSP/CPs who are competing. The case of $\beta^N = 1.00 / \beta^C = 1.00$ can be considered identical to the game without σ, see Section 4.1, as well as to the games where all prices are factually identical, as discussed in [4] and [3]. Moreover, note that by introducing the σ functions the market for each provider type (NSP/CP) is split into segments occupied by several players; hence, the overall utilities need to be summed up for a comparison of the overall market situation.

Remember that the paradox of side payments originally has been defined as an equilibrium situation where the NSPs (receiver of side payments) end up with a lower profit than the CPs (sender of side payments). Observe that such a paradox arises whenever $\beta^C = 0.75$, but also at $\beta^N = 1.25/\beta^C = 1$, thus when $\beta^N \geq \beta^C$ holds. On the other hand, we see from Figure 2 that side paradoxes vanish at very high p_s.

It is interesting to note that Figure 2 allows to identify also a second type of paradox which results in decreasing NSP utilities as a function of p_s; this is often the case for small to medium p_s. In the opposite case ($\beta^N \leq \beta^C$), the NSP profits from the competitive situation. Thus, providers facing discounters are better off in general.

We also observe the magnitude of the side payment paradox shift increases with the growing discrepancy of the competitive situations between provider types, i.e. CP and NSP markets. In particular, the potential to yield paradox outcomes increases with premium players in the NSP market and discounters in the CP market. As a consequence, the $\beta^N = 1.25 / \beta^C = 0.75$ case obviously leads to the highest paradox of all inspected cases, while the opposite case would benefit targeted NSPs at least for sufficiently low p_s. However, as our main conclusions from this numerical analysis we would like to emphasize that it is the competition between NSPs and/or CPs (expressed in terms of the σ functions) which is responsible for creating paradoxical situations, while the aggregation of providers leads to non-paradoxical results.

By varying the β^C in an extended range, i.e., $\beta^C \in [0.5, 1.5]$, while holding β^N constant in the initially used range, Figure 3 illustrates the utility difference between NSP 1 and CP 1, where negative values indicate a paradoxical situation. Note that with

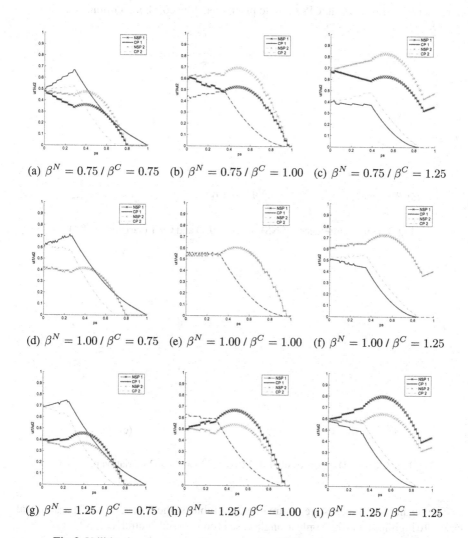

(a) $\beta^N = 0.75 / \beta^C = 0.75$ (b) $\beta^N = 0.75 / \beta^C = 1.00$ (c) $\beta^N = 0.75 / \beta^C = 1.25$

(d) $\beta^N = 1.00 / \beta^C = 0.75$ (e) $\beta^N = 1.00 / \beta^C = 1.00$ (f) $\beta^N = 1.00 / \beta^C = 1.25$

(g) $\beta^N = 1.25 / \beta^C = 0.75$ (h) $\beta^N = 1.25 / \beta^C = 1.00$ (i) $\beta^N = 1.25 / \beta^C = 1.25$

Fig. 2. Utilities for nine cases of two competing NSPs and two competing CPs

increasing β^N, the range of the side payments paradox increases as well (i.e., the partitions below the x-axis of Figure 3). Correspondingly, the difference between NSP 2 and CP 2 is depicted in Figure 4), resulting from a shift of the point $p_s = 0$, while limited effects are inferred after the point of convergence. In contrast, β^C has the capability to lead to a shift of the curve's level being reinforced by an alternation of the slope with an increase of p_s. Beyond that, CPs seem to profit from low cost competition, i.e., $\beta^C < 1$.

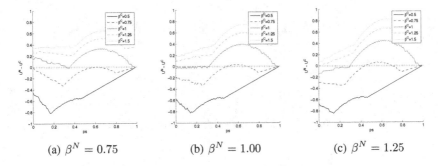

(a) $\beta^N = 0.75$ (b) $\beta^N = 1.00$ (c) $\beta^N = 1.25$

Fig. 3. Utility Differences of NSP 1 (fixed β^N) and CP 1 (variation of β^C)

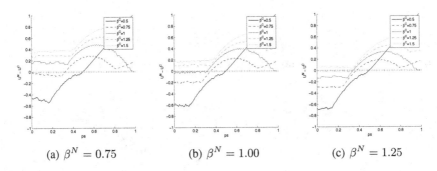

(a) $\beta^N = 0.75$ (b) $\beta^N = 1.00$ (c) $\beta^N = 1.25$

Fig. 4. Utility Differences of NSP 2 (fixed β^N) and CP 2 (variation of β^C)

The results for all cases are summarized in Table 1; the four identified paradoxical cases are highlighted, while only a single case is considered neutral, i.e., $\beta^N = \beta^C = 1$.

4.3   Revising the Customer Distribution Function

Having identified the key significance of the σ functions for establishing the Paradox of Side Payments, we now further investigate this issue by employing an alternative

Table 1. Summary of results

β^N / β^C	0.75	1.00	1.25
0.75	paradox (max. ≈ 0.2)	NSP gains	NSP gains heavily
1.00	paradox (max. ≈ 0.3)	neutral/base case	NSP gains heavily
1.25	paradox (max. ≈ 0.4)	paradox (max. ≈ 0.12)	NSP gains

version of these functions for the case of two competing NSPs and two competing CPs. To this end, remember that [4] defines σ_i^N and σ_j^C as the distribution of the end customers among the various NSPs and CPs, respectively, which fulfils two additional requirements: (i) if all providers charge the same price, the distribution is assumed to be uniform; (ii) a more expensive provider has less customers than a cheaper one. Obviously, the definition provided in (3) fulfils these conditions but of course is not the only such function. Suppose for instance there are two NSPs (or CPs, resp.; to improve clarity, we omit for now the superscripts N or C) competing against each other which have set prices $p_1, p_2 \geq 0$ with $p_2 \leq 2p_1$, resulting in a distribution of σ_1 and σ_2 with $\sigma_1 + \sigma_2 = 1$. Assume that, w.l.o.g., provider 1 keeps her price fixed at p_1 while provider 2 changes her price by Δp_2. Then, it is reasonable to assume that the resulting change of σ_2, i.e., $\Delta \sigma_2$, is directly proportional to the difference between p_1 and p_2 (i.e., the larger this price difference, the stronger the trigger for customers to change providers):

$$\Delta \sigma_2' = -\alpha \cdot |p_2 - p_1| \Delta p_2 \quad , \tag{8}$$

with $\alpha > 0$ as constant of proportionality. Note how the direction of change depends on whether p_2 is larger or smaller than p_1. Hence, we may formulate the following differential equation for σ_2':

$$\frac{d\sigma_2'}{dp_2} = -\alpha \cdot |p_2 - p_1| \quad . \tag{9}$$

For the solution of equation (9), we have to take the above condition (i) into account and distinguish two cases:

$$p_2 \geq p_1 \Rightarrow \sigma_2' = \alpha(p_1 p_2 - \frac{1}{2}p_2^2) + \frac{1}{2} - \frac{\alpha}{2}p_1^2 \tag{10}$$

$$p_2 \leq p_1 \Rightarrow \sigma_2' = -\alpha(p_1 p_2 - \frac{1}{2}p_2^2) + \frac{1}{2} + \frac{\alpha}{2}p_1^2 \tag{11}$$

Note that in both cases, $p_1 = p_2$ leads to $\sigma_2' = 0.5$ which is in line with condition (i). Finally, if we consider $p_2 = 0 \Rightarrow \sigma_2' = 1$ as additional boundary condition (i.e., if provider 2 is offering the service for free, she attracts all customers), we can calculate the constant of proportionality, which turns out to be $\alpha = 1/p_1^2$, and thus determine the final form of σ_2' and $\sigma_1' = 1 - \sigma_2'$ as follows (with $\beta = p_2/p_1$ as defined already earlier in the paper):

$$\beta \geq 1 \Rightarrow \sigma_2' = \beta - \frac{1}{2}\beta^2 \text{ and } \sigma_1' = 1 - (\beta - \frac{1}{2}\beta^2) \tag{12}$$

$$\beta \leq 1 \Rightarrow \sigma'_2 = 1 - (\beta - \frac{1}{2}\beta^2) \text{ and } \sigma'_1 = \beta - \frac{1}{2}\beta^2 \tag{13}$$

Observe the mutual identities between each σ'_2 and the σ'_1 belonging to the opposite case which nicely reflects the fact that for calculating σ'_1 directly it is required to change the roles of p_1 and p_2. Altogether, equations (12) and (13) describe a novel type of distribution which evidently fulfils also condition (ii) and thus can be used as an alternative definition replacing the original σ proposed by Caron et al. in equation (3).

By this replacement of σ the characteristics of the loyalty relationship between price and the market share of individual providers changes. This is depicted in Figure 5 where the new $\sigma'_{1/2}$ (right figure) demonstrates stability around the neutral point (identical prices; $\beta = 1.00$), but non-linearly diverges in both directions (unlike the original $\sigma_{1/2}$ as shown in the left figure). Moreover, the σ' finally converges to zero when the price difference becomes sufficiently large ($\beta \geq 2$).

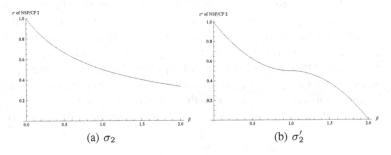

(a) σ_2 (b) σ'_2

Fig. 5. Characteristics of the revised σ'_2 (right) compared to the original σ_2 (left) depending on β

This alternative version of σ'_1 and σ'_2 has been simulated for the same range of values as before and is depicted in Figure 6. While in general, most revised figures pretty much resemble their counterparts in Figure 2, we observe also some significant differences: While for the original version of σ, a paradox is achieved for all competing CPs whenever it occurs for one, in the revised case, only the "representative player" can substantially profit from a paradox. Secondly, this representative player may then substantially profit more from competition advantages, e.g., higher utilities for the presentative player in the paradox case. Thirdly, the case $\beta^N = 1.25 / \beta^C = 1.00$ only yields an insignificant paradox in the revised calculation.

In none of the discussed cases (whether with revised σ' or original σ, with or without allowance of zero prices, or with various competition constellations) we have been able to observe that side payments need to stay below around 4% of p_{max} as a necessary condition for the appearance of the paradox, which is in contrast to Theorem 1 in [4] (probably due to specific assumptions about the competition behaviour). This is particularly obvious from Figures 3 and 4 where paradoxical states correspond to curve partitions below the x-axis. Higher side payments still seem to yield stable pure NEs with adequate utility levels. Very high utility levels, however, will obviously be unbeneficial for all players. However, with the revised calculation of σ' the potential for a paradox over all players seems to be lowered by the natural increase of side payments, i.e., the competitor typically soon falls below the utility levels of both NSPs.

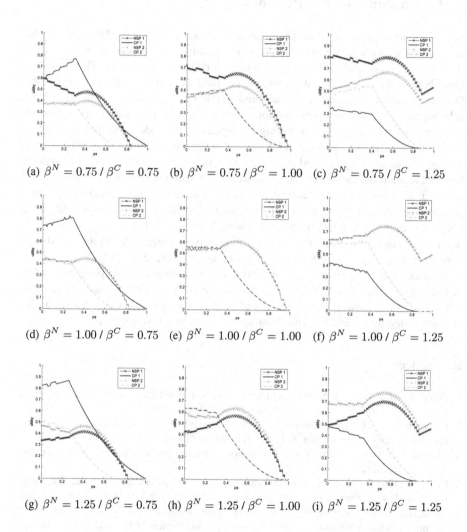

(a) $\beta^N = 0.75 / \beta^C = 0.75$ (b) $\beta^N = 0.75 / \beta^C = 1.00$ (c) $\beta^N = 0.75 / \beta^C = 1.25$

(d) $\beta^N = 1.00 / \beta^C = 0.75$ (e) $\beta^N = 1.00 / \beta^C = 1.00$ (f) $\beta^N = 1.00 / \beta^C = 1.25$

(g) $\beta^N = 1.25 / \beta^C = 0.75$ (h) $\beta^N = 1.25 / \beta^C = 1.00$ (i) $\beta^N = 1.25 / \beta^C = 1.25$

Fig. 6. The nine cases for the alternative version of σ'^N and σ'^C

Despite the non-zero assumption of prices used in the corresponding works [3] and [4], we claim that even negative prices may be considered in order extend the range of acceptable side payments for both players.

5 Conclusions and Future Work

In the case of network services, providers may intend to provide different quality levels, where individual end users may prefer one quality level over another, i.e., varying willingness to pay, and NSPs may have to face different cost levels. Thus, the Nash Equilibria identified by [3] and [4] and their conditions may not fully be transferrable. Despite the advantages of having clear and simple recommendations, the handling of side payments seems to be more complex than previously anticipated, and our results illustrate that recommendations are highly dependent on underlying assumptions and modelling details, like the weak relationship between provider types or the questionable formulation of loyalty and provider competition, e.g., among NSPs. In order to further facilitate the entanglement of networks ignoring previously applied hierarchical separation (i.e., tiers of classical providers), a sufficient understanding of how to perfectly enable side payments will be required. Thus, future work has to address the integration of well recognised competition models and user behaviours for make loyalty relationships more realistic. Due to the involved solving complexity, numerical simulations have proven to be appropriate tools for required further extensions.

Summarising our main findings, it turns out that a paradox of side payments indeed exists, however based on our numerical results we conclude that it is subject to rather subtle conditions. Thus, it should be viewed as substantially more nuanced and complex than suggested by [3] and [4], and definitely needs further investigation.

References

1. Wong, S., Altman, E., Rojas-Mora, J.: Internet access: Where law, economy, culture and technology meet. Elsevier Computer Networks 55(2), 470–479 (2011)
2. Chemerinsky, E.: Content neutrality as a central problem of freedom of speech: Problems in the supreme court's application. S. Cal. L. Rev. 74, 49 (2000)
3. Altman, E., Caron, S., Kesidis, G.: Application Neutrality and a Paradox of Side Payments. Technical report (2010)
4. Caron, S., Kesidis, G., Altman, E.: Application Neutrality and a Paradox of Side Payments. In: Proceedings of the Re-Architecting the Internet (ReARCH 2010). ACM (2010)
5. Musacchio, J., Schwartz, G., Walrand, J.: A two-sided market analysis of provider investment incentives with an application to the net-neutrality issue. Review of Network Economics 8(1) (2009)
6. Lee, R.S., Wu, T.: Subsidizing Creativity through Network Design: Zero-Pricing and Net Neutrality. Journal of Economic Perspectives 23(3), 61–76 (2009)
7. Zwickl, P., Reichl, P.: An Instance-Based Approach for the Quantitative Assessment of Key Value Network Dependencies. In: Becvar, Z., Bestak, R., Kencl, L. (eds.) NETWORKING 2012 Workshops. LNCS, vol. 7291, pp. 97–104. Springer, Heidelberg (2012)
8. Akerlof, G.A.: The market for lemons. Quarterly Journal of Economics, 480–500 (1970)

Securing Address Registration in Location/ID Split Protocol Using ID-Based Cryptography

Mahdi Aiash[1], Ameer Al-Nemrat, and David Preston[2]

[1] School of Science and Technology, Middlesex University, London, UK
M.Aiash@mdx.ac.uk
[2] School of Architecture, Computing and Engineering, University of East London, London, UK
{A.Al-Nemrat,D.Preston}@uel.ac.uk

Abstract. The Locator/ID Separation Protocol (LISP) is a routing architecture that provides new semantics for IP addressing. In order to simplify routing operations and improve scalability in future Internet, the LISP separates the device identity from its location using two different numbering spaces. The LISP also, introduces a mapping system to match the two spaces. In the initial stage, each LISP-capable router needs to register with a Map Server, this is known as the Registration stage. However, this stage is vulnerable to masquerading and content poisoning attacks. Therefore, a new security method for protecting the LISP Registration stage is presented in this paper. The proposed method uses the ID-Based Cryptography (IBC) which allows the mapping system to authenticate the source of the data. The proposal has been verified using formal methods approach based on the well-developed Casper/FDR tool.

Keywords: Location/ID Split Protocol, Casper/FDR, Future Internet, Address Registration, Masquerading attacks.

1 Introduction

Since the public Internet first became part of the global infrastructure, its dramatic growth has created a number of scaling challenges. Among the most fundamental of these is helping to ensure that the routing and addressing system continues to function efficiently even as the number of connected devices continues to increase. An IETF working group along with the research group at Cisco, are working on the Locator/ID Separation Protocol (LISP) [1]. Unlike IP addresses, which combine hosts' locations and devices IDs in a single namespace, the LISP separates hosts' locations and identities. The LISP specifies an architecture and mechanism for replacing the addresses currently used by IP with two separate name spaces: Endpoint IDs (EIDs), used within EID sites, and Routing Locators (RLOCs), used on the transit networks such as the Internet infrastructure. To achieve this separation, LISP defines protocol mechanisms for EID-to-RLOC mapping. Furthermore, LISP assumes the existence of a mapping system in the form of distributed database to store and propagate those

V. Tsaoussidis et al. (Eds.): WWIC 2013, LNCS 7889, pp. 129–139, 2013.

mappings globally. The functionality of the mapping system goes through two stages:

1. Registration Stage: in this stage, the Map Server learns the EIDs-to-RLOC mappings from an authoritative LISP-Capable Router and publishes them in the database.
2. Addresses resolving Stage: the Map Server (MS) accepts Map-Requests from routers, looks up the database and returns the requested mapping.

These two stages will be explained in more details in section 2.2.

Currently, the research concentrates mainly on defining the LISP overall architecture as well as the structure of the LISP packets such as the Map-Register, Map-Notify and Map-Reply. However, the security-related research is still at an early stage, the research in [2] [3] have highlighted the potential threats to be addressed at a later stage of the research. Therefore, this paper investigates the security side of implementing the LISP architecture. Our main concern here is the security of the address Registration stage, where an LISP-capable router publishes all its hosts' EIDs to the Map Server via a Map-Register as will be discussed in section 1. For a secure Registration, two information elements are critical: the hosts' EIDs and the the router's address (RLOC). Indeed, a malicious router might spoof different RLOC and supply wrong EID- prefixes to the MS. This is very similar to poisoning attacks against Domain Name Server (DNS) or routing tables [4]. To stop such attacks, we need to thwart masquerading threats; therefore, a new approach based on the ID-Based Cryptography (IBC) [5] is proposed in this paper. The IBC helps to certify the messages sender as the real owner of the RLOC that will update the Map Server. The main advantage of using the IBC over traditional Public Key Infrastructure is that since the public key will be derived from the nodes' identifiers, IBC eliminates the need for a public key distribution infrastructure, more details are in section 2.3. The proposed solution is formally verified using formal methods approach based on the well-developed Casper/FDR tool [7].

The rest of the paper is organised as follows: Section 2 describes some related work in the literature. Section 3 presents the proposed security protocol along with its formal analysis. The paper concludes in Section 4.

2   Related Work

2.1   An Overview of The LISP

To improve routing scalability while facilitating flexible address assignment in multi-homing and mobility scenarios, the LISP describes changes to the Internet architecture in which IP addresses are replaced by routing locators (RLOCs) for routing through the global Internet and by endpoint identifiers (EIDs) for identifying network sessions between devices [8]. As shown in Fig 1, three essential components exist in the LISP environment: the LISP sites (EID space), the non-LISP sites (RLOC space), and the LISP Mapping System which comprises Map Servers and databases.

– **The LISP sites (EID space):** they represent customer end-sites in exactly the same way that end-sites are defined today. However, the IP addresses in the EID space are not advertised to the non-LISP sites, but are published into the LISP Mapping Systems which perform the EID-to-RLOC mapping. The LISP functionality is deployed on the site's gateway or edge routers. Therefore, based on their roles, two types of routers are defined: firstly, the Ingress Tunnel Routers (ITRs) which receive packets from hosts and send LISP packets toward the Map Server. Secondly, the Egress Tunnel Routers (ETRs) which receive LISP packets from the Map Server and pass them to hosts [1] [8].
– **Non-LISP sites (RLOC space):** they represent current sites where the IP addresses are advertised and used for routing purpose.
– **LISP Mapping Systems:** These are represented by Map Servers (MS) and a globally distributed database that contains all known EID prefixes to RLOC mappings. Similar to the current Domain Name System (DNS), the Mapping systems are queried by LISP-capable devices for an EID-to-RLOC mapping.

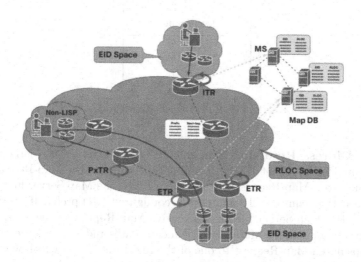

Fig. 1. The LISP Network Architecture Design [8]

2.2 Interactions with Other LISP Components

The functionality of the LISP goes through two stages:

1. **The EID Prefix Configuration and ETR Registration Stage**
   As explained in [9], an ETR publishes its EID-prefixes on a Map Server (MS) by sending LISP Map-Register messages which include the ETR's RLOC and a list of its EID-prefixes. Initially, it has been presumed that prior to sending

a Map-Register message, the ETR and the Map Server must be configured with a shared secret or other relevant authentication information. Upon the receipt of a Map-Register from an ETR, the Map Server checks the validity of the Map-Register message and acknowledges it by sending a Map-Notify message. When registering with a Map-Server, an ETR might request a no-proxy reply service which implies that the Map Server will forward all the EID-to-RLOC mapping requests to the relevant ETR rather than dealing with them.

Since no security protocol has been proposed yet to authenticate the ETR and secure the connection with the MS, the registration stage, shown in Fig 2, is vulnerable to serious security threats such as replay and poisoning attacks. Therefore, a security protocol will be introduced in section 3.

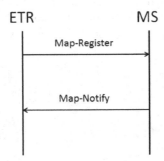

Fig. 2. The ETR Registration Process

2. **The Address Resolving Stage:** Once a Map Server has EID-prefixes registered by its client ETRs, it will accept and process Map-Requests. In response to a Map-Request (sent from an ITR), the Map Server first checks to see if the required EID matches a configured EID-prefix. If there is no match, the Map Server returns a negative Map-Reply message to the ITR. In case of a match, the Map Server re-encapsulates and forwards the resulting Encapsulated Map-Request to one of the registered ETRs which will return Map-Replay directly to the requestion ITR as shown in Fig 3.

The LISP working group in [1] has defined the structure of all the LISP Packets including the Map-Request, the Map-Notify, the Map-Register and the MAP-Reply. However, for the security analysis in section 3, only security-related parameters of the LISP messages are explicitly mentioned.

2.3   ID-Based Cryptography (IBC)

The IBC is a cryptographic scheme was first proposed by Adi Shamir [5]. The scheme enables users to communicate securely and verify each other's signature

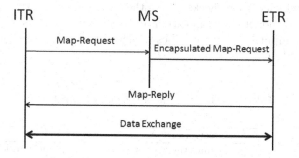

Fig. 3. The No Proxy Map Server Processing

without exchanging public or private keys. However, the scheme requires the presence of Trusted Key Generation (TKG) centres.

IBC's Operation: Unlike the normal Public Key Infrastructure (PKI) where a TKG randomly generates pairs of public/private keys, each node in IBC chooses its identifier (address or name) as a public key. Practically, any publicly known information that uniquely identifies the node could be used as a public key. The TKG generates the corresponding private key and securely distributes it to the node.

When a node (A) wants to communicate with another node (B), node A will sign the message using its private key and encrypt the result with the node B's public key. Upon receiving the message, node B will decrypt the message using its private key and verify the signature using node A's public key.

The IBC represents an efficient and easy to implement system which removes some of the overhead encountered in PKI for key management and digital certificate issuance/revocation. However, the security of the IBC is based on the secrecy of the private key. To deal with this issue, the node needs to combine additional information such as timestamps to their identifiers when generating the public key. This procedure will guarantee a periodic update of the public key. However, it introduces a key-management problem where all users must have the most recent public key for the node.

2.4 Verifying Security Protocols Using Casper/FDR

Previously, analysing security protocols used to go through two stages. Firstly, modelling the protocol using a theoretical notation or language such as the CSP [10]. Secondly, verifying the protocol using a model checker such as Failures-Divergence Refinement (FDR) [11]. However, describing a system or a protocol using CSP is a quite difficult and error-prone task; therefore, Gavin Lowe [7] has developed the CASPER/FDR tool to model security protocols, it accepts a simple and human-friendly input file that describes the system and compiles it into CSP code which is then checked using the FDR model checker. Casper/FDR has been used to model communication and security protocols as in [12], [13]. The CASPER's input file that describes the systems consists of eight headers as explained in Table 1.

Table 1. The Headers of Casper's Input File

The Header	Description
# Free Variables	Defines the agents, variables and functions in the protocol
# Processes	Represents each agent as a process
# Protocol Description	Shows all the messages exchanged between the agents
# Specification	Specifies the security properties to be checked
# Actual Variables	Defines the real variables, in the actual system to be checked
# Functions	Defines all the functions used in the protocol
# System	Lists the agents participating in the actual system with their parameters instantiated
# Intruder Information	Specifies the intruder's knowledge and capabilities

3   The Proposed Solution

This section discusses our proposal of using the IBC protocol to secure the Registration procedure of the LISP.

3.1   System Definition

As shown in Fig 2, and based on the notations in Table 2, the secure Registration procedure using the IBC goes as follows:

```
Msg1. TKG→ ETR : {SK(ETR)}{K1}
Msg2. TKG → MS : {SK(MS)}{K2}
```

The TKG provides the two communicating parties (ETR, MS) with their private keys SK(ETR), SK(MS) in messages 1 and 2. These messages are encrypted using the pre-shared secret keys K1, K2, respectively.

```
Msg3. ETR → MS : {Map-Register}{PK(MS)}, {h(Map-Register)}{SK(ETR)}
```

The ETR sends an LISP Map-Register packets in Msg3. The content of this message is encrypted using the MS's public key (which is publicly known) and digitally signed using the private key of the ETR. As described in [9], the Map-Register packet includes the ETR's address (RLOC), a random number (n1) and a list of EID-Prefix, managed by the ETR.

Msg4. MS → ETR : {Map-Notify}{PK(ETR)}, {h(Map-Notify)}{SK(MS)}

Upon receiving msg3, the MS will use its private key SK(MS) to decrypt the message and then verify the signature using the ETR's public key PK(ETR). Finally, the MS will hash the included Map-Register and compare the result with the received signed value. Only if the two values are equal, the MS composes a Map-Notify packet as msg4 which includes the received random number (n1). This message is encrypted using the ETR's public key and digitally signed using the MS's private key. The ETR will check the included random number and only when the check succeeds, the ETR authenticates the MS.

Table 2. Notation

The Notation	Definition
TKG	The Trusted Ticket Granting
SK(ETR), SK(MS)	The Private keys of the ETR, MS, respectively. These keys are derived by the TKG
K1, K2	Pre-shared keys to secure the connections between the TKG and ETR, MS
ETR	The Egress Tunnel Router in the destination EID Space
MS	The Map Server
n1	A fresh random number
h(m)	Hash value of the message (m)
{m}{K}	The message (m) being encrypted with the key (K)

3.2 Formal Analysis Using Casper/FDR

To formally analyse the proposed solution, we simulate the system using Casper/FDR tool. The full Casper input file describing the system is included in the Appendix. For conciseness, only the #Protocol Description, the #Specification and the #Intruder Information headings are described here, while the rest are of a less significance in terms of understanding the verification process.

The #Protocol description heading defines the system and the transactions between the entities. It is worth pointing out that for security simulation we need to explicitly define the security parameters. Therefore, we mention the security-related contents of the Map-Register and Map-Notify as shown below in msg 3, 4. Where (m) and (m1) refer to Map-Register and Map-Notify packets, respectively. EIDPre refers to the EID-Prefix sent by the ETR.

```
#Protocol description
0. -> ETR : MS, TKG
1. TKG -> ETR : {SK(ETR)}{K1}
2. TKG -> MS : {SK(MS)}{K2}
```

3. ETR -> MS : {m,ETR, n1,EIDPre}{PK(MS)}, {h(m, ETR, n1, EIDPre)}{SK(ETR)}%z
[$decryptable(z, PK(ETR))$]

4. MS -> ETR : {m1, n1}{PK(ETR)}, {h(m1, n1)}{SK(MS)}%w
[$decryptable(w, PK(MS))$]

The security requirements of the system are defined under the # Specification heading. The lines starting with the keyword **Secret** define the secrecy properties of the protocol. The Secret(MS, n1, [ETR]) specifies the n1 nonce as a secret between the ETR and the MS. The lines starting with the **Agreement** define the protocol's authenticity properties; for instance Agreement(MS, ETR, [n1]) specifies that, the MS is correctly authenticated to the ETR using the random number n1. The WeakAgreement(ETR, Ms) assertion could be interpreted as follows: if ETR has completed a run of the protocol with MS, then MS has previously been running the protocol, apparently with ETR.

```
#Specification
Secret(MS, n1, [ETR])
WeakAgreement(ETR, MS)
WeakAgreement(MS, ETR)
Agreement(MS, ETR, [n1])
```

The # Intruder Information heading specifies the intruder's identity, knowledge and capability. The first line identifies the intruder as Mallory, the intruder knowledge defines the Intruder's initial knowledge, i.e., we assume the intruder knows the identity of the participants, its own private key and can fabricate Map-Register and Map-Notify messages.

```
#Intruder Information
Intruder = Mallory
IntruderKnowledge = {ETR, MS, Mallory, PK ,SK(Mallory), Map-Register,
Map-Notify}
```

After generating the CSP description of the systems using Casper and asking FDR to check the security assertions, no attack was found against the proposed solution as shown in Fig 4.

Security Considerations. Despite the fact that no attack has been discovered against the proposed solution in section 3.2, this result needs to be considered carefully. The formal verification result is based on the system defined in 3.1. In this system, it is assumed that the ETR knows the authoritative MS in its network or domain. In a very similar way to the current Domain Naming System (DNS), where clients are preconfigured with the authoritative DNS server. However, we simulated the case when the ETR is not sure of the identity of its authoritative MS. The following attack against the Secret(MS, n1, [ETR]), Agreement(MS, ETR, [n1]) and WeakAgreement(ETR, MS) assertions was discovered

```
0. -> ETR : Mallory, TKG
1a. TKG -> I_ETR : {SK(ETR)}{K1}
1b. I_TKG -> ETR : {SK(ETR)}{K1}
```

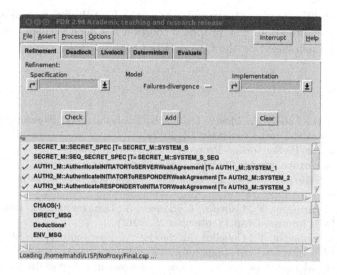

Fig. 4. The FDR Formal Verification

2a. TKG -> I_MS : {SK(MS)}{K2}

2b. I_TKG -> MS : {SK(MS)}{K2}

3a. ETR -> Mallory : {M, ETR, n1, EIDpre}{PK(Mallory)}, {h(M, ETR, N1, EIDpre)}{SK(ETR)}

3b. I_ETR -> MS : {M, ETR, n1, EIDpre}{PK(MS)}, {h(M, ETR, n1, EIDpre)} {SK(ETR)}

4. MS -> I_ETR : {M2, n1}{PK(ETR)}, {h(M2, n1)}{SK(MS)}

Where the notations I_ Ms, I_ETR and I_TKG represent the case where the Intruder impersonates the Ms, ETR and TKG, respectively. This is an active Man-in-the-Middle attack; the Intruder intercepts and replays messages 1 and 2. Since the ETR is not sure of the identity of the MS, the intruder manages to impersonate the MS and fools the ETR to use its (rather than the MS's) public key to encrypt message 3a. Consequently, the random number (n1) will be compromised, and the ETR will run the protocol mistakenly believing it is with the MS, while in reality it is with the Intruder. In order to stop such attacks, the ETRs should be configured to use the authoritative Map Server in its domain or network. This could be simply achieved during the network configuration in a similar way to configuring the default DNS server or the default Gateway in a network.

4   Conclusion

This paper analysed the security of the address Registration in the LISP protocol. We presented a new security method, based on the IBC, allowing a Map

Server to check the received information (i.e., the EID-Prefix) as well as providing source authentication. The proposed solution has been verified using formal methods approach based on the Casper/FDR tool.

References

1. Farinacci, D., Fuller, V., Meyer, D., Lewis, D.: Locator/ID Separation Protocol (LISP). Internet-Draft (November 13, 2012)
2. Cisco Locator/ID Separation Protocol Security At-A-Glance, http://www.cisco.com/en/US/prod/collateral/iosswrel/ps6537/ps6554/ps6599/ps10800/at_a_glance_c45-645204.pdf (last accessed on January 13, 2013)
3. Maino, F., Ermagan, V., Cabellos, A., Saucez, A., Bonaventure, O.: LISP-Security (LISP-SEC). Internet-Draft (September 12, 2012)
4. Maino, F., Ermagan, V., Cabellos, A., Saucez, A., Bonaventure, O.: LISP-Security (LISP-SEC). Internet-Draft (September 12, 2012)
5. Shamir, A.: Identity-based cryptosystems and signature schemes. In: Blakely, G.R., Chaum, D. (eds.) CRYPTO 1984. LNCS, vol. 196, pp. 47–53. Springer, Heidelberg (1985)
6. Arends, R., Austein, R., Larson, M., Massey, D., Rose, S.: DNS Security Introduction and Requirements, Internet Engineering Task Force, RFC 4033 (March 2005)
7. Lowe, G., Broadfoot, P., Dilloway, C., Hui, M.L.: Casper: A compiler for the analysis of security protocols, 1.12 edn. (September 2009)
8. Cisco Locator/ID Separation Protocol Revolutionary Network Architecture to Power the Network, http://www.cisco.com/en/US/prod/collateral/iosswrel/ps6537/ps6554/ps6599/ps10800/aag_c45-635298.pdf (last accessed on January 13, 2013)
9. Farinacci, D., Fuller, V.: LISP Map Server Interface. Internet-Draft (March 4, 2012)
10. Goldsmith, M., Lowe, G., Roscoe, A.W., Ryan, P., Schneider, S.: The modelling and analysis of security protocols. PEARSON Ltd. (2010)
11. Formal Systems, Failures-divergence refinement. FDR2 user manual and tutorial, Version 1.3 (June 1993)
12. Aiash, M., Mapp, G., Lasebae, A., Phan, P., Loo, J.: Casper: A formally verified AKA protocol for vertical handover in heterogeneous environments using Casper/FDR. EURASIP Journal on Wireless Communications and Networking 2012, 57 (2012)
13. Aiash, M., Mapp, G., Lasebae, A., Phan, P., Loo, J.: A Formally Verified Device Authentication Protocol Using Casper/FDR. In: 11th IEEE International Conference on Trust, Security and Privacy in Computing and Communications (TrustCom), June 25-27 (2012)

Appendix: The Casper Description of the Proposed Solution

```
#Free variables
ETR, MS : Agent
na, nb, seq2, n1 : Nonce
```

```
PK: Agent -> PublicKey
SK: Agent -> PrivateKey
K1, K2: PreSharedKey
TKG: Server
m,m2, Ack: Messages
InverseKeys = (PK,SK), (K1, K1),(K2, K2)
h : HashFunction
EIDPre: EIDPrefix
hash1: HashValues
#Processes
INITIATOR(ETR, MS,TKG, K1,nb, m, Ack, n1, EIDPre)knows PK(ETR), PK(MS), SK(ETR)
RESPONDER(MS,TKG, K2, m2) knows PK(ETR), PK(MS), SK(MS)
SERVER(TKG, ETR, MS, K1, K2, na) knows PK, SK(ETR), SK(MS)
#Protocol description
0. -> ETR : MS, TKG
1. TKG -> ETR : {SK(ETR)}{K1}
2. TKG -> MS : {SK(MS)}{K2}
3. ETR -> MS : {m,ETR, n1,EIDPre}{PK(MS)}, {h(m, ETR, n1, EIDPre)}{SK(ETR)}%z
```
$[decryptable(z, PK(ETR))]$
```
4. MS -> ETR : {m2, n1}{PK(ETR)}, {h(m2, n1)}{SK(MS)}%w
```
$[decryptable(w, PK(MS))]$
```
#Specification
WeakAgreement(ETR, MS)
Secret(MS, n1, [ETR])
WeakAgreement(MS, ETR)
Agreement(MS, ETR, [n1])
#Actual variables
etr, ms, Mallory : Agent
Na, Nb, Seq2, N1 : Nonce
k1, k2: PreSharedKey
tkg: Server
InverseKeys = (k1, k1),(k2, k2)
EIDpre: EIDPrefix
M, M2, ack: Messages
haash1: HashValues
#Functions
symbolic SK, PK
#System
INITIATOR(etr,ms, tkg, k1, Nb, M, ack, N1, EIDpre)
RESPONDER(ms,tkg,k2,M2)
SERVER(tkg, etr, ms, k1,k2, Na))
#Intruder Information
Intruder = Mallory
IntruderKnowledge = {etr, ms, Mallory, PK ,SK(Mallory), M, M2}
```

Application-Layer Security for the WoT: Extending CoAP to Support End-to-End Message Security for Internet-Integrated Sensing Applications

Jorge Granjal, Edmundo Monteiro, and Jorge Sá Silva

DEI/CISUC, University of Coimbra
Polo 2, Pinhal de Marrocos, 3030-290 Coimbra, Portugal
{jgranjal,edmundo,sasilva}@dei.uc.pt

Abstract. Future Web of Things (WoT) applications employing constrained wireless sensing devices will require end-to-end communications with more powerful devices as Internet hosts. While the Constrained Application Protocol (CoAP) is currently being designed with this purpose, its current approach to security is to adopt a transport-layer solution. Transport-layer security may be limitative, considering that it does not provide a granular and flexible approach to security that many applications may require or benefit from. In this context, we target the design and experimental evaluation of alternative security mechanisms to enable the usage of end-to-end secure communications at the application-layer using CoAP. Rather than replacing security at the transport-layer, it is our goal that the proposed mechanisms may be employed in the context of a broader security architecture supporting Internet-integrated wireless sensing applications. Ours is, as far as we known, the first proposal with such goals.

Keywords: CoAP security, DTLS, end-to-end application-layer security, message security, granular security.

1 Introduction

Although many of the applications currently envisioned for the Web of Things (WoT) are critical in respect to security, the fact that they are envisioned to employ very constrained sensing platforms and wireless communications complicates the design of appropriate security solutions. In practice, many applications are required to accept compromises between security and the usage of resources on constrained sensing platforms. With wireless sensing devices as the TelosB [1] energy is a scarce resource. Such devices are employed in the context of low-energy personal area networks (LoWPANs) using link-layer communications standards such as IEEE 802.15.4 [2]. IEEE 802.15.4 supports low-energy wireless communications at low transmission rates using small packets in order to minimize transmission errors, and technologies for the integration of LoWPANs with the Internet are starting to appear and are expected to play an important role in the fulfillment of the WoT vision.

V. Tsaoussidis et al. (Eds.): WWIC 2013, LNCS 7889, pp. 140–153, 2013.

Communications and security technologies for the WoT are currently in the design phase and consequently a communications and security architecture for the WoT is currently not completely defined. In this context, of particular relevance are technologies currently being designed at the 6LoWPAN (IPv6 over Low Power Personal Area Networks) [3] and Core (Constrained RESTful Environments) [4] working groups of the IETF. Such technologies target the usage of LoWPAN devices in the context of its integration with the Internet, and as such are of most relevance to the WoT. 6LoWPAN provides adaptation mechanisms to enable the transmission of IPv6 packets over LoWPAN environments as IEEE 802.15.4 [2], while CoRE is currently designing the Constrained Application Protocol (CoAP) [5] with the purpose of enabling RESTful HTTP-based web communications on such environments. Focusing on how CoAP approaches security, we observe that the current choice to support end-to-end security is to adopt the Datagram Transport Layer Security (DTLS) Protocol [6]. Thus, security is not integrated at the application-layer protocol itself, but rather transparently applied to all CoAP messages at the transport layer. Given that 6LoWPAN environments currently employ UDP, DTLS appears as a logical choice in protecting communications at higher layers, at least from the standpoint of standardization. As we address in the paper, this approach misses all the advantages available in the usage of security at the application layer. With this in mind, we propose and experimentally evaluate new security mechanisms for the CoAP application-layer protocol.

The paper proceeds as follows. Section 2 describes related work, and Section 3 discusses end-to-end security in the context of Internet-integrated LoWPANs using 6LoWPAN and CoAP. The proposed mechanisms are described in Section 4 and experimentally evaluated in Section 5. Finally, Section 6 concludes the paper.

2   Related Work

Although security for Wireless Sensor Networks (WSN) is a prolific research area, investigation concerning the integration of LoWPAN environments with the Internet is very recent, and in consequence less proposals are available that target security in this context, and in particular security for end-to-end communications between LoWPAN wireless sensing devices and Internet hosts. Nevertheless, we find it important to address proposals with goals similar as ours, even if not addressing application-layer security using the (currently being designed) CoAP protocol.

The first of such proposals is Sizzle [7], which implements a compact web server providing HTTP accesses protected by SSL using 160-bit ECC (Elliptic Curve Cryptography) keys for authentication and key negotiation, but requiring a reliable transport-layer protocol and therefore being incompatible with CoAP and 6LoWPAN. Sizzle also does not support two-way authentication as will be required by many Machine-to-Machine (M2M) applications on the WoT. On the other end, SSNAIL [8] supports two-way authentication using an ECC-enabled handshake, but also requiring a reliable transport-layer protocol. More in line with the 6LoWPAN and CoAP technologies, authors in [9] propose the compression of DTLS headers with the goal of saving payload space and in consequence reducing the communications overhead. The architecture proposed in [10] supports two-way authentication with DTLS for end-to-end communications with constrained sensing devices employing specialized trusted-platform modules (TPM) to support hardware-assisted RSA cryptography. A previous internet-draft [11] proposed the integration of security with CoAP using options for the activation/deactivation of security contexts and for the protection of CoAP messages. Although this proposal shares some goals with ours, it assumes that all exchanged CoAP messages are protected in a similar fashion, as security is handled in the context of security sessions previously established between CoAP communicating entities. We may thus consider that this proposal is more in line with transport-layer security than with how application-layer security may be handled for individual CoAP messages. Other limitation of this proposal is that it doesn't enable a CoAP message to securely transverse multiple trust domains. Overall, none of the previously discussed proposals addresses application-layer security using CoAP with our goals.

3   End-to-End Communications for Internet-Integrated Wireless Sensing and Actuating Applications

The current Internet architecture illustrates the importance of employing complementary security mechanisms at diverse protocol layers. This aspect may also be considered when planning security for Internet-integrated LoWPANs, and in particular regarding the protection of end-to-end communications. End-to-end transport-layer security using DTLS as currently proposed for CoAP may be appropriate to applications requiring the transparent encryption of all CoAP communications, while on the other side applications may benefit from a more granular approach to security. Applications may require that security be applied according to the semantics of the CoAP protocol, or to the type of message or its contents. Overall, different approaches to end-to-end security may not only enrich the set of solutions available for Internet communications in the context of Internet-integrated LoWPANs, but also contribute to a more intelligent allocation of resources to security, given the computational and energetic impact of the cryptographic operations. Before proceeding with a discussion on how we approach application-layer CoAP security, we find it important to discuss how 6LoWPAN and CoAP are employed to support end-to-end communications with external (Internet) devices, as Figure 1 illustrates.

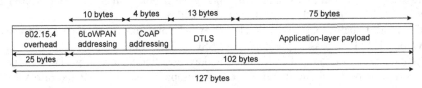

Fig. 1. Payload space usage for end-to-end communications in IEEE 802.15.4 environments

We may observe that payload space is a scarce resource in LoWPAN IEEE 802.15.4 environments, and as a consequence 6LoWPAN and CoAP incorporate header and address compression whenever viable. IEEE 802.15.4 provides 127-bytes of payload space at the link-layer, from which 25 bytes are required for the purpose of link-layer addressing. Therefore, 102-bytes of payload space are available for the 6LoWPAN adaptation layer and Protocols such as DTLS and CoAP at above layers. 6LoWPAN IPHC shared-context header compression [12] enables the compression of the UDP/IPv6 header down to 10 bytes, while CoAP employs a 4-byte fixed header and DTLS a 13-byte header. Without transport-layer security 88 bytes are available for applications using CoAP without incurring in costly 6LoWPAN fragmentations.

3.1   The CoAP Protocol

The CoAP Protocol [5] provides a request/response communications model between application endpoints and enables key concepts of the web such as the usage of URIs to identify resources in LoWPAN wireless sensing devices. In the context of an Internet-integrated LoWPAN sensing application, end-to-end communications may take place purely with CoAP or in alternative by translating HTTP to CoAP at a reverse or forward proxy, for example supported by a 6LBR (6LoWPAN border router). Such proxy entities as employed by CoAP may also be used in the benefit of security, as we discuss next in the context of our proposal. A CoAP request requiring an acknowledgment may be sent in a confirmable message, while data for which eventual delivery is sufficient may be sent in a non-confirmable message. A reset message may also be sent to identify unavailable resources or error conditions. Similarly to HTTP, CoAP also defines a set of method and response codes.

An important concept of CoAP is that, other than a basic set of information, most of the information is transported by options. CoAP options may be critical, elective, safe or unsafe. In short, a critical option is one that an endpoint must understand, while an elective option may be ignored by an endpoint not recognizing it. Safe and unsafe options determine how an option may be processed by an intermediary entity. An unsafe option needs to be understood by the proxy in order to safely forward it, while a safe option may be forwarded even if the proxy is unable to process it.

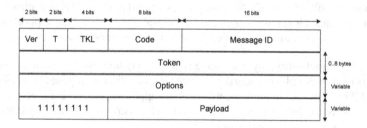

Fig. 2. CoAP message

The CoAP header and message format as currently proposed [5] is illustrated in Figure 2. The top row illustrates the 4-byte CoAP fixed header, constituted by the version field (2 bits), the message type field (2 bits), the token length field (4 bits), the Code field (8 bits) and the Message ID (16 bits). The token enables a CoAP entity to perform request/reply matching, while the message ID field may enable duplicate and optional reliability. Each option instance in a CoAP message specifies the Option Number of the CoAP option, the length of the Option Value and the Option Value itself. CoAP options are employed to support mechanisms designed at the application-layer, and new options can be introduced to support new functionalities in the future.

3.2   Limitations of CoAP Transport-Layer Security

The current CoAP specification [5] defines bindings to the DTLS (Datagram Transport-Layer Security) Protocol in order to enable security at the transport-layer. DTLS may apply security to all messages in a given security session, thus providing confidentiality, authentication and integrity for all CoAP communications. While DTLS is a good choice in respect to its support of efficient AES/CCM cryptography as available at the hardware in IEEE 802.15.4 sensing platforms, we may identify a few aspects motivating our alternative approach:

- Security is transparently applied to all CoAP messages: DTLS security is applied to all messages of a given communication session. A cipher suite is negotiated during the DTLS handshake and is employed to protect all CoAP messages, irrespective of the semantics of the Protocol or the type and contents of the messages. Applications are thus unable to define granular security policies and security may be more costly than what would be required by applications.

- Applications are required to employ a static security configuration: After the DTLS handshake all messages are protected using a particular cipher suite and the corresponding cryptographic algorithms and keys. Applications are thus unable to employ different security algorithms and keys to protect different messages in the context of a single CoAP wireless sensing application.

- Security is incompatible with the employment of CoAP intermediaries: Although CoAP defines the usage of proxies in forward and reverse modes [5], end-to-end security as currently proposed at the transport-layer is problematic in this context. Although end-to-end communications are at the hearth of IPv6, the exposure of constrained LoWPANs to the Internet is likely to require appropriate protection mechanisms based on the usage of security gateways. Such gateways may also support the 6LBR and CoAP proxy roles, thus breaking DTLS security. Other aspect is that such gateways may provide a strategic place for the support of heavy cryptographic operations offloaded from constrained sensing devices.

We believe that application-layer message security may address the previous discussed limitations of transport-layer security. Rather than constituting a panacea, application-layer CoAP security may complement DTLS in supporting effective end-to-end secure communications for Internet-integrated LoWPANs, according to the requirements of particular wireless sensing application.

4   CoAP Application-Layer Message Security

Our proposed mechanisms to integrate security at the application-layer with the CoAP Protocol target the issues previously discussed and may provide various benefits, which we also address in the context of the experimental evaluation of our proposal. Packet payload space usage is one aspect to address, as security-related information at the application-layer may be transported in the same context as headers and control information of the CoAP protocol itself. The overhead in terms of the required energy and computational time on constrained sensing devices is also worth investigating, given the significance of such aspects on the lifetime and the communications rate of wireless sensing applications. We proceed by describing the format and usage of the new CoAP security options. All such options are critical, unsafe and non-mandatory, given that applications may opt for security mechanisms at different layers (DTLS at the transport-layer or IPSec at the 6LoWPAN adaptation layer, for example).

4.1 *SecurityOn* CoAP Security Option

The *SecurityOn* option states that the given CoAP message is protected by application-layer security. The format of this option is illustrated in Figure 3. This option states the following about a CoAP message: how security is applied, what entity should process or verify security for the message, the security context that the message belongs to and temporal information relevant to ascertain about the validity of the message. CoAP options are formatted in the TLV (Type, Length, Value) format and thus the length of the *Destination Entity* field in Figure 3 may be obtained from the total length of the option.

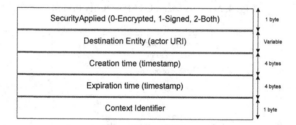

Fig. 3. *SecurityOn* CoAP security option

The *Destination Entity* field identifies the actor CoAP URI (in the form of a NULL-terminated string) that the destination must handle. This option enables the usage of application-layer security in scenarios where security associations may or may not be handled in an end-to-end fashion. The actor URI may identify the final entity receiving the CoAP message or on the other end an intermediary, thus enabling the usage of CoAP secure communications that are managed by an intermediary. This field thus states "this CoAP secured message is meant for any endpoint acting in the capacity indicated by this URI". This option may be employed more than once in a given CoAP message to enable the transversal of different trust domains possibly using also different encryption keys. The *SecurityOn* option also transports temporal values that enable verifying the legitimacy of the message. The creation and expiration time of the message are inserted by its creator and may enable an intermediary or the final CoAP ascertain the validity of the message. The context identifier enables the client, server and/or intermediaries to contextualize the message in terms of security, in particular in determining the appropriate ciphers and keys.

4.2 *SecurityToken* CoAP Security Option

The *SecurityToken* option enables the usage of identity and authorization mechanisms at the application-layer, on a per message basis. Using this option a CoAP requestor (client) may state "who am I" and "what I know" in order to obtain access to a given CoAP resource. With granular security applications may provide accesses to CoAP resources with different criteria, according to the identity of the client and to the criticality of the sensing data requested. Thus, although a security context between communicating entities is required, this option enables request authorization on a per message basis, thus contributing to the implementation of more detailed security policies. The format of this option is illustrated in Figure 4.

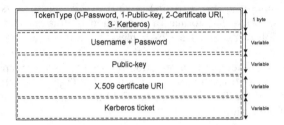

Fig. 4. *SecurityToken* CoAP security option

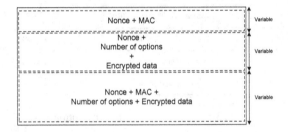

Fig. 5. *SecurityEncap* CoAP security option

A CoAP message only transports data related with one particular authorization mechanism at a time, and thus the length of the corresponding field is obtained from the total length of the option. A CoAP destination or intermediary entity along the path of the message may enforce the usage of a *SecurityToken* option in order to authorize CoAP requests. As Figure 4 illustrates, the currently defined format for this options enables a client to authenticate itself using a simple username plus password scheme, using its public-key, its X.509 certificate referred by a URI (NULL-terminated string), or a *kerberos* ticket previously obtained form a domain server (in binary format). Further authorization mechanisms may be designed or adopted in the future by defining appropriate identification values and the format of the authorization data to be transported.

A CoAP requestor may be authorized at a destination or intermediary using its public-key or X.509 certificate to validate an encrypted MAC (Message Authentication Code) transported by a *SecurityEncap* option that we discuss later. An URI to the certificate is transported rather then the certificate itself, given the payload restrictions already discussed. When authenticating requestors using public-keys or certificates, the *SecurityToken* option must be sent in a CoAP message also transporting an encrypted MAC (signature). In order to support Kerberos-based authentication domains, a *kerberos* ticket may identify and authorize CoAP requests. As with the *SecurityOn* option, a CoAP message may transport more than one *SecurityToken* option, thus supporting multiple trust domains and intermediaries.

4.3 *SecurityEncap* CoAP Security Option

The *SecurityEncap* option transports the security-related data required for the processing of a CoAP message, according to the contents of the *SecurityOn* option. The format of this option is illustrated in Figure 5 and, as for the previous option, only one of the variable-length fields in required for a given CoAP message. The length of this field is thus derived from the length of the option itself.

When providing sender authentication, replay protection and integrity for a CoAP message (in the *SecurityOn* option the *SecurityApplied* field value is 1) this option may be used to transport an encrypted MAC plus a nonce value for freshness. If only encryption is required (the *SecurityApplied* value is 0 in the *SecurityOn* option) this option transports a nonce plus the number of options following in the encrypted part of the payload. As all other options plus the CoAP packet payload are encrypted, the number of options is transported as information helping in the processing of the message by a CoAP intermediary or final entity. In the last scenario the CoAP message is fully protected and all security-related data is transported. The MAC value is computed using the hash or keyed hash algorithm associated with the security context negotiated by the communicating entities and identified in the *SecurityOn* option. The MAC value is computed considering the complete CoAP message plus the options, considering also the *SecurityEncap* option itself with the MAC value field set to all zeros.

4.4 Default Security with AES/CCM

The current proposals to standardize security mechanisms for LoWPAN environments and communications are strongly based on the usage of AES/CCM, given its availability at the hardware in wireless sensing platforms supporting IEEE 802.15.4 [2]. Although AES/CCM is available on such platforms to protect messages transmitted at the link-layer, it may also be employed to protect messages of communication protocols at higher layers, by using AES/CCM in the standalone mode. We consider that AES/CCM is the cipher supporting the default CoAP security context, identified with the value 1 and employed when no specific security context has been negotiated. This may be of interest to simple applications employing key pre-configuration or for the initial secure bootstrap of applications employing more complex context negotiation and key management mechanisms. In the default security context AES/CCM is employed with a 12-byte nonce value and an 8-byte MAC. This is in line with the capabilities of current sensing platforms and with the usage of AES/CCM with TLS [13][14], thus enabling the design of cross-layer security mechanisms in the future, for example to support authentication and key management mechanisms for the transport and application-layer. We also consider that applications using the default security context may omit the *Destination Entity* identification on the *SecurityOn* option. This may be appropriate for applications where devices only answer for a default actor URI, while we must note that the final CoAP address is always part of the CoAP request.

5   Evaluation of CoAP Application-Layer Message Security

Our experimental evaluation allowed us to measure the energetic and computational impact of end-to-end security using CoAP security and DTLS. As our goal is to evaluate end-to-end security in the context of Internet-integrated wireless sensing applications, we consider the usage of a CoAP client residing on an external Internet host and requesting resources from a CoAP server on a LoWPAN wireless sensing device, as illustrated in Figure 6.

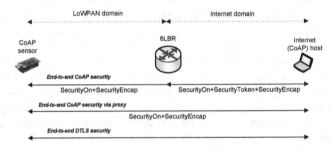

Fig. 6. CoAP and DTLS security end-to-end usage scenarios

As Figure 6 illustrates, end-to-end security may be achieved in a pure fashion either using DTLS at the transport-layer or the proposed CoAP security options at the application-layer. Alternatively, we also consider the usage of a CoAP intermediary (a forward proxy) in the processing of security. The security intermediary provides authorization of CoAP clients and control of accesses to resources on the LoWPAN via the *SecurityToken* option. We consider the usage of AES/CCM cipher in the default CoAP security context, due on the one side to the availability of this cipher in the TelosB [1] and on the other to guarantee a fair comparison of CoAP security against DTLS as currently proposed for CoAP [5].

5.1   Impact of End-to-End Security on CoAP Packet Payload Space

As packet payload space is a scarce resource in LoWPANs environments, our initial evaluation is on the impact of end-to-end security on CoAP packet payload space. Our goal is to analyze if application-layer security leaves enough payload space to transport data from CoAP applications while not requiring costly fragmentations at the 6LoWPAN adaptation layer. Figure 7 illustrates the impact of security on the payload space available for CoAP applications in the presence of end-to-end security. The values illustrated are in percentage of the maximum available payload without security and correspond to the usage scenarios previously illustrated in Figure 6.

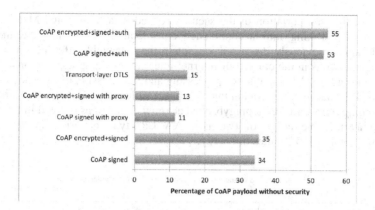

Fig. 7. Impact of end-to-end security on packet payload space available to CoAP

As we may observe in Figure 7, end-to-end security usage scenarios involving the participation of a CoAP security intermediary (proxy) performs better than DTLS. The usage of a security intermediate thus provides the benefit of permitting the offloading of computationally heavy computations to a more specialized entity while guaranteeing a very small impact on CoAP payload space. The impact of end-to-end security without a proxy on CoAP packet payload space is greater, mostly due to the usage of the *Destination Entity* field in the *SecurityOn* option. We consider that this field requires an average of 20 bytes to transport the URI. Although the impact in this usage scenario is greater, in the worst case 65% of the original 6LoWPAN payload of 88 bytes is still available. Thus, we verify that CoAP security is a viable approach for end-to-end security from the point of view of its impact on packet payload space.

5.2 Impact of End-to-End Security on the Lifetime of Sensing Applications

As energy is a critical resource on LoWPAN environments, it directly dictates the lifetime of wireless sensing applications and, in consequence, security mechanisms must be tested against its impact on energy. In our experimental evaluation study we obtained the energy consumption for security using experimental measurements of the voltage across a current sensing resistor placed in series with the battery pack and the circuit board of the TelosB [1]. The energy required for the processing of a 102-byte 6LoWPAN message and related headers (including DTLS and CoAP security headers plus options) was measured as 0.007 nJ (Nano joules). The energy required for the processing of security using AES/CCM in standalone mode for a similar message was measured as 0.2 mJ (Micro joules), while the energy required for the transmission of a packet has been measured as 0.004 nJ (Nano joules) per bit. These experimentally obtained measurements enable us to predict the impact of end-to-end security on the lifetime of CoAP sensing applications.

From the values illustrated in Figure 7 we are able to obtain the maximum payload space that CoAP applications may employ without enforcing costly fragmentation operations at the 6LoWPAN adaptation layer. This corresponds to the usage scenario where end-to-end CoAP security performs encryption, integrity and authentication without the usage of a proxy, for which 45% of the original 6LoWPAN payload (or 40 bytes) is available to transport CoAP data. From this value we subtract 20 bytes required for the transportation of the security-related data (nonce and MAC values) for AES/CCM. Taking into account such considerations and the experimentally obtained values previously discussed we obtain the expectable lifetime for wireless sensing applications in the context of Internet-integrated sensing applications, that we illustrate in Figure 8. We assume the processing and transmission of two messages for each CoAP request, one containing a confirmable request and the other the corresponding reply carrying a piggybacked acknowledgment as defined in CoAP [5]. We also assume the usage of two new AA LR6-type batteries on the TelosB providing a total of 6912 joules of energy.

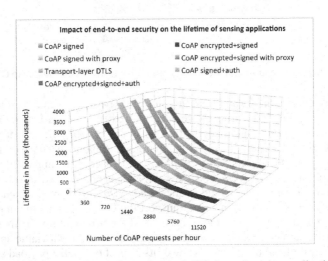

Fig. 8. Impact of end-to-end security on the lifetime of sensing applications

As in the previous analysis, we observe that end-to-end CoAP security performs better that DTLS when employing a security proxy providing support for the processing of the *SecurityToken* option. Pure end-to-end CoAP security without a security intermediate causes a greater impact on the expected lifetime of sensing applications, particularly for lower communication rates where the cumulative impact of AES/CCM encryption is lower when compared to the impact of the energy required to process and transmit CoAP security options. Despite this observation, the obtained values allow us to conclude that CoAP security provides acceptable lifetime values in all usage scenarios, particularly considering WoT applications designed to require low or moderate wireless communications rates.

As previously discussed, one major motivation of the design of application-layer message security for CoAP is in the support of granular security policies. Security policies may define how each message must be protected, according to the semantics of the CoAP protocol, the type of message, its contents or particular requirements of the application. In this context, our next evaluation considers the following four usage profiles for end-to-end security:

• Applications that only require integrity for CoAP replies containing sensorial data from LoWPAN CoAP devices. In such applications sensorial data is not confidential but must be protected against tampering or communication errors.

- Applications requiring confidentiality and integrity for the same type of CoAP messages. In such applications sensorial data is of sensitive-nature, thus also requiring protection against disclosure.

- Applications requiring confidentiality and integrity but only for CoAP requests transporting authentication-related data using the *SecurityToken* CoAP option. In this case we are concerned with the protection of identity and authorization data against disclosure or tampering.

- Applications requiring confidentiality and integrity for all CoAP messages irrespective of its type or contents. In such applications all messages are considered sensitive from the point of view of security.

In Figure 9 we illustrate the impact of end-to-end security according to the usage profiles previously identified. We are able to clearly observe the advantage of granular security in terms of the lifetime of sensing applications, in comparison with transport-layer DTLS where this approach is unavailable. The only security profile performing worst than DTLS is with CoAP encrypting and signing all messages, due to the difference in terms of the payload space required accommodating security. Despite this, in this scenario the expectable lifetime for applications is large, even considering applications protecting many CoAP messages per hour.

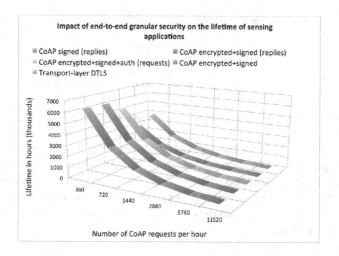

Fig. 9. Impact of (granular) end-to-end security on the lifetime of sensing applications

Overall, our comparative analysis clearly illustrates the advantages of application-layer message security in protecting CoAP communications. When compared with DTLS, our approach introduces flexibility while providing security functionalities not possible with the transport-layer approach. The usage of security intermediaries participating in security also benefits energy and in consequence the lifetime of sensing applications. We also observe that even when CoAP security is employed to protect all messages as with DTLS, it provides comparable performance.

5.3 Impact of End-to-End Security on the Communications Rate of Wireless Sensing Applications

Our final evaluation is on how CoAP security influences the communications rate achievable by applications. When considering wireless communications using IEEE 802.15.4 at 250Kbit/s, we need to consider the overhead introduced by IEEE 802.15.4 on the bandwidth available for 6LoWPAN and upper protocols, which is of 19.6% of the total bandwidth, given that 25 bytes are required for link-layer information with each 127-byte 6LoWPAN packet. Figure 10 illustrates the maximum transmission rate achievable using DTLS versus the previously described CoAP security profiles. The values illustrated in this Figure are obtained considering our experimental evaluation results and that CoAP transports an average of 20 bytes of payload data per message. We also consider the time required for the application of AES/CCM cryptography to CoAP messages, according to the security usage profiles.

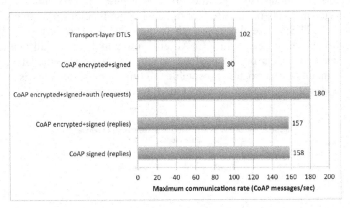

Fig. 10. Impact of end-to-end security on the communications rate of sensing applications.

We may again observe the superior performance of the security profiles requiring the usage of granular application-layer security. CoAP signing and encryption of all messages (as using DTLS) provides inferior performance, but despite this it still allows for 90 CoAP protected messages per second, a limit we may safely consider to be clearly above the requirements of most CoAP wireless sensing applications envisioned for the WoT.

6   Conclusions

The availability of secure end-to-end communications with sensing devices may provide an important contribution to enable WoT wireless sensing applications, as many of such applications may benefit from the availability of direct communications with Internet hosts or external backend servers. Our proposal seeks to provide a contribution in the context of a security architecture supporting Internet-integrated wireless sensing LoWPANs and applications. Our experimental evaluation allowed us to observe that CoAP application-layer security may perform similarly or better than transport-layer security, while supporting functionalities that are not possible with a transport-layer approach. Further research work remains to be done in the context of our proposal, for example in the design of appropriate key management and clock synchronization mechanisms.

Acknowledgements. The work presented in this paper was partly financed by the iCIS project (CENTRO-07-ST24-FEDER-002003) which is co-financed by QREN, in the scope of the Mais Centro Program and European Union's FEDER.

References

1. TelosB Mote Platform, http://www.xbow.com/pdf/Telos_PR.pdf
2. Wireless Medium Access Control (MAC) and Physical Layer (PHY) Specifications for Low-Rate Wireless Personal Area Networks (WPANs), IEEE std. 802.15.4 (2006)
3. IPv6 over Low power WPAN (6lowpan), https://datatracker.ietf.org/wg/6lowpan/charter/
4. Constrained RESTful Environments (core),
   https://datatracker.ietf.org/wg/core/charter/
5. Shelby, Z., et al.: Constrained Application Protocol (CoAP), draft-ietf-core-coap-13 (2013)
6. Rescorla, E., et al.: Datagram Transport Layer Security Version 1.2, RFC 6347 (2012)
7. Gupta, V., et al.: Sizzle: a standards-based end-to-end security architecture for the embedded Internet. In: Proceedings of the 3rd IEEE International Conference on Pervasive Computing and Communications (PerCom 2005), Kauai Island, HI, USA (2005), doi:10.1109/PERCOM.2005.41
8. Jung, et al.: SSL-based Lightweight Security of IP-based Wireless Sensor Networks. In: Proceedings of the International Conference on Advanced Information Networking and Applications Workshop (WAINA 2009), Bradford, UK (2009)
9. Raza, S., et al.: 6LoWPAN Compressed DTLS for CoAP. In: Proceedings of the IEEE 8th International Conference on Distributed Computing in Sensor Systems (DCOSS 2012), Hangzhou, China (2012), doi:10.1109/DCOSS.2012.55
10. Kothmayr, T., et al.: A DTLS Based End-To-End Security Architecture for the Internet of Things with Two-Way Authentication. In: Proceedings of the Seventh IEEE International Workshop on Practical Issues in Building Sensor Network Applications (IEEE SenseApp 2012), Clearwater, FL, USA (2012)
11. Yegin, A., Shelby, Z.: CoAP Security Options, draft-yegin-coap-security-options-00 (expired April 2012)
12. Hui, J., et al.: Compression Format for IPv6 Datagrams over IEEE 802.15.4-Based Networks, RFC 6282 (2011)
13. Dierks, T., Rescorla, E.: The Transport Layer Security (TLS) Protocol Version 1.2, RFC 5246 (2008)
14. McGrew, D., Beiley, D.: AES-CCM Cipher Suites for Transport Layer Security (TLS), RFC 6655 (2012)

Energy Evaluation Model for an Improved Centralized Clustering Hierarchical Algorithm in WSN

Mian Ahmad Jan, Priyadarsi Nanda, and Xiangjian He

Centre for Innovation in IT Services and Applications (iNEXT)
University of Technology, Sydney
Sydney, Australia
Mian.A.Jan@student.uts.edu.au,
{Priyadarsi.Nanda,Xiangjian.He}@uts.edu.au

Abstract. Wireless Sensor Networks (WSN) consists of battery-powered sensor nodes which collect data and route the data to the Base Station. Centralized Cluster-based routing protocols efficiently utilize limited energy of the nodes by selecting Cluster Heads (CHs) in each round. Selection of CHs and Cluster formation is performed by the Base Station. In each round, nodes transmit their location information and their residual energy to the Base Station. This operation is a considerable burden on these resource hungry sensor nodes. In this paper we propose a scheme whereby a small number of High-Energy nodes gather location information and residual energy status of the sensing nodes and transmit to the Base Station. This scheme eliminates CH advertisement phase in order to conserve energy. Based on the energy consumption by various types of nodes, we have derived an energy model for our algorithm which depicts the total energy consumption in the network.

Keywords: Wireless Sensor Network, LEACH, Cluster Head, Base Station.

1 Introduction

Micro-Electro-Mechanical Systems (MEMS) technology has seen phenomenal growth in recent years which has enabled the deployment of small, battery powered sensor nodes. These tiny sensor nodes have brought a revolution in the world of Wireless Communication System [1]. Sensor nodes are constraint with resources like energy, storage, processing capabilities and available bandwidth. Sensor nodes collaborate with each other to form Wireless Sensor Network (WSN) which outperforms many existing Wired and Wireless technologies in terms of their use. These networks are deployed in environments which cannot be monitored with traditional networks. They have numerous applications like volcanic monitoring, battlefield surveillance, home appliances, industrial monitoring, agriculture, health and many more. These networks possess some unique characteristics like self-healing, self-organizing and fault tolerance. WSN is considered as a next wave of computing. WSN market is expected to grow from its current half a billion dollars to around two billion dollars by 2021 [2]. Sensor nodes are randomly deployed in most applications and left unattended. Hence it becomes necessary that the energy of the nodes should

V. Tsaoussidis et al. (Eds.): WWIC 2013, LNCS 7889, pp. 154–167, 2013.

be utilized efficiently to extend the lifetime of the network. Energy-efficient routes need to be setup and the data should be reliably transferred from the nodes to the Base Station [3]. If all these nodes route their data directly to the Base Station, large amount of energy will be consumed due to long range communication. Hence nodes are grouped together to form Clusters. In Clustering protocols, one node is elected as Cluster Head (CH) which gather, aggregate and route the data to the Base Station [4] These CHs can either transmit the data directly to the Base Station or route their data to the upper level CHs and hence form a hierarchy of Clusters to reach the Base Station.

In existing Clustering Hierarchical protocols, the CH is either selected randomly or this task being performed by Base Station. Base Station uses the residual energy and location information of the nodes as selection criteria. However in this scheme, the nodes have to transmit their location information and energy status at the start of each round to the Base Station. Although, this mechanism results in an optimal number of CHs in each round but it consumes a considerable amount of energy.

In this paper, we have proposed a centralized solution for CH selection. In our approach, CH selection and Cluster formation are performed by the Base Station. Here, we have considered five percent of the nodes as High-Energy nodes in addition to sensing nodes in any sensor network. As per the above statistics, a network of hundred sensing nodes would require an additional five High-Energy nodes and a network of two hundred sensing nodes would require an additional ten such nodes. The number of such nodes in any network depends on its scalability. These High-Energy nodes transmit the location and residual energy of the sensing nodes to the Base Station in each round. They are located in the sensor field in order to enable the sensing nodes to minimize their energy consumption during communication. Once they transmit the sensing node's location and energy information to the Base Station, they go to sleep mode till the beginning of next round. The Base Station selects optimal number of CHs.

Also, our proposed algorithm eliminates "CH-Advertisement". CHs are no longer required to advertise themselves to their respective Cluster members. This approach enables the CH nodes to conserve their energy. We have calculated the energy consumption by different nodes in the network and formulated a new energy model. Our model then depicts the total amount of energy consumed in the network.

This paper is organized into six sections. In section 2 we presented related works and refined our objectives for a new Centralized CH selection and Cluster formation approach. In Section 3 we presented radio model for sensor nodes of our algorithm. In Section 4 we have described the network architecture model and the operations performed by the Base Station for Cluster formation and CH selection. In Section 5, we have derived an energy model for our algorithm. We concluded our work in section 6 with future directions.

2   Related Works

A Centralized Low Energy Adaptive Clustering Hierarchy (LEACH-C) protocol was presented in [5]. In this protocol, the Base Station elects the optimal number of Clusters and CHs using simulated annealing algorithm [6]. At the start of each round, the nodes send their remaining energy levels and location information to the Base Station which in turn calculates the average of these residual energy levels. All those nodes whose energy levels are greater than average value are elected as CHs. Practically this approach cannot guarantee the optimal number of CHs. It is highly probable that in each round, there will be a considerable number of CHs exceeding the optimal value. Also, this protocol lacks the detail mechanism of its operation. This protocol is an improvement over LEACH [7], where each node autonomously elects itself as CH. LEACH results in poor Cluster formation and nodes with very low energy are frequently selected as CHs.

Base-Station Controlled Dynamic Clustering Protocol (BCDCP) was proposed in [8]. BCDCP uses the same centralized approach for Cluster formation as of LEACH-C. Additionally, the Base Station maintains a set S, which contains all those nodes whose energy levels are greater than average energy value. The task of the Base Station is to elect an optimal number of Cluster Heads (N_{CH}) from S and arrange all the remaining nodes of the network around them. BCDCP implements an iterative Cluster splitting algorithm which splits the sensor network into two sub-Clusters and proceed further until sufficient numbers of small Clusters are formed. The number of sub-Clusters depends on the number of N_{CH} nodes. BCDCP uses balanced Clustering technique [9] to establish Clusters having approximately equal number of nodes. This protocol consumes a considerable amount of time in Cluster formation and CHs selection and hence does not suit time critical applications.

Base-Station Initiated Dynamic Routing Protocol (BIDRP) is proposed in [10]. All the above protocols emphasis on the homogenous sensor networks where all the nodes have the same initial energy. BIDRP is specifically used for heterogeneous sensor networks where some nodes have higher energy in the network. These higher energy nodes are always elected as CHs in each round. The Base Station broadcasts a packet which is specifically meant for these higher energy CH nodes which in turn calculate their distance from the Base Station based on the Received Signal Strength (RSS) of the packet. This enables the CHs to adjust their transmission power in order to reach Base Station in one hop. Next, these CHs transmit the same packet to the CHs which are one level higher. They also perform the same function and adjust their transmission power and this process continues till the highest level of CHs. Base Station is at Level 0, the CHs which are one hop away from Base Station are at Level 1 and so on. Cluster Heads aggregate their data from their respective Clustering nodes and deliver it to the CHs which are one-hop up the tree. Data always flow from higher levels to lower level until it is delivered at the Base Station. BIDRP lacks the concept of CH rotation. Same higher energy nodes are used as CHs in each round, ultimately their energy will drain after some time. For video streaming and multimedia applications, this protocol does not produce the best results as these applications have considerable amount of data and require constant availability of services. BIDRP does not provide an alternative solution in situations where these higher energy CH nodes die. Clustering Protocol with Mode Selection (CPMS) is proposed in [11]. This protocol is based on [8] for CH selection and on [10] for levels formation. CPMS improve the selection of Leader node based on Energy-Distance (E-D) ratio. Residual energy of each CH node is divided by their respective levels to obtain E-D ratio. The one whose E-D ratio is highest is elected as the Leader node which will gather the data from all CHs and transmit to Base Station. The drawback of this approach is that

CHs does not rotate like [10] and CH nodes far away from Base Station have less chance to be elected as Leader nodes.

All these protocols have one major drawback in common: all the nodes transmit their residual energy status to the Base Station at the start of each round which is a considerable burden on these energy-constraint sensor nodes. Alternatively, there should be additional solution to broadcast energy status of sensor nodes in each round which can minimize the energy consumption. Our algorithm is based on the latter, where a small number of High-Energy nodes perform transmission of location and residual energy information of the sensing nodes to the base station. Base Station evaluates the energy level of all the nodes and calculates an average threshold value. Nodes are selected as Cluster Heads based on their energy values. If their energy level is greater than threshold value, they are eligible to be elected as Cluster Heads. More than one node in the same cluster cannot be elected as Cluster Head. Nodes having energy values greater than average threshold energy level are elected as Candidate nodes. The choice of Cluster Head node among the Candidate nodes depends on various factors like the specific number of Candidate nodes in a particular Cluster, Candidate node elected as Cluster Head in previous round, its present energy status.

3   Sensor Node Radio Model

The radio model used by the sensor nodes in our network is shown in Figure 1 and is based on [12].

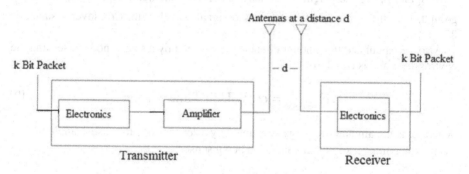

Fig. 1. Sensor Node Radio Model

In Figure 1, k is the length of message and d is the distance between the receiver and transmitter nodes. E_{Tx} and E_{Rx} are the energy consumed by the transmitter and receiver nodes respectively. E_{Tx} is equal to the sum of energy dissipated by the Transmitter's electronic (E_{elec}) and its amplifier (ε_{amp}) while E_{Rx} is equal to the energy dissipated by the receiver's electronics (E_{elec}). Their values are given below in the equation 1 and 2 respectively [12].

$$E_{Tx}(k, d) = E_{elec} k + \varepsilon_{amp} k d^n \tag{1}$$

$$E_{Rx}(k) = E_{elec}\, k \qquad (2)$$

The amount of energy consumed by the transmitter's amplifier depends on the distance (d) between the transmitter and receiver node. If the distance (d) is less than crossover distance ($d_{crossover}$), then path loss (n) is modeled by free space [12]. FS-amp stands for energy consumed by amplifier in free space. The amount of energy consumed by the transmitter in this case is given by equation 3:

$$E_{Tx}(k, d) = E_{elec}\, k + \varepsilon_{FS\text{-}amp}\, k\, d^2 \qquad (3)$$

If the distance d is greater than or equal to $d_{crossover}$, then Two-Ray model (multipath) is used. Here equation 1 is modified as following:

$$E_{Tx}(k, d) = E_{elec}\, k + \varepsilon_{Two\text{-}Ray\text{-}amp}\, k\, d^4 \qquad (4)$$

In free space, there is a line of sight connection between transmitter and receiver while in Two-Ray ground propagation model, signal travel through multi paths due to deflection through obstacles. The crossover distance is given in equation 5:

$$d_{crossover} = 4\pi\, \sqrt{L}\, h_t\, h_r\, /\lambda \qquad (5)$$

Here h_t and h_r are the height of sender and receiver antennas respectively above the ground, L is the system loss and λ is the signal wavelength. Crossover distance is 87m [12].

Also we calculated the amount of energy consumed by a sensor node in sensing the environment and is equal to

$$E_{sense} = \alpha .\, I\, /\, \text{Unit Time} \qquad (6)$$

Where α is the amount of energy consumed by a sensor node to sense a single bit and I is the total number of bits in a message being sensed.

4   Network Architecture

The network architecture of our proposed model is based on the following assumptions:

- o Base Station is located far away from sensor field and is immobile.
- o Sensor nodes are energy-constrained and have the same initial energy.
- o Communication channels are symmetric in nature i.e.: energy consumed in transmission on a particular channel is equal to energy consumed for reception on it.

    o Sensor nodes have the capabilities to adjust their transmission power.
    o Sensor nodes sense the environment at a fixed rate and always have data to send.

Additionally, our network consists of a small percentage of High Energy nodes (other than sensor nodes) which have higher energy than the sensor nodes deployed. Also, optimal number of CHs in each round is assumed around five percent of the sensor nodes. The reason we have chosen five percent of high energy nodes to balance between computational complexity to run our algorithm and lower data aggregation ratio against high energy efficiency and transmission distance.

Our proposed algorithm is based on centralized approach: Cluster formation and CHs selection is performed by the Base Station. We believe our approach is unique because it uses a hybrid methodology: For Cluster formation and CHs selection, it is homogenous because only sensing nodes can be elected as CHs and belongs to any of the Clusters formed by the BS. All these sensing nodes have the same initial energy at the time of deployment. For transmission of energy status of nodes and location information, it is heterogeneous because such information is only transmitted by High-Energy nodes which have higher energy than sensing nodes. High-Energy nodes do not perform any sensing and only perform transmission of location information and residual energy to BS at the start of each round.

In this section the flowchart for our proposed algorithm is presented. The flowchart illustrates the Setup phase of our algorithm followed by the network operation. Evaluation of residual energy levels by the Base Station is also presented here which explain the queuing mechanism being deployed by the Base Station and the selection criteria for a node to be elected as Cluster Head. The BS maintains a single queue which contains the location information and residual energy information of each node. Base Station chooses CHs from the queue by evaluating each node's residual energy against average energy threshold value. Location information of each sensing node (other than High-Energy nodes) is also maintained in the queue. Once BS elects the CHs nodes, location information of each node is used to transmit this information to each individual node. High-Energy nodes do not participate in CH election or Cluster formation. The flowchart, network operation and evaluation procedure by the Base Station in our proposed approach are presented in this section.

4.1   Flowchart of the Algorithm

In this sub-section, a detail flowchart for our algorithm is presented. In the flowchart

- L stands for Location
- RE stands for Residual Energy of Nodes
- HEN stands for High-Energy Nodes
- CN stands for Candidate Node(s)
- A is connector

The algorithm describing our scheme is presented through the flow chart in Figure 2.

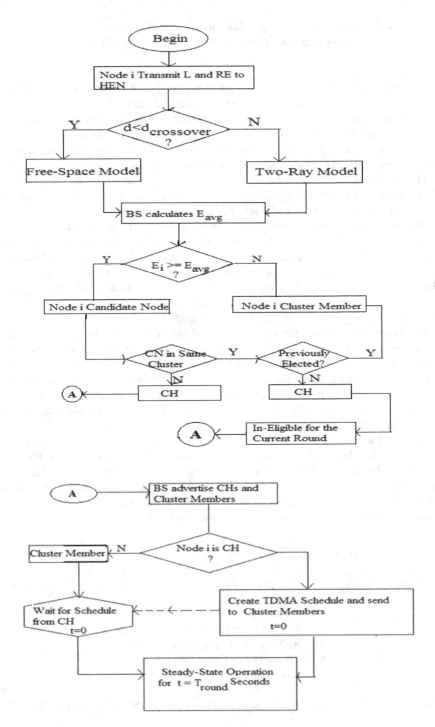

Fig. 2. Flowchart of the Proposed Algorithm

4.2   Network Operation

Our proposed algorithm operates in two phases: Setup phase and Steady-State phase. Setup phase consists of the following sub-phases: Status, Cluster formation, Cluster Head selection and Schedule creation.

In Status sub-phase, all the nodes transmit their location information and residual energy at the start of each round to the High-Energy nodes instead of Base Station. These High-Energy nodes are uniformly deployed in the network as shown in Figure 3. High-Energy nodes can be deployed outside the sensor field. However in that case, the sensor nodes have to transmit over a longer range to reach them. Also, at later stages when the nodes are low on energy, they cannot afford to transmit over longer range. In-network deployment High-Energy nodes enhance the lifetime of the network. These nodes are used only to transmit Status message containing residual energy and location information of nodes to the Base Station.

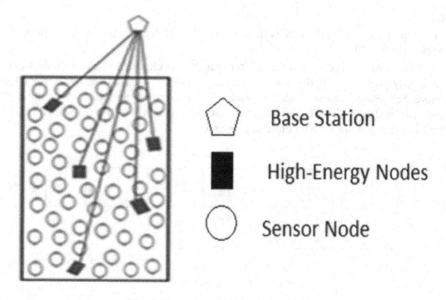

Fig. 3. Operation of High-Energy Nodes

The Status message contains Source ID, destination ID and residual energy of the node as shown in Figure 4. Destination ID is always the ID of one of the High-Energy nodes. Source ID is of the source node which transmits status message. Residual energy field is variable in length.

Source ID	Destination ID	Residual Energy

Fig. 4. Frame Format of Status Message

Once the High-Energy nodes deliver the Status message to the Base Station, they go to sleep mode until the start of next round. The Base Station maintains a queue containing all the nodes having their location information and energy status (Figure 5a). In our network, there are 100 nodes other than the High-Energy nodes. High-Energy nodes in our proposed algorithm are only five percent in addition to the normal sensing node but it can be increased up to ten percent. The reason we have chosen five percent of such nodes is because greater the number of High-Energy nodes means higher the network cost as these nodes are relatively expensive than normal sensing nodes. The Base Station calculates the average (E_{avg}) of all the energy levels of the nodes using the formula

$$E_{avg} = \sum_{i=0}^{i=100} \left(\frac{E_i}{N}\right) \tag{7}$$

Where;

E_i is the energy of node i, N is the total number of sensing nodes in the network and is equal to 100.

Any node whose energy level is greater than E_{avg} is eligible to be elected as a CH. It is highly probable that there will be a large number of candidate nodes for CHs (Figure 5c). Base Station evaluates such candidate nodes and selects an optimal number of nodes as CHs. In our network, optimal value is five (Figure5d). All these various operations are shown below in Figure 5.

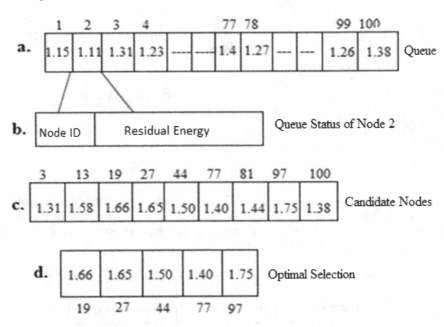

Fig. 5. Cluster Head Selection Procedure by Base Station

4.3   Evaluation of Residual Energy by Base Station

The Base Station evaluates energy levels of the nodes and results in nine nodes eligible as CH candidates as shown in Figure 5c. Candidate nodes are those having residual energy greater than average value. As the optimal number of CHs in each round are five so the Base Station further evaluates these nine nodes and finalize five of them. Like BCDCP, CPMS and BIDRP, our algorithm is also based on balanced Clustering Technique [9]. However, the procedure for evaluation of Candidate nodes is totally different. In Equation 5, the average threshold energy value for a sensor node to be nominated as a Candidate node for CH is 1.30 Joule. This value is calculated by the Base Station by taking the average of all energy values of sensing nodes. However, it is important to note that the average threshold value for a CH Candidate node changes in each round. In the beginning the sensor nodes have higher energy, so the average threshold energy value is higher. In the latter rounds when the energy level of the nodes reduces due to extensive network operations, the average threshold energy values also reduces.

Among the Candidate nodes, 3, 13 and 19 lies in the same Cluster. Nodes 81, 97 and 100 also lie in the same Cluster (Figure 6). Only one node in each Cluster has to be elected as CH by the Base Station. Since nodes 19 and 97 have higher energy in their respective Clusters so they are chosen as CH nodes. Selection of Nodes in a particular Cluster depends on their residual energy and whether it has been elected as CH in previous rounds or not. If in case, node 19 and 97 are elected in previous rounds, they become ineligible to become CHs in this round. In this figure, Candidate nodes in Cluster 1 and 5 are represented by dark circles with numerical numbers. Bold numeric digit in each cluster represents their respective Cluster number. All these tasks are performed by the Base Station which has sufficient energy to perform this complex computation task.

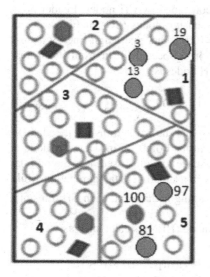

● Candidate Nodes in Cluster 1 and 5 Competing with each others

Fig. 6. Candidate Nodes

The term "Cluster" used in Figure 6 and preceding figures are from the prospective of Base Station. At the time of evaluation by the Base Station, there are neither CHs nor Clusters. Once the Base Station evaluates the energy levels, then CHs are selected and Clusters are formed. In the beginning, all these nodes lie in the "Region" of sensor network. So Region is the most suitable word to be mentioned in place of Cluster in these Figures. However, for simplicity we have used the word Cluster.

Once CHs are selected, the Base Station transmits a message to each node about the notification of their respective CHs. This message contains each node ID and their respective Cluster Head ID. The reason we have chosen this method is because the Base Station already has location information of all the nodes. So it is the job of Base Station to assign Cluster Head to each node. CHs will conserve lot of energy as they are no longer required to broadcast "CH-advertisement" messages to their respective Cluster members. Once the nodes receive this message from the Base Station, they associate themselves with their respective CHs (being assigned by the Base Station). During all these operations by the Base Station, sensor nodes and the High-Energy nodes remain in sleep mode in order to conserve their energy. The CHs create Time Division Multiple Access (TDMA) schedule for their respective Cluster members to transmit data during their respective slots.

Once Setup phase is completed, Steady-State phase starts. In this phase, the CHs gather data from their respective Clustering nodes and transmit to one of the CH node which is elected by the Base Station as the Leader node. Unlike other protocols, our Leader node changes in each round and is always elected by the Base Station based on the residual energy of CH nodes. This balances the energy load uniformly among all the Leader nodes.

5   Energy Model

Based on [12], we have calculated the energy consumed by CH nodes, Leader node (LN), High-Energy nodes (HENs) and normal sensing nodes (SN) of Figure 7. As previously said, our network has 100 nodes (N=100) (other than High-Energy nodes) in a 100m x 100m sensor field. The base station is located 90 m from its nearest sensor neighbor. The energy consumed by the CH nodes is

$$E_{CH} = m\,E_{elec}\,(N/k) + m\,E_{DA}\,((N/k)\text{-}1) + m\,\varepsilon_{FS\text{-}amp}\,d^2_{to\,-LN} \quad (8)$$

Unlike LEACH-C and its variants, the CHs in our network transmit the data to another CH having large energy (Leader node) instead of BS. Since Leader node is located in the field of above dimensions so free space model is used. k is the optimal number of Clusters (here k=5), E_{DA} is the energy consumed in data aggregation while m is the message being transmitted by each Clustering node. Next, each CH transmits the aggregated data to the Leader node (LN).

The energy consumption of the High-Energy node (HEN) is calculated as:

$$E_{HEN} = m\,E_{elec} + m\,\varepsilon_{Two\text{-}Ray\text{-}amp}\,d^4_{to\,-BS} \quad (9)$$

Here, m is the message sent by each node containing its location information and residual energy during Status sub-phase. R is the number of nodes. Here R is variable as the numbers of nodes, which transmit their location and energy information to HEN nodes varies. As HEN nodes transmit this information directly to Base Station which is far away from sensor field, so Two-Ray ground propagation model is used ($d > d_{crossover}$). If the HEN nodes are near the Base Station, then Free Space model is used. In our algorithm, Two-Ray ground propagation model will always be used due to our network specification (Distance of Base Station from Sensor field).

The energy consumed by the Leader node is

$$E_{LN} = m\ E_{elec}\ (N/k) + m\ E_{DA}\ ((N/k)-1) + n\ E_{DA}\ \sum_{i=1}^{i=k-1} CH$$
$$+ m\ \varepsilon_{Two-Ray-amp}\ d^4_{to\ -BS}\quad ;\ d > d_{crossover} \qquad (10)$$

As the sensor nodes are at a distance greater than crossover from Base Station, so Two-Ray ground propagation model is used to model the energy consumption of the Leader node.

In equation 10, the Leader node collects data from its Clustering members as well (since Leader node is one of the CH nodes having high energy) and also it gathers data from other CH nodes. In equation 10, n is the number of messages transmitted by the CH nodes and k-1 is the number of optimal Clusters from which the data is send. If k is 5, this means four CHs will transmit data to the Leader node.

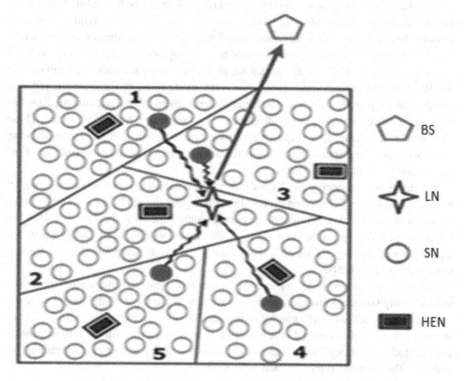

Fig. 7. Steady-State Data Transfer of Our Proposed Algorithm

The energy consumed by any sensing node during Status sub-phase is given by:

$$E_{\text{Sensing-Node}} = m\,E_{\text{elec}} + m\,\varepsilon_{\text{FS-amp}}\,d^2_{\text{to}-\text{HEN}} \qquad (11)$$

Sensing node can be any node in the network other than HEN nodes because during Status sub-phase there is neither CH nor Leader node. Once Clusters are formed and the Clustering nodes start transmitting their data to the CH, their energy consumption is calculated as:

$$E_{\text{Non-CH}} = m\,E_{\text{elec}} + m\,\varepsilon_{\text{FS-amp}}\,d^2_{\text{to}-\text{CH}} \qquad (12)$$

Finally, the total energy consumed in the network is equal to the sum of energy consumed by all the nodes of the network and is given in Equation 13.

$$E_{\text{Total}} = E_{\text{Sensing-Node}} + E_{\text{CH}} + E_{\text{Non-CH}} + E_{\text{LN}} + E_{\text{HEN}} \qquad (13)$$

6   Conclusion

All Centralized Cluster-based routing protocols efficiently utilize limited energy of the nodes by rotating nodes as CHs. However, these protocols require nodes to transmit location and energy information to Base Station at the start of each round. In order to reduce the burden on sensor nodes, we proposed an algorithm in which a small percentage of High-energy nodes are used to convey each node's information to the Base Station. These nodes remain in sleep mode most of the time. In order to reduce energy load further, Cluster Head advertisement phase is eliminated as this function is performed by Base Station which has sufficient energy resources. These CHs gather data from their respective Clusters and transmit to a Leader node being selected by the Base Station based on its residual energy. This node transmits the final aggregated data to the Base Station.

We developed an energy model for our proposed approach and this energy model can be applied to any clustering protocol depending on the application and the choice of nodes to be used. We believe, the proposed energy model is the first of its kind in Cluster-based routing protocols. However, we have also calculated energy levels for Leader node, Sensing Node and High-Energy node to compute overall energy consumptions in a WSN.

Currently we are working on the validation and improvements on our proposed scheme using simulation models. In future, we aim to use these High-Energy nodes as CHs at later rounds when the energy of the sensing nodes is very low. Also as part of future work, we will investigate the behavior of our algorithm with the introduction of mobile nodes along with investigation of various security aspects and measures for our algorithm to make it more robust and secure.

References

[1] Akyildiz, I.F., Su, W., Sankarasubramaniam, Y., Cayirci, E.: Wireless sensor networks: a survey. Elsevier Computer Networks 38, 393–422 (2002)

[2] Harrison, E.: Wireless Sensor Networks to Grow to $2B in 2021: Report TMCNET FEATURE (August 2011)

[3] Akkaya, K., Younis, M.: A survey on routing protocols for wireless sensor networks. Elsevier Ad Hoc Networks 3, 325–349 (2005)

[4] Boyinbode, O., Le, H., Mbogho, A., Takizawa, M., Poliah, R.: A Survey on Clustering Algorithms for Wireless Sensor Networks. In: Proceedings of 13th International Conference on Network Based Information Systems (2010)

[5] Heinzelman, W.R., Chandrakasan, A., Balakrishnan, H.: An Application-Specific Protocol Architecture for Wireless Microsensor Networks. Proceedings of IEEE Transaction on Wireless Communication 1(4), 660–670 (2002)

[6] Murata, T., Ishibuchi, H.: Performance Evaluation of Genetic Algorithms for Flow shop Scheduling Problems. In: Proceedings of First IEEE Conference on Evolutionary Computation, vol. 2, pp. 812–817 (1994)

[7] Heinzelman, W.R., Chandrakasan, A., Balakrishnan, H.: Energy-Efficient Communication Protocol for Wireless Microsensor Networks. In: Proceedings of 33rd Hawaii International Conference on System Sciences (2000)

[8] Muruganathan, S.D., Daniel, C.F., Rolly, M.A., Bhasin, I., Fapojuwo, A.O.: A Centralized Energy-Efficient Routing protocol for Wireless Sensor Networks. In: Proceedings of IEEE Radio Communications (2005)

[9] Ghiasi, S., et al.: Optimal Energy Aware Clustering in Sensor Networks. MDPI Sensors 2(7), 258–269 (2002)

[10] Varma, S., Nigam, N., Tiwary, U.S.: Base Station Initiated Dynamic Routing Protocol for Heterogeneous Wireless Sensor Network using Clustering. In: Proceedings of IEEE Wireless Communication and Sensor Networks (2008)

[11] Kusdaryono, A., Lee, K.O.: A Clustering Protocol with Mode Selection for Wireless Sensor Network. Proc. Journal of Information Processing Systems 7(1) (March 2011)

[12] Heinzelman, W.R.: Application-Specific Protocol Architectures for Wireless Networks. PhD. Dissertation (2000)

Applying a Continuous Working Time Model to Dynamic Clustering in Energy Constrained Wireless Sensor Networks

Arezoo Vejdanparast[1] and Ali Karami[2]

[1] Departement of Computer Engineering, Qazvin Branch Islamic Azad University (QIAU), Qazvin, Iran
[2] Department of Computer Science, University of York, York, UK
arezoo.vejdanparast@gmail.com, ak552@york.ac.uk

Abstract. In Wireless Sensor Networks (WSNs), the sensor nodes are extremely energy restricted. Therefore, minimizing energy dissipation and maximizing network lifetime are the main goals of most energy efficient algorithms designed for these networks. Clustering techniques could significantly reduce the energy consumption of each individual sensor in WSNs. In this paper, we propose an energy efficient Continuous Working Time (C.W.T) strategy that could apply to the data transmission phase of the LEACH algorithm to improve its performance and save more energy. In our model, unlike LEACH, the cluster head keeps working continuously until its residual energy reaches pre-determined threshold. With this mechanism the frequency of updating clusters and the energy dissipation for new cluster head establishment can be reduced. The results of simulation demonstrate that using C.W.T model can reduce the energy consumption of each cluster effectively and increase the system useful lifetime.

Keywords: Wireless sensor networks, Energy-Efficient algorithms, Low-Energy consumption, Dynamic clustering, Network lifetime.

1   Introduction

Wireless Sensor Network (WSN) is composed of a large number of sensor nodes remotely deployed in unattended environments to monitor the surrounding area and collect data or some predefined events and send the information to the base station autonomously. The energy source of the sensor nodes are powered by batteries which are very difficult or often impossible to recharge or replace. Once sensors are deployed, the network can keep operating while the powers of batteries are adequate [1]. In addition to various architectures proposed for energy-efficient data gathering, clustering is shown to be a scalable and energy-efficient architecture for WSNs. The implementation of cluster-based network requires dividing the sensor network into smaller subnets (clusters) and selecting a candidate sensor from each cluster to act as its cluster head. The cluster head node in the cluster consumes more energy compared with other members. As depicted in figure 1, the data collected by sensors is transmitted to the cluster head and after receiving data from all members the cluster

V. Tsaoussidis et al. (Eds.): WWIC 2013, LNCS 7889, pp. 168–179, 2013.

head filters and aggregates the data in order to extract useful information and the refined data is then sent it to the base station using a one-hop communication. Unlike other types of networks (wired, cellular, WLAN, etc.), energy conservation in WSN is a critical issue that has been addressed by significant research works [2].

LEACH (low-energy adaptive clustering hierarchy), is one of the fundamental energy-efficient clustering algorithms proposed for WSN. It plays a great role in reducing the total energy consumption of nodes and extending the useful lifetime of the network [3]. This algorithm tries to distribute the energy load, between all nodes in the network. However LEACH is round based algorithm and selects the cluster heads at the end of each round dynamically and frequently using a round mechanism. It makes the cluster head to send the advertisement message to all ordinary nodes during the cluster setup phase of every single round with additional energy consumption.

In this paper, we will refer to the sensor network model depicted in Fig.1 which consists of one sink node (base station) and a large number of sensor nodes deployed randomly over a large unattended area (monitoring field). The captured data are transferred from sensor nodes to the sink node through certain cluster heads. We assume that the sensor nodes and sink node are static and there is no mobility defined for them.

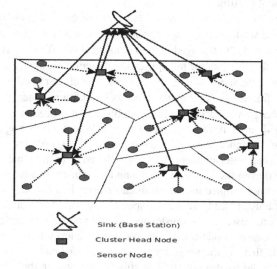

Fig. 1. Clustering technique in wireless sensor network

In this paper, we take the advantages of LEACH algorithm as a basic clustering algorithm of WSN and propose a new method to reduce the frequency of cluster updating and save the energy dissipated at the new cluster head selection phase. In our proposed model, the selected cluster head will keep working continuously until its residual energy reaches a threshold. The cluster then loses its structure and all sensors with no cluster are grouped into new clusters according to the LEACH algorithm.

The rest of this paper is organized as follows: Section 2 reviews the related works. Section 3 describes the frequent cluster head updating problem and explains our networks assumptions. Section 4 presents our Continuous Working Time (C.W.T) model. In section 5 we evaluate the performance of our model by applying to both

LEACH and S-LEACH algorithms and comparing the results with the original ones. Finally, Section 6 concludes the paper.

2   Related Works

The main goals of many clustering algorithms that have been proposed for WSNs are to maintain the energy consumption of sensor nodes and decrease the number of transmitted data to the base station. We reviewed some of the most relevant papers in this section.

Kumar et. al. [4], proposes an energy efficient clustering protocol by considering fixed size clusters. In this approach there are static clusters and the role of cluster head rotates among members. Using fixed clusters and rotating cluster head role within the cluster, in some cases, impose more transmission power to the member nodes to transmit the collected data to their cluster head. This results in an increment to the energy dissipation of member nodes. Besides, as the system ages and the number of dead nodes increases, it is difficult to control the cluster size or bound to maximize the system lifetime.

The cluster head rotation must ensure that energy consumption of all sensors is balanced over the network. In the actual application, network may contain large number of sensors that are randomly deployed in high density. It is difficult to realize the energy balance in large scale. The author in [5] uses the dynamic clustering technique to keep the energy load more balanced among the clusters. The cluster head will be replaced at end of each round frequently. This method results in additional energy consumption for the cluster setup phase and new cluster head establishment procedure.

Xiang et. al [6], also introduces an energy efficient clustering algorithm with optimum one-hop distance and clustering angle, designed for reducing power consumption between inter-clusters and intra-clusters. In this method, cluster are formed only once during the life of the WSN and the cluster heads which acts as local control center, will not replace by the candidate cluster head at the end of round until the time of being cluster head, reach the specific threshold. It could reduce the total energy consumption, however the cluster were fixed and only the role of cluster head were rotated, may cause a node use a large amount of energy to communicate with its cluster head, while there is the neighbor cluster's cluster head is close by. Therefore, using fixed clusters and rotating the role of cluster head within the cluster may require more transmit power which increase the energy dissipation of algorithm and will affect the total performance of the algorithm.

Gamwarige et. al. [7] uses predetermine *periodic time based* cluster head role rotation. The role of cluster head rotates after predetermined number of data transmission rounds. In such algorithms, if the role of cluster head changed after small number of data transmission rounds, it might cause cluster formation over head during frequent re-clustering at the cluster set up phase. On the other hand if increase the number of data transmission rounds, the cluster head depleted quickly and would not have enough energy to act as ordinary sensor nodes for the next rounds. Therefore, selecting optimum number of data transmission round is the main challenges in this approach.

3   Problem Description and Assumptions

As stated in section1, the LEACH algorithm is one of the fundamental clustering protocols in wireless sensor networks that uses clustering technique and frequent rotations of cluster heads to distribute the energy load uniformly among all nodes. However, there are some challenges on the procedure of cluster head selection and the cluster head rotation mechanism of this algorithm. The first problem is that LEACH algorithm does not consider the current energy of nodes at the time of cluster head selection which may cause the early death problem for some nodes. Also, it does not take into account the density and location of nodes which might lead to a sparse distribution of clusters. The second problem is that, in this algorithm the cluster head is selected dynamically by a round mechanism that dissipates some energy for broadcasting the advertising message to ordinary nodes or other cluster heads during set up phase.

Vejdanparast and Zeinali [5] overcome the former problem by proposing a new combinational metric that considers both residual energy and distance parameters of the nodes at the time of cluster head selection. Using the residual energy metric causes the nodes with high sources of energy to have higher chances to become cluster heads. Taking the distance metric into account leads to the selection of a candidate that is close to the densest part of the cluster (sensor-wise). The results demonstrate that the improved algorithm, which for the purpose of this paper we call S-LEACH (Selection-LEACH), could effectively reduce the total energy consumption and avoid early death problem. However, like LEACH, S-LEACH algorithm is round based and selected cluster heads are replaced dynamically at end of data transmission round. Therefore, the latter problem is still unsolved in this algorithm. In this research an energy efficient method has been developed for the data transmission phase to overcome this problem. The idea is that instead of frequently updating the cluster head, it works uninterrupted and is not replaced by other candidates until its residual energy reaches a certain threshold. It results in saving the amount of energy dissipated during the set up phase.

There are some assumptions we have to make, to proceed with our model analysis:

(1) All nodes are homogeneous and have the same resources and capabilities. They transmit the same data packet length frequently.
(2) Live sensors are immobile and have static locations.
(3) For perfect transmission of data, we assume MAC layer conditions.
(4) One-hop communication and symmetric propagation channel is considered.

4   Our Proposed Algorithm

4.1   Energy Model

We assume a simple model for the radio energy dissipation. Our model is similar to Heinzelman et al.'s [8]. Since all nodes have a uniform data generation rate and amount of energy consumed by sensing has been balanced among all sensor nodes, it is not necessary to consider the energy consumption for the data sensing.

Depending on the distance between the transmitter and the receiver, both the free space and the multipath fading models are used. If the distance is less than the threshold d_o, the free space model (fs) is used. Otherwise, the multipath (mp) model is used. The energy consumed for transmitting a l-bit message to distance d is:

$$E_{TX}(l,d) = E_{Tx-elec}(l) + E_{Tx-amp}(l,d)$$

$$= \begin{cases} l.E_{elec} + l_{\epsilon fs}d^2 & d < d_o \\ l.E_{elec} + l_{\epsilon mp}d^4 & d \geq d_o \end{cases} \tag{1}$$

$$d_o = \sqrt{\frac{E_{fs}}{E_{mp}}}$$

and to receive this message the radio expends:

$$E_{Rx}(l) = E_{Rx-elec}(l) = l.E_{elec} \tag{2}$$

where E_{elec} is the energy being used to run the transmitter and receiver circuit and E_{Tx-amp} is the energy used by transmission amplifier for an acceptable E_b/N_0 at the receiver's demodulator.

4.2   A Continuous Working Time Model

The LEACH algorithm expends some energy for the new cluster head establishment at the end of each round. If the current cluster head acts continuously as the local control center, then the frequency of the cluster head update would be reduced. On the other hand, once the cluster head is depleted, the whole cluster loses connection to the base station. Therefore, keeping the cluster head alive (operational) is the main goal for keeping the connectivity of the network. Thus, the lifetime of a cluster is defined as the time interval between the selection and death (losing the remaining energy) of its cluster head. Considering this tradeoff we propose an analytical iterative model that takes into account the working process of sensor networks in a time round manner. In this method, time is partitioned into fixed intervals of equal lengths called *rounds*. The residual energy parameter of current cluster head is considered to determine the suitable round to call for the new cluster head set up phase.

Let n_k be the number of nodes in the cluster k. The total amount of energy consumed in the cluster head during one round can be denoted as

$$E_{cost}(CH) = (n_k - 1) \times l \times E_{elec} + n_k \times l \times E_{D.A} + l \times E_{elec} + l_{\epsilon mp} \times d_{toBS}^4 \tag{3}$$

where E_{DA} is the energy used for data aggregation. The energy used in each ordinary (non-cluster head) node during one round is

$$E_{cost}(non - CH) = E_{elec} \times l + E_{elec} \times d_{toCH}^{2} \tag{4}$$

The average continuous working time (rounds) of each node that acts as a cluster head can be denoted as

$$f_{CH} \approx \frac{E_r(CH)}{E_{cost}(CH)} \tag{5}$$

The average continuous working time of an ordinary node can be denoted as

$$f_{non-CH} \approx \frac{E_r(non - CH)}{E_{cost}(non - CH)} \tag{6}$$

Based on Eqs.(5) , if the continuous working time of the first cluster head approaches f_{CH} , the residual energy of this cluster head must be the lowest and it will die quickly. Therefore, we consider the residual energy of the current cluster head at the time of threshold definition.

$$X = \frac{r_{max} - r_{current}}{\mu} \tag{7}$$

$$\mu = \frac{E_{cost}(CH)}{E_{cost}(non - CH)} \tag{8}$$

where X is defined as a combinational parameter based on the number of desired data transmission rounds and the residual energies of cluster head and cluster members. μ is the ratio of the energy cost of a cluster head to an ordinary node which is a round independent constant value. So, as the system ages and of $r_{current}$ is increased, the value of X parameter is reduced.

$$\frac{E_r(CH)}{E_{cost}(CH)} \geq X \tag{9}$$

As mentioned above, the cluster head is more energy intensive than the ordinary nodes. Thus, for instance, if the node i acts as a cluster head for X rounds until energy depletion, node i could be an ordinary node for μX rounds with the same initial energy.

$$\frac{E_r(CH)}{E_{cost}(CH)} \geq \frac{r_{max} - r_{current}}{\frac{E_{cost}(CH)}{E_{cost}(non-CH)}} \tag{10}$$

The final threshold is shown as

$$E_r(CH) \geq (r_{max} - r_{current}). E_{cost}(non - CH) \tag{11}$$

Once the residual energy of the current cluster head becomes less than the discussed threshold, cluster set up phase will be called to establish the new cluster heads and form new clusters. Whit this proposed mechanism and continuous acting as cluster head, the frequency of updating cluster head and energy consumption for new cluster head establishment is effectively reduced. The pseudocode of LEACH algorithm and our model is given in Figure 2, and Figure 3.

```
1.   Nodes ← set of all nodes with NotClustered status
2.   for n in Nodes do
3.       p ← rand(0,1)
4.       if p < LEACH.threshold
5.           create a cluster c
6.           Add n to c.Nodes
7.           n.Status ← ClusterHead
8.           Remove n from Nodes
9.       endif
10.  end
11.  for n in nodes do
12.      c ← cluster with closest ClusterHead
13.      Add n to c.Nodes
14.      n.Status ← Clustered
15.  end
```

Fig. 2. LEACH Algorithm pseudocode

```
1.   for c in Clusters do
2.       c.Energy ← current residual energy of node c
3.       if c.Energy ≥ threshold
4.           keep cluster c as it is for the next round
5.       else
6.           for n in c.Nodes do
7.               Remove n from c.Nodes
8.               n.Status ← NotClustered
9.           end
10.      end
11.  end
```

Fig. 3. Continuous Working Time pseudocode

Let $X_{r,i}$ be the continuous working time of an instance node i that serves as a cluster head in the rth round. Based on Eqs. (3) and (4), $E_{cost}(CH) > E_{cost}(non - CH)$. Also we have $X_{0,i} > X_{1,i} > \cdots > X_{r,i}$, based on these equations, node i will be soon depleted. By considering the residual energy of node i at the time of cluster head selection, it could be replaced before complete discharge. Consequently, prevent early death problem.

5   Simulation and Performance Evaluation

In this section, we evaluate the performance of our model by applying it to LEACH and one of its improvements, S-LEACH algorithms and compare the results of simulations. Four algorithms are implemented as follows:

- LEACH algorithm, as base line of our research.
- Continuous Working Time LEACH (C.W.T. LEACH) as the improved LEACH by applying the cluster head continuous working time method in the data transmission phase.
- S-LEACH as the improved LEACH in terms of cluster head selection phase.
- Continuous Working Time S-LEACH (C.W.T S-LEACH) as our proposed model applied to the data transmission phase of S-LEACH.

To illustrate the performance of "continuous Working Time" model, the simulations are performed in MATLAB and utilized a network with 100 sensor nodes. We present the results of our experiments by applying our model on both LEACH and S-LEACH algorithms and evaluated the performance of new ones by comparing with the original ones. Moreover, to be able to compare these algorithms in our simulation we need to run them on the same networks. This is achieved by using equal random seeds for each run in all algorithms. The simulation parameters are presented in Table1.

Table 1. Experiment simulation parameters

Parameter	Value
Number of nodes	100
Monitoring area	(100,100) m
Position of Sink node	(50,150) m
Initial energy	0.3 J
Length of Data packet	4000 bits
Simulation end conditio	Number of nodes < 3
E_{elec}	50nJ/bit
ϵ_{fs}	10PJ/bit/m^2
ϵ_{mp}	0.0013PJ/bit/m^4

5.1   Network Lifetime

One of the main goals of our works is to increase the lifetime of the sensor network by reducing the total amount of energy consumption. The simulation ends when the number of live nodes becomes less than three. This means that the network loses its connectivity and is no longer operational. In this section we introduce First Node Dead (FND) and Half Node Alive (HNA) as two important parameters in terms of evaluating the performance of our model.

One of the main design features of "Continuous Working Time" model is to avoid the hot spots problem. Such avoidance can prevent the early death problems. As it is demonstrated in Figure 4, by applying our model to LEACH and S-LEACH, the life time of the network in terms of FND and HNA increases effectively compared with the original algorithms. Applying our model to both LEACH and S-LEACH algorithms improves the gradient of their diagrams, which leads to a more balanced distribution of energy loads among the clusters.

Figure 5 shows the comparison histogram, comparing FND and HNA parameters of these algorithms. This gives us an idea of the gradient of the curve. If the difference between FND and HNA is small (they are close to each other), a steep slope can be observed at the end of the curve and if the difference is noticeable, a smooth slope is observed.

Applying our model to LEACH improves the FND parameter by %44 and on S-LEACH by %7 and improves the HNA parameter by %17 and on S-LEACH %3. As stated in this paper, the S-LEACH is one of the improvements of LEACH algorithm that makes some changes in the cluster set up phase of LEACH and increases the FND parameter effectively compared with LEACH. However, this algorithm is still dynamic and works based on round mechanism. In this experiment, as we could observe, applying our model to S-LEACH could still increase the FND parameter, although, this improvement is not much comparing with LEACH.

5.2   Total Residual Energy

The energy reduction rate of the network is considered as a useful metric to compare the energy efficient algorithms in WSN. Uniform energy consumption is very important for network load balancing and less energy consumption per round which leads to a better network performance. To measure the amount of residual energy of active (live) sensor nodes generated by C.W.T LEACH and C.W.T. S-LEACH, we run these two protocols periodically. Figure 6 depicts the rate of energy reduction curves. It indicates smooth slopes for the new algorithm comparing with the original ones. This is because the energy consumption is more balanced among the clusters.

Also C.W.T LEACH and C.W.T.S-LEACH could outperform original ones during spending %68 and %84 of their initial energy respectively in term of energy saving. This could be explained by our proposed model. We keep the cluster head in each cluster working continuously in order to reduce the frequency of updating cluster head and re-clustering procedure and save the energy consumed for new cluster establishment. Thus, as illustrated in Figure 6, the amount of average residual energy in the active (live) nodes of the new algorithms is greater than active nodes of the original algorithms. Results demonstrate that applying the C.W.T model causes the energy to be consumed efficiently in the network.

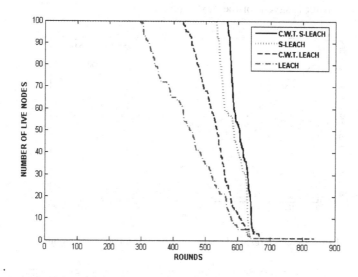

Fig. 4. Number of active (live) nodes per round

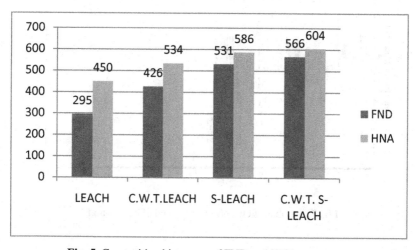

Fig. 5. Competition histogram of FND and HNA parameters

5.3 Number of Clusters Saved

In this section, as an instance, we presented the number of the clusters kept in C.W.T LEACH at end of each round and compared with original LEACH. The results are demonstrated in Figure 7. As we could observe, because of dynamic nature of

LEACH there is no cluster kept at end of each round, new clusters are formed at end of every single round. In the C.W.T LEACH algorithm, the predefined threshold is applied on the cluster head at end of each round and any cluster head that satisfy the threshold will be working continuously as the cluster head for the next round. Therefore this cluster is saved for the next round.

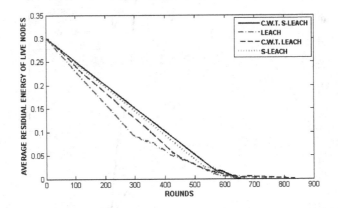

Fig. 6. Average residual energy of active (live) nodes per round

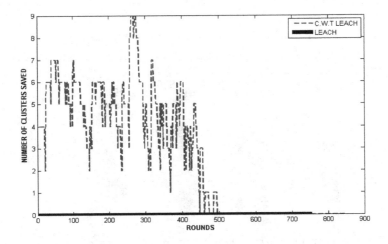

Fig. 7. Number of clusters saved at end of each round

6   Conclusion

In this paper we employ a Continuous Working Time model in the data transmission phase of the LEACH algorithm. In LEACH, the cluster head is replaced dynamically at the end of each round which entails additional energy dissipation for new cluster set up and cluster head establishment. In C.W.T model the cluster head keeps working continuously until its residual energy reaches a pre-defined threshold. If the cluster head works continuously as a local control center, then the frequency of cluster updating and the amount of energy consumed for new cluster head establishment is reduced. Therefore the lifetime of the networks is increased. We assume the channel is lossless and don't consider the packet loss and retransmission in our implementation. The performance evaluation shows that by applying our model to the data transmission phase of both LEACH and S-LEACH, the lifetime of the network in terms of FND and HNA is increased effectively.

References

1. Anastasi, G., Conti, M., Francesco, M.-D., Passarella, A.: Energy Conservation in Wireless Sensor Networks: A Survey. Ad Hoc Networks 7, 537–568 (2009)
2. Merrett, G., Harris, N., Hashimi, B., White, N.: Energy Manage Reporting for WSNs. Sensors and Actuators 142, 379–389 (2008)
3. Nayebi, A., Sarbazi-Azad, H.: Performance Modeling of LEACH Protocol for Mobile WSN. Journal of Parallel and Distributed Computing 71, 812–821 (2011)
4. Kumar, A., Chand, N., Kumar, V.: Location Based Clustering in WSN. World Academy Science, Engineering, Technology 60, 1977–1984 (2011)
5. Vejdanparast, A., Zeinali Kh., E.: A New Approach to Clustering with Respect to the Balance of Energy in Wireless Sensor Networks. In: Bravo, J., López-de-Ipiña, D., Moya, F. (eds.) UCAmI 2012. LNCS, vol. 7656, pp. 25–32. Springer, Heidelberg (2012)
6. Xiang, M., Shi, W., Jiang, C., Zhang, Y.: Energy Efficient Clustering Algorithm for Maximizing Lifetime of WSN. Int. J. of Electronic and Communication 64, 289–298 (2010)
7. Gamwarige, S., Kulasekere, C.: Optimization of Cluster Head Rotation in Energy Constrained WSN. In: IFIP Int. Conference on Wireless and Optical Communications Networks, pp. 1–5 (2007)
8. Heinzelman, W., Chandrakasan, A., Balacrishnan, H.: An Application-Specific Protocol Architecture for Wireless Microsensor Networks. IEEE Trans. on Wireless Communications, 660–670 (2002)
9. Chen, J.: Improvement of LEACH Routing Algorithm Based on Use of Balanced Energy in Wireless Sensor Networks. In: Huang, D.-S., Gan, Y., Bevilacqua, V., Figueroa, J.C. (eds.) ICIC 2011. LNCS, vol. 6838, pp. 71–76. Springer, Heidelberg (2011)

Construction of a Sensor Network to Forecast Landslide Disasters

Sensor Terminal Development and On-Site Experiments

Hikofumi Suzuki[1], Daichi Kuroyanagi[2], David K. Asano[3], Mitsuru Komatsu[4],
Yuji Takeshita[4], Kazuaki Sawada[5], Masato Futagawa[6],
Hiroaki Nose[7], and Yasushi Fuwa[1]

[1] Integrated Intelligence Center, Shinshu University, 3-1-1, Asahi, Matsumoto, 390-8621 Japan
[2] Graduate School of Science and Technology, Shinshu University, 4-17-1, Wakasato, Nagano, 380-8553 Japan
[3] Department of Computer Science & Engineering, Shinshu University, 4-17-1, Wakasato, Nagano, 380-8553 Japan
[4] Graduate School of Environmental and Life Science, Okayama University, 3-1-1, Tsushima-Naka, Kita-ku, Okayama, 700-8530 Japan
[5] Department of Electrical and Electronic Information Engineering, Toyohashi University of Technology, 1-1 Hibarigaoka, Tempaku, Toyohashi, Aichi, 441-8580 Japan
[6] Head Office for "Tailor-Made and Baton-Zone" Graduate Course, Toyohashi University of Technology, 1-1 Hibarigaoka, Tempaku, Toyohashi, Aichi, 441-8580 Japan
[7] Nagano Prefectural Institute of Technology, 813-8 Shimonogo, Ueda Nagano, Japan
{h-suzuki,fuwa}@shinshu-u.ac.jp, 11ta520h@shinshu-u.ac.jp,
david@cs.shinshu-u.ac.jp, mkomatsu@okayama-u.ac.jp,
yujitake@cc.okayama-u.ac.jp, sawada@ee.tut.ac.jp,
futagawa@batonzone.tut.ac.jp, nose@cs.pit-nagano.ac.jp

Abstract. We believe it is extremely important to quickly communicate information — on matters such as the extent of the damage and the safety of affected persons — when a large-scale earthquake or other disaster occurs. However, if electric power is lost, communication will be impossible with existing information networks. For this reason, we have built an Ad-Hoc network in Shiojiri City enabling communication even if electric power is lost due to a large-scale disaster. Using this Ad-Hoc network, we are building a sensor network to forecast landslide disasters. Among the various sensors installed to the sensor terminals, this paper reports in particular on observation results with EC sensors.

Keywords: Ad-hoc Network, Sensor Network, EC Sensor, Landslide Hazard Prediction.

1 Introduction

At times of disasters, such as earthquakes, it is necessary for local governments to respond to the disaster and to communicate a variety of information (a proper understanding of the disaster situation, information communication to disaster victims,

V. Tsaoussidis et al. (Eds.): WWIC 2013, LNCS 7889, pp. 180–191, 2013.

confirmation of the safety of the citizens, etc.) in real time. This means an information network that allows for the real-time communication of information is required. However, in the cases of Mid Niigata Prefecture Earthquake in 2004 and the 2011 off the Pacific coast of Tohoku Earthquake, the disaster situation caused the electricity that was the foundation of that network to fail, resulting in the network being cut off.

Because of the information network being cut off, there were many cases of necessary information not reaching the necessary locations. Furthermore, in the case of the Tohoku Earthquake, the tsunami even caused the network infrastructure itself to collapse. Because of this backgrounds, we developed an Ad-Hoc network with high fault-tolerance [1-8]. This Ad-Hoc network was established all across the urban area of Shiojiri City, and started operating in 2008. In Shiojiri City, the Children Trackinng System [1-8] and Bus Location System [9] were introduced and utilized as daily-life applications that use this Ad-Hoc network.

On the other hand, localized torrential downpours are causing landslide disasters and causing a lot of damage all over Japan. Heretofore, however, the detection of landslide disasters has basically only been used to detect the actual occurrence of landslide disasters, but it is not sufficient for forecasting them. This is why we are now researching and developing a sensor network with the purpose of forecasting landslide disasters as an application that uses the Ad-Hoc network that is being used in Shiojiri City [10]. For this research, we devised a system that uses sensor terminals with EC sensors to measure the volume of water inside the soil, then send the data via the existing Ad-Hoc network. This enables us to collects the necessary information for predicting landslide disasters.   In this paper, we will touch on the establishment status of landslide disaster sensor terminals and on packet loss rate of this sensor network.

2   The Purpose of the Sensor Network

In recent years, landslide disasters caused by localized torrential downpours have been occurring all over Japan. The detection method for landslide disasters that is currently the most common basically only detects the actual occurrence of landslide disasters. However, in order to minimize disaster damage, we considered it necessary for local government to provide landslide disaster forecasts to the citizens. Keeping this in mind, the purpose of the landslide disaster network that we are aiming for is not detection, but forecasting. This is why we placed the sensor terminals. The sensor terminals measure the volume of water inside the soil at that location and then send that value to the server. Then, the prediction system that is implemented in the server uses the values it received from many servers to predict the slope failure of a mountain.

3   Tasks in the Sensor Network

In order to perform the forecasting of landslide disasters, we considered it necessary to place sensor terminals with numerous sensors in a mountainous area and to establish a network system that sends the soil water content to the server in real time. The sensor terminals need to fulfill the following conditions:

- 1 sensor terminal must measure multiple depths regularly and send them to the Ad-Hoc network.
- In order to facilitate placement, the sensor terminal must operate on dry cells and remain buried for 3 years.
- Considering that multiple terminals have to be placed, each terminal must be inexpensive.

Considering this, the tasks that we face in the research and development of a landslide disaster sensor network can be organized as follows:

(1)   Development of a sensor with long operating life for measuring soil water content.
(1-1) Must consume little electricity.
(1-2) Must be able to measure stable values while being buried for a long time.
(2)   Development of stable data transmission technology from inside mountains.
(2-1) Wireless installations placed on the surface of mountains must be able to send packets to the relay device even when covered in grass and trees.
(2-2) Development of a protocol that enables sensors that are placed along mountain ridges and ravines to transmit stable data.

Regarding the above tasks, (1) will be explained in detail in 3.1 and (2) in 3.2.

3.1   Development of a Sensor with Long Operating Life for Measuring Soil Water Content

The sensor network for forecasting landslide disasters that we are aiming for has to be able to operate on a long-term basis. Therefore, the sensor network needs to fulfill the following basic requirements (1-1) and (1-2).

(1-1) Must consume little electricity
Up until now, sensors that measure soil water content have utilized dielectric sensors that make use of the fact that the dielectric constant is almost completely proportional to the soil water content. Because the dielectric sensor needs to release an electrical current in the soil that is to be measured, it uses a certain amount of electricity. The power consumption of the average dielectric sensor is 3 V, 10 mA. Sensors that use this kind of power cannot operate on a long-term basis.

(1-2) Must be able to measure stable values while being buried for a long time
Normally, when a sensor is buried in soil for a long time, the measured values change because of corrosion and drifting. However, the sensor network of this research requires to be buried on a long-term basis, so it poses the problem of necessitating maintenance. This means that a sensor is required that allows for the output of stable values even while being buried for a long time, without performing maintenance.

3.2   Development of Stable Data Transmission Technology from Inside Mountains

Sensor terminals in the sensor network for forecasting landslide disasters will not be placed in urban areas but in the mountains, where the transmission environment is not good (changes in the natural situation or rugged mountains). In order to deliver stable data from the mountains to the server, this sensor network needs to fulfill the following requirements (2-1) and (2-2).

(2-1) Wireless installations placed on the surface of the mountains must be able to send packets to the relay device even when covered in grass and trees
For ZigBee, which is widely used for sensor networks, a 2.4 GHz or 900 MHz zone is used. However, in case of the high-frequency 2.4 GHz, communication may be destabilized due to the large amount of attenuation caused by being covered in plants and trees that contain a lot of moisture. This means that it is necessary to construct the sensor network through a wireless system, which allows for communication even when the sensor terminal is covered in plants and trees.

(2-2) Development of a protocol that enables sensors that are placed along mountain ridges and ravines to transmit stable data
In the case of wireless communication, even if the relay devices and each separate terminal can detect each other's carriers and communicate among one another, there is still the hidden terminal problem of interference occurring because the terminals can't detect each other's communication carriers. Especially in this sensor network, because the terminals are placed on mountain ridges and ravines, hidden terminal problems are expected to occur frequently between sensors due to the rise and fall of the landscape. Therefore, a communication protocol that solves this problem is required.

4   Sensor Terminal Development and the On-Site Status of Sensor Terminals in Shiojiri City

In 2011, we developed the sensor terminals that are able to transmit information using the Ad-Hoc network that is widely used in Shiojiri City (Fig.1). In order to realize research task (1) as indicated in chapter 3, we decided to use an EC(Electrical Conduction) sensor that conserves electricity and contains data for long-term use [11,12]. This sensor was developed by the Toyohashi University of Technology.

Normally in this kind of research, the moisture volume is measured using a dielectric sensor, but this doesn't fulfill the requirement of low electricity consumption stipulated in (1-1).   This EC sensor was developed for agricultural purposes and is not used for landslide disasters and such. However, we decided to use the EC sensor for this research because there was sufficient basic data to deal with task (1) of this research.

Regarding task (2) of this research, we used the Ad-Hoc network established by Shinshu University (Matsumoto Campus) for testing purposes, to test the communication status at 950 MHz and 429 MHz. The results showed that communication of the Ad-Hoc network at 950 MHz was obstructed by trees, and that it was considerably worse than communication at 429 MHz. So we decided to handle task (2-1) by using communication at 429 MHz.

We then placed this sensor terminal together with a representative of Shiojiri City after selecting a placement location from the areas that are feared to have a high risk of landslide disasters. In the following paragraphs, we will touch on the on-site locations, on-site status and the data transmission timing of the sensor terminal.

4.1   Placement of the Sensor Terminals

We created 5 sensor terminal prototypes as shown in Fig.1, and placed them in the mountains in the Ono area of Shiojiri City on May 15, 2012. The mountains of the Ono area of Shiojiri City are an area that has a high risk of landslide disasters and this area requires immediate attention. Therefore, we decided that this area was extremely effective for the testing of a landslide disaster sensor network.

Fig.2 indicates the locations where the 5 sensor terminal prototypes were placed. Fig.3 and 4 show their on-site statuses. As shown in Fig.2, sensor terminal prototypes No. 1-3 were placed from the top of the mountain to the ridge, No. 4 was placed on a slope of the ridge and No. 5 was placed in a valley (No. 1-4 were placed on ridgelines, No. 5 was placed on a trough line). Sensor terminal prototypes No. 1-3 were placed on relatively gentle slopes (Fig.3), but No. 4 and 5 were placed on a steep slope of 40° (Fig.4). The EC sensors were buried at a depth of 30 cm, based on the results of a soil boring test.

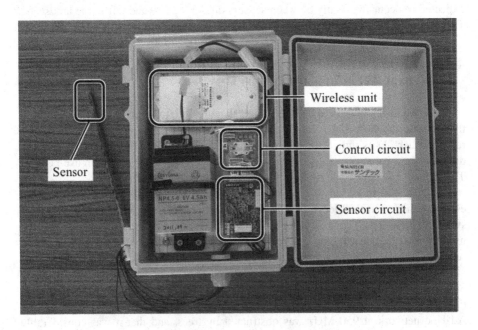

Fig. 1. A landslide disaster sensor terminal prototype

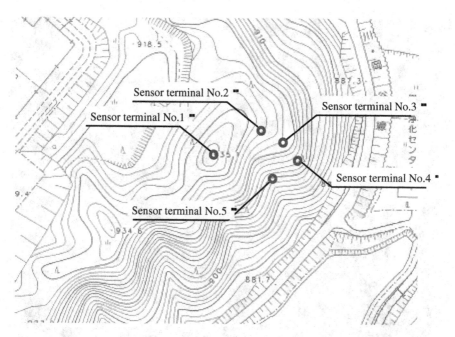

Sensor terminal No.2

Sensor terminal No.1

Sensor terminal No.3

Sensor terminal No.4

Sensor terminal No.5

Fig. 2. On-site locations of the sensor terminal prototypes in the Ono area of Shiojiri City

Fig. 3. A placed sensor terminal prototype (Prototype No. 3)

Fig. 4. On-site status of a sensor terminal prototype (Prototype No. 5, The picture was taken at a horizontal angle)

4.2   Data Transmission from the Sensor Terminal

The sensor terminal prototypes that were made for this research contain 2 definitions for the timing at which the measured EC values are transmitted. Which of the two definitions is used depends on the EC value that is measured by each individual sensor terminal.

(A)   If the EC values are less than 0.1 mS/cm, the data for the EC values etc. are sent periodically each hour.

(B)   If the EC values are 0.1 mS/cm or above, the data for the EC values etc. are sent periodically every 10 minutes.

(A) assumes a situation with little to no rain. (B) assumes torrential rainfall. When an amount of rain falls that could lead to landslide disasters, it is necessary to send more detailed information in order for the local government to provide adequate evacuation instructions. Therefore, in case of heavy rainfall or, in other words, when a high EC value is detected by the sensor terminals, the sensor terminals won't send information once per hour, but they will send EC values every 10 minutes to ensure larger particle sizes.

5   Packet Loss Rate and Evaluation

In order to forecast landslide disasters in the mountains of Shiojiri City, we constructed a sensor network that gathers information from sensor terminals using the Ad-Hoc network. In this chapter, we will evaluate the packet loss rate of the sensor network, we will mention our response to research task (2) outlined in chapter 3, and we will take note of future tasks as well.

In order to perform a proper forecast of landslide disasters in the sensor network, the loss rate of packet containing data acquired sensor terminals must be as low as possible. Fig.5 shows the packet loss rate of the sensor network from July to early October 2012. The loss rates were aggregated every week.

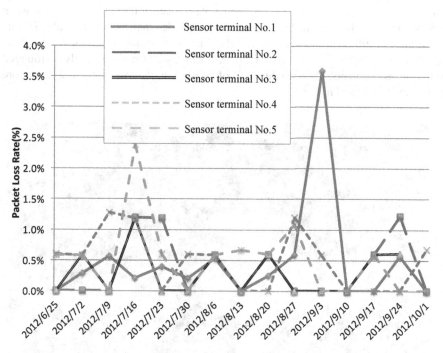

Fig. 5. Sensor network packet loss rate (June 20 - October 5 2012)

The loss rate is calculated while keeping the following points in mind.

- The total amount of the packet that is generated during data transmission is counted on the assumption data is transmitted every 10 minutes for EC values of over 0.1 mS/cm, or every hour for EC values below 0.1 mS/cm
- Sensor terminals that are not operative due to malfunction or battery problems are not taken into the equation.
- If the EC value data transmission communication from 1 sensor is received and sent to the server by multiple relay stations, this will be regarded as overlapping data, which will not be counted (identical data deduplication)

The sensor terminals send out data at regular intervals of 10 minutes or 1 hour, depending on the EC values. This means that data loss can be confirmed by comparing the EC values and the time difference of the packet that was sent last. Furthermore, since the sensor terminals that have currently been set are prototypes, any problems during operation (malfunctions, battery damage etc.) are excluded from the sensor network loss calculation. If the packet from a sensor terminal in the Ad-Hoc network that is currently being used in Shiojiri City is received by multiple relay stations, the packet will be sent to a server as separate packets. The duplicate packets that arrive in this way are recorded as multiple arrival packets, but these were regarded as the same single packet. This is how the loss rate was calculated.

As can be understood from the loss rate in Fig.5, some of the sensor terminals experience a sudden protrusion in loss. However, the loss rate is 2.5% for sensor terminal No. 5 in the week of July 16 2012 and 3.5% for sensor terminal No. 1 in the week of September 3 2012. Judging by this, we have concluded that, even if this value is at its worst, there is still no problem in the actual use of the terminals. Fig.6 shows the status of sensor terminal No. 5 on October 6 2012. This sensor terminal is thinly surrounded by low-growing plants, but with this kind of vegetation, the loss rate will not be more than what is indicated in Fig.5.

Fig. 6. Status of sensor terminal prototype No. 5 (Picture taken on October 6 2012)

Also, loss rates due to the change in seasons (i.e. changes in vegetation) are almost double for the weeks from July 9 – July 23 2012, the week of August 27 2012 and the week of September 24 2012. However, even in this case, the loss rate is below 1.5%, so we have concluded that there are few problems with the practical use of these terminals.

Judging by the above, we can summarize our observations regarding the research tasks (2-1) and (2-2) from chapter 3 in the following way:

(2)   Development of stable data transmission technology from inside mountains.
(2-1) Wireless installations placed on the surface of mountains must be able to send packets to the relay device even when covered in grass and trees.

For this operation test, we performed communication using 429 MHz. And, excluding problems with the sensor terminal itself, the loss rate turned out to be below 3.5% at its worst and less than 1% almost all of the time. We also used the Ad-Hoc network of Shinshu University, Matsumoto Campus to examine the communication status when using 950 MHz. The results showed that the communication status became unstable at 950 MHz due to the trees. This effect was not seen for 429 MHz.

(2-2) Development of a protocol that enables sensors that are placed along mountain ridges and ravines to transmit stable data.

We used 5 sensor terminals for this operation test. We confirmed that these 5 sensor terminals have no communication problems even with the communication protocols that we developed so far. However, in order to accomplish our research goal, we need to place multiple sensor terminals. This is why we are currently assuming the use of multiple sensor terminals, and performing simulation tests in order to develop the ideal communication protocol.

The loss rate of this operation test did not yield any issues that could turn into major problems in the on-site of the sensor terminals. Therefore, we expect to be able to resolve research task (2) from chapter 3 by using radio communication of 429MHz. However, since there was not enough diversity in the observation period and on-site environment, we will continue our research with the following points in mind.

1. Data collection throughout the year (data collection will also be performed annually)
2. Checking the vegetation situation and placing the sensor terminals in a varied vegetation environment (investigating the automation of vegetation data collection at the on-site location)
3. Examining the effect of placing even more sensor terminals over a wider area

Especially point 3 is an extremely important task for the Ad-Hoc network when placing a large number of inexpensive sensor terminals, which is one of the goals of this research. Contrary to the urban areas where the Ad-Hoc network has been used so far, there are elevation differences on ridge lines and trough lines, meaning that the level of exposure/concealment of the sensor terminals and relay stations becomes more complicated. At present, having constructed this communication model, we are using simulations to gain an understanding of the effects in advance in order to develop the ideal communication protocol [10].

6   Summary and Future Goals

We have discussed the construction of a sensor network aimed at forecasting landslide disasters. We have researched and developed an Ad-Hoc network with high fault-tolerance which we constructed and applied in the wide urban area of Shiojiri City. And now we are researching a landslide disaster sensor network as an application of this Ad-Hoc network.

Our research group contains landslide disaster experts and sensor experts who are currently performing analysis regarding the relation between EC values and disaster prediction, the theme of this research.

In 2011, we created sensor terminals for establishing a landslide disaster sensor network, and with the cooperation of Shiojiri City, we placed the terminals in a mountainous area in Shiojiri City that has a high risk of landslide disasters. Up until this point, not every EC sensor on the sensor terminals has necessarily provided effective values. However, it is expected that this problem can be solved by our research method of placing multiple inexpensive sensor terminals. Furthermore, the calculation results so far have shown that there is little to no loss of the sensor network. Of course, the sensor terminals are still prototypes, so the tasks mentioned in 5.1 and 5.2 still remain. However, by resolving these issues, it will be possible to create an adequate landslide disaster forecasting system.

These sensor terminals possess many interfaces and can be mounted with a variety of sensors other than EC sensors. The final goal of this research is to obtain effective forecasts for landslide disasters and flood damage by using these sensor terminals to obtain a variety of data, allowing not only for the measuring of soil water content, but of the water level of rivers as well.

Acknowledgements. Part of this research was performed with the assistance of the Ministry of Internal Affairs and Communications Strategic Information and Communications R&D Promotion Program "Development of a High Fault Tolerance Wireless Ad-Hoc Network Targeting the Whole Region of a Municipality for Revitalization of Safe and Anxiety-free Towns (072304002) (2007–2008)," "Research and Development of a High Fault Tolerance Regional Disaster Communication Network using Ad-Hoc Networks and Sensor Networks (092304014) (2009–2010)" and "Research and Development of a Sensor Network System that realizes Safety of the Entire Region, Disaster Prevention/Reduction that Ensures Safety and Wildlife Sensing (112304003) (2011–2012). The city of Shiojiri, Nagano Prefecture, has also been of great help in the system's experiments and application. We extend our deepest thanks to all who have been involved in this project.

References

1. Nakanishi, K., Horio, S., Niimura, M., Kunimune, H., Motoyama, E., Fuwa, Y.: Development and Evaluation Regional Protection System Using a Wireless Ad-Hoc Network. IEICE Technical Report, CS 108(279), 13–18 (2008)

2. Fuwa, Y., Horio, S., Nakanishi, K., Niimura, M., Kunimune, H., Motoyama, E.: [Invited Lecture] Regional protection system using a wireless Ad-Hoc Network. IEICE Technical Report, USN 108(252), 69–76 (2008)

3. Fuwa, Y., Aguirre, H., Oda, H., Takeda, T., Fuwa, K., Motoyama, E.: Evaluation and Improvement of Wireless Communication Access Protocol ARIB STD-T67 in case of Many Terminals. IEICE Technical Report, RCS 107(402), 91–96 (2007)

4. Fuwa, Y., Niimura, M., Kunimune, H., Kikuta, K., Oda, H., Takeda, T., Fuwa, K., Miyagi, M., Motoyama, E.: Improvement of Wireless Communication Access Protocol ARIB STD-T67: Reducing Packet-loss in High-Load Multihop Network Environment. IEICE Technical Report, NS 107(524), 313–318 (2008)

5. Nose, H., Fuwa, Y., Niimura, M., Kunimune, H., Motoyama, E., Kaneko, H.: Development of Regional Protection System Using a Wireless Ad-Hoc Network. IEICE Trans. B J95-B(1), 30–47 (2012)

6. Nose, H., Motoyama, E., Suzuki, H., Fuwa, Y.: Development and Evaluation of Regional Protection System Using a Wireless Ad-Hoc Network. Information and Communication Systems for Safe and Secure Life (ICSSSL) [IEICE], ICSSSL2011-01 (December 2011)

7. Nose, H., Fuwa, Y.: Regional Protection System Using a Wireless Ad-hoc Network. J. IEICE 95(9), 797–802 (2012)

8. Suzuki, H., Fuwa, Y.: Examination of a Routing decision algorithm for Improvement of Network Performance of a Regional Protection System. In: International Technical Conference on Circuits/Systems, Computers and Communications 2012 (ITC-CSCC 2012), Proceedings CD of ITC-CSCC 2012, E-M1-01, Sapporo, Japan (July 2012)

9. Yamamoto, H., Motoyama, E., Suzuki, H., Fuwa, Y.: Bus Location System Using Wireless Ad-Hoc Network. Information and Communication Systems for Safe and Secure Life (ICSSSL) [IEICE], ICSSSL2011-03 (December 2011)

10. Kuroyanagi, D., Asano, D.K., Suzuki, H., Fuwa, Y.: A Sensor Network Terminal for Disaster Detection. Information and Communication Systems for Safe and Secure Life (ICSSSL) [IEICE], ICSSSL2011-04 (December 2011)

11. Futagawa, M., Iwasaki, T., Noda, T., Takao, H., Ishida, M., Sawada, K.: Miniaturization of Electrical Conductivity Sensors for a Multimodal Smart Microchip. Japanese Journal of Applied Physics 48, 04C184 (2009)

12. Kawashima, K., Futagawa, M., Ban, Y., Asano, Y., Sawada, K.: Measurement of Electrical Conductivity into Tomato Cultivation Beds using Small Insertion Type Electrical Conductivity Sensor Designed for Agriculture. IEE J. Trans. Sens. Micromach. 131(6), 211–217 (2011)

Spotique: A New Approach to Local Messaging

Manfred Sneps-Sneppe[1] and Dmitry Namiot[2]

[1] Ventspils University College
Ventspils International Radioastronomy Centre
Ventspils, Latvia
manfreds.sneps@gmail.com
[2] Lomonosov Moscow State University
Faculty of Computational Mathematics and Cybernetics
Moscow, Russia
dnamiot@gmail.com

Abstract. This paper describes a new approach to local messaging. Our application combines passive monitoring for smart phones and cloud based messaging for mobile OS (operational system). Passive monitoring can determine the location of mobile subscribers (mobile phones, actually) without the active participation of the users. Mobile users do not need to mark own location on social networks (check-in), they do not need to run on their phones the location track applications. In the same time, Cloud Messaging allows interested parties to directly deliver their information to mobile users who find themselves near a selected point. This is the main content of the service - how to combine the monitoring and notifications.

Keywords: Wi-Fi, monitoring, proximity, location, messaging.

1   Introduction

In the first paper that introduced the term 'context-aware' (Schilit and Theimer [1]), authors describe context as location, identities of nearby people and objects, and changes to those objects. There are several definitions from other authors, but most of them define context awareness as a complementary element to location awareness. Location serves as a determinant for the main processes and context adds more flexibility with mobile computing and smart communicators [2].

There are models of applications, where the concept of location can be replaced by that of proximity. At the first hand, this applies to use cases where the detection for exact location is difficult, even impossible or not economically viable [2]. Very often, this change is related to privacy. For example, a privacy-aware proximity detection service determines if two mobile users are close to each other without requiring them to disclose their exact locations [3]. As per developed algorithms for privacy-aware proximity detection methods we can mention papers [4] and [5], for example. They allow two online users to determine if they are close to each other without requiring them to disclose their exact locations to a service provider or other friends. Usually, the main goal for such systems is to generate proximity messages when friends

V. Tsaoussidis et al. (Eds.): WWIC 2013, LNCS 7889, pp. 192–203, 2013.

approach each other closer than some predefined distance threshold. Technically, this threshold can be defined individually for each user (for group of users).

Of course, the term "distance" here depends on the metric used for the measurements. The classical example includes shortest path metric and two users on the different sides (banks) of the river. It is anti-pattern. The distance between users could be within the given threshold, but such "proximity" is useless.

Note, that for privacy oriented, users can still share information about the positioning with service provider. Some of the approaches deploy sophisticated cloaking services for hiding the location ([4], [5]). Our own approach presented in [6] proposes a new paradigm: keep location data anonymously and share identification data on the peer to peer basic. WATN (Where Are They Now) model creates a special form of distributed database that splits location info and identity information. In this distributed data store identity info is always saved locally where the social graph data store is still centralized.

Note, that proximity defined on the threshold distance only could be very limited in some use cases. What can we do for getting users in the proximity with similar interests? At least, we have to add a new dimension (interest) to our measurements.

Metric measurements for privacy can be replaced with some approximation by wireless proximity (network proximity). For this paper network proximity definition is very intuitive. It is a measure of how mobile nodes are close or far away from the elements of network infrastructure. For example, let us assume that we have one Wi-Fi access point (AP). Network proximity is this case is a measure how our mobile phones are close of far away from this AP. Technically, it is based on the observation that measurements of the wireless channels between a radio frequency source and devices in proximity are highly correlated [7].

There are several systems that can use network proximity as a base for mobile services. At the first hand we can mention here our own system SpotEx (Spot Expert) [8]. According to this model, any existing or even especially created Wi-Fi hot spot could be used as presence sensor that can trigger access for some user-generated information snippets. In this approach mobile users can discover hyper local data as information snippets that are relevant for mobile subscribers being at this moment nearby some Wi-Fi access point. And an especially developed mobile application (context-aware browser) can present that information to mobile subscribers.

The typical application in this area uses collected database of so called Wi-Fi "fingerprints", including MAC addresses and the received signal strengths (RSSI) of nearby access points. This database could be used for Wi-Fi based positioning as well as for discovering the user's behavioral patterns [9]. A classical approach to Wi-Fi fingerprinting [10] involves RSSI (signal strength). The basic principles are transparent. At a given point, a mobile application may hear ("see") different access points with certain signal strengths. This set of access points and their associated signal strengths represents a label ("fingerprint") that is unique to that position. The metric that could be used for comparing various fingerprints is k-nearest-neighbors in signal space. It means that two compared fingerprints should have the same set of visible access points. As the next step they could be compared by calculating the Euclidian distance for signal strengths. At the same time, the need for the collection of fingerprints is the biggest problem for this approach.

The rest of the paper is organized as follows. Section 2 contains an analysis of monitoring for Wi-Fi devices. In Section 3 we describe Cloud Messaging platforms. In Section 4 we discuss a new project – Spotique as a mashup for monitoring and Cloud Messaging.

2   Wi-Fi Devices and Monitoring

Problems associated with the collection of fingerprints, are fairly obvious. It is the price of the calibration process, the need for rework after the changes in the network and, most importantly, lack of support for dynamic networks. For example, most of the modern smart phones let users open Wi-Fi access point right on the phone:

Fig. 1. Wi-Fi Access Point on the phone

We cannot create stable base of fingerprints for dynamic access points. Data linked to such dynamic access points become linked to the phones. It is, in fact, a typical dynamic location based system (LBS). The available services move with the moved phone. Services automatically follow the phone. It is one of the basic models for SpotEx service [11].

In our new service we've decided to use another fingerprints-less model: sniffing for beacon frames. Typically, during the calibration phase of Wi-Fi fingerprinting, beacon frames are collected from nearby access points at each survey position. As the next step, the MAC address, RSSI (signal strength), and timestamp could be are extracted from each beacon. In our system we use the reverse schema. We would like to analyze beacons transmitted by Wi-Fi devices, rather than beacons collected by them.

Collecting traces of Wi-Fi beacons is the well-know approach for getting the locations of Wi-Fi access points. Beacon frames are used to announce the presence of a Wi-Fi network. As a result, an 802.11 client receives the beacons sent from all nearby access points. Client receives beacons even when it is not connected to any network. In fact, even when a client is connected to a specific AP, it periodically scans all the channels to receive beacons from other nearby APs. It lets clients keep track of networks in its vicinity. But in the same time Wi-Fi client periodically broadcasts an 802.11 probe request frame. Client expects to get back an appropriate probe request response from Wi-Fi access point. As per Wi-Fi spec, a station (client) sends a probe request frame when it needs to obtain information from another station. For example, a radio network interface card would send a probe request to determine which access points are within range.

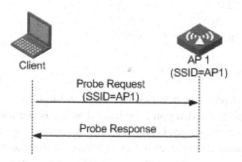

Fig. 2. Probe request/response

A Probe Request frame contains two fields: the SSID and the rates supported by the mobile station. Stations that receive Probe Requests use the information to determine whether the mobile station can join the network. To make a happy union, the mobile station must support all the data rates required by the network and must want to join the network identified by the SSID. This may be set to the SSID of a specific network or set to join any compatible network. Drivers that allow cards to join any network use the broadcast SSID in Probe Requests [12].

Technically, probe request frame contains the following information:

- source address (MAC-address)
- SSID
- supported rates
- additional request information
- extended support rates
- vendor specific information

Figure 3 contains a snapshot for decoded packages:

Our access point can analyze received probe request. Obviously, that any new request (any new MAC-address) corresponds to a new wireless customer nearby.

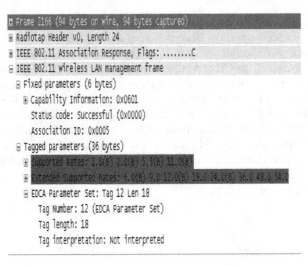

Fig. 3. Probe request example [13]

For sending probe requests network interface on the client side works in active mode. But for the client itself it could be treated as a passive mode. Client does not require load specific applications. Client does not require run specific applications. In other words, client-side activity does not exist here. These systems use only common, off-the-shelf access point hardware to both collect and deliver detections. Thus, in addition to high detection rates, it potentially offers very low equipment and installation cost [14].

Note, that Bluetooth devices could be monitored by the same principles.

Wi-Fi based device detections are made by capturing Wi-Fi transmissions from the device in question. This detection uses only a part from the above mentioned probe request. It is a device-unique address (MAC address). This unique information lets us re-identify devices (mobile phones) across our monitors.

We should note also, that passive Wi-Fi detection is not 100% reliable. Mobile phones (mobile OS, actually) can transmit probe requests at their discretion. See below the Table 1 from [14] illustrates iOS behavior related to probe requests.

Wi-Fi transmissions depends on transmit power, path loss and fading effects. Also, Wi-Fi tracking deployments are likely to be sparse, potentially leading to extended periods of time without any detection at all. As per detection rate we can cite [14] again. In one 12-hour trial using 7 monitors across 2.8 kilometers of arterial road, over 23,000 unique phones were observed. On average, if Wi-Fi is turned on, a monitor detects a passing smartphone 69% of the time.

There are commercial of-the-shelf components that can provide passive Wi-Fi monitoring. For example, it is Meshlium Xtreme [15]. These devices can be detected without the need of being connected to a specific access point, enabling the detection of any smartphone, laptop or hands-free device which comes into the coverage area.

Table 1. Probe requests on iOS

State	Behavior
Idle	Sends probe request every 8 minutes for 30-60 minutes. Radio is off other times.
Idle (some iOS 5.0 phones)	Sends probe requests every minute, radio is off other times.
Active from standby	Wi-Fi is on and scanning (with probe requests).
Background app (email)	Wi-Fi is on probe requests are sent when app need to data access

The information read from each user contains:

- the MAC address of the wireless interface, which allows to identify it uniquely
- the strength of the signal (RSSI), which gives us the average distance of the device from the scanning point
- the vendor of the Smartphone (Apple, Nokia, etc)
- the Wi-Fi Access Point where the user is connected to (if any) and the Bluetooth friendly name. Users no connected to an AP will be showed as "free users"
- the Class of Device (CoD) in case of Bluetooth which allows us to differentiate the type of device (Smartphone, Handsfree, Computer, LAN/Network AP). With this parameter we can differentiate among pedestrians and vehicles.

Fig. 4. Smartphones detection

Here is an example of information saved by Wi-Fi scanner:

DB ID: 53483
Timestamp: 2012-04-24 07:56:25
MAC: C4:2C:03:96:0E:4A
AP: MyCafe
RSSI :   69
Vendor: Apple

Note, that the key moment here is MAC-address for mobile device. We will use it for re-identification only. It means, by the way, that for keeping the privacy we do not need to save in our database an original address. It is enough just to keep some hash-code for this address.

The typical tasks this approach could be applied for are:

- get a number of people passing daily in a street
- detect an average time of the stance of the people in a street or in a building
- differentiate between residents (daily matches) and visitants (sporadic matches)
- detect the walking routes of people in shopping malls and average time in each area

In general, it could be described as a real analytics for the real places. It is what makes Google Analytics for web sites, but applied for the real places and real visitors.

In this paper we propose a new model (use case) for passive monitoring. It is messaging for the real places and real visitors.

3   Cloud Messaging

Google Cloud Messaging for Android (GCM) is a service that allows you to send data from your server to your users' Android-powered device. This could be a lightweight message telling your app there is new data to be fetched from the server (for instance, a movie uploaded by a friend), or it could be a message containing up to 4kb of payload data (so apps like instant messaging can consume the message directly).

The GCM service handles all aspects of queuing of messages and delivery to the target Android application running on the target device. GCM is completely free no matter how big your messaging needs are, and there are no quotas [16].

Apple Push Notification Service (APN) is a robust and highly efficient service for propagating information to devices such as iPhone, iPad, and iPod touch devices. Each device establishes an accredited and encrypted IP connection with the service and receives notifications over this persistent connection. If a notification for an application arrives when that application is not running, the device alerts the user that the application has data waiting for it [17].

We can mention here also Microsoft's Push Notification Service (MPNS) for Windows Mobile [18], Blackberry's Push Service (BPS) [19], and Nokia's Notifications API (NNA) for Symbian and Meego devices [20].

Architectures of these push notification services have common features. At the first hand, application servers send a notification message with an intended receiver (or the target mobile device) to one of the cloud-based messaging servers. Messaging servers pushes the message to the target mobile device. The push notification service eliminates the needs of application servers to keep track of the state of a mobile device (i.e., online or offline). Furthermore, mobile devices do not need to periodically probe (poll) the application servers for messages. It reduces the workloads of the application servers and seriously simplifies the mobile application development.

We describe below Google Cloud Messaging Service as a main system used in our development. In the same time principles are the equal for all the above-mentioned services.

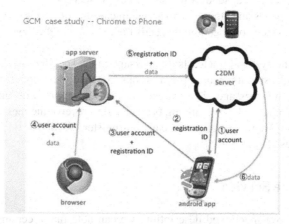

Fig. 5. GCM architecture

Here are the primary characteristics of GCM as per Google's manual:

It allows 3rd-party application servers to send messages to their Android applications.

An Android application on an Android device doesn't need to be running to receive messages. The system will wake up the Android application via Intent broadcast when the message arrives, as long as the application is set up with the proper broadcast receiver and permissions.

The first time the Android application needs to use the messaging service, it fires off a registration Intent to a GM server. This registration Intent) includes the sender ID, and the Android application ID.

If the registration is successful, the GCM server broadcasts an intent which gives the Android application a registration ID.

The Android application should store this ID for later use. To complete the registration, the Android application sends the registration ID to the application server. The application server typically stores the registration ID in a database.

The registration ID lasts until the Android application explicitly un-registers itself, or until Google refreshes the registration ID for your Android application.

For an application server to send a message to an Android application, the following things must be in place:

- The Android application has a registration ID that allows it to receive messages for a particular device.
- The 3rd-party application server has stored the registration ID.
- An API key. This is something that the developer must have already set up on the application server for the Android application. Now it will get used to send messages to the device.

Here is the sequence of events that occurs when the application server sends a message:

- The application server sends a message to GCM servers.
- Google en-queues and stores the message in case the device is offline.
- When the device is online, Google sends the message to the device.

On the device, the system broadcasts the message to the specified Android application via Intent broadcast with proper permissions, so that only the targeted Android application gets the message. This wakes the Android application up. The Android application does not need to be running beforehand to receive the message.

And the same Android application cans un-register GCM if it no longer wants to receive messages [16].

4   Spotique Service

Based on the above-mentioned description, we can note that receiving the messages requires the registration phase. Android application (read – mobile phone with installed application) should inform GCM about the possibility to obtain messages. Usually, this contract is presented in the form of some ID (registration ID). IDs are stored in database. So, our service can select all the stored IDs and distribute some custom message (messages) to applications.

What if we include into process of registration MAC-address too? This decision lets us simply compare subscription info with the locally detected (presented) mobile subscribers.

The whole schema is actually very transparent.

1) Mobile user informs CGM about his intention to receive messages.

2) Messages are divided by topics. Each topic actually corresponds to some location with passive Wi-Fi monitoring.

3) Our sender saves registration ID, topic and MAC-address in central database.

4) Wi-Fi monitoring detects the presence for mobile phones.

5) Our daemon scans detection log, extracts MAC-addresses and compares them with subscription database

6) As soon as we discover that subscriber is detected (he is somewhere nearby) we can use CGM for delivering some custom messages

Note, that MAC-address in this schema is used for the re-identification only. So, for keeping the privacy, we can replace it with some hash-code (for both processes: monitoring and subscription).

The typical use cases are proximity marketing and news delivery in Smart City projects for example.

The push notification services of other platforms are similar to GCM in the architectural design. When an application launches in a mobile device, it needs to register to the push service to get a unique ID. This ID may have different names in different platforms, e.g., device token in iOS and push URI in Windows, and then sends it to the application server. When the application server wants to send a push notification to an application, it sends the ID together with the payload to a push server. Push server forwards the payload to the application [21].

What are the advantages for this approach? At the first hand, it is so-called passive monitoring. We do not need to develop some special applications for mobile subscribers. We do not need to ask for any special actions from mobile subscribers, like running some application, checking-in in social networks etc. The messaging will target only subscribers physically presented in the covered area. The process for subscription and un-subscription is very straightforward. The "check-in" process (passive discovering) is secure. It does not keep records in social networks like ordinary check-ins in Foursquare, Facebook, etc. It does not require user's identification too.

What are the disadvantages? At the first hand, the passive monitoring (as we wrote above) is not 100% reliable. Push messaging delivery requires internet connectivity. But in the same time, installing active Wi-Fi access point on-site, mobile users can connect to, will improve the discovery process.

The future development will introduce customized messaging servers for passive Wi-Fi monitoring.

5   Conclusion

In this article we present a new solution that combines passive Wi-Fi monitoring for mobile devices and notifications. Passive monitoring uses probe requests from Wi-Fi specifications for detecting nearby clients. Notification module uses cloud messaging (push notifications) from mobile operational systems. This approach does not require from mobile subscribers use special applications for setting own location or publish location info in the social network. Practical use cases for this application are proximity marketing and Smart City projects. The proposed approach automatically guaranties that custom messages will target online subscribers in the nearby area only.

Acknowledgement. The paper is financed from EDRF's project SATTEH (No. 2010/0189/2DP/2.1.1.2.0./10/APIA/VIAA/019) being implemented in Engineering Research Institute «Ventspils International Radio Astronomy Centre» of Ventspils University College (VIRAC).

References

[1] Schilit, G., Theimer, B.: Disseminating Active Map Information to Mobile Hosts. IEEE Network 8(5), 22–32 (1994)

[2] Namiot, D., Sneps-Sneppe, M.: Context-aware data discovery. In: 2012 16th International Conference on Intelligence in Next Generation Networks (ICIN), pp. 134–141 (2012), doi:10.1109/ICIN.2012.6376016

[3] Šikšnys, L., Thomsen, J., Šaltenis, S., Yiu, M.: Private and Flexible Proximity Detection in Mobile Social Networks. In: 2010 Eleventh International Conference on Mobile Data Management (MDM), pp. 75–84 (2010)

[4] Mascetti, S., Bettini, C., Freni, D., Wang, X.S., Jajodia, S.: Privacy-aware proximity based services. In: MDM, pp. 31–40 (2009)

[5] Ruppel, P., Treu, G., Küpper, A., Linnhoff-Popien, C.: Anonymous User Tracking for Location-Based Community Services. In: Hazas, M., Krumm, J., Strang, T. (eds.) LoCA 2006. LNCS, vol. 3987, pp. 116–133. Springer, Heidelberg (2006)

[6] Namiot, D., Sneps-Sneppe, M.: Where Are They Now – Safe Location Sharing. In: Andreev, S., Balandin, S., Koucheryavy, Y. (eds.) NEW2AN/ruSMART 2012. LNCS, vol. 7469, pp. 63–74. Springer, Heidelberg (2012)

[7] Mathur, S., Miller, R., Varshavsky, A., Trappe, W., Mandayam, N.: ProxiMate: Proximity-based Secure Pairing using Ambient Wireless Signals. In: MobiSys 2011 Proceedings of the 9th International Conference on Mobile Systems, Applications, and Services, pp. 211–224 (2011), doi:10.1145/1999995.2000016

[8] Namiot, D., Schneps-Schneppe, M.: About location-aware mobile messages. In: International Conference and Exhibition on Next Generation Mobile Applications, Services and Technologies (NGMAST), September 14-16, pp. 48–53 (2011), doi:10.1109/NGMAST.2011.19

[9] Rekimoto, J., Miyaki, T., Ishizawa, T.: LifeTag: WiFi-Based Continuous Location Logging for Life Pattern Analysis. In: Hightower, J., Schiele, B., Strang, T. (eds.) LoCA 2007. LNCS, vol. 4718, pp. 35–49. Springer, Heidelberg (2007)

[10] Chen, Y., Chawathe, Y., LaMarca, A., Krumm, J.: Accuracy characterization for metropolitan-scale Wi-Fi localization. In: ACM MobiSys (2005)

[11] Namiot, D., Sneps-Sneppe, M.: Using Network Proximity for Context-aware Browsing. International Journal on Advances in Telecommunications 5(3&4), 163–172 (2012)

[12] Gast, M.: 802.11 Wireless Networks: The Definitive Guide, 654 p. O'Reilly Media, Inc. (2005)

[13] Wi-Fi probe request, http://wiresharklab.blogspot.ru/ (retrieved: January 2013)

[14] Musa, A., Eriksson, J.: Tracking Unmodified Smartphones Using Wi-Fi Monitors. In: SenSys 2012, Toronto, November 6-9 (2012)

[15] Lubelium routers, http://www.libelium.com (retrieved: January 2013)

[16] Google Cloud Messaging, http://developer.android.com/google/gcm/index.html (retrieved: January 2013)

[17] Apple Push Notification Service, http://developer.apple.com/library/mac/#documentation/NetworkingInternet/Conceptual/RemoteNotificationsPG/ApplePushService/ApplePushService.html (retrieved: January 2012)

[18] Microsoft Inc. Push Notifications Overview for Windows Phone,
      `http://msdn.microsoft.com/en-us/library/windowsphone/`
      `develop/ff402558(v=vs.105).aspx` (retrieved: January 2013)
[19] Reserach In Motion Inc. Blackberry push service, `http://us.blackberry.com/`
      `developers/platform/pushapi.jsp` (retrieved: January 2013)
[20] Nokia Inc. Notifications api, `https://projects.developer.nokia.com/`
      `notificationsapi/wiki` (retrieved: January 2013)
[21] Zhao, S., Lee, P., Lui, J., Guan, X., Ma, X., Tao, J.: Cloud-Based Push-Styled Mobile
      Botnets: A Case Study of Exploiting the Cloud to Device Messaging Service. In:
      ACSAC 2012, Orlando, Florida, USA, December 3-7 (2012)
[22] Namiot, D.: Context-Aware Browsing – A Practical Approach. In: 2012 6th International
      Conference on Next Generation Mobile Applications, Services and Technologies
      (NGMAST), pp. 18–23 (2012), doi:10.1109/NGMAST.2012.13

Local SIP Overload Control

Luca De Cicco, Giuseppe Cofano, and Saverio Mascolo

Dipartimento di Elettrotecnica ed Elettronica, Politecnico di Bari
Via Orabona n.4, 70125 Bari, Italy
{l.decicco,g.cofano,mascolo}@poliba.it

Abstract. The Session Initiation Protocol (SIP) is a signaling framework that allows two or more parties to establish, alter, and terminate various types of media sessions. The mechanism employed by the standard SIP is not effective in handling overload situations that occur when the incoming flow of requests overcomes the processing resources of the server. In this paper we present a local overload control system based on feedback control theory. The algorithm has been implemented in Kamailio (OpenSER) and a performance comparison with Ohta and Occupancy (OCC) overload control algorithms has been performed. The proposed control system efficiently counteracts overload situations providing a goodput which is close to the optimal while maintaining low call establishment delays and retransmission ratios. On the other hand, Ohta and OCC algorithms provide higher call establishment delays and retransmission ratio and lower goodputs.

1 Introduction

The Session Initiation Protocol (SIP) [1] is a signaling framework that allows two or more parties to establish, alter, and terminate various types of media sessions. Nowadays, SIP is the main signaling protocol for multimedia sessions such as Voice over IP, instant messaging and video conferencing in the Internet and IP telephony.

A key open issue of SIP is the proper handling of overload situations. Overload typically occurs when the incoming request rate to a SIP server exceeds its processing capacity. Possible causes for overload include poor capacity planning, component failures, avalanche restart, flash crowds and denial of service attacks [2]. It has been shown that the overload gets worse when SIP is used with UDP due to the presence of a retransmissions mechanism which is employed to cope with packet losses. During overload episodes retransmissions occur and the total incoming load increases, potentially leading the entire network to collapse [2][3]. The 503 response code *"Service Unavailable"* is sent by the overloaded SIP servers to the user agent (UA) to reject messages, thus preventing messages retransmissions. Unfortunately, it is well-known that this mechanism is not able to effectively mitigate overload situations [2][3].

With the purpose of addressing this issue, researchers have recently proposed several overload control algorithms and the SIP Overload Control IETF working group has been established . Overload control algorithms can be designed

V. Tsaoussidis et al. (Eds.): WWIC 2013, LNCS 7889, pp. 204–215, 2013.

following three different approaches (see [3] for a comparison): 1) *local overload control*: the algorithm is executed locally on the SIP server and it does not receive any feedback from other SIP servers; 2) *hop-by-hop*: the control loop is closed between two connected SIP servers; 3) *end-to-end*: the overload algorithm is executed at the UA and the control loop is closed between the UA and the final SIP server, thus each server on the routing path can reject a message before arriving to the destination.

In this paper we propose a local SIP overload controller by employing a feedback control approach: the controller drives the queue length and the CPU utilization to opportune targets to both avoid overload and ensure a target response time.

The rest of the paper is organized as follows: in Section 2 a brief overview of the SIP protocol is given along with the state of the art of overload control methods proposed in the literature; Section 3 presents the proposed feedback overload control algorithm; Section 4 shows the results of an experimental evaluation; Section 5 draws the conclusion of the paper.

2   SIP Overview and Related Work

SIP is a client-server message-based protocol for managing media sessions. Two logical entities participate in SIP communications: SIP User Agents (UAs) and SIP servers. SIP servers can be further classified as: proxy servers, for session routing, and registration servers, for UA registration.

Figure 1 shows the time sequence diagram of the establishment of a SIP call session. An originating UA sends an *INVITE* request to a terminating UA via a proxy server. The proxy server returns a provisional *100 Trying* response to confirm. In the case the proxy is stateful, the terminating UA returns a *180*

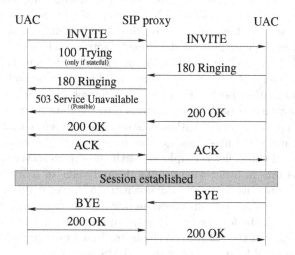

Fig. 1. Time sequence diagram of the establishment of a SIP call

ringing response after confirming that the parameters are appropriate. It also sends a *200 OK* message to answer the call. At that point, after receiving the *200 OK* message, the originating UA sends an *ACK* response to the terminating UA and the call is established. Finally, the *BYE* request is sent to close the session.

In the case the SIP messages are sent over a UDP socket, SIP employs a retransmission mechanism to cope with packet losses. In particular, SIP uses the *Timer A* to trigger an *INVITE* retransmission every time it expires [1]. The first retransmission occurs when the initial default value of $T_1 = 500$ms is reached. After each retransmission *Timer A* is doubled. Retransmissions are stopped when a provisional response is received or when the timeout value exceeds 32s. In case of overload, SIP servers are mandated to send a *503 "Service Unavailable"* that avoids the start of retransmissions. The incoming message is said to be rejected.

Several local overload control algorithms have been proposed so far. The first local overload control mechanism specifically designed for SIP was proposed by Ohta [4]: the algorithm decides to either reject or accept a new SIP session based on the queue length. Another well-known example of local control is Local Occupancy (OCC), in the version described in [3]. It is based on CPU utilization: when it becomes higher than the desired target value, the algorithm reacts by rejecting a fraction of *INVITE*s according to a simple control law. Authors proved that a distributed version of the same control mechanism, though more complex, can achieve better performance.

Distributed overload control algorithms have attracted a great deal of attention due to the promise of achieving better performance. The first paper exploring the hop-by-hop approach was [5]. Authors group overload into two categories: (i) server to server overload and (ii) client to server overload. In [5] only the first case was considered and three hop-by-hop window-based feedback algorithms were proposed. The idea is that the sender server employs a feedback information which is sent by downstream servers to dynamically set the transmission window size to counteract overload. The window adjustment is made according to three different policies. The three algorithms were compared to two rate-based algorithms, showing better results. A hop-by-hop strategy is followed in [6], where several algorithms are developed. Metrics such as queue delay, CPU utilization and fraction of successful calls are employed to throttle the traffic in the upstream servers. However, techniques in [5] require the communication of a feedback information between servers. A different approach is proposed in [7] which employs a feedback-based approach to regulate retransmissions ratio when overload episodes occur. Authors distinguish between redundant and non-redundant retransmitted messages, i.e. due to overload delay or due to message loss recovery: a PI controller is employed at the upstream server to regulate the retransmissions rate in order to track the desired value of redundant messages rate, thus preventing overload over the downstream server without requiring explicit feedback. In [8] authors proposed an overload mechanism combining local and remote control, the former based on the appropriate queuing structure and buffer management of the SIP proxy, the latter based on a prediction technique in the remote control loop according to a NLMS algorithm.

An end-to-end overload control proposal was made in [9] which does not require any modification of the SIP protocol. The author adapted to the SIP networks context an algorithm employed for multi-hop radio networks making use of a backpressure-based technique. Finally, it is worth to mention that the performance of the proposed controllers in [4,5,3,7,9] were evaluated by means of discrete events simulators, and an experimental evaluation is not provided.

3   The Proposed Control System

In this Section we propose a local overload control algorithm based on a feedback control approach. We adopt a local control approach since it does not require any modification in SIP protocol and it can be rapidly deployed in SIP proxies. Moreover, local control should be always implemented in a large SIP network in order to protect the servers in the case the distributed controllers do not work properly.

Without loss of generality, in this paper we focus only on *INVITE* transactions since they are the most CPU-expensive messages to be handled by a SIP proxy [10]. Furthermore, we make the modelling assumption, which is experimentally validated , that the cost for forwarding one *INVITE* message is unitary, while rejecting one *INVITE* has a cost $\frac{1}{\beta}$ ($\beta>1$) which is a fraction of the forward cost. Let $\rho(t)$ denote the incoming load of *INVITE* messages measured in cps (calls per second) and $C(t) \in [0,1]$ the instantaneous CPU load. As $\rho(t)$ increases, $C(t)$ will increase until the point it reaches its maximum value 1 and overload occurs. We denote with ρ_M the maximum offered load the SIP proxy can manage without suffering overload, and we define the normalized incoming *INVITEs* rate $r(t) = \rho(t)/\rho_M$. Finally, the normalized goodput $g(t)$ is the rate of successfully established calls divided by ρ_M. From now on, we will consider only the normalized load $r(t)$ and goodput $g(t)$.

Let us now consider the overall model composed of a generic rate-based local overload controller and the proposed CPU model. The controller computes the fraction $\alpha(t)$ of incoming *INVITE* rate $r(t)$ to be rejected. The CPU load can be modelled as follows:

$$C(t) = (1 - \alpha(t))r(t) + \frac{1}{\beta}\alpha(t)r(t) + d(t) \tag{1}$$

where the first term is the load due to the accepted rate, the second is due to rejected rate, and the third models the CPU load due to other processes in execution.

The overall control system is made of two control loops aiming at controlling both the queue length $q(t)$ of incoming *INVITE* messages and the CPU utilization $C(t)$.

We start by assuming that the SIP proxy server is able to store incoming messages in a queue that will be drained by an asynchronous worker thread. The amount of messages drained and the reject ratio are the output of the two controllers. Figure 2 depicts the proposed control architecture consisting of two

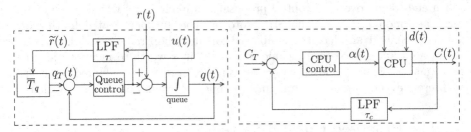

Fig. 2. The proposed control architecture

feedback loops: the goal of the first controller, depicted in the box at the left in Figure 2, is to steer the queue level $q(t)$ to a target $q_T(t)$; the other aims at steering the CPU load $C(t)$ to the desired target C_T.

Let us now focus on the first controller: the goal of this control loop is to compute the queue draining rate $u(t)$, i.e. the rate of *INVITE*s to be processed by the CPU, so that the queuing time of incoming *INVITE* messages is lower than the first retransmission timeout $T_1 = 500\text{ms}$. The queue is modelled by the integrator which is drained at the rate $u(t)$ decided by the controller and filled at the incoming rate $r(t)$.

It is possible to steer the queuing delay $T_q(t)$ to a set-point $\overline{T}_q$, the desired queuing delay, at steady state by considering a variable set-point for the queue control loop. We are able to indirectly control $T_q(t)$ by using a set-point $q_T(t) = \overline{T}_q \tilde{r}(t)$ where $\tilde{r}(t)$ is a low-pass filtered version of the measured instantaneous *INVITE*s incoming rate $\tilde{r}(t)$. We have set $\overline{T}_q = 50\text{ms}$ which is 10 times lower than the first retransmission timer T_1 to avoid retransmissions. We employ a first order low-pass filter (LPF) with a time constant $\tau = 0.4$ s to filter out the high frequency components of the incoming rate $r(t)$.

We employ a proportional-integrative controller so that $q(t)$ can track $q_T(t)$ with zero steady state error [11]:

$$u(t) = K_{pq}e_q(t) + K_{iq} \int_0^t e_q(\tau)d\tau \qquad (2)$$

where $e_q(t) = q_T(t) - q(t)$ is the error and K_{pq} and K_{iq} denote the proportional and integral gains of the controller respectively.

The second control loop computes the fraction of messages to reject $\alpha(t)$, using 503 messages, in order to steer the CPU usage $C(t)$ to the desired value C_T. The queue draining rate $u(t)$ can be considered as a disturbance acting on such control loop.

Let us now focus on the proposed controller: it computes the reject ratio $\alpha(t)$ based on the error $e_c(t) = \tilde{C}(t) - C_T$, where C_T is the set-point and $\tilde{C}(t)$ is the CPU load $C(t)$ passed through a first order low-pass filter with time constant $\tau_c = 0.1$ s, to filter out the high frequency components of $C(t)$. Again, we employ a proportional-integrative controller, whose equation is given by $\alpha(t) = K_{pc}e_c(t) + K_{ic} \int_0^t e_c(\tau)d\tau$.

4   Performance Evaluation

The proposed overload control system has been implemented in a module of the open source Kamailio SIP proxy[1] with the purpose of carrying out the controller optimization and a comparison with Ohta and OCC overload controllers. This section is organized as follows: Section 4.1 describes the experimental testbed employed in the performance evaluation; in Section 4.2 the implementation details of the considered overload controllers are provided; in Section 4.3 a comparison of the proposed control system with Ohta and OCC algorithm is provided.

4.1   Experimental Scenario and Metrics

Figure 3 shows the testbed employed for the experimental evaluation. Two Linux PCs are connected over a 1000 BaseT Ethernet LAN. We adopted a point-to-point topology by using SIPp[2] to generate the *INVITE* stream at a configurable rate. SIPp was also used to emulate the upstream SIP server behavior. The SIPp client and server ran over the faster PC, a Intel Pentium 4 with 3.60 GHz clock speed and 2 GB of RAM. The modified Kamailio SIP server, configured in the transaction-stateless mode with no authentication, ran as proxy server over the slower PC, a Intel Pentium III with CPU clock speed of 1 GHz and 756 MB of RAM. The SIP server PC employs Ubuntu Server 11.10.

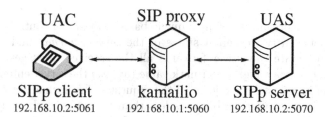

Fig. 3. The testbed employed for the experimental evaluation

We have adopted the goodput as the main metric to evaluate and compare the performance of the three algorithms. We also considered 1) the retransmissions ratio defined as the ratio between the number of retransmissions and the total received calls and 2) the response time, i.e. the time required to establish a call.

For each $r_i \in R_i = \{0.53, 0.79, ..., 2.61\}$ we ran $m = 5$ experiments, whose duration was 120s, and we measured the obtained goodput $g_k(r_i)$ for $k = 1, ..., m$. We then evaluated the $g(r_i)$ as the average of the goodputs $g_k(r_i)$. Finally, in the case of the proposed control system and OCC, we have carried out the experiments considering the CPU target equal to 0.8 and 0.9.

---

[1] http://www.kamailio.org/
[2] http://sipp.sourceforge.net/

4.2 Implementation Details

Kamailio is an open source SIP proxy server written in C language for Unix-like operating systems. It is distributed under the GPL license and it is widely employed both for scientific and commercial purposes. Kamailio employs an architecture which is made of a *core*, which provides basic SIP server functionalities, and several pluggable modules, extending the core. The Kamailio core does not implement a queuing structure, since it processes the incoming messages synchronously with their arrival. Since both Ohta and the proposed control system require the incoming messages to be enqueued before being processed, we implemented in the core a queue where the *INVITE* messages are stored[3]. The three overload controllers were implemented in a Kamailio module called `ratelimit`. In the following we provide a description of the considered algorithms and their implementation details.

The Proposed Control System. Both the PI controllers were discretized and provided with an anti-wind up scheme to cope with saturation of the actuation variables. A timer function ensures a sampling time of $T_c = 20$ms, while another timer samples the CPU load every $T_m = 10$ms. The maximum queue length was set to 800 calls. The parameters of the controllers described in Section 3.2 have been optimized by means of the iterative algorithm Extremum Seeking [12] with the aim of maximizing the obtained goodput. The optimal parameters obtained were $K_{pq} = 20$, $K_{iq} = 130$ $K_{pc} = 5$, $K_{ic} = 5$.

Ohta. Ohta's algorithm is a simple queue-based bang-bang controller that differentiates between two different states of the server: *normal* and *congestion*. During normal state the server forwards all the received messages. When the queue length exceeds a high watermark value (`hi_wm`) the server enters into congestion state: in this state it rejects all the requests. The normal state is entered again when the queue length becomes less than the watermark value (`lo_wm`). Since it is based on a queuing structure as our algorithm, Ohta was implemented in a similar way in the "ratelimit" module. Queue buffer size was set to 1000, `lo_wm` and `hi_wm` to 400 and 800 respectively as suggested in [3].

OCC. The algorithm dynamically adjusts the probability f of accepting an incoming *INVITE* request based on measurements of the CPU load to drive it to a target utilization ρ_{targ}.If the CPU utilization ρ is larger than the target value ρ_{targ}, the load is reduced by rejecting a higher percentage of incoming requests. The control law is a discrete time nonlinear controller described by the following equation:

$$f^{k+1} = \begin{cases} f_{min} & \phi^k f^k < f_{min} \\ 1 & \phi^k f^k > 1 \\ \phi^k f^k & \text{otherwise} \end{cases}$$

---

[3] The other messages are forwarded as usual.

where f^k is the acceptance ratio, $\phi^k = \min(\frac{\rho_{targ}}{\rho}, \phi_{max})$. f_{min} avoids to have zero minimal acceptance ratio, whereas $\phi_{max} > 1$ is the maximum multiplicative increase factor. The CPU occupancy is measured every measurement interval T_m, whereas the algorithm actuation variable is update every control interval T_c.

OCC was implemented in the `ratelimit` module without using a queuing structure, since messages are forwarded synchronously with their arrival. We employed a control interval $T_c = 1\mathrm{sec}$, a measurement interval $T_m = 0.1\mathrm{sec}$, $f_{min} = 0.02$, and $\phi_{max} = 5$ as suggested in [3].

4.3   Comparison with Ohta and OCC

In this section we compare the proposed control system, named PI in the following, with Ohta and OCC algorithms.

Figure 4, Figure 5 (a), and Figure 5 (b) show respectively the goodput curves, the retransmission ratio, and the response time W for each of the considered SIP overload controllers. Figure 4 shows that the proposed control system achieves significantly better performance in terms of goodput, retransmissions ratio, and response time.

In particular, the proposed control system achieves a normalized goodput equal to 0.4 when $r = 2$, whereas OCC and Ohta are overloaded. When OCC is used with CPU load target equal to 0.9 the goodput degrades significantly for input rates greater than 1.3, due to its low responsiveness. OCC 80% betters handle overload *wrt* OCC 90%, and it is able to support input rates up to

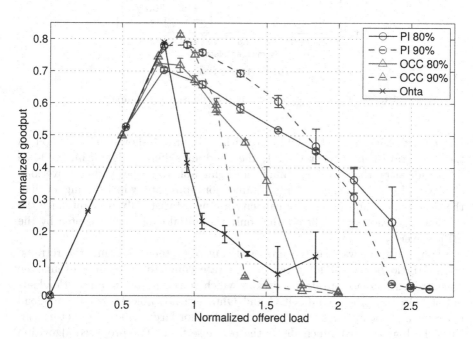

Fig. 4. Goodput comparison

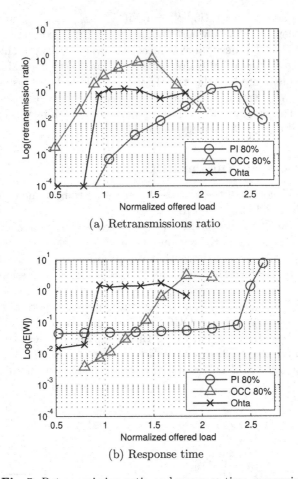

(a) Retransmissions ratio

(b) Response time

Fig. 5. Retransmission ratio and response time comparison

1.7. For what concerns the Ohta algorithm, Figure 4 shows that as soon as the input rate gets greater than 1, the goodput suffers a significant step-like drop, indicating that the algorithm is not being able to properly handle overload episodes. Moreover, measurements obtained for input rates which are higher than the server maximum processing capacity are not statistically relevant since the overload situation was so heavy that only the initial calls were accepted by the SIPp server.

Figure 5 (a) shows that the proposed control system maintains the retransmission ratio below 0.1 for a normalized rate equal to 2, i.e. it prevents the uncontrolled increase of retransmissions which is a symptom of an overload situation. On the other hand, OCC and Ohta are not able to handle overload correctly and retransmissions are not controlled for large values of r. Let us consider the Figure 5 (b) which shows the response time. The proposed algorithm maintains a response time which matches the target value $T_q = 0.05$s for every

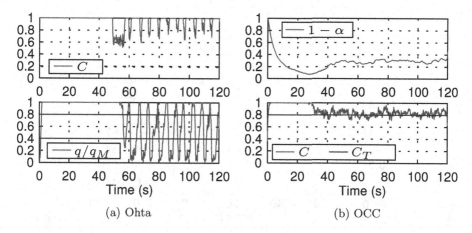

(a) Ohta

(b) OCC

Fig. 6. Ohta ($r = 1.1$) and OCC ($r = 1.57$) dynamic behaviour

input load: this confirms that the first control loop tracks the reference signal $q_T(t)$. On the other hand, OCC exhibits very high average response time.

Figure 7, Figure 8, and Figure 6 show the dynamic behaviour of the considered algorithms. Figure 7 (b) confirms that the queue control loop of the proposed control system tracks the reference signal $q_T(t)$, thus indirectly tracking the target queuing time $\overline{T}_q = 0.05$s. Moreover, Figure 7 (a) shows that the CPU control loop quickly steers the CPU load $C(t)$ to the target C_T effectively avoiding overload. Figure 8 shows the estimated arrival rates, drawn with solid lines, for several input rates, drawn with dashed lines. It is important to notice that the estimated arrival rate $\tilde{r}$ is the sum of the incoming rate and the retransmission rate. The figure shows that retransmissions are very low for rates less

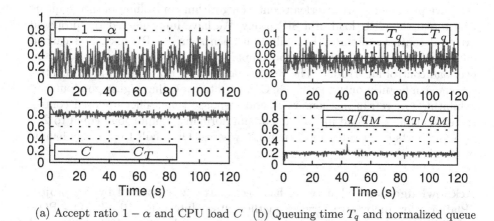

(a) Accept ratio $1 - \alpha$ and CPU load C (b) Queuing time T_q and normalized queue length q/q_M

Fig. 7. The proposed control system dynamic behaviour ($r = 1.57$)

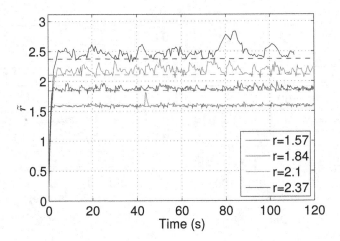

Fig. 8. The estimated arrival rate $\tilde{r}$ for the proposed control system

than $r = 2.01$, whereas for $r \geq 2.01$ larger retransmission rates occur. However, the figure shows that these retransmissions are effectively controlled and they are rejected at steady state.

Figure 6 (b) shows the dynamics of OCC for a normalized input rate $r = 1.57$: the figure shows that the accept ratio dynamics for OCC is slow and, as a consequence, during the first 25s the CPU is overloaded ($C(t) = 1$). Finally, Figure 6 (a) shows the dynamics of Ohta obtained when $r = 1.1$. The queue length exhibits remarkable oscillations and the overload is not avoided.

5   Conclusions

We have proposed a SIP overload control algorithm controlling both the queue length and the CPU load of a SIP proxy. We have implemented the proposed overload control system in Kamailio, an open source SIP proxy, and carried out a performance evaluation and a comparison with OCC and Ohta, two local overload control algorithms. The results have shown that the proposed control system significantly outperforms OCC and Ohta providing higher goodput and exhibiting low retransmissions ratio and response time. The proposed control system handles overload up to a maximum normalized input load equal to 2.3, OCC supports input rates lower than 1.7, whereas Ohta fails to properly handle overload.

Acknowledgement. This work has been partially supported by the project "Platform for Innovative services in the Future Internet" (PLATINO - PON 2007IT161PO006) funded by Italian Ministry of Education, Universities and Research (MIUR).

References

1. Rosenberg, J., et al.: SIP: Session Initiation Protocol. RFC 3261 (June 2002)
2. Rosenberg, J.: Requirements for Management of Overload in the Session Initiation Protocol. RFC 5390, Internet Engineering Task Force (December 2008)
3. Hilt, V., Widjaja, I.: Controlling Overload in Networks of SIP Servers. In: Proc. IEEE ICNP, pp. 83–93 (October 2008)
4. Ohta, M.: Overload control in a SIP signaling network. Enformatika Transactions in Enginnering, Computing and Technology, 205–210 (2006)
5. Shen, C., Schulzrinne, H., Nahum, E.: Session initiation protocol (SIP) server overload control: Design and evaluation. In: Schulzrinne, H., State, R., Niccolini, S. (eds.) IPTComm 2008. LNCS, vol. 5310, pp. 149–173. Springer, Heidelberg (2008)
6. Noel, E., Johnson, C.: Novel overload controls for SIP networks. In: 21st International Teletraffic Congress, ITC 21 2009, pp. 1–8. IEEE (2009)
7. Hong, Y., Huang, C., Yan, J.: Mitigating sip overload using a control-theoretic approach. In: Proc. of IEEE GLOBECOM 2010, pp. 1–5 (2010)
8. Garroppo, R., Giordano, S., Niccolini, S., Spagna, S.: A prediction-based overload control algorithm for SIP servers. IEEE Transactions on Network and Service Management (99), 1–13 (2011)
9. Wang, Y.: SIP overload control: a backpressure-based approach. In: Proc. of ACM SIGCOMM 2010, pp. 399–400 (2010)
10. Jiang, H., et al.: Load Balancing for SIP Server Clusters. In: Proc. IEEE INFOCOM, pp. 2286–2294 (April 2009)
11. Franklin, G., Powell, J., Emami-Naeini, A.: Feedback control of dynamic systems. Addison-Wesley (1994)
12. Killingsworth, N., Krstic, M.: PID tuning using extremum seeking: online, model-free performance optimization. IEEE Control Systems 26(1), 70–79 (2006)

Profiling Packet Processing Workloads on Commodity Servers

Ahmed Abujoda and Panagiotis Papadimitriou

Institute of Communications Technology, Leibniz Universität Hannover, Germany
{firstname.lastname}@ikt.uni-hannover.de

Abstract. The advanced programmability and high level of parallelism can turn commodity servers into powerful and extensible packet processing platforms. A commodity server can consolidate multiple processing functions, performing the role of a multiple-purpose "software middlebox". To this end, the knowledge of the workloads' computational requirements is a prerequisite for efficient resource utilization and admission control. Workload computational requirements can vary depending on packet I/O techniques and optimizations, and therefore, previously reported CPU cycle measurements may not be applicable to packet processing systems where a different I/O technique is exercised.

In this paper, we discuss the implications and challenges arising from workload profiling on commodity servers. We exemplify a technique that circumvents the difficulty of profiling packet processing workloads. Applying this technique to our packet processing platform, we gauge the computational requirements of selected workloads and corroborate the effect of various I/O optimizations on workload CPU utilization.

1 Introduction

Over the last few years we have seen an increasing interest in packet processing on general-purpose hardware. Commodity servers, in particular, offer advanced level of programmability and multi-Gigabit forwarding rates, exploiting the parallelism afforded by multi-core CPUs and hardware multi-queuing on network interface cards (NICs) [2], [5], [3]. This ample processing power in conjunction with the availability of packet processing software (e.g., Click Modular Router [10], Snort [13]) enable commodity servers to perform various packet processing operations beyond IPv4 forwarding, such as encryption, intrusion detection and prevention, packet aggregation, and redundancy elimination. As such, a commodity server can be turned into an extensible "software middlebox" that consolidates multiple processing functions [7].

Such software middleboxes can be incrementally deployed at enterprise networks alleviating the customization and manageability limitations of existing ad-hoc deployments [12]. Alternatively, software middleboxes can comprise a viable platform for in-network services, allowing customers, such as enterprise network operators, to outsource network functionality [14], [7], [6]. In both deployment scenarios, the knowledge of the workloads' computational requirements

V. Tsaoussidis et al. (Eds.): WWIC 2013, LNCS 7889, pp. 216–228, 2013.

can enhance resource utilization expanding the level of consolidation and further provides the ability to perform admission control on incoming processing requests. Previous studies [2], [8] have reported the computational requirements of selected packet processing workloads, such as IPv4 forwarding and IPsec. However, workload computational requirements may vary depending on packet I/O techniques and optimizations (e.g., packet handling in batches) [2], [8], [11]. As such, previously reported workload computational requirements may not be applicable to packet processing systems where a different I/O technique is exercised.

Profiling packet processing workloads on commodity servers is not trivial. For example, high-performance packet processing systems typically rely on polling for packet handling along the receive path. This entails significant implications on workload profiling, since the CPU appears to be fully utilized, irrespective of the processing load. In this paper, we discuss the implications and challenges of workload profiling on commodity servers and we exemplify a technique for gauging the computational requirements of packet processing workloads. Furthermore, we present the computational requirements of selected packet processing workloads and show the effect of various I/O optimizations on workload CPU utilization. Our workload profiling technique is implemented on a packet processing platform based on Click [10]. However, our profiling method is widely applicable to any packet processing system that uses polling and batch processing.

The remainder of this paper is organized as follows. Section 2 provides an overview of packet I/O handling on Click-based packet processing systems. In Section 3, we discuss the challenges of workload profiling and present our profiling technique. In Section 4, we discuss our workload profiling results. Finally, in Section 5, we highlight our conclusions.

2   Packet I/O on Commodity Servers

Packets I/O handling is an essential operation for any packet processing workload and accounts for a significant proportion of the workload's computational requirements. Hereby, we discuss how commodity servers handle packet I/O.

2.1   Packet I/O Handling Overview

In principle, packet I/O consists of the receive and the transmit path, as shown in Fig. 1.

Receive Path. The receive path essentially comprises two operations: (i) packets are transferred from NIC to main memory using Direct Memory Access (DMA) (arrow 1 in Fig. 1) and (ii) the CPU accesses the packets copied to memory (arrow 2 in Fig. 1). In more detail, packets are transferred from the NIC hardware queues to a chained ring of buffers, called Rx ring, allocated in the main memory. Each Rx buffer is managed through a data structure called receive (Rx) descriptor. The Rx descriptor holds information about the packet data

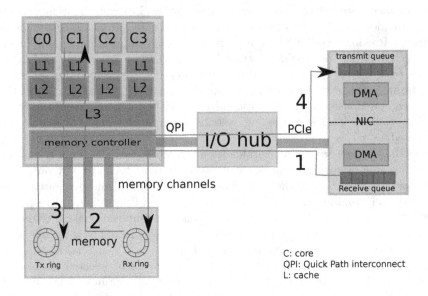

Fig. 1. Packet I/O handling on commodity servers

buffer address, length, checksum and status. The status field indicates whether the packet transfer is completed. As soon as the packets are copied into memory, the CPU accesses and processes each packet.

Transmit Path. Similar to the reception path, the transmit path consists of the following operations: (i) upon processing, the CPU writes packets to memory (arrow 3 in Fig. 1) and (ii) packets are copied from memory to NIC using DMA (arrow 4 in Fig. 1). More precisely, the CPU places the packets in another chained ring of buffers, called Tx ring, allocated in the main memory. Subsequently, the packets are transferred from the Tx ring to the NIC hardware queue. The Tx ring buffers are managed through the corresponding data structure, i.e., the transmit (Tx) descriptor, which maintains the packet data buffer address, length, checksum and status. As with the Rx descriptor, the Tx status field indicates whether the NIC has transmitted the packet. Upon packet transmission, Tx buffers are recycled and reused for the transmission of subsequent packets.

A crucial aspect of packet I/O handling is the interaction between the NIC and the CPU. In particular, the CPU should be able to know when new packets are copied into memory and when their transmission has been completed. Since interrupts yield low packet forwarding performance, modern packet processing systems typically rely on polling. Polling eliminates the processing overhead incurred by interrupt handling and prevents receive livelock.

Fig. 2. Exemplary Click forwarding path

2.2 Packet I/O Handling with Click

We further discuss packet I/O handling in the context of Click Modular Router [10], which is widely used for the implementation of packet processing systems on commodity servers. Click offers a large set of packet processing elements which can be connected in a graph forming a fully customizable forwarding plane. The Click elements that compose a given forwarding-plane configuration can be assigned to multiple threads, allowing a high level of parallelism with multi-core CPUs. Click can run in the Linux kernel offering very high packet forwarding rates.

With respect to packet I/O, Click uses two elements to handle packets: *PollDevice* for reception and *ToDevice* for transmission. Whenever *PollDevice* is scheduled, it initiates a NIC device driver call which checks the status field of the Rx descriptor and passes the incoming packets along with their metadata structures (*sk_buff* in Linux) from the Rx ring to *PollDevice*. *PollDevice* can be configured to poll packets in batches (i.e., batch processing).

On the transmit path, *ToDevice* transfers packets enqueued by Click to the Tx ring. Similar to *PollDevice*, packets may be copied to the Tx ring in batches. *ToDevice* receives information from the NIC device driver regarding the status of packet transmission and upon its completion, *ToDevice* recycles the Tx ring buffers. Finally, the NIC device driver returns the recycled buffers to the Rx ring.

An exemplary Click forwarding path comprising a *PollDevice*, a queue, and a *ToDevice* is illustrated in Fig. 2. *Polls* represent the packet transfers from the Rx ring by *PollDevice*, while *dequeues* denote the packets fetched from the Click queue by *ToDevice*.

3   Workload Profiling

In this section, we discuss the challenges and implications with respect to workload profiling on commodity servers. Furthermore, we exemplify our workload profiling technique for Click-based packet processing systems.

3.1   Workload Profiling Implications

The difficulty in workload profiling mainly stems from the implications and side-effects of polling and batch processing, which comprise common techniques for handling packet I/O on commodity servers, as discussed in Section 2.

Polling. Polling enforces checks for new incoming packets, as frequently as possible, irrespective of the packet arrival rate. Therefore, polling utilizes all idle CPU cycles, regardless of the traffic rate and the packet processing application. Similarly to polling, transferring packets to the Tx ring (i.e., *ToDevice*) also tends to consume idle CPU cycles in order to speed up the packet transmission. Consequently, the full CPU utilization during packet transactions along the receive and transmit path inhibits the accurate estimation of workloads' computational requirements.

Batch Processing. Processing packets into batches reduces significantly the processing cost per packet. For example, multiple packets can be polled at once from the Rx ring reducing the bookkeeping cost per packet. Batch processing can be also exercised at the application layer (e.g., encrypting packets in batches) or at the NIC to mitigate the PCIe transaction cost per packet. However, batch processing becomes less effective for low packet forwarding rates, since the number of packets per batch is smaller. Certainly, the effect of batch processing can be optimized by reducing the number of CPU cycles allocated to the workload. However, this may increase latency and result in packet drops. Essentially, the variable processing cost per packet, depending on the effectiveness of batch processing, complicates workload profiling.

It is important to note that these factors do not affect workload profiling in isolation. In fact, we need to take into account the confluence of polling and batch processing on workload profiling. A major challenge in this respect is to estimate the computational requirements of a workload under near-optimal operation, where the CPU resources entitled to the workload maximize the batch processing effectiveness without causing packet loss.

3.2   Workload Profiling Methods

Based on these observations, we investigate methods to circumvent the difficulty of profiling packet processing workloads on commodity servers. First, we define *empty polls* as the number of accesses to the Rx ring (initiated by *PollDevice*) in which no packet was found. Similarly, we define *empty dequeues* as the number of unsuccessful attempts to fetch packets from the Click queue (initiated by *ToDevice*). A Click-based packet processing system typically yields *empty polls* and *empty dequeues*, due to the effect of polling.

Since polling results in full CPU utilization, there are two main approaches for the computation of workloads' requirements: (i) to estimate and deduct the number of CPU cycles consumed for all tasks that are not associated with the workload, and (ii) to restrict the cycles entitled to the workload such that *empty polls* and *empty dequeues* are minimal while the packet forwarding rate matches the target rate. Both approaches require the monitoring of *empty polls* and *empty dequeues*. To this end, we implemented counters for both variables and the number of packets transferred within each batch, so that we can quantify the degree of batch processing.

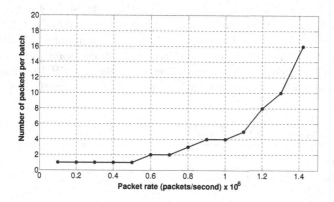

Fig. 3. Average number of packets per batch vs. packet rate

According to the first approach, we merely have to estimate the number of cycles consumed by *empty polls* and *empty dequeues*, and subsequently deduct them from the nominal cycles of the core (under the condition that the workload runs alone in a core). In particular, this amount can be estimated by measuring the number of cycles utilized by an *empty poll* and *empty dequeue* and multiplying by the number of monitored *empty polls* and *empty dequeues*. We found that this approach provides accurate results only for high packet forwarding rates (i.e., more that 10^6 packets/sec for IPv4), where batch processing is effective. When the polling rate is substantially higher than the receiving rate, the small number of packets per batch increases the computational cost per packet. Fig. 3 illustrates the packets per batch versus the packet rate. It can be observed that for rates below 5×10^5 packets/sec batch processing is eliminated. Note that this method was used by RouteBricks [2] (but without taking the *empty dequeues* into account) in order to compute the CPU cycles/packet for selected packet processing workloads at the maximum packet forwarding rate.

Due to the inefficiencies of this method, we rely on the second approach, so that we can obtain accurate results for a wide range of packet forwarding rates. Instead of estimating the number of cycles consumed by a workload, we aim to adjust the CPU resources entitled to the workload, such that the following conditions are satisfied: (i) there is no perceptible reduction in the packet forwarding rate, (ii) the number of *empty polls* and *empty dequeues* is minimal, and (iii) the number of packets per batch approximates an optimal value (i.e., 16 packets in our system).

We use an auxiliary workload to iteratively achieve the transition to this state. In particular, as auxiliary workload we use a Click forwarding path that comprises a *PollDevice* element. In principle, any workload that stresses the CPU and remains active for the whole measurement period can be used. The measurements are conducted on a single core which is shared by the packet processing and auxiliary workloads. We iteratively adapt the resources entitled to the auxiliary workload by adjusting the scheduling priorities accordingly. During each iteration, we examine the packet rate, *empty polls*, *empty dequeues* and packets per batch to identify whether the system has approached the desired state. Once the packet processing system has reached this state, the number of CPU cycles consumed by the packet processing workload (W_p) correspond to its minimum computational requirements, since the effect of polling on CPU utilization has been eliminated while batch processing has maximized its effectiveness.

Algorithm 1. Workload Profiling

---

while True **do**
 if $W_p.Rate > TargetRate$ **then**
  decrease $W_p.Cycles$
  if $(W_p.EP \leq EP_{thresh})$ and $(W_p.ED \leq ED_{thresh})$ **then**
   $MeasuredCycles = W_p.Cycles$
   if $W_p.B \geq B_{thresh}$ **then**
    return $W_p.CPU$
   else
    while $W_p.Rate > TargetRate$ **do**
     decrease $W_p.Cycles$
     if $W_p.B \geq B_{thresh}$ **then**
      return $W_p.Cycles$
    return $MeasuredCycles$
 elseif $W_p.Rate \leq TargetRate$ **then**
  Increase $W_p.Cycles$
  if $(W_p.Rate > TargetRate)$ and $(W_p.EP \leq EP_{thresh})$ and
  $(W_p.ED \leq ED_{thresh})$ **then**
   $MeasuredCycles = W_p.Cycles$
   if $W_p.B \geq B_{thresh}$ **then**
    return $W_p.Cycles$
   else
    while $W_p.Rate > TargetRate$ **do**
     decrease $W_p.Cycles$
     if $W_p.B \geq B_{thresh}$ **then**
      return $W_p.Cycles$
    return $MeasuredCycles$

Our workload profiling method is depicted in Algorithm 1. We initially seek to minimize the rate of *empty polls* (EP) and *empty dequeues* (ED) while achieving the target forwarding rate, and we subsequently record the current CPU utilization. Then we adjust the workload's CPU cycles in order to maximize the packets per batch (B). If we manage to optimize the effect of batching while maintaining a minimal number of EP and ED, we have reached the desired state and we thereby measure the CPU cycles of W_p; otherwise the algorithm returns the previously recorded sub-optimal CPU utilization. Since it is not feasible to achieve zero EP and ED, and an optimal B, as seen from experiments in our packet processing platform, we use thresholds for all these values. In our system, we have set EP_{thresh} and ED_{thresh} to 40000 empty_polls/empty_dequeues per sec (which is a sufficiently low value compared to a maximum measured value of 3.5M), while B_{thresh} is adjusted to 10 packets.

4   Experimental Results

In this section, we present the computational requirements of selected packet processing workloads using our workload profiling technique.

4.1   Experimental Setup

Our experimental setup consists of three commodity NUMA-based (Non-Uniform Memory Architecture) servers (i.e., source, packet processing platform and sink), each one equipped with a Xeon E5520 quad-core CPU at 2.26 GHz. Each core has dedicated 32 KB L1 and 256 KB L2 cache, while all four cores share 8 MB L3 cache. Furthermore, each server has 6 GB DDR3 RAM at 1333 MHz and two quad 1G port NICs based on Intel 82571EB. Traffic is generated by a quad 1G port NetFPGA card. The number of buffers in the Rx and Tx ring is set to 4096.

We use Click Modular Router version 1.7 for the implementation of the packet processing applications. Click runs on Linux kernel version 2.6.24.7 in order to achieve high performance. We further rely on Intel VTune Amplifier XE 2011 [9] for CPU cycle measurement and analysis.

We implement and profile the following workloads:

- **Raw forwarding:** Packet forwarding without any layer-2 or layer-3 processing.

- **IPv4 forwarding:** IPv4 forwarding including IP lookup in a table with 380K entries, checksum computation, Time-to-Live (TTL) decrement, and destination MAC address rewrite. Packets are generated with random destination IP addresses to stress the system.

- **AES encryption:** Packet encryption based on the Advanced Encryption Standard (AES).

- **CRC:** Checksum calculation for the whole packet payload.

4.2   Results and Discussion

Using our workload profiling technique, as exemplified in Section 3, we gauge the computational requirements of raw forwarding, IPv4, AES and CRC for diverse packet forwarding rates. Fig. 4 illustrates the CPU cycles/sec versus the packet forwarding rate for raw forwarding, IPv4, and CRC with 64-byte packets. The standard deviation among different runs is negligible. As expected, raw forwarding incurs the lowest CPU utilization among all workloads, since it basically

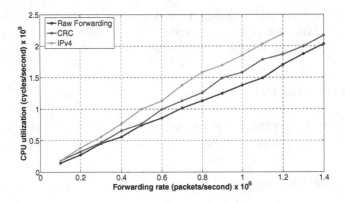

Fig. 4. CPU cycles/sec for raw forwarding, IPv4 and CRC vs. packet forwarding rate with 64-byte packets

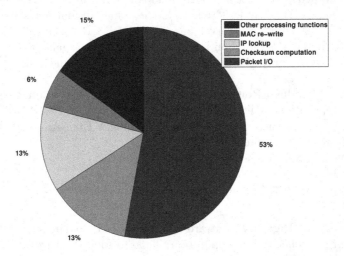

Fig. 5. CPU cycles/sec distribution for IPv4

comprises packet I/O handling along the receive and transmit path. In particular, packet I/O accounts roughly for 83% of the CPU cycles/sec consumed for raw forwarding, according to our measurements. In comparison, IPv4 forwarding consumes more CPU cycles, due to the additional processing operations performed on packets. In this respect, Fig. 5 shows the distribution of CPU cycles for IPv4[1]. Approximately 32% of the measured CPU cycles are consumed for IP lookup, checksum computation and destination MAC address rewrite, resulting in an increased CPU utilization for IPv4 compared to raw forwarding. Furthermore, Fig. 6 illustrates the NIC driver and processing functions that incur main

---

[1] The 15% of the CPU cycles/sec that correspond to "other processing functions" are consumed for packet enqueueing/dequeueing, timestamps, TTL decrement, Click counters and other operations with insignificant processing load.

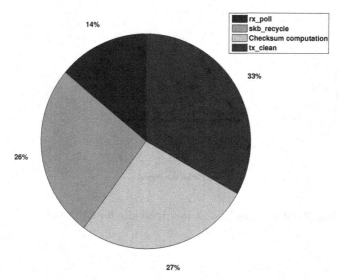

Fig. 6. Main memory access distribution for IPv4

memory accesses for IPv4. Particularly, we measured approximately 3.79 main memory accesses per packet. Note that this number represents the main memory accesses initiated by the CPU (i.e., excluding the memory accesses initiated by the NIC). The large fraction of CPU cycles (i.e., 53% for IPv4) utilized for packet I/O indicates the significance of packet I/O handling for such workloads.

As shown in Fig. 4, CRC yields relatively low computational requirements, due to the minimum packet size. In fact, CRC incurs less processing load compared to IPv4 for this packet length. However, measurements with larger packets (Fig. 7) show that CRC requires a substantially larger number of CPU cycles per packet.

Fig. 8 depicts the computational requirements of AES versus the packet forwarding rate with 64-byte packets. Fig. 8 corroborates that AES is a CPU-intensive workload. Similar to CRC, AES requires more CPU cycles per packet for larger packets, as shown in Fig. 7.

Based on the measurements in Figs. 4 and 8, Table 1 shows the average number of CPU cycles per packet for all four workloads with 64-byte packets. The study in [1], which also relies on a Click-based packet processing system without any advanced packet I/O handling, reports similar computational requirements for IPv4 (i.e., 1813 cycles/packet). These computational requirements can decrease (especially for workloads in which packet I/O accounts for a significant fraction of consumed cycles), when more efficient packet I/O techniques are applied [2], [8], [11]. In this respect, Table 2 depicts the average number of CPU cycles per packet for raw forwarding when the I/O optimizations of Netmap [11] and RouteBricks [2] are employed. Both I/O techniques transfer packets from NIC to memory in batches, while additional I/O optimizations of Netmap include static buffer allocation and the reduction of the data structure size for packet descriptors. Note that Click runs in user-space when Netmap is used. Compared to standard Click packet I/O handling, both Netmap and RouteBricks yield

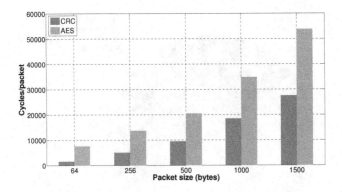

Fig. 7. CPU cycles/packet vs. packet size for CRC and AES

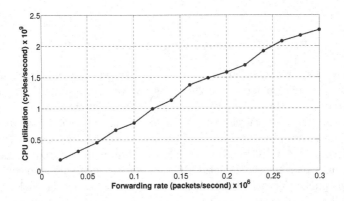

Fig. 8. CPU cycles/sec for AES vs. packet forwarding rate with 64-byte packets

substantially lower computational requirements. This corroborates the strong impact of packet I/O handling on workload CPU utilization and manifests the need for efficient workload profiling methods.

So far, we discussed the computational requirements of packet processing applications that run alone on a single core. Depending on resource availability, a packet processing system can host multiple applications, performing the role of a multi-purpose software middlebox. In this context, we briefly discuss the impact of CPU resource sharing on the workloads' computational requirements. For workloads running on different cores (i.e., one workload per core), recent work [1] shows that the computational requirements of packet processing workloads increase, due to L3 cache contention. The computational requirements of workloads sharing a single core may increase depending on scheduling and the size of their working sets. If their working sets do not fit into L3 cache, the additional main memory accesses will incur a performance penalty, increasing the required amount of CPU cycles to sustain a desired packet processing rate.

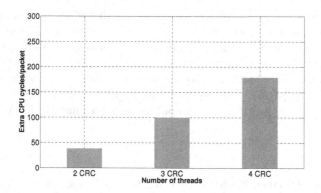

Fig. 9. Extra CPU cycles/packet required for CRC with multi-threading

Table 1. Average CPU cycles/packet (64-byte packets)

Workload	cycles/packet
Raw forwarding	1415
IPv4	1874
AES	7931
CRC	1577

Table 2. Average CPU cycles/packet for raw forwarding with diverse I/O optimizations (64-byte packets)

System	cycles/packet
Click	1415
Netmap	907
RouteBricks	926

In terms of scheduling, multiple workloads can be assigned to a single (kernel) thread or to different (kernel) threads. The former requires a task scheduler, so that multiple workloads can be executed within the same thread. Click provides such a scheduler, allowing multiple workloads to share a single core, without context switching. This does not incur a perceptible effect on the computational requirements of workloads. However, in this case, the migration of processing applications across cores is complicated and can result in traffic disruption. To facilitate migrations, a packet processing system can assign workloads (that share the same CPU core) to separate threads. To investigate the processing requirements under multi-threading, we compare the CPU cycles required for CRC with a single and multiple threads, running always on the same CPU core. Fig. 9 depicts the extra cycles consumed with a diverse number of threads, due to context switching. Note that this experiment does not incur any L3 cache contention, since there is no application running on any of the other 3 cores.

5   Conclusions

In this paper, we exemplified methods to circumvent the difficulty of profiling packet processing workloads on commodity servers. We discussed the implications of polling and batch processing on workload profiling and we further showed that workload profiling can produce inaccurate results when the confluence of these two factors is not taken into account. Our experimental results demonstrate that our workload profiling technique can measure the computational requirements of various workloads for a wide range of packet forwarding rates. We believe that our workload profiling method can comprise a prominent component of a modern packet processing system, improving its ability to perform admission control and to utilize the computing resources more efficiently.

References

1. Dobrescu, M., Argyraki, K., Ratnasamy, S.: Toward Predictable Performance in Software Packet-Processing Platforms. In: Proc. USENIX NSDI, San Jose (April 2012)
2. Dobrescu, M., Egi, N., Argyraki, K., Chun, B., Fall, K., Iannaccone, G., Knies, A., Manesh, M., Ratnasamy, S.: RouteBricks: Exploiting Parallelism to Scale Software Routers. In: Proc. USENIX SOSP 2009, Big Sky, MT, USA (October 2009)
3. Dobrescu, M., Argyraki, K., Iannaccone, G., Manesh, M., Ratnasamy, S.: Controlling Parallelism in a Multicore Software Router. In: Proc. ACM CoNEXT PRESTO 2010, Philadelphia, USA (December 2010)
4. Egi, E., Greenhalgh, A., Handley, M., Hoerdt, M., Huici, F., Mathy, L.: Towards High Performance Virtual Routers on Commodity Hardware. In: Proc. ACM CoNEXT 2008, Madrid, Spain (December 2008)
5. Egi, N., Greenhalgh, A., Handley, M., Hoerdt, M., Huici, F., Mathy, L., Papadimitriou, P.: Forwarding Path Architectures for Multi-core Software Routers. In: Proc. ACM CoNEXT PRESTO 2010, Philadelphia, USA (December 2010)
6. Gibb, G., Zeng, H., McKewon, N.: Outsourcing Network Functionality. In: Proc. ACM SIGCOMM HotSDN, Helsinki, Finland (August 2012)
7. Greenhalgh, A., Huici, F., Hoerdt, M., Papadimitriou, P., Handley, M., Mathy, L.: Flow Processing and the Rise of Commodity Network Hardware. ACM SIGCOMM Computer Communication Review 39(2) (April 2009)
8. Han, S., Jang, K., Park, K., Moon, S.: PacketShader: A GPU-Accelerated Software Router. In: Proc. ACM SIGCOMM, New Delhi, India (September 2010)
9. Intel VTune Amplifier XE 2011 (2011),
   http://software.intel.com/en-us/intel-vtune-amplifier-xe
10. Kohler, E., Morris, R., Chen, B., Jahnotti, J., Kasshoek, M.F.: The Click Modular Router. ACM Transaction on Computer Systems 18(3) (2000)
11. Rizzo, L., Carbone, M., Catalli, G.: Transparent Acceleration of Software Packet Forwarding Using Netmap. In: Proc. IEEE INFOCOM, Orlando, USA (March 2012)
12. Sekar, V., Egi, N., Ratnasamy, S., Reiter, M., Shi, G.: The Design and Implementation of a Consolidated Middlebox Architecture. In: Proc. USENIX NSDI, San Jose (April 2012)
13. Snort, http://www.snort.org/
14. Wolf, T.: In-Network Services for Customization in Next-Generation Networks. IEEE Network 24(4) (July 2010)

Fractional Frequency Reuse in Integrated Femtocell/Macrocell Environments

Christos Bouras, Vasileios Kokkinos, Andreas Papazois, and Georgia Tseliou

Computer Technology Institute & Press "Diophantus", Patras, Greece and
Computer Engineering and Informatics Department, University of Patras, Greece
{bouras,kokkinos}@cti.gr, {papazois,tseliou}@ceid.upatras.gr

Abstract. Femtocells have a strong potential for increasing the efficiency, cell coverage and network capacity of next-generation mobile networks. In Long Term Evolution technology, the adaptation of Fractional Frequency Reuse techniques has been proposed in order to overcome the co-channel interference and augment the total throughput of the network. In this work, we propose a Fractional Frequency Reuse method that on the one hand calculates the optimal inner region radius and frequency allocation of a macrocell and on the other hand assigns frequency resources to the femtocells in order to mitigate the co-channel interference. We apply this method in an integrated femtocell/macrocell environment and evaluate it based on the optimization of three metrics, depending on the network operator's needs.

Keywords: Fractional frequency reuse, channel interference, throughput.

1   Introduction

The integrated femtocell/macrocell environments comprise of a conventional cellular network overlaid with shorter-range self-configurable base stations (BS), called femtocells [1]. These kinds of networks offer an efficient way to improve cellular system capacity. The limiting factor in such networks is the interference between macrocells and femtocells that can suffocate the capacity due to the near-far problem. This means that femtocells should use a different frequency channel than the one of the potentially nearby high-power macrocell users (MUs). Fractional Frequency Reuse (FFR) techniques are discussed in Long Term Evolution (LTE) networks to overcome the Co-Channel Interference (CCI) problems, i.e., interference from transmitters located in neighbor cells with the same frequency bands as the reference cell of interest, and Inter-Cell Interference (ICI) problems, i.e., interference from neighboring cells. In FFR techniques the cell space is divided into two regions: inner, which is close to the macrocell BS and outer, which is situated to the cell borders.

There are several published related works that concern FFR techniques for interference mitigation in femtocell/macrocell deployments. In [2], the authors propose a scheme that adapts radio frequency parameters taking into account all the user and channel conditions. Furthermore in [3], a hybrid frequency assignment framework is introduced for femtocells and different scenarios of femtocell CCI are

V. Tsaoussidis et al. (Eds.): WWIC 2013, LNCS 7889, pp. 229–240, 2013.
© Springer-Verlag Berlin Heidelberg 2013

analyzed. The authors of [4] propose a frequency planning mechanism, in which femtocells choose the frequency sub-bands that will not be used in the sub-region of a macrocell using FFR in an integrated macrocell/femtocell network. Work in [5] proposes a novel frequency partitioning method, in which both sub-channels for inner cell region and sub-channels for outer region are allowed to be used in the inner region of cells while sub-channels for outer region are defined differently from cell to cell to reduce CCI. Another FFR scheme is introduced in [6], by noting that the inner and the outer regions can be served in a different way, not only in terms of frequency sub-bands but also in terms of time slots. This scheme is extended further in [7], by employing the concept of making cell sectors. Finally, the authors of [8] propose an interference avoidance scheme for LTE downlink using dynamic inter-cell coordination, facilitated through the interface between neighboring LTE BS.

Although these works provide very useful ideas regarding FFR techniques, they do not offer methods that take into consideration real parameters from the network operator's side nor do they optimize the network conditions according to them. In this paper, we focus on the downlink process of an integrated femtocell/macrocell environment by evaluating several metrics related to the fairness of the network resources. We propose an FFR method that calculates the optimal inner region radius and bandwidth allocation as well as assigns the proper frequency resources to the overlaid femtocells in order to reduce the total interference. The proposed method is evaluated for three different approaches. The 1st approach finds the optimal inner region radius and frequency allocation based on the maximization of the network's total throughput, the 2nd one based on the Jain's Fairness Index and the 3rd one based on a new metric, which is called weighted throughput. This metric aims to make a trade-off between the total cell throughput values and the per-user throughput values that occur from the two previous approaches, so as higher cell throughput are achieved simultaneously with similar per-user throughput values. The proposed FFR method aims to enhance the total cell throughput and allocate the network resources in a fair way among the MUs and femtocell users (FUs).

The paper is organized as follows. Section 2 introduces the downlink interference scenarios and the proposed frequency allocation scheme. Section 3 presents the theoretical approach of the proposed FFR method. The evaluation of the proposed method is presented in Section 4 and the final conclusions and proposals for future work are drawn up in Section 5.

2   Frequency Allocation in Femtocell/Macrocell Environments

In FFR the whole frequency band is divided into several sub-bands, and each one is exclusively assigned to inner and outer region of the cell respectively. In order to ensure that the mutual interference between users and BSs remains below a harmful level, adjacent cells use different frequencies. The interference scenarios that appear in such integrated femtocell/macrocell environments during the downlink session are described in Fig. 1. In more detail, the interference caused to a FU by a macrocell BS (Scenario 1), the interference caused to a MU by a femtocell BS (Scenario 2) and the interference caused to a FU by a neighboring femtocell BS (Scenario 3) are depicted.

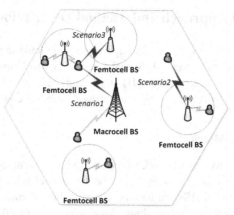

Fig. 1. Downlink interference scenarios in an integrated femtocell/macrocell environment

In order to mitigate these kinds of interference, we apply a specific frequency allocation scheme for the MUs and FUs. As shown in Fig. 2, each cell of the architecture is divided into inner and outer region. The total available bandwidth of the system is split into four uneven spectrums (or resource sets), denoted by yellow (A), blue (B), red (C) and green (D) colors. All the MUs that are located in the inner region of each cell, are assigned sub-band A. The MUs located in the outer region will be assigned one of the rest sub-bands (B, C or D). If a FU is located in the outer region of a cell, then the sub-band used for the inner region plus the sub-bands that are used in the outer region of the neighboring cells can be reused. According to this allocation, each femtocell BS adopts an effective frequency assignment, assuring that MUs/FUs use different frequencies and the CCI is reduced.

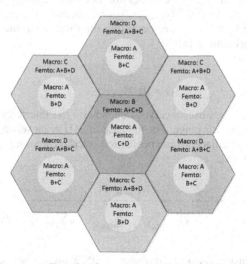

Fig. 2. Proposed frequency allocation for an integrated femtocell/macrocell environment

3   Theoretical Approach and Method Description

In this section we describe the theoretical approach for calculating the metrics that are related to the proposed FFR method: Signal Interference to Noise Ratio (SINR), cell total throughput, Jain's Fairness Index (JI) and Weighted Throughput (WT). Then, we introduce the proposed FFR method by presenting its pseudo-code.

3.1   Calculation of Metrics

We assume that the overall network is composed of N adjacent cells. Each cell contains a number of users (either MUs or FUs) seeking to share a group of subcarriers. The macrocell BSs are located at the center of each cell. Femtocell BSs are uniformly distributed in the topology. Moreover, we consider that the MUs are outdoor users whereas the FUs are located indoors. We use the path loss suburban model described in [9], for the calculation of the path loss between an outdoor MU and a macro BS (with frequency of 2GHz):

$$PL_{MU}[dB] = 15.3 + 37.6 \log_{10}(d[m]) + S^{out} \tag{1}$$

where d is the distance between the transmitter and the receiver and S^{out} factor represents the outdoor shadowing which is characterized by the Gaussian distribution with zero mean and standard deviation. In the same way, we calculate the path loss between an indoor FU and a femto BS:

$$PL_{FU}[dB] = 38.46 + 20 \log_{10}(d[m]) + 0.7 d_{2D,indoor} + 18.3 n^{((n+2)/(n+1)-0.46)} \tag{2}$$

where n is the number of penetrated floors and in case of a single-floor house, the last term equals to zero. The term $0.7 d_{2D,indoor}$ takes into account the penetration loss by the walls inside a house with $d_{2D,indoor}$ representing the distance in the house. So now we can define the channel gain as [8]:

$$G = 10^{-\frac{PL}{10}} \tag{3}$$

The downlink SINR that a user receives depends on the interference of the cells that include the user within their range. For the case of MU m on subcarrier n, we consider both the impact of the adjacent macrocells and overlaid femtocells. So the SINR for this case is defined as [8]:

$$SINR_{m,n} = \frac{G_{M,m,n} \cdot P_{M,n}}{\sigma_n^2 + \sum_{neigM} G_{m,neigM,n} \cdot P_{neigM,n} + \sum_{F} G_{m,F,n} \cdot P_{F,n}} \tag{4}$$

where $P_{X,n}$ is the transmit power of the serving BS X on subcarrier n (X can be either the macrocell M or the neighboring macrocell $neigM$ or the femtocell F). The term $G_{x,X,n}$ refers to the channel gain between user x and the serving cell X (where x can be an MU or a FU and X his serving BS). It is calculated from (1) for the MU and from (2) for the FU. Finally, the term σ_n^2 is the power of the Additive White Gaussian Noise (AWGN). Consequently, the expression for the SINR of a FU is expressed as follows, taking into account the interference caused by neighboring femtocells (*neigF*) and the macrocells that use the same frequency bands:

$$SINR_{f,n} = \frac{G_{F,f,n} \cdot P_{F,n}}{\sigma_n^2 + \sum_{neigF} G_{f,neigF,n} \cdot P_{neigF,n} + \sum_{M} G_{f,M,n} \cdot P_{M,n}}$$

(5)

After the SINR estimation, we proceed to the throughput calculation. The capacity of user x on subcarrier n can be calculated by the following [10]:

$$C_{x,n} = \Delta f \cdot \log_2(1 + aSINR_{x,n})$$

(6)

where, Δf refers to the subcarrier spacing. The constant term α is connected with the target bit error rate (*BER*) as follows $\alpha = -1.5/\ln(5BER)$. Moreover, the overall throughput of a serving macrocell can be expressed as follows [4]:

$$T_M = \sum_m \sum_n \beta_{m,n} \cdot C_{m,n}$$

(7)

where, $\beta_{m,n}$ represents the subcarrier assignment to MU m. When $\beta_{m,n}=1$, the subcarrier n is assigned to MU m. Otherwise, $\beta_{m,n}=0$. A similar expression can be derived for FUs. To obtain a metric of fairness for the proposed FFR method we use the JI metric, firstly introduced in [11]. Assuming the allocated throughput for user i is x_i, then JI is defined as:

$$JI = \frac{\left(\sum_{i=1}^{\#users} x_i\right)^2}{\#users \cdot \sum_{i=1}^{users} x_i^2}$$

(8)

This metric is very interesting for the evaluation of the proposed method due to its properties. It is scale-independent, applicable for different number of users and it is bounded between [0, 1], where 0 means "total unfairness" and 1 means "total fairness" in terms of throughput division among the users. In the following section, we are going to prove that the optimization of the throughput favors the users that are located next to the BS whereas the optimization of JI assigns similar per-user throughput values but the total cell throughput remains quite low. In order to make a trade-off between the achieved total cell throughput and the per-user throughput values that occur from the previous approaches, we introduce one more named WT and we define it as:

$$WT_x = JI_x \cdot T_x$$

(9)

where x is the corresponding user (either FU or MU), which we calculate the metric for. By introducing this metric, we aim not only at the low variance of the per-user throughput values but also at higher values of the cell total throughput.

3.2 Proposed FFR Method

The proposed FFR method receives as input the integrated femtocell/macrocell environment with all its parameters (i.e., the number of femtocells, macrocells, FUs, MUs, and their positions in the deployment). In order to find the optimal FFR scheme, the method divides each cell into two regions (inner and outer) and scans all the inner region radiuses and frequency allocations. The frequency allocation is examined in terms of resource blocks (RBs), the minimum allocation unit in LTE both for protocol side and system resource allocation [9]. For each RB, the method calculates the per-user throughput, the cell total throughput, JI and WT. This procedure is repeated for successive inner region radiuses (0 to R, where R is the cell radius). After the above calculations, the method chooses the optimal FFR scheme that maximizes the cell total throughput, the JI and the WT. The pseudo-code that follows describes the main idea of the proposed FFR method.

```
% Pseudo-code for the proposed FFR method
1:generate_network();
2:generate_MUs();
3:generate_FUs();
4:for r=0:R                    %scan all the radiuses
5:    for b=0:50              %scan all the RBs
6:        allocate_RBs();      %according to Fig. 2
7:        for x=1:X %for all users
8:            calculate_sinr(x);
9:            calculate_capacity(x);
10:          calculate_througput(x);
11:      end
12:      calculate_total_througput(r,b);
13:      calculate_JI(r,b);
14:      calculate_WT(r,b);
15:  end
16:end
17:select_optimal_radius&rb_throuputApproach();  %1st
                                             % approach
18:select_optimal_radius&rb_JIApproach();        %2nd
                                             % approach
19:select_optimal_radius&rb_WTApproach();         %3rd
                                             % approach
```

4   Performance Evaluation

4.1   Simulation Parameters

The simulation parameters for the examined system that are necessary for the conduction of the experiments are presented in Table 1. We consider a topology of 16 cells sites with 360 uniformly distributed users and 90 uniformly distributed femtocells (Fig. 3). Our experiments focus on one cell of the topology (second row and third column). This cell contains 7 femtocells, 5 FUs and 22 MUs.

Table 1. Simulation parameters

Parameter	Units	Value
System bandwidth	MHz	10
Resource Blocks (RB)		50
Carrier frequency	MHz	2000
Macrocell / Femtocell Radius	m	250 / 40
Correlation distance	m	40
Channel model		3GPP Typical Urban
Path loss	dB	Suburban deployment
Macrocell BS transmit power	W	20
Femtocell BS transmit power	mW	20
Power Noise Density	dbm/Hz	-174
Intersite Distance	m	500

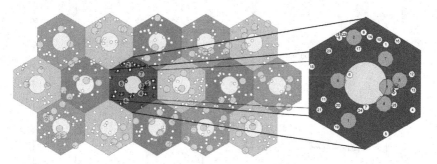

Fig. 3. Multicell integrated femtocell/macrocell environment

4.2   Operation of the Proposed FFR Method

Selection of Optimal Inner Region Radius and RB

The first experiment shows how the proposed FFR method chooses the optimal inner region radius and frequency allocation for the three approaches. Fig. 4 depicts the selection of the optimal inner region radius whereas Fig. 5 shows how each metric change while the number of RBs allocated to the inner region varies from 0 to 50.

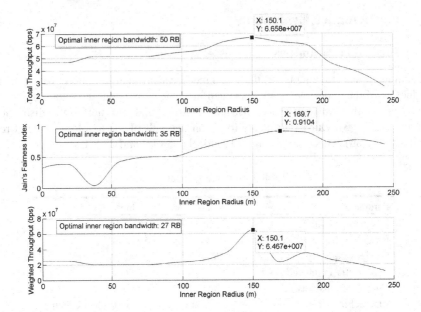

Fig. 4. Selection of optimal inner region radius

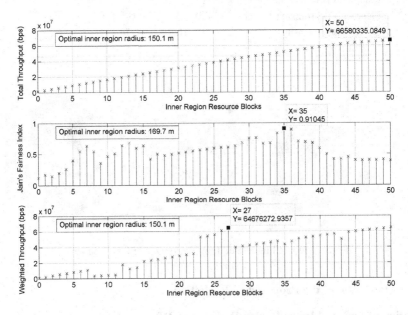

Fig. 5. Selection of optimal inner region RB

In both figures, we mark the optimal combination of inner region radius and RB for each approach. In the 1st approach, the maximum value of the cell total throughput is 66.58Mbps (150.1m radius and 50 RBs). This means that the method assigns all the

RBs to the inner region due to the fact that almost all the users are located in the inner region. In the 2nd approach, the JI is maximized (0.9104) for 169.7m radius and 35 RBs. Finally, the 3rd approach maximizes the WT (64.67Mbps) for 150.1m radius and 27 RBs.

Per-User throughput for Each Approach
After demonstrating the operation of the proposed FFR method for the three approaches, we examine the per-user throughput achieved by each one of the approaches. In Fig. 6 we depict the per-user throughput of an environment consisting of 5FUs (users 5, 6, 12, 15 and 22) and 22MUs for the three approaches. The 1st approach that chooses the optimal inner region radius and RB based on the total throughput, leads to an unfair distribution of the available frequency resources. It is remarkable, that in this case the users are treated in two different ways; there are users that achieve very high throughput values whereas there are others with quite low values. This is rational, because the 1st approach assigns all the available bandwidth to the inner region and the users of the outer region are not served. Consequently the femtocells BS of the outer region are allocated with the biggest bandwidth part whereas the ones located in the inner region achieve quite low values (Fig. 2). That is the reason why FU 22, covered by femtocell 2 (Fig. 3) achieves the highest throughput value (24.198 Mbps). For this approach the average user throughput equals to 2.466Mbps and the minimum throughput value is 1.905Kbps.

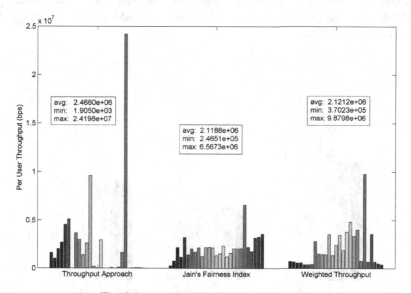

Fig. 6. Per-user throughput for each approach

In the 2nd approach, the FFR method finds the optimal inner region radius and frequency allocation based on the JI. We can observe that this approach allocates the frequency resources in a way that allows all users to have similar throughput values. The average throughput value equals to 2.1188Mbps, when the maximum is

6.5673Mbps and the minimum is 0.24651Mbps. So, this approach not only assures the serving of inner region users but also the ones located in the outer region. However, the total cell throughput is lower compared to the 1st approach. This is the reason why we have introduced WT approach where the throughput values are ranged between the ones occurred by the previous approaches. In this case the average per-user throughput is 2.1212Mbps, whereas the maximum equals to 9.8798Mbps and the minimum to 0.37023Mbps. To sum up, this approach makes a trade-off between the previous two, because it ensures both high cell total throughput and similar per-user throughput values among FUs and MUs.

Scalable Number of Femtocells

For this part of the experimental evaluation, we assume an integrated femtocell/macrocell environment consisting of a scalable number of femtocells. Fig. 7 shows how the cell total throughput changes as the number of femtocells per macrocell increases from 1 to 7, for each one of the three approaches. Moreover, Fig. 8 presents the combination of inner region radius and RBs for each added femtocell. According to this figures, for the 1st approach the maximum value (66.581Mbps) is achieved when the 6th femtocell is added to the environment (for 151.2m radius and 50RBs). The throughput value when the 7th femtocell is added to the environment is quite close to the maximum one. For the 2nd approach, the highest achieved throughput value equals to 52.622Mbps for 169.5m inner region radius and 33 RBs (6th femtocell). Finally, for the 3rd approach, the maximum total throughput (59.675Mbps) is succeeded when the 6th femtocell is added to the topology, for 150.9m radius and 25RBs.

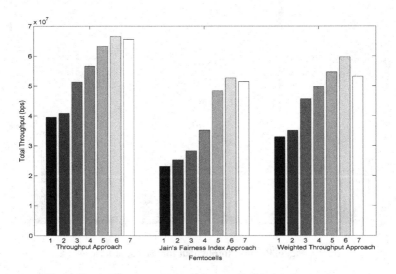

Fig. 7. Total throughout for each femtocell added to the topology

The proposed FFR method adapts as we add femtocells to the integrated femtocell/macrocell environment. As Fig. 8 shows, while the FFR method finds the optimal inner region radius and RBs based on WT, the inner region radius and RBs remain in similar values since the addition of the 4th femtocell. It is worth noting, that in this case, the method can succeed satisfying total cell throughput values without the need of altering the inner region radius and frequency allocation of the examined environment which is a demanding task by the network operator's side. So, we conclude that this approach seems the most efficient from the network operator's side.

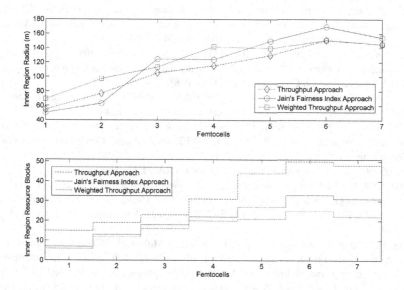

Fig. 8. Inner region radius and RBs for each femtocell

5   Conclusions and Future Work

In this paper we proposed an FFR method that calculates the optimal inner region radius and frequency allocation based on three different metrics: the cell total throughput, JI and a newly introduced metric called WT. Moreover, we described a potential frequency allocation scheme for both femtocell and macrocell BS so as the total network interference is reduced. The application of the FFR method based on WT makes a trade-off between the other two approaches, due to the fact that it increases the cell total throughput and decreases the variance of per-user throughput values.

A potential future step for this work is to integrate several realistic network parameters in the proposed method and evaluate it in real conditions. Also, we can create a dynamic frequency allocation scheme instead of the proposed static one, for the frequency assignment.

240   C. Bouras et al.

References

1. Chandrasekhar, V., Andrews, J.G.: Femtocell networks: A survey. IEEE Communications Magazine 46(9), 59–67 (2008)
2. Lopez-Perez, D., Valcarce, A., Roche, G., Zhang, J.: OFDMA femtocells: A roadmap on interference avoidance. IEEE Communications Magazine 47(9), 41–48 (2009)
3. Guvenc, I., Jeong, M.-R., Watanabe, F., Inamura, H.: A hybrid frequency assignment for femtocells and coverage area analysis for co-channel operation. IEEE Communications Letters 12 (2008)
4. Lee, P., Lee, T., Jeong, J., Shin, J.: Interference management in LTE femtocell systems using fractional frequency reuse. In: International Conference on Advanced Communication Technology (ICACT 2010), pp. 1047–1051 (2010)
5. Han, S.S., Park, J., Lee, T.-J., Ahn, H.G., Jang, K.: A new frequency partitioning and allocation of subcarriers for fractional frequency reuse in mobile communication systems. IEICE Transactions on Communications E 91-B(8), 2748–2751 (2008)
6. Giuliano, R., Monti, C., Loreti, P.: WiMAX fractional frequency reuse for rural environments. IEEE Wireless Communications 15(3), 60–65 (2008)
7. Hamoudal, S., Yeh, C., Kim, J., Wooram, S., Kwon, D.S.: Dynamic hard fractional frequency reuse for mobile WiMAX. In: IEEE International Conference on Pervasive Computing and Communications (PerCom 2009), pp. 1–6 (2009)
8. R1-050507, Soft Frequency Reuse Scheme for UTRAN LTE, Huawei
9. 3GPP TR 36.814 V9.0.0 Technical Report 3rd Generation Partnership Project; Technical Specification Group Radio Access Network; Evolved Universal Terrestrial Radio Access (E-UTRA); Further advancements for E-UTRA physical layer aspects (Release 9) (March 2010)
10. Lei, H., Zhang, L., Zhang, X., Yang, D.: A Novel Multi-Cell OFDMA System Structure Using Fractional Frequency Reuse. In: Proceedings of the 18th Annual IEEE International Symposium on Personal, Indoor and Mobile Radio Communications, PIMRC 2007 (2007)
11. Jain, R., Chiu, D.M., Hawe, W.R.: A Quantitative measure of fairness and discrimination for resource allocation in shared computer systems. Digital equipment corporation technical report TR-301 (September 1984)

Performance Evaluation of Bit Error Rate in Relay-Based Cooperative Diversity Systems over Rayleigh Fading Channels with Interference

Rami Mohaisen and Mamoun F. Al-Mistarihi

Jordan University of Science and Technology/ Electrical Engineering Department, Irbid, Jordan
rami.fayez@hotmail.com, mistarihi@just.edu.jo

Abstract. Adaptive relaying schemes of the cooperative diversity networks have drawn a considerable attention since they provide an efficient way in allocating the channel resources effectively when needed. The incremental relaying form of the cooperative networks uses a feedback channel from the destination in order to use the relay only when the direct path from the source to the destination is in outage which in turn will combine the two received signal by the maximum ratio combiner (MRC) to proactively improve the signal reception at the destination. This paper derives a closed form expression for the bit error rate (BER) in decode-and-forward incremental relaying systems over Rayleigh fading channels and incorporating the effects of the multiple L interferers near the destination which will degrade the system performance due to the Co-channel interference. Numerical results are provided to consolidate the assumptions.

Keywords: Incremental relaying, cooperative wireless networks, decode-and-forward, signal to interference ratio, Rayleigh fading channel.

1 Introduction

The implementation of the cooperative wireless networks in general consists of the source, destination and the relay node which helps the source in relaying its signal to the destination and depending on how and when the relay will send the source signal, many cooperative protocols arose [1, 2].

For instance, the work in [3, 4] elaborate on a variety of protocols and schemes of the cooperative diversity, out of which are the amplify-and-forward (AF), the decode-and-forward (DF) and the fixed relaying schemes. Authors of [5] discussed the case of the amplify-and-forward fixed relaying over Rayleigh channels where a closed form expressions of the BER and the outage probability were derived.

Fixed relaying systems have a performance drawback since they allocate the channel resource in a deterministic manner which eventually will lead to a dimensioned performance due to the fact that, most of the time the direct path is usable and hence the whole utilization of the relay path will be considered a waste of resources.

Performance analysis in terms of symbol error probability and outage probability for the AF and DF relaying over Rayleigh and Nakagami-m fading channels have been thoroughly analyzed and discussed [6-9].

V. Tsaoussidis et al. (Eds.): WWIC 2013, LNCS 7889, pp. 241–250, 2013.
© Springer-Verlag Berlin Heidelberg 2013

In order to mitigate for the previously mentioned restrictions, the incremental relaying scheme come into play to effectively optimize the performance by using the relay path only when needed. Authors of [10, 11] elaborated on the decode-and-forward incremental relaying over Rayleigh fading channel with one single relaying node where close forms of the BER and the outage probability were provided.

In this paper, we discuss the performance of the decode and forward incremental relaying over Rayleigh fading channel with the presence of the multiple L interferers near the destination with the them to the destination is a assumed to be identically and independently Rayleigh random variables. Numerical results are there to validate our theory.

This paper is further organized as follows; Section 2 provides the system model. Section 3 provides the performance analysis and derived tight closed form expression of bit error rate. Results and discussion are presented in section 4. Finally we concluded this paper in section 5.

2   System Model

Fig. 1 shows the cooperative wireless network where the source send its data to the destination and the relay where the latter stay passive till it receives a negative feedback from the destination indicating the necessity to send the source signal to the destination which in turn will combine the two received signals by the MRC. The channel coefficients between the source - relay, the relay - destination, and the source - destination are assumed to follow the Rayleigh distribution and are independent of each other.

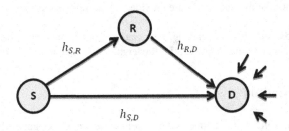

Fig. 1. Cooperative Diversity Network with Multiple L Interferers Located near the Destination

Multiple L interferers exist near the destination with the assumption that the channel coefficients from those interferers to the destination are identical and independent Rayleigh random variables. The multiple access technique is time division multiple access TDMA and the noise at the destination is assumed to be AWGN with a unity variance, and the nodes are all equipped with one antenna.

Since the TDMA is used, then upon receiving the source signal by the relay and the destination, the latter will report the signal quality to both the source and the relay in order for the relay to participate in the transmission or not.

Expressing the above scenario, the two received signals at both the relay and the destination are denoted as:

$$y_{S,D}(t_1) = h_{S,D}\sqrt{E_s}\, x(t_1) + n_1(t_1) + I(t_1) \tag{1}$$

$$y_{S,R}(t_1) = h_{S,R}\sqrt{E_s}\, x(t_1) + n_2(t_1) \tag{2}$$

where E_s is being the energy of the source signal, $x(t_1)$ and $I(t_1)$ are the symbol of the signal and interference effects, respectively, within the first time slot, and the noise terms are all assumed to be AWGN.

If the direct path was in outage, the relay will receive a negative feedback from the destination, requesting it to send the source signal within the second time slot. Expressing the received signal at the destination from the relay path within the second time slot as follows:

$$y_{R,D}(t_2) = h_{R,D}\sqrt{E_s}\, x_r(t_2) + n_3(t_2) + I(t_2) \tag{3}$$

where $x_r(t_2)$ is the regenerated symbol at the destination, the interference effects within the second time slot are represented by $I(t_2)$.

The bottom line in assessing the direct path usability is by comparing the direct path SNR with γ_0 which represents the minimum threshold beyond which the destination can receive and process the source signal effectively without the participation of the relay.

3   Performance Analysis

In the proposed system model, rather than working on the signal to noise and interference ration at the destination (SINR), we will use the signal to interference ratio (SIR) because the noise effects at the destination will not be as much as the effects of the Co-channel interference imposed by the multiple L interferers near the destination, and hence we will transgress the noise at the destination to focus merely on the SIR at the destination from the direct and the relay paths.

In the following subsections, we derive the SIR's PDFs at the destination from both the source and the destination along with their CDFs.

3.1   Probability Density Function of SIR's $\eta_{S,D}$ and $\eta_{R,D}$

The PDF of the SIR ($\eta_{S,D}$) at the destination from the source path is given as follows:

$$f_{\eta_{S,D}}(\eta_{S,D}) = \varsigma_{S,D}\left(\frac{1}{\lambda_{S,D}+\eta_{S,D}}\right)^{L+1} \tag{4}$$

where $\lambda_{S,D} = \frac{\overline{\gamma_{S,D}}}{\overline{\gamma_C}}$, $\varsigma_{S,D} = L\left(\lambda_{S,D}\right)^L$

The PDF of the SIR ($\eta_{R,D}$) at the destination from the relay path is given as follows:

$$f_{\eta_{R,D}}(\eta_{R,D}) = \varsigma_{R,D}\left(\frac{1}{\lambda_{R,D}+\eta_{R,D}}\right)^{L+1} \tag{5}$$

where $\lambda_{R,D} = \frac{\overline{\gamma_{R,D}}}{\overline{\gamma_C}}$, $\varsigma_{R,D} = L\left(\lambda_{R,D}\right)^L$

Proof

Given that the SNR of the direct path $\gamma_{S,D}$ and the relay path $\gamma_{R,D}$ at the destination from both the source and the relay, respectively, follow the exponential distribution and the fading channels from the interferers to the destination $(\gamma_b = \sum_1^L \gamma_k)$ is assumed to be a sum of identically and independently distributed exponential random variables. The PDF of the SIR $(\eta_{S,D})$ can be calculated as [14]:

$$f_{\eta_{S,D}}(\eta_{S,D}) = \int_0^\infty \gamma_b f_{\gamma_{S,D}}(\gamma_b \eta_{S,D}) f_{\gamma_b}(\gamma_b) d\gamma_b \tag{6}$$

And the PDF of the SIR $(\eta_{R,D})$ can be calculated as:

$$f_{\eta_{R,D}}(\eta_{R,D}) = \int_0^\infty \gamma_b f_{\gamma_{R,D}}(\gamma_b \eta_{R,D}) f_{\gamma_b}(\gamma_b) d\gamma_b \tag{7}$$

The PDFs of $\gamma_{S,D}$, $\gamma_{R,D}$ and γ_b are denoted as:

$$f_{\gamma_{S,D}}(\gamma_{S,D}) = \frac{1}{\overline{\gamma}_{S,D}} \exp\left(-\frac{\gamma_{S,D}}{\overline{\gamma}_{S,D}}\right), \; \gamma_{S,D} > 0 \tag{8}$$

$$f_{\gamma_{R,D}}(\gamma_{R,D}) = \frac{1}{\overline{\gamma}_{R,D}} \exp\left(-\frac{\gamma_{R,D}}{\overline{\gamma}_{R,D}}\right), \; \gamma_{R,D} > 0 \tag{9}$$

$$f_{\gamma_b}(\gamma_b) = \frac{\gamma_b^{L-1}}{\overline{\gamma}_c^L (L-1)!} \exp\left(\frac{-\gamma_b}{\overline{\gamma}_c}\right) \tag{10}$$

where $\overline{\gamma}_c$ is the average SNR of each independent interfering channel.

Solving the integrals in (6) and (7) to get the compact form of the SIR's PDF at the destination from the direct path as in (4) and from the relay path as in (5) by using [15,(3.351.1)].

3.2   The Cumulative Distribution Function of SIR's $\eta_{S,D}$, $\eta_{R,D}$

The CDF of the SIR $(\eta_{S,D})$ at the destination from the source path is given as follows:

$$F_{\eta_{S,D}}(\eta_{S,D}) = \left[\frac{(\lambda_{S,D}+\eta_{S,D})^L - \lambda_{S,D}^L}{(\lambda_{S,D}+\eta_{S,D})^L}\right] \tag{11}$$

The CDF of the SIR $(\eta_{R,D})$ at the destination from the relay path is given as follows:

$$F_{\eta_{R,D}}(\eta_{R,D}) = \left[\frac{(\lambda_{R,D}+\eta_{R,D})^L - \lambda_{R,D}^L}{(\lambda_{R,D}+\eta_{R,D})^L}\right] \tag{12}$$

Proof

The CDF of $\eta_{S,D}$ can be calculated as [14]:

$$F_{\eta_{S,D}}(\eta_{S,D}) = \int_0^{\eta_{S,D}} f_{\eta_{S,D}}(y) dy \tag{13}$$

where $f_{\eta_{S,D}}(y)$ is given as in (4).

The CDF of $\eta_{R,D}$ is found by integrating the PDF of $\eta_{R,D}$ given in (5) as follows:

$$F_{\eta_{R,D}}(\eta_{R,D}) = \int_0^{\eta_{R,D}} f_{\eta_{R,D}}(y) dy \tag{14}$$

Solving the integrals in (13) and (14) using [15,(2.117.2)], the compact form of the CDF of $\eta_{S,D}$ will be as in (11) and that of $\eta_{R,D}$ will be as in (12).

3.3   Bit Error Rate Analysis

The bit error rate for the incremental relaying system can be denoted as:

$$p_e = \Pr(\eta_{S,D} \leq \gamma_o) \times P_{div}(e) + \left(1 - \Pr(\eta_{S,D} \leq \gamma_o)\right) \times P_{direct}(e) \tag{15}$$

This expression encompasses all the average unconditional bit error rate cases at the destination that depend on whether the relays will participate in the transmission or not. For instance, if the destination relays only on the direct path, then the bit error rate at the destination is represented by the second term of (15). On the other hand, if the relay path is used, the destination will combine the two received signals by the MRC for which the bit error rate at the destination is represented by the first term of (15).

$P_{div}(e)$ is the average probability that an error occurs in the combined diversity transmission from the source and the relay to the destination by the MRC. $P_{direct}(e)$ is the probability of error at the destination given that the destination decides that the relay should not forward the source signal, in such a case the destination depends only on the direct transmission.

$P_{direct}(e)$ can be expressed as:

$$P_{direct}(e) = \int_0^\infty P_{direct}(e|\eta) f_{\eta_{S,D}}(\eta|\eta_{S,D} > \gamma_o) d\eta_{S,D} \tag{16}$$

where $P_{direct}(e|\eta)$ is the conditional error probability which takes the form $\alpha \, Q\left(\sqrt{\beta \eta_{S,D}}\right)$ with the constellation parameters α and β. $f_{\eta_{S,D}}(\eta|\eta_{S,D} > \gamma_o)$ is the conditional PDF of $\eta_{S,D}$ given that $\eta_{S,D}$ is greater than the threshold γ_o to emphasize that the direct path is not in outage which is expressed as:

$$f_{\eta_{S,D}}(\eta|\eta_{S,D} > \gamma_o) = \begin{cases} 0 & , \eta_{S,D} \leq \gamma_o \\ \rho \left(\dfrac{1}{\lambda_{S,D}+\eta_{S,D}}\right)^{L+1} & , \eta_{S,D} \geq \gamma_o \end{cases} \tag{17}$$

where $\rho = \dfrac{\varsigma_{S,D}}{1 - \left[\dfrac{(\lambda_{S,D}+\gamma_o)^L - \lambda_{S,D}{}^L}{(\lambda_{S,D}+\gamma_o)^L}\right]}$

Substituting (17) into (16) and using the Prony approximation of the Q-function and [15, (3.353.1)], the approximated expression of $P_{direct}(e)$ is as follows:

$$P_{direct}(e) \approx \alpha\rho \sum_{i=1}^2 A_i \left\{ e^{-\gamma_o a_i \beta} \sum_{k=1}^L \frac{(k-1)!(-a_i\beta)^{L-k}}{(L)!(\gamma_o+\lambda_{S,D})^k} - \frac{(-a_i\beta)^L}{(L)!} e^{a_i\beta\lambda_{S,D}} E_i[-a_i\beta(\gamma_o + \lambda_{S,D})] \right\}$$

$$\tag{18}$$

where $E_i[x]$ is the exponential integral function [15, (8.211.1)] and the terms A_i and a_i are the Prony approximation parameters.

When the relay helps in relaying the source signal, the MRC at the destination will combine the two signals and the probability of error $P_{div}(e)$ is expressed as:

$$P_{div}(e) = p_{SR}(e)p_x(e) + (1 - p_{SR}(e))p_{com}(e) \tag{19}$$

where $p_{SR}(e)$ characterizes the probability of error at the relay and $p_x(e)$ is the probability of error at the destination given that the relay decoded unsuccessfully and is bounded by 0.5 as stated in [18] and [19]. The term that represents the error probability at the destination given that the relay decode correctly is $p_{com}(e)$.

$p_{SR}(e)$ is expressed as [12]:

$$p_{SR}(e) = \frac{1}{2}\left(1 - \mu\left(\frac{\alpha^2 \overline{\gamma_{S,R}}}{2}\right)\right) \tag{20}$$

where $\mu\left(\frac{\alpha^2 \overline{\gamma_{S,R}}}{2}\right) \triangleq \sqrt{\frac{\alpha^2 \overline{\gamma_{S,R}}/2}{1 + \alpha^2 \overline{\gamma_{S,R}}/2}}$. $\overline{\gamma_{S,R}}$ is the average SNR at the relay from the direct path.

$p_{com}(e)$ can be expressed as:

$$p_{com}(e) = \alpha \int_0^\infty f_x(x|\eta_{S,D} \leq \gamma_0)\, Q(\sqrt{\beta x})dx \tag{21}$$

where $x = \eta_{S,D} + \eta_{R,D}$. Since $\eta_{S,D}$ is much less than $\eta_{R,D}$ at the MRC, we will make a transgression to work merely on $\eta_{R,D}$ and hence, $p_{com}(e)$ will be expressed as:

$$p_{com}(e) \approx \alpha \int_0^\infty f_{\eta_{R,D}}(\eta_{R,D}|\eta_{S,D} \leq \gamma_0)\, Q(\sqrt{\beta \eta_{R,D}})d\eta_{R,D} \tag{22}$$

where

$$f_{\eta_{R,D}}(\eta_{R,D}|\eta_{S,D} \leq \gamma_0) = f_{\eta_{R,D}}(\eta_{R,D}) = \zeta_{R,D}\left(\frac{\eta_{R,D}^{m-1}}{(\eta_{R,D} + \lambda_{R,D})^{L+m}}\right) \tag{23}$$

Since the two random variables are independent [14].

Solving the integral in (22) and using the Prony approximation of the Q-function and [15,(3.353.2)], the approximated expression of $p_{com}(e)$ is as follows:

$$p_{com}(e) \approx \alpha \zeta_{R,D} \sum_{i=1}^2 A_i \left[\frac{1}{(L)!} \sum_{k=1}^L (k-1)!\,(-a_i\beta)^{L-k} \frac{1}{(\lambda_{S,D})^k} \right.$$
$$\left. - \frac{(-a_i\beta)^L}{(L)!} e^{a_i\beta\lambda_{S,D}} E_i\left[-a_i\beta\lambda_{S,D}\right] \right] \tag{24}$$

where $E_i[x]$ is the exponential integral function [15].

To get the overall expression of the BER substitute (24), (20), and (18) into (15).

The detailed mathematical derivations of (4), (5), (11), (12), (18), and (24) will be submitted to a journal for publication.

4   Numerical Results

In this section we analyze the performance of the decode-and-forward incremental relaying system over Rayleigh fading channel with interference near the destination. The effect of changing the threshold value γ_0, number of interferers L, and the average SNR at the destination from the interferers $\overline{\gamma_c}$ on the system behavior is investigated too.

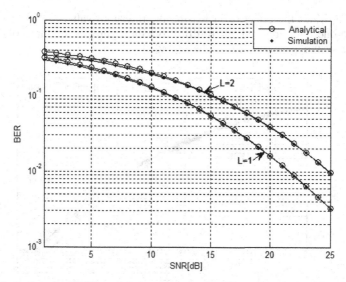

Fig. 2. Bit Error Rate for BPSK modulation scheme with different numbers of interferers (L=1, 2), γ_o=10dB, and $\overline{\gamma_C}$=10 dB

Fig. 2 and 3 depict the effects of increasing the number of interferers near the destination on the system performance for BPSK using (γ_o=10 dB, $\overline{\gamma_C}$=10 dB) and (γ_o=15 dB, $\overline{\gamma_C}$=15 dB), respectively. From the two figures, as the number of interferers' increases, the system performance in terms of the BER will drastically be degraded in response to the Co-channel interference. For example, in Fig. 2, for BER of 10^{-1}, a system with (L=1) outperforms a system with (L=2) by (3 dB).

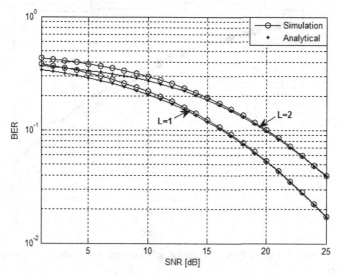

Fig. 3. Bit Error Rate for BPSK modulation scheme with different numbers of interferers (L=1, 2), γ_o=15dB, and $\overline{\gamma_C}$=15 dB

Fig. 4 illustrates the effect of increasing the threshold values on the BER for the BPSK with one interferer and $\overline{\gamma_c}$=10 dB. From the figure, as the threshold value increases, the system performance will be degraded.

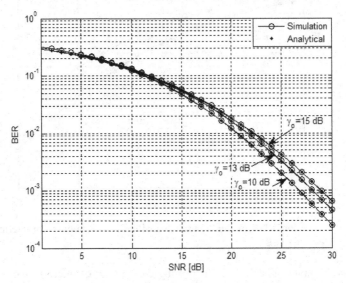

Fig. 4. Bit Error Rate for the BPSK modulation scheme with one interferer, (γ_o=10dB, 13dB, 15dB), and $\overline{\gamma_c}$=10 dB

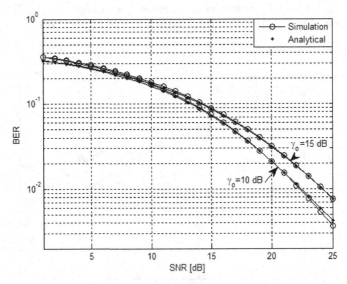

Fig. 5. Bit Error Rate for the 4-PSK modulation scheme with one interferer, (γ_o=10dB, 15dB), and $\overline{\gamma_c}$=10 dB

Figs. 5 and 6 illustrate the effect of increasing the threshold values on the BER behavior for the 4-PSK modulation scheme with one interferer and two interferers, respectively. From the two figures, as the threshold value increases, the system performance will be degraded. Also, as the number of interferers' increases, the system performance in terms of the BER will drastically be degraded in response to the Co-channel interference.

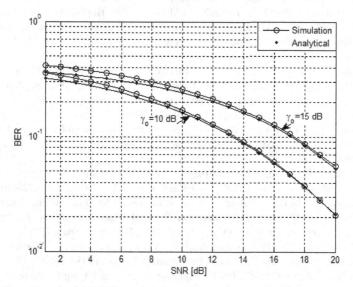

Fig. 6. Bit Error Rate for the 4-PSK modulation scheme with two interferers, (γ_o=10dB, 15dB), and $\overline{\gamma_c}$=10 dB

5   Conclusion

This paper analyzes the performance of the decode-and-forward incremental relaying with the presence of multiple interferers near the destination. The incremental relaying systems achieve the spatial diversity at the destination and utilize the channel resources. Closed form expression of the bit error rate is derived. Due to the effect of the co-channel interference, the overall system performance will be degraded. Numerical results show that as we decrease the number of interferers near the destination and γ_o, the system performance will be improved consequently.

References

1. Laneman, J.N., Tse, D.N.C., Wornell, G.W.: Cooperative diversity in wireless networks: efficient protocols and outage behavior. IEEE Trans. Inf. Theory 50 (2004)
2. Laneman, J.N., Tse, D.N.C., Wornell, G.W.: Distributed spacetime-coded protocols for exploiting cooperative diversity in wireless networks. IEEE Trans. Inf. Theory 49, 2415–2425 (2003)
3. Sendonaris, A., Erkip, E., Aazhang, B.: User cooperation diversity, part I: system description. IEEE Trans. Commun. 51(11), 1927–1938 (2003)

4. Hasna, M.O., Alouini, M.-S.: End-to-end performance of transmission systems with relays over Rayleigh-fading channels. IEEE Trans. Wireless Commun. 2(6), 1126–1131 (2003)
5. Adinoyi, A., Yanikomeroglu, H.: Cooperative relaying in multiantenna fixed relay networks. IEEE Transactions on Wireless Communications 6(2), 533–544 (2007)
6. Al-Mistarihi, M.F., Sharaqa, A., Mohaisen, R., Abu-Alnadi, O., Abu-Seba, H.: Performance Analysis of Multiuser Diversity in Multiuser Two-Hop Amplify and Forward Cooperative Multi-Relay Wireless Networks. In: Proc. 35th Jubilee International Convention on Information and Communication Technology, Electronics and Microelectronics, MIPRO 2012, Opatija, Croatia (2012)
7. Al-Mistarihi, M.F., Mohaisen, R.: Performance Analysis of Multiuser Diversity in Multiuser Two-Hop Decode-and-forward Cooperative Multi-Relay Wireless Networks. In: Proc. International Conference on Wireless Communication and Mobile Computing, ICWCMC 2011, Bangkok, Thailand, pp. 238–242 (2011)
8. Beaulieu, N.C., Hu, J.: A closed-form expression for the outage probability of decode-and-forward relaying in dissimilar Rayleigh fading channels. IEEE Commun. Lett. 10, 813–815 (2006)
9. Suraweera, H.A., Smith, P.J., Armstrong, J.: Outage probability of cooperative relay networks in Nakagami-m fading channels. IEEE Commun. Lett. 10, 834–836 (2006)
10. Ikki, S., Ahmad, M.H.: Performance Analysis of Decode-and-Forward Incremental Relaying Cooperative-Diversity Networks over Rayleigh Fading Channels. In: Proc. IEEE Technology Conference-Spring (VTC-Spring 2009), Barcelona, Spain (2009)
11. Ikki, S., Ahmed, M.H.: Performance Analysis of Cooperative Diversity Wireless Networks over Nakagami-m Fading Channel. IEEE Commun. Letter 11, 334–336 (2007)
12. Simon, M.K., Alouini, M.-S.: Digital Communication over Fading Channels. John Wiley and Sons, New York (2000)
13. Miejer's G-Function Tables of Integrals, a comprehensive online compendium of formulas involving the special functions of mathematics. For a key to the notations used here, http://functions.wolfram.com/Notations/
14. Papoulis, A.: Probability, Random Variables, and Stochastic Processes, 4th edn. McGraw-Hill, New York (2002)
15. Gradshteyn, I.S., Ryzhik, I.M.: Table of Integrals, Series, and Products, 7th edn. Academic Press (2007)

Optimal Joint Sensing Threshold and Sub-channel Power Allocation in Multi-channel Cognitive Radio

Xin Liu, Guoan Bi, Rui Lin, and Yongliang Guan

School of Electrical and Electronic Engineering, Nanyang Technological
University, 637553, Singapore
EGBI@ntu.edu.sg,
liuxinstar1984@gmail.com

Abstract. An optimal joint sensing threshold and sub-band power allocation is proposed for multi-channel cognitive radio (CR) system by formulating a mixed-variable optimization problem to maximize the total throughput of the CR while constraining the total interference to the PU, the total power of the CR, and the probabilities of false alarm and detection of each sub-channel. Based on the bi-level optimization method, the proposed optimization problem is divided into two single-variable convex optimization sub-problems: the upper level for threshold optimization and the lower level for power optimization. The simulation results show that the proposed joint optimization can achieve desirable improvement on the throughput with different sub-channel gains.

Keywords: cognitive radio, energy detection, joint optimization.

1   Introduction

Cognitive Radio (CR) has been proposed to improve the spectrum utilization by exploiting the temporarily unused radio spectrum allocated to the primary user (PU) [1]. The CR has to continuously sense the spectrum to identify the presence of the PU in order to avoid any harmful interference to the PU [2]. Energy detection has been widely used for spectrum sensing because of its simplicity without using any prior information of the PU's signal[3]. False alarm probability and detection probability are commonly used to measure the detection performance [4].

Multi-channel CR is used over multiple idle sub-channels to make improvement on throughput. An optimal multiband joint detection for spectrum sensing has been proposed in [5,6] by formulating the spectrum sensing problem as a class of optimization problems about sensing threshold for maximizing the aggregated throughput of the CR while constraining the interference to the PU. However, the work reported in [5,6] assumes that the CR has a fixed transmission power and rate in each sub-channel, and the gain of dynamic power allocation has not been exploited.

In this paper, a joint optimization on sensing threshold and sub-band power allocation is proposed, which maximizes the total throughput of the multi-channel CR subject to the constraints on the total interference to the PU, the total power of the CR, and the probabilities of false alarm and detection of each sub-channel. The sensing

V. Tsaoussidis et al. (Eds.): WWIC 2013, LNCS 7889, pp. 251–261, 2013.

threshold and sub-band power are dynamically allocated according to the gains of sub-channels in order to make full use of the spectrum resources. The proposed algorithm gives the joint sensing and transmission optimization, which involves both the physical layer and link layer of the wideband CR networking.

2   System Model

Considering a PU system operating over multiple sub-channels, some of the sub-channels may be unused by the PU at a particular time and area. Hence, these idle sub-channels are to be used for the spectrum access of the multi-channel CR, as shown in Fig. 1.

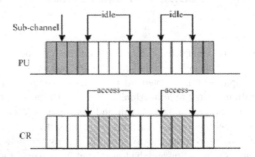

Fig. 1. Spectrum access of multi-channel cognitive radio

Supposing that there are L sub-channels, the energy detection in each sub-channel is seen as a binary hypotheses testing, which is described by

$$y_l(m) = \begin{cases} n_l(m), & H_0 \\ s_l(m) + n_l(m), & H_1 \end{cases} \quad \begin{array}{l} l = 1, 2, ..., L \\ m = 1, 2, ..., M \end{array} \tag{1}$$

where $y_l(m)$ is the received signal, $s_l(m)$ is the PU's signal with a variance of e_l^2, $n_l(m)$ is the Gaussian noise with a zero mean and a variance of σ_l^2, M is the number of the sampling nodes, and H_0 and H_1 denote the absence and presence of the PU, respectively. Energy detection firstly generates the energy statistic by accumulating the power of the M sampling nodes as follows

$$\kappa(y_l) = \frac{1}{M} \sum_{m=1}^{M} |y_l(m)|^2. \tag{2}$$

By comparing $\kappa(y_l)$ to a sensing threshold λ_l, the activity of the PU is determined by

$$\begin{cases} H_0 : \kappa(y_l) < \lambda_l \\ H_1 : \kappa(y_l) \geq \lambda_l \end{cases} \tag{3}$$

If M is large enough, according to the center limit theorem, $\kappa(y_l)$ approximately obeysthe Gaussian distribution

$$\kappa(y_l) \sim \begin{cases} \mathcal{N}\left(\sigma_l^2, \; \sigma_l^4/M\right), & H_0 \\ \mathcal{N}\left((1+\gamma_l)\sigma_l^2, \; (1+2\gamma_l)\sigma_l^4/M\right), & H_1 \end{cases} \tag{4}$$

where $\mathcal{N}(a,b)$ is the Gaussian distribution with a mean of a and a variance of b, and $\gamma_l = e_l^2/\sigma_l^2$ is the received SNR of sub-channel l.

Hence the false alarm probability P_l^f and the detection probability P_l^d for the *lth* sub-channel are respectively given by [7]

$$\begin{bmatrix} P_l^f(\lambda_l) = Q\left(\left(\frac{\lambda_l}{\sigma_l^2}-1\right)\sqrt{M}\right) \\ P_l^d(\lambda_l) = Q\left(\left(\frac{\lambda_l}{\sigma_l^2}-\gamma_l-1\right)\sqrt{\frac{M}{2\gamma_l+1}}\right) \end{bmatrix} \tag{5}$$

where $Q(x) = \frac{1}{\sqrt{2\pi}}\int_x^\infty \exp\left(-x^2/2\right)dx$. In practice, the CR may transmit data in sub-channel l with the following two scenarios.

- The CR makes correct decision on the absence of the PU with a probability of $1-P_l^f$ and then uses the sub-channel with a rate of

$$r_l^0(p_l) = \mathrm{lb}\left(1+\frac{p_l h_l^2}{\sigma_l^2}\right) \tag{6}$$

where p_l and h_l are the transmission power and the gain of sub-channel l, respectively. Since the CR may not bring the interference to the PU, its data transmission is valid.

- The CR falsely detects the absence of the PU with a probability of $1-P_l^d$ and the transmits data with a rate of

$$r_l^1(p_l) = \mathrm{lb}\left(1+\frac{p_l h_l^2}{\sigma_l^2(1+\gamma_l)}\right) \tag{7}$$

In this case, the CR will disturb the normal operation of the PU. Hence, over L sub-channels, the total throughput, R, of the CR and the total interference, I, to PU are respectively given by

$$R(\boldsymbol{\lambda}, \boldsymbol{p}) = \mathcal{P}_0 \sum_{l=1}^L r_l^0(p_l)\left(1-P_l^f(\lambda_l)\right) \tag{8}$$

$$I(\boldsymbol{\lambda}, \boldsymbol{p}) = \mathcal{P}_1 \sum_{l=1}^L r_l^1(p_l)\left(1-P_l^d(\lambda_l)\right) \tag{9}$$

where $\lambda = \{\lambda_1, \lambda_2, ..., \lambda_L\}$, $\boldsymbol{p} = \{p_1, p_2, ..., p_L\}$, and $\mathcal{P}_0$ and $\mathcal{P}_1$ are the appearance probabilities of the hypotheses H_0 and H_1, respectively.

If the PU appears in the channel frequently, we have $\mathcal{P}_0 \ll \mathcal{P}_1$ that denotes the throughput of the CR decreases, while the interference to the PU increases. In this case, the probabilities of false alarm and detection must be decreased and increased respectively for guaranteeing both the communications of the PU and the CR.

3   Optimal Joint Allocation Algorithm

The goal of the optimal allocation is to select the optimal threshold and power for each sub-channel in order to maximize the total throughput of the CR over the L sub-channels while keeping the total interference to the PU, the total transmission power, and the probabilities of false alarm and detection of each sub-channel within the constraints. The optimization problem is formulated as follows

$$\max_{\boldsymbol{p}\lambda} R(\boldsymbol{p}, \lambda) = \mathcal{P}_0 \sum_{l=1}^{L} r_l^0(p_l)\left(1 - P_l^f(\lambda_l)\right)$$

$$s.t. \quad (a)\mathcal{P}_1 \sum_{l=1}^{L} r_l^1(p_l)\left(1 - P_l^d(\lambda_l)\right) \le \varepsilon; \tag{10}$$

$$(b)\sum_{l=1}^{L} p_l \le p_{\max}; \quad (c)\begin{cases} P_l^f \le \alpha \\ P_l^d \ge \beta \text{ for } l = 1, 2, ..., L \\ p_l \ge 0 \end{cases}$$

where ε, α and β are the upper limit of the interference, the upper limit of the false alarm probability and the lower limit of the detection probability, respectively, and $p_{\max}$ is the maximal total power of the CR. Since the CR needs higher spectrum utilization and lower interference to PU, we often set $\alpha \le 0.5$ and $\beta \ge 0.5$.

In the previous research, a well-known multi-channel joint spectrum sensing method has been proposed in [5], which maximizes the throughput of the CR by selecting the optimal sensing threshold for each sub-channel. Because the uniform power was allocated to each sub-channel, however, the gain of dynamic power allocation has not been exploited. In [5], the joint optimization problem about sensing threshold is given as follows

$$\max_{\lambda} R(\lambda) = \mathcal{P}_0 \sum_{l=1}^{L} \text{lb}\left(1 + \frac{p_l h_l^2}{\sigma_l^2}\right)\left(1 - P_l^f(\lambda_l)\right)$$

$$s.t. \quad \mathcal{P}_1 \sum_{l=1}^{L} \text{lb}\left(1 + \frac{p_l h_l^2}{\sigma_l^2(1 + \gamma_l)}\right)\left(1 - P_l^d(\lambda_l)\right) \le \varepsilon; \tag{11}$$

$$\begin{cases} P_l^f \le \alpha \\ P_l^d \ge \beta \end{cases} \text{ for } l = 1, 2, ..., L$$

where $p_l = p_{\max}/L$ for $l=1,2,...,L$.

Another conventional scheme is to allocate the uniform threshold and power for each sub-channel, and the throughput of the CR is given as follows

$$R = \mathcal{P}_0 \sum_{l=1}^{L} \text{lb}\left(1 + \frac{p_{\max} h_l^2}{L\sigma_l^2}\right)\left(1 - P_l^f(\lambda)\right) \tag{12}$$

where λ is obtained by the equation as follows

$$\sum_{l=1}^{L} \text{lb}\left(1 + \frac{p_{\max} h_l^2}{L\sigma_l^2(1 + \gamma_l)}\right)\left(1 - P_l^d(\lambda)\right) = \varepsilon / \mathcal{P}_1 \tag{13}$$

3.1   Sub-optimization Problem of Sensing Threshold

The optimization problem in (10)is a mixed-variable optimization problem, which is usually NP-hard to solve directly. As in [8],the bi-level optimization method is adopted to find the optimal approximate solution, which divides (10) into two single-variable convex optimization sub-problems. If p is given, as the upper level, the optimization problem about λ is given by

$$\max_{\lambda} R(\lambda) = \mathcal{P}_0 \sum_{l=1}^{L} r_l^0 \left(1 - P_l^f(\lambda_l)\right)$$

$$s.t. \quad (a)\mathcal{P}_1 \sum_{l=1}^{L} r_l^1 \left(1 - P_l^d(\lambda_l)\right) \leq \varepsilon; \ (b) \begin{cases} P_l^f \leq \alpha \\ P_l^d \geq \beta \end{cases} \text{for } l = 1, 2, ..., L \tag{14}$$

According to(5), with the constraints $P_l^f(\lambda_l) \leq \alpha$ and $P_l^d(\lambda_l) \geq \beta$, the minimum $\lambda_l^{\min}$ and the maximum $\lambda_l^{\max}$ of the sensing threshold in sub-channel l are respectively given as follows

$$\begin{cases} \lambda_l^{\min} = \left(Q^{-1}(\alpha)/\sqrt{M} + 1\right)\sigma_l^2 \\ \lambda_l^{\max} = \left(Q^{-1}(\beta)\sqrt{2\gamma_l + 1}/\sqrt{M} + \gamma_l + 1\right)\sigma_l^2 \end{cases} \tag{15}$$

By substituting (15)into (14), the optimization problem is rewritten as follows

$$\min_{\lambda} \sum_{l=1}^{L} r_l^0 P_l^f(\lambda_l)$$

$$s.t. \quad (a) \sum_{l=1}^{L} r_l^1 \left(1 - P_l^d(\lambda_l)\right) \leq \varepsilon / \mathcal{P}_1 \tag{16}$$

$$(b) \ \lambda_l^{\min} \leq \lambda_l \leq \lambda_l^{\max} \text{ for } l = 1, 2, ..., L$$

To solve optimization problem(16), we firstly prove that (16)is a convex optimization problem.

Lemma 1. *If* $\alpha \leq 0.5$ *and* $\beta \geq 0.5$, $P_l^f(\lambda_l)$ *and* $P_l^d(\lambda_l)$ *are convex and concave functions about* λ_l *respectively.*

Proof. See appendix A.

From Lemma 1, we also know that $1 - P_l^d(\lambda_l)$ is convex. Note that the nonnegative weighed sum of a set of convex functions is also convex[8], and therefore both of the objective function and the nonlinear constraint (a) are convex. Hence, (16) is a convex optimization problem.

Lagrange multiplier method is used to obtain the optimal solution to(16). Considering the objective function and the constraint (a), the Lagrange optimization function about the threshold vector $\boldsymbol{\lambda}$ is given by

$$\psi(\boldsymbol{\lambda}) = \sum_{l=1}^{L} r_l^0 P_l^f\left(\lambda_l\right) + \mu\left(\sum_{l=1}^{L} r_l^1\left(1 - P_l^d\left(\lambda_l\right)\right) - \varepsilon/\mathcal{P}_1\right) \tag{17}$$

where $\mu > 0$ is the Lagrange coefficient. The optimal solution to(17) can be obtained by

$$\left.\frac{\partial\psi(\boldsymbol{\lambda})}{\partial\lambda_l}\right|_{\lambda_l} = 0, \quad l = 1, 2, \ldots, L \tag{18}$$

where we derive λ_l as follows

$$\lambda_l = \frac{\sigma_l^2}{2}\left(1 + \sqrt{1 + 2\gamma_l + \frac{8\gamma_l + 4}{M\gamma_l}\ln\left(\frac{r_l^0}{\mu r_l^1}\sqrt{2\gamma_l + 1}\right)}\right), \quad l = 1, 2, \ldots, L \tag{19}$$

where μ can be obtained by substituting(19) into the constraint (a) in(16). Since the linear constraint $\lambda_l^{\min} \leq \lambda_l \leq \lambda_l^{\max}$ must be satisfied, the optimal solution to(16) is given by

$$\lambda_l^* = \begin{cases} \lambda_l^{\min}, & \text{if } \lambda_l < \lambda_l^{\min} \\ \lambda_l, & \text{if } \lambda_l^{\min} \leq \lambda_l \leq \lambda_l^{\max}, \quad l = 1, 2, \ldots, L. \\ \lambda_l^{\max}, & \text{if } \lambda_l > \lambda_l^{\max} \end{cases} \tag{20}$$

3.2   Sub-optimization Problem of Sub-channel Power

When the optimal sensing threshold is obtained by(20), the next step is to optimize the sub-channel power, which is seen as the lower level. If $\boldsymbol{\lambda}$ is given, the optimization problem (10)is transformed into a single-variable optimization problem about $\boldsymbol{p}$

$$\max_{p} R(p) = \mathcal{P}_0 \sum_{l=1}^{L} \left(1 - P_l^f\right) \mathrm{lb}\left[1 + \frac{p_l h_l^2}{\sigma_l^2}\right]$$

$$s.t. \quad (a) \sum_{l=1}^{L} \left(1 - P_l^d\right) \mathrm{lb}\left[1 + \frac{p_l h_l^2}{\sigma_l^2(1 + \gamma_l)}\right] \le \varepsilon/\mathcal{P}_1; \qquad (21)$$

$$(b) \sum_{l=1}^{L} p_l \le p_{\max}; \quad (c) p_l \ge 0, l = 1, 2, ..., L.$$

Since $\mathrm{lb}(x)$ is a convex function, it is easily known that both of the objective function and the nonlinear constraint (a) are convex. Hence, the problem (21) is also a convex optimization. Considering the objective function and the constraints (a) and (b), the Lagrange optimization function about the power vector p is given by

$$\varphi(p) = \sum_{l=1}^{L} \left(1 - P_l^f\right) \mathrm{lb}\left[1 + \frac{p_l h_l^2}{\sigma_l^2}\right] -$$
$$\mu_1 \left(\sum_{l=1}^{L} \left(1 - P_l^d\right) \mathrm{lb}\left[1 + \frac{p_l h_l^2}{\sigma_l^2(1 + \gamma_l)}\right] - \varepsilon/\mathcal{P}_1\right) - \mu_2 \left(\sum_{l=1}^{L} p_l - p_{\max}\right) \qquad (22)$$

where $\mu_1 > 0$ and $\mu_2 > 0$ are both the Lagrange coefficients. The optimal solution to (22) is obtained by

$$\left.\frac{\partial \varphi(p)}{\partial p_l}\right|_{p_l} = 0, \quad l = 1, 2, ..., L \qquad (23)$$

By substituting (22)into(23), we get the solution as

$$p_l = \frac{1}{2\mu_2} \sqrt{\left(A_l - B_l\right)^2 + \frac{2\mu_2 \gamma_l \sigma_l^2}{h_l^2}\left(A_l + B_l\right) + \frac{\mu_2^2 \gamma_l^2 \sigma_l^4}{h_l^4}} +$$
$$\frac{A_l - B_l}{2\mu_2} - \frac{\left(1 + 0.5\gamma_l\right)\sigma_l^2}{h_l^2}, \qquad l = 1, 2, ..., L \qquad (24)$$

where $A_l = 1 - P_l^f$ and $B_l = 1 - P_l^d$; μ_1 and μ_2 are obtained by substituting (24) into the constraints (a) and (b), respectively. According to(24), especially if $\gamma_l \approx 0$ and $P_l^d \approx 1$, the CR can use all the sub-channels with the sub-channel power as follows

$$p_l = \frac{A_l}{\mu_2} - \frac{\sigma_l^2}{h_l^2}, \quad l = 1, 2, ..., L \qquad (25)$$

which is the conventional water-filling algorithm in multi-channel system. Since the constraint $p_l \ge 0$ is needed, the optimal solution to(21) is given by

$$p_l^* = \max\left\{p_l, 0\right\}, l = 1, 2, ..., L. \qquad (26)$$

The bi-level optimization method is applied to solve the optimization problem(10), where the upper level problem (14)and the lower level problem (21)are alternately optimized until the objective value is converged [20]. The optimal joint allocation algorithm of λ and p is described in Table 1.

Table 1. Optimal joint sensing threshold and sub-channel power allocation

Algorithm 1: Joint allocation algorithm
1.   Initialize: $p^{(0)}$ ($p_l^{(0)} = p_{\max}\big/L$ for $l=1,2,...,L$), the iteration number $k=0$ and the estimation error $\delta = 10^{-3}$;
2.   Fixing $p^{(k)}$, calculate $\lambda^* = \{\lambda_l^*\}_{l=1}^L$ by(20);
3.   Set $\lambda^{(k+1)} = \lambda^*$;
4.   Fixing $\lambda^{(k+1)}$, calculate $p^* = \{p_l^*\}_{l=1}^L$ by(26);
5.   Set $p^{(k+1)} = p^*$ and $k=k+1$;
6.   Repeat 2~5 until $\left|\lambda^{(k)} - \lambda^{(k-1)}\right| \le \delta$ and $\left|p^{(k)} - p^{(k-1)}\right| \le \delta$;
7.   Output: $\lambda^* = \lambda^{(k)}$ and $p^* = p^{(k)}$.

4   Simulations and Discussions

In this section, we numerically evaluate the proposed joint optimization scheme. It is assumed that the number of the sub-channels $L=10$, the number of the sampling nodes $M=128$, the noise variance $\sigma_l^2 = 0.01\text{mW}$, the received SNR $\gamma_l = -10 \sim 0\text{dB}$, the upper limit of false alarm probability $\alpha = 0.5$, the lower limit of detection probability $\beta = 0.8$, and the maximal total power $p_{\max} = 100\text{mW}$.

Let us study the performance of the different sensing schemes in multi-channel CR. The proposed joint optimization algorithm of sensing threshold and sub-band power(A1) is examined by comparing with two other algorithms: the threshold optimization algorithm with a uniform power of each sub-channel proposed in [5] (A2), and the conventional scheme with the uniform threshold and power of each sub-channel (A3). The throughput of the proposed joint optimization algorithm is calculated by Algorithm 1, the throughput of the algorithm in [5] is calculated by (11), and the throughput of the conventional scheme is calculated by (12).

Fig. 2 compares the throughput of the three algorithms mentioned above with the same gain -10dB of each sub-channel. It is seen that the performances of the proposed joint optimization and the threshold optimization with the uniform power are nearly same, because the proposed power allocation is related to the gain of each sub-channel, and therefore the performance of the joint optimization make slight improvement if the sub-channel gain is same. However, the performance of the joint optimization is much better than that of the conventional scheme with the uniform threshold and power, because the threshold optimization improves detection performance greatly.

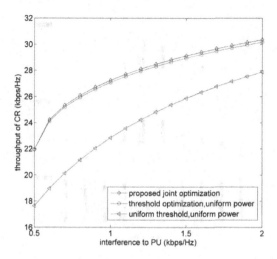

Fig. 2. Throughput of CR with the same gain for each sub-channel

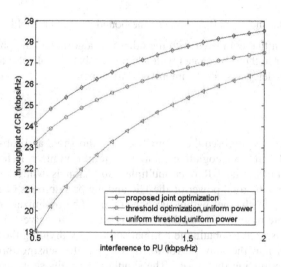

Fig. 3. Throughput of CR with the different gains for each sub-channel

Fig. 3 indicates the throughput comparison of the CR with different gains for each sub-channel as [-4,-8,-10,-12,-20,-20,-12,-10,-6,-4]dB. It is seen that the performance of the proposed joint optimization is much better than the other two. In Fig. 2 and Fig. 3, the throughput is improved with the increase of the interference because the probabilities of false alarm and detection have the same monotony. Fig. 4shows the probabilities of false alarm and miss detection and the power of each sub-channel achieved by the three algorithms mentioned above. Since $P_d \geq \beta = 0.8$, we have $P_m \leq 0.2$. It is seen that the sensing probabilities of the proposed joint optimization algorithm is kept within their

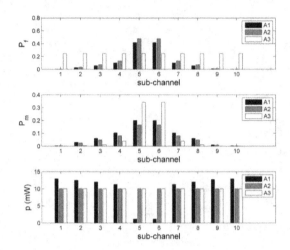

Fig. 4. The probabilities of false alarm and detection and the power of each sub-channel

limits, i.e., $P_f \le 0.5$ and $P_m \le 0.2$, because the bound of the threshold is constrained in (15). It is also seen that compared with the other two algorithms, the proposed one can allocate less power to the sub-channel with a higher probability of false alarm (or higher probability of miss detection) for the improved throughput.

5   Conclusion

In this paper, we have proposed the optimal sensing threshold and sub-channel power allocation in multi-channel cognitive radio. The joint optimization has achieved the maximal throughput of the CR over multiple sub-channels while keeping the total interference to PU, the total power of the CR and the probabilities of false alarm and detection of each sub-channel within the constraints. The optimization is formulated as a mixed-variable optimization problem that is NP-hard to solve. The bi-level optimization method is used to obtain the optimal solution by dividing the proposed optimization problem into the upper level for optimizing the sensing threshold and the lower lever for optimizing the power. The simulation results show that the proposed joint optimization can achieve desirable improvement on the throughput at the different sub-channel gain by allocating less power to the sub-channel with a higher probability of false alarm.

Appendix A

Proof: Taking the second derivatives of $P_l^f(\lambda_l)$ and $P_l^d(\lambda_l)$, respectively, in λ_l from(5), we have

$$\frac{\partial^2 P_l^f}{\partial^2 \lambda_l} = \frac{\left(\lambda_l - \sigma_l^2\right) M^{1.5}}{\sigma_l^6 \sqrt{2\pi}} \exp\left(-\frac{M}{2}\left(\frac{\lambda_l}{\sigma_l^2} - 1\right)^2\right) \tag{27}$$

$$\frac{\partial^2 P_l^d}{\partial^2 \lambda_l} = \frac{\left(\lambda_l - \left(\gamma_l + 1\right)\sigma_l^2\right) M^{1.5}}{\sigma_l^6 \sqrt{2\pi \left(2\gamma_l + 1\right)^3}} \exp\left(-\frac{M}{4\gamma_l + 2}\left(\frac{\lambda_l}{\sigma_l^2} - \gamma_l - 1\right)^2\right). \tag{28}$$

Since $\alpha \leq 0.5$ and $\beta \geq 0.5$, we have the constraint from (15),

$$\sigma_l^2 \leq \lambda_l \leq \sigma_l^2 \left(\gamma_l + 1\right). \tag{29}$$

By substituting (29) into (27)and (28), respectively, we have

$$\frac{\partial^2 P_l^f(\lambda_l)}{\partial^2 \lambda_l} \geq 0, \quad \frac{\partial^2 P_l^d(\lambda_l)}{\partial^2 \lambda_l} \leq 0 \tag{30}$$

which indicates that $P_l^f(\lambda_l)$ and $P_l^d(\lambda_l)$ are convex and concave in λ_l respectively.

References

1. Mitola, J., Maguire, G.Q.: Cognitive radio: making software radios more personal. IEEE Person. Communication 6(4), 13–18 (1999)
2. Haykin, S.: Cognitive radio: brain-empowered wireless communications. IEEE Journal on Selected Areas in Communications 23(2), 201–220 (2005)
3. Urkowitz, H.: Energy detection of unknown deterministic signals. Proceedings of the IEEE 55(4), 523–531 (1967)
4. Zhang, S.Q., Wu, T.Y., Vincent, K.N.: A low-overhead energy detection based cooperative sensing protocol for cognitive radio systems. IEEE Transactions on Wireless Communications 8(11), 5575–5581 (2009)
5. Quan, Z., Cui, S., Sayed, A.H., Poor, H.V.: Optimal multiband joint detection for spectrum sensing in cognitive radio networks. IEEE Trans. Signal Process. 57(3), 1128–1140 (2009)
6. Quan, Z., Cui, S., Sayed, A.H., Poor, H.V.: Wideband Spectrum Sensing in Cognitive Radio Networks. In: IEEE International Conference on Communications (ICC), Beijing, China, pp. 901–906 (May 2008)
7. Liu, X., Tan, X.Z.: Optimization for weighed cooperative spectrum sensing in cognitive radio network. Applied Computational Electromagnetics Society Journal 26(10), 800–814 (2011)
8. Boyd, S., Vandenberghe, L.: Convex Optimization. Cambridge Univ. Press, Cambridge (2003)

Crosstalk-Steady Receivers
for Small-Scale WCAN Networks

Evgeny Bakin, Konstantin Gurnov, and Grigory Evseev

State University of Aerospace Instrumentation (SUAI), St. Petersburg, Russia
{jenyb,kocta4212,egs}@vu.spb.ru

Abstract. In the paper we consider small-scale wireless chip-area network (WCAN), consisting with a few couples of simplex communicating devices. In WCAN ultra-wideband technologies are usually used. Since all the couples operate in one frequency band performance of such communication system can sufficiently suffer from crosstalk. We proposed two receivers, named Maximum A-Posteriori (MAP) and Max-Log-MAP, considering crosstalk structure. Simulation results show, that usage of proposed receivers can significantly increase maximum date rate in the system comparing to conventional correlation receiver.

Keywords: Wireless Chip Area Network, WCAN, Ultra-wideband, UWB, Crosstalk, MAP, Max-Log-MAP.

1 Introduction

Rapid growth of complexity of modern digital electronic devices brings to increasing of density of chips on board and requirements to data rates between them. Conventionally used wired communication channel faces more and more limitations due to influence of printed circuit board (PCB) material frequency properties and traces configuration [1,2,3]. Wireless communication between chips is an attractive alternative to wired communication. This caused a born of new communication system type, Wireless Chip Area Networks (WCAN) [4,5]. According to this idea, chips which critical placement does not allow to use conventional communication channels, are to be equipped with wireless transceivers. Hence, wireless network of chips appears in case of device [5].

Usually for wireless inter-chip communication Ultra Wide-Band schemes are proposed because of their ability to achieve high data rates on short distances. In these schemes such modulations types as Binary Phase Shift Keying (BPSK), Pulse Amplitude Modulation (PAM), Pulse Position Modulation (PPM) are usually used [6,7]. Choice of particular modulation depends on channel properties and requirements to data rate and reliability. In this paper pulse-position modulation is considered as one of the most widely used [7,8].

WCAN has the following important features:

1. Chips are closely situated.
2. In the device case channel is static and some parameters of channel responses between chips can be measured in advance.

V. Tsaoussidis et al. (Eds.): WWIC 2013, LNCS 7889, pp. 262–275, 2013.

3. Number of chips in network is relatively small.
4. Since complex electronic device usually has plugged power supply, transceiver energy consumption is not critical.
5. WCAN transceiver has to be cheap and simple for not to overcome cost of equipped chip.

Unfortunately in devoted papers WCAN systems are considered as conventional UWB networks and described features are not completely taken into account. For example, channel is considered to be unknown and its properties are not used in the receivers. Also, crosstalk is usually assumed to normalize but in WCAN this assumption can be frequently violated due to feature 3. In this paper it will be shown that appropriate usage of the features can sufficiently improve performance of WCAN systems. Especially we focus on consideration of specifics in crosstalk structure for mitigating error floor effect, typical for conventional UWB receivers working in WCAN environment.

The remainder of the paper is organized as follows. In Section 2, we outline the considered modulation scheme and the network model. In Section 3 conventional correlation receiver is described. In Section 4 we propose MAP and Max-Log-MAP receivers which use information about structure of crosstalk between communicating chips. In Section 5 simulation results are given. Finally, some conclusions are given in Section 6.

2 System Description

2.1 Pulse-Position Modulation

Let us describe PPM scheme used in investigated WCAN UWB system. In PPM time is divided into frames with duration T_f. Each frame is divided into M slots with duration T_s ($M \geq 2, T_f = MT_s$). In each frame transmitter pseudo randomly chooses number of slot for symbol transmission. If transmitted symbol is equal to 0, then short pulse is transmitted in left sub-slot of chosen slot, otherwise in right sub-slot. Usually PN repetition code with rate $1/N$ is used in such systems. Hence, one information bit is transmitted during N frames ($M \times N$ slots) and data rate is $\frac{1}{MNT_s}$ bps (see fig. 1) [7].

Corresponding PPM transmitter is shown in figure 2. It consists of two pseudo random numbers generators (PRNG1 for PN repetition coder, PRNG2 for slot in frame choice), coder and pulse-delay modulator.

Here b_i denotes $i - th$ information bit ($b_i \in \{0, 1\}$, usually in communication systems preliminary scrambling is used, making b_i uniformly distributed), $n_{i,1}, n_{i,2}, \ldots, n_{i,N}$ - PN sequence, generated for $i - th$ information bit transmission, $c_{i,1}, c_{i,2}, \ldots, c_{i,N}$ - corresponding sequence of code symbols ($c_{i,j} = b_i \oplus n_{i,j}, j = \overline{1, N}$), $\Delta_{i,j}$ - number of slot in frame for transmission of $j - th$ code symbol of $i - th$ information bit. Then, transmitted signal can be expressed in the following way:

$$s_{TX}(t) = \sum_i \sum_{j=1}^N h\left(t - iNT_f - jMT_s - \Delta_{i,j}T_s - c_{i,j}\frac{T_s}{2}\right) \qquad (1)$$

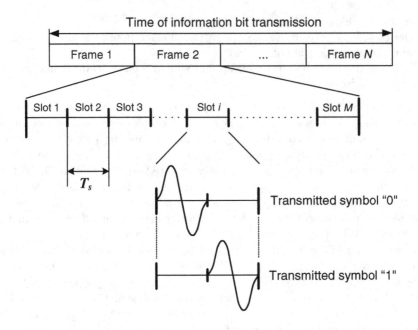

Fig. 1. Time diagram of pulse position modulation

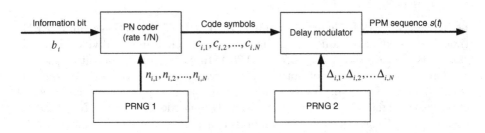

Fig. 2. PPM transmitter

Here $h(t)$ denotes shape of pulse, used for code symbols transmission. Usually $h(t)$ can be approximated with gaussian monocycle [7]. Duration of $h(t)$ doesn't exceed $\frac{T_s}{2}$. For the sake of brevity let us refer to $\tau_{i,j}$ as a beginning of slot for j-th code symbol of i-th information bit transmission ($\tau_{i,j} = iNT_f + jMT_s + \Delta_{i,j}T_s$).

2.2 Communication Channel Model

In considered WCAN system the whole set of chips can be split up into K couples of chips in each of which unidirectional point-to-point communication is set up. Since all the couples operate in one frequency band, mixture of all K signals present at receiving chip. Let us discuss structure of this mixture.

Within each couple chips are strictly synchronized. It means that at transmitting chip and at receiving chip PRNGs work synchronously and bounds of frames and slots are perfectly known on receiving side. This can be achieved by means of initial synchronization procedure which is set up immediately after device turning on [10,11]. However, slots bounds of particular couples can be shifted relatively to each other due to dispersion of delays in signal propagation (see fig. 3).

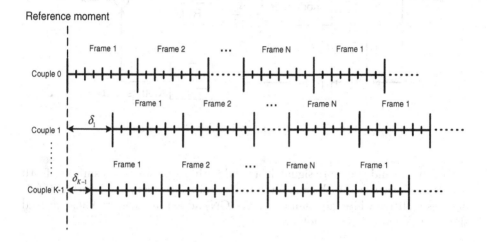

Fig. 3. Slots bounds relation between couples

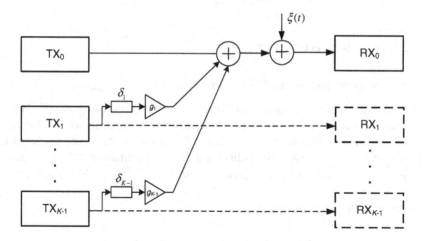

Fig. 4. Model of communication system

Due to different path losses transmitted signals are summed in receiver with different weights. In figure 4 we show used model of system if parameters of channel (delay and pathloss), connecting couple number 0 are chosen as reference.

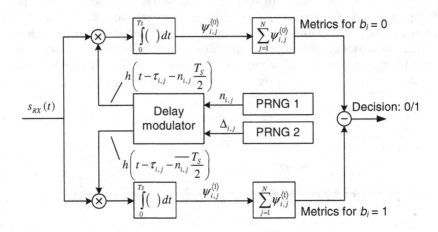

Fig. 5. Correlation receiver for PPM signal

In figure δ_i and g_i denote signal delay and pathloss between transmitter of i-th couple and receiver of 0-th couple relatively to it's own delay and pathloss. $\xi(t)$ denotes additive white gaussian noise (AWGN) added in receiver. Thus received signal can be expressed as follows:

$$s_{RX}(t) = s_0(t) + \sum_{k=1}^{K-1} g_k s_k(t - \delta_k) + \xi(t) \tag{2}$$

3   Correlation Receiver

Usually in papers devoted to UWB distortion $\eta(t) = \sum_{k=1}^{K-1} g_k s_k(t - \delta_k) + \xi(t)$ in (2) is considered to normalize due to large K and intensive $\xi(t)$ [12]. Hence, correlation receiver would be an optimal one in sense of minimization of bit-error rate (BER). In correlation receiver (see fig. 5, where its structure is given) for each i-th bit correlation coefficients between received signal and reference signals for transmitted bits 0 and 1 are chosen as metrics ($\Psi_i^{(0)}$ and $\Psi_i^{(1)}$ respectively) (see fig. 5).

Let us consider structure of correlation receiver metrics.

$$\Psi_i^{(0)} = \int_{iNT_f}^{(i+1)NT_f} (s_0(t) + \eta(t)) \sum_{j=1}^{N} h\left(t - \tau_{i,j} - n_{i,j}\frac{T_s}{2}\right) dt =$$

$$= \int_{iNT_f}^{(i+1)NT_f} s_0(t) \sum_{j=1}^{N} h\left(t - \tau_{i,j} - n_{i,j}\frac{T_s}{2}\right) dt + \int_{iNT_f}^{(i+1)NT_f} \eta(t) \sum_{j=1}^{N} h\left(t - \tau_{i,j} - n_{i,j}\frac{T_s}{2}\right) dt$$

Let us consider first term of the sum.

$$\int\limits_{iNT_f}^{(i+1)NT_f} s_0(t) \sum_{j=1}^{N} h\left(t - \tau_{i,j} - n_{i,j}\frac{T_s}{2}\right) dt = \sum_{j=1}^{N} \int\limits_{\tau_{i,j}}^{\tau_{i,j}+T_s} s_0(t) h\left(t - \tau_{i,j} - n_{i,j}\frac{T_s}{2}\right) dt =$$

$$= \sum_{j=1}^{N} \int\limits_{\tau_{i,j}}^{\tau_{i,j}+T_s} h\left(t - \tau_{i,j} - c_{i,j}\frac{T_s}{2}\right) h\left(t - \tau_{i,j} - n_{i,j}\frac{T_s}{2}\right) dt$$

Each term of the sum is equal to $\int_0^{T_s} h^2(t)dt = E$ if $b_i = 0$ and equal to zero otherwise (here E denotes energy of one pulse).

Considering the second term:

$$\int\limits_{iNT_f}^{(i+1)NT_f} \eta(t) \sum_{j=1}^{N} h\left(t - \tau_{i,j} - n_{i,j}\frac{T_s}{2}\right) dt = \sum_{j=1}^{N} \int\limits_{\tau_{i,j}}^{\tau_{i,j}+T_s} \eta(t) h\left(t - \tau_{i,j} - n_{i,j}\frac{T_s}{2}\right) dt =$$

$$= \sum_{j=1}^{N} \int\limits_{\tau_{i,j}}^{\tau_{i,j}+T_s} \left[\sum_{k=1}^{K-1} g_k s_k (t - \delta_k) + \xi(t)\right] h\left(t - \tau_{i,j} - n_{i,j}\frac{T_s}{2}\right) dt =$$

$$= \sum_{j=1}^{N} \left[\sum_{k=1}^{K-1} \int\limits_{\tau_{i,j}}^{\tau_{i,j}+T_s} g_k s_k (t - \delta_k) h\left(t - \tau_{i,j} - n_{i,j}\frac{T_s}{2}\right) dt + \int\limits_{\tau_{i,j}}^{\tau_{i,j}+T_s} \xi(t) h\left(t - \tau_{i,j} - n_{i,j}\frac{T_s}{2}\right) dt\right] =$$

$$= \sum_{j=1}^{N} \left[\sum_{k=1}^{K-1} x_{k,i,j}^{\langle 0 \rangle} + \xi_{i,j}^{\langle 0 \rangle}\right]$$

Here $x_{k,i,j}^{\langle 0 \rangle}$ reflects impact of cross-talk interfering signal from k-th chip on output of correlator, adjusted for $b_i = 0$, $\xi_{i,j}^{\langle 0 \rangle}$ - impact of AWGN.

Finally,

$$\Psi_i^{\langle 0 \rangle} = \sum_{j=1}^{N} \psi_{i,j}^{\langle 0 \rangle} \tag{3}$$

where,

$$\psi_{i,j}^{\langle 0 \rangle} = \begin{cases} E + \sum_{k=1}^{K-1} x_{k,i,j}^{\langle 0 \rangle} + \xi_{i,j}^{\langle 0 \rangle} & \text{if } b_i = 0 \\ \sum_{k=1}^{K-1} x_{k,i,j}^{\langle 0 \rangle} + \xi_{i,j}^{\langle 0 \rangle} & \text{otherwise} \end{cases} \tag{4}$$

Similarly,

$$\Psi_i^{\langle 1 \rangle} = \sum_{j=1}^{N} \psi_{i,j}^{\langle 1 \rangle} \tag{5}$$

where,

$$\psi_{i,j}^{\langle 1 \rangle} = \begin{cases} E + \sum_{k=1}^{K-1} x_{k,i,j}^{\langle 1 \rangle} + \xi_{i,j}^{\langle 1 \rangle} & \text{if } b_i = 1 \\ \sum_{k=1}^{K-1} x_{k,i,j}^{\langle 1 \rangle} + \xi_{i,j}^{\langle 1 \rangle} & \text{otherwise} \end{cases} \tag{6}$$

In each frame receiver chooses slot in which current symbol is transmitted (it is possible, since PRNG2 works synchronously at receiver and transmitter). In this slot correlation coefficient between current part of $s_{RX}(t)$ and reference signals for information bit 0 and information bit 1 are found ($\psi_{i,j}^{\langle 0 \rangle}$ and $\psi_{i,j}^{\langle 1 \rangle}$ respectively). Summing over all N frames we obtain metrics for information bit 0 and for information bit 1.

Unfortunately in particular case of wireless inter-chip communication distortion $\eta(t)$ doesn't tend to normalize (see features 1 and 3 from Introduction). Crosstalk $\sum\limits_{k=1}^{K-1} g_k s_k (t - \delta_k)$, which distribution can be quite far from gaussian dominates in the mixture. Thus performance of the receiver can be sufficiently improved by means of accurate accounting of distribution of $\psi_{i,j}^{\langle 0 \rangle}$ and $\psi_{i,j}^{\langle 1 \rangle}$ instead of simple summing over all N.

4   Effective Demodulators in Presence of Crosstalk

4.1   MAP Receiver

In the work we propose to use outputs $\psi_{i,j}^{\langle 0 \rangle}$ and $\psi_{i,j}^{\langle 1 \rangle}$ for producing smarter metrics than direct summing as in correlation receiver. By definition Maximum A-Posteriori receiver (MAP) uses the following metrics:

$$M_i^{\langle 0 \rangle} = p \left(b_i = 0 | \psi_{i,1}^{\langle 0 \rangle}, \ldots, \psi_{i,N}^{\langle 0 \rangle}, \psi_{i,1}^{\langle 1 \rangle}, \ldots, \psi_{i,N}^{\langle 1 \rangle} \right)$$
$$M_i^{\langle 1 \rangle} = p \left(b_i = 1 | \psi_{i,1}^{\langle 0 \rangle}, \ldots, \psi_{i,N}^{\langle 0 \rangle}, \psi_{i,1}^{\langle 1 \rangle}, \ldots, \psi_{i,N}^{\langle 1 \rangle} \right)$$

Here $p()$ denotes conditional probability density function (PDF). Thus the decision rule can be expressed as follows:

$$\hat{b}_i = \arg \max_{b \in \{0,1\}} p \left(b_i = b | \psi_{i,1}^{\langle 0 \rangle}, \ldots, \psi_{i,N}^{\langle 0 \rangle}, \psi_{i,1}^{\langle 1 \rangle}, \ldots, \psi_{i,N}^{\langle 1 \rangle} \right) \qquad (7)$$

Since in transmitter scrambler of data is usually used, $Pr\{b_i = 0\} = Pr\{b_i = 1\} = 1/2$. Hence, using Bayes formula rule (7) can be rearranged as follows:

$$\hat{b}_i = \arg \max_{b \in \{0,1\}} p \left(\psi_{i,1}^{\langle 0 \rangle}, \ldots, \psi_{i,N}^{\langle 0 \rangle}, \psi_{i,1}^{\langle 1 \rangle}, \ldots, \psi_{i,N}^{\langle 1 \rangle} | b_i = b \right)$$

Assuming, that PRNG1 and PRNG2 produce sequences of independent random variables initial PDF can be split up into N PDFs:

$$p \left(\psi_{i,1}^{\langle 0 \rangle}, \ldots, \psi_{i,N}^{\langle 0 \rangle}, \psi_{i,1}^{\langle 1 \rangle}, \ldots, \psi_{i,N}^{\langle 1 \rangle} | b_i = b \right) = \prod_{j=1}^{N} p \left(\psi_{i,j}^{\langle 0 \rangle}, \psi_{i,j}^{\langle 1 \rangle} | b_i = b \right) \qquad (8)$$

For further processing of terms $p \left(\psi_{i,j}^{\langle 0 \rangle}, \psi_{i,j}^{\langle 1 \rangle} | b_i = b \right)$ in (8) let us study structure of distortion $\eta(t)$ deeper.

In each frame each of the $K - 1$ signals transmitted by the other stations $(s_1(t), \ldots, s_{K-1}(t))$ may interfere with information signal $(s_0(t))$ in one of four ways (see figure 6):

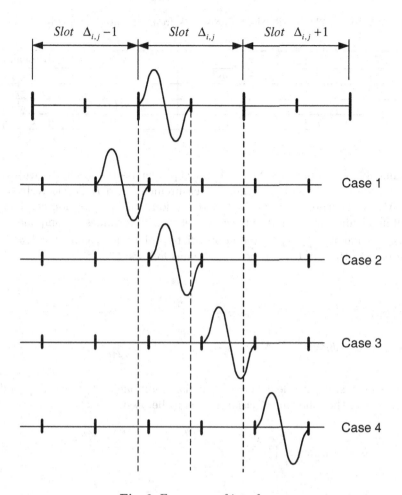

Fig. 6. Four cases of interference

1. interfering pulse impacts left sub-slot;
2. interfering pulse impacts both sub-slots;
3. interfering pulse impacts right sub-slot;
4. interfering pulse misses.

Depending on a case four different summands of cross-talk would appear in $\psi_{i,j}^{\langle 0 \rangle}$ and $\psi_{i,j}^{\langle 1 \rangle}$. In table 1 2D distribution of cross-talk is given.

Here $R()$ denotes autocorrelation function of pulse $h(t)$ ($R(\tau) = \int\limits_{-\infty}^{+\infty} h(t)h(t-\tau)dt$). All the couples of chips work independently. Hence, sums $\sum\limits_{k=1}^{K-1} x_{k,i,j}^{\langle 0 \rangle}$ and $\sum\limits_{k=1}^{K-1} x_{k,i,j}^{\langle 1 \rangle}$ in general case have 2D distribution

Table 1. 2D distribution of cross-talk from one interfering chip

Case	$x_{k,i,j}^{\langle 0 \rangle}$	$x_{k,i,j}^{\langle 1 \rangle}$	Probability
1	$R\left(\frac{T_s}{2} - \delta_k\right)$	0	$\frac{1}{2M}$
2	$R\left(\delta_k\right)$	$R\left(\frac{T_s}{2} - \delta_k\right)$	$\frac{1}{2M}$
3	0	$R\left(\delta_k\right)$	$\frac{1}{2M}$
4	0	0	$1 - \frac{3}{2M}$

containing 4^{K-1} components. Since channels properties (delays and pathlosses) can be known by means of preliminary measurements and K is relatively small in WCAN (see features 2, 3 and 5 in Introduction) this distribution can be calculated in advance and stored in receiver. Let us denote values of components in this distribution as $\{v_t^{\langle 0 \rangle}, v_t^{\langle 1 \rangle}\}$ and appropriate probabilities as p_t ($t = \overline{1, 4^{K-1}}$). Hence, each PDF in (8) can be described as follows:

$$p\left(\psi_{i,j}^{\langle 0 \rangle}, \psi_{i,j}^{\langle 1 \rangle} | b_i = 0\right) = \sum_{t=1}^{4^{K-1}} p_t \frac{1}{\sqrt{2\pi}\sigma} e^{-\frac{\left(\psi_{i,j}^{\langle 0 \rangle} - E - v_t^{\langle 0 \rangle}\right)^2}{2\sigma^2}} \frac{1}{\sqrt{2\pi}\sigma} e^{-\frac{\left(\psi_{i,j}^{\langle 1 \rangle} - v_t^{\langle 1 \rangle}\right)^2}{2\sigma^2}}$$

$$p\left(\psi_{i,j}^{\langle 0 \rangle}, \psi_{i,j}^{\langle 1 \rangle} | b_i = 1\right) = \sum_{t=1}^{4^{K-1}} p_t \frac{1}{\sqrt{2\pi}\sigma} e^{-\frac{\left(\psi_{i,j}^{\langle 0 \rangle} - v_t^{\langle 0 \rangle}\right)^2}{2\sigma^2}} \frac{1}{\sqrt{2\pi}\sigma} e^{-\frac{\left(\psi_{i,j}^{\langle 1 \rangle} - E - v_t^{\langle 1 \rangle}\right)^2}{2\sigma^2}}$$

Here σ denotes standard deviation of gaussian components $\xi_{i,j}^{\langle 0 \rangle}$ and $\xi_{i,j}^{\langle 1 \rangle}$ in distortion. Hence, the following decision rule is to be used:

$$
\begin{aligned}
\hat{b}_i &= \arg\max_{b \in \{0,1\}} \prod_{j=1}^{N} \sum_{t=1}^{4^{K-1}} p_t e^{-\frac{\left(\psi_{i,j}^{\langle \overline{b} \rangle} - v_t^{\langle \overline{b} \rangle}\right)^2 + \left(\psi_{i,j}^{\langle b \rangle} - E - v_t^{\langle b \rangle}\right)^2}{2\sigma^2}} = \\
&= \arg\max_{b \in \{0,1\}} \sum_{j=1}^{N} \log \sum_{t=1}^{4^{K-1}} e^{-\frac{\left(\psi_{i,j}^{\langle \overline{b} \rangle} - v_t^{\langle \overline{b} \rangle}\right)^2 + \left(\psi_{i,j}^{\langle b \rangle} - E - v_t^{\langle b \rangle}\right)^2 - 2\sigma^2 \log p_t}{2\sigma^2}}
\end{aligned}
\tag{9}
$$

Unfortunately rule (9) can be too complex for implementation due to necessity to calculate exponents and to know noise deviation σ. However, performance of this receiver can be treated as upper bound of receivers performances for such model.

4.2   Max-Log-MAP Receiver

For simplification of rule (9) the following known approximation can be used [9]:

$$\log\left(e^a + e^b\right) \approx \max(a, b)$$

Hence,

$$
\log \sum_{t=1}^{4^{K-1}} e^{-\frac{\left(\psi_{i,j}^{\langle \bar{b} \rangle} - v_t^{\langle \bar{b} \rangle}\right)^2 + \left(\psi_{i,j}^{\langle b \rangle} - E - v_t^{\langle b \rangle}\right)^2 - 2\sigma^2 \log p_t}{2\sigma^2}} \approx
$$

$$
\approx \frac{1}{2\sigma^2} \max_{t=1,4^{K-1}} - \left[\left(\psi_{i,j}^{\langle \bar{b} \rangle} - v_t^{\langle \bar{b} \rangle}\right)^2 + \left(\psi_{i,j}^{\langle b \rangle} - E - v_t^{\langle b \rangle}\right)^2 - 2\sigma^2 \log p_t \right] =
$$

$$
= -\frac{1}{2\sigma^2} \min_{t=1,4^{K-1}} \left[\left(\psi_{i,j}^{\langle \bar{b} \rangle} - v_t^{\langle \bar{b} \rangle}\right)^2 + \left(\psi_{i,j}^{\langle b \rangle} - E - v_t^{\langle b \rangle}\right)^2 - 2\sigma^2 \log p_t \right]
$$

Rule (9) transforms into:

$$
\arg \max_{b \in \{0,1\}} \sum_{j=1}^{N} \log \sum_{t=1}^{4^{K-1}} e^{-\frac{\left(\psi_{i,j}^{\langle \bar{b} \rangle} - v_t^{\langle \bar{b} \rangle}\right)^2 + \left(\psi_{i,j}^{\langle b \rangle} - E - v_t^{\langle b \rangle}\right)^2 - 2\sigma^2 \log p_t}{2\sigma^2}} \approx
$$

$$
\approx \arg \max_{b \in \{0,1\}} \sum_{j=1}^{N} \left(-\frac{1}{2\sigma^2} \min_{t=1,4^{K-1}} \left[\left(\psi_{i,j}^{\langle \bar{b} \rangle} - v_t^{\langle \bar{b} \rangle}\right)^2 + \left(\psi_{i,j}^{\langle b \rangle} - E - v_t^{\langle b \rangle}\right)^2 - 2\sigma^2 \log p_t \right] \right)
$$

Finally,

$$
\hat{b}_i = \arg \min_{b \in \{0,1\}} \sum_{j=1}^{N} \min_{t=\overline{1,4^{K-1}}} \left[\left(\psi_{i,j}^{\langle \bar{b} \rangle} - v_t^{\langle \bar{b} \rangle}\right)^2 + \left(\psi_{i,j}^{\langle b \rangle} - E - v_t^{\langle b \rangle}\right)^2 - 2\sigma^2 \log p_t \right] \tag{10}
$$

As one can see rule (10) is simpler than rule (9) and more attractive in practice. Note, that in case of high SNR $\sigma \approx 0$ and (10) can be additionally simplified.

$$
\hat{b}_i' = \arg \min_{b \in \{0,1\}} \sum_{j=1}^{N} \min_{t=\overline{1,4^{K-1}}} \left[\left(\psi_{i,j}^{\langle \bar{b} \rangle} - v_t^{\langle \bar{b} \rangle}\right)^2 + \left(\psi_{i,j}^{\langle b \rangle} - E - v_t^{\langle b \rangle}\right)^2 \right] \tag{11}
$$

Summarizing the discussion of the receivers the following table can be represented.

Table 2. Comparison of three receivers

Receiver	Noise variance knowledge	Complexity	Calculation of transcendental functions	Consideration of crosstalk structure
Correlation receiver	Not required	$O(N)$	Not required	No
MAP receiver	Required	$O(N4^{K-1})$	Required	Yes
Max-Log-MAP receiver	Not required	$O(N4^{K-1})$	Not required	Yes

5   Simulation Results

For estimation of efficiency of proposed receivers the simulation with the following typical parameters was performed [12]:

– Number of chips: 10 ($K = 5$).
– Slot duration: $T_s = 1ns$.
– Required $MN = 24$ (data rate $\approx$ 50 Mbps).

The required data rate can be obtained in one of 6 ways ($[M = 2, N = 12], [M = 3, N = 8], [M = 4, N = 6], [M = 6, N = 4], [M = 8, N = 3]$ and $[M = 12, N = 2]$). For three receivers (correlation, MAP and Max-Log-MAP) a set of plots reflecting BER/SNR dependency was built to find optimal M/N ratio (see fig. 7, fig. 8 and fig. 9 respectively). In simulation SNR was determined as ratio of energy of one pulse E to power spectral density of AWGN. In simulation model depicted in figure 4 was used. Pathlosses were assumed to be equal: $g_1 = g_2 = g_3 = 1$, i.e. power level of each component of crosstalk is equal to power level of signal. Delays $\delta_1, \delta_2, \delta_3$ - uniformly distributed random variables in range $\left[0, \frac{T_s}{2}\right]$.

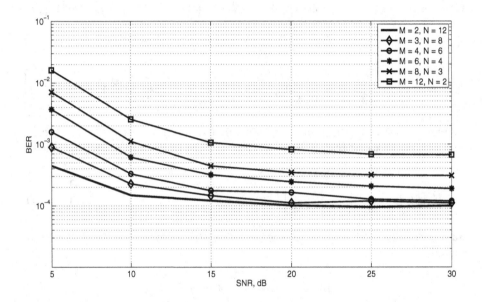

Fig. 7. Correlation receiver

As one can see, for all three types of the receivers combination $[M = 2, N = 12]$ is an optimal one. However, curves for correlation receiver are characterized with error floor, because of its inability to cope with crosstalk even if SNR is quite high. Considering the crosstalk allows breaking error floor to both proposed receivers. In figure 10 the best results for all three receivers are given.

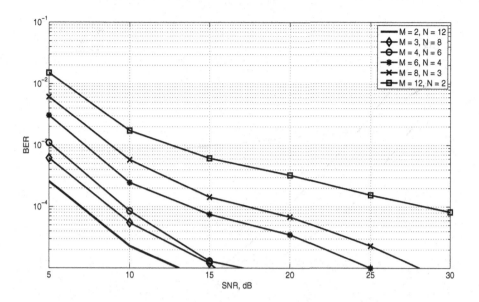

Fig. 8. MAP receiver

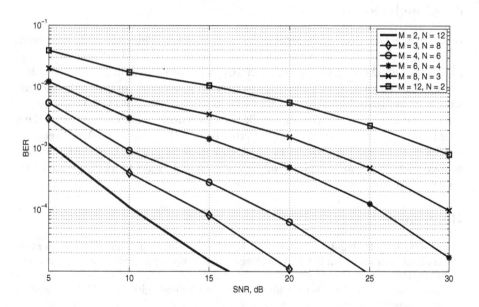

Fig. 9. Max-Log-MAP receiver

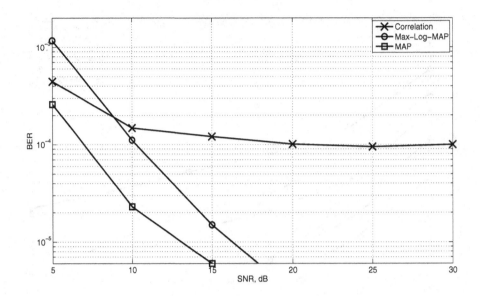

Fig. 10. Comparison of three receivers

6 Conclusion

In the paper three receivers for small-scaled Wireless Chip Area Network were considered: conventional (correlation) and two proposed (MAP and Max-Log-MAP). For all the receivers decision metrics were described and discussed. Simulation showed that conventional receiver heavily suffers from crosstalk and has sufficient data rate limitation even in case of high SNR. However, proposed receivers are able to cope with crosstalk thus increasing maximum possible data rate in system. MAP receiver shows better results than Max-Log-MAP receiver but faces sufficient limitations due to high complexity. Max-Log-MAP receiver is more attractive for practical applications and has no more than 3dB loss relatively to MAP one.

References

1. Moore, S., Sellathamby, C., Iniewski, K.: Chip-to-chip communications for terabit transmission rates. In: IEEE Asia Pacific Conference on Circuits and Systems, pp. 1558–1561 (2008)
2. Carusone, T.: Future chip-to-chip interconnect technologies. In: CMOS Emerging Technologies Spring Conference (2009)
3. Yordanov, H., Russer, P.: Wireless inter-chip and intra-chip communication. In: Proceedings of the 39th European Microwave Conference (2009)
4. Chang, M.F., Roychowdhury, V.P., Zhang, L., Shin, H., Qian, Y.: RF/wireless interconnect for inter- and intra-chip communications. Proc. IEEE 89, 4656–4661 (2001)

5. Chen, Z.M., Zhang, Y.P.: Inter-chip wireless communication channel, measurement, characterization, and modeling, antennas and propagation. IEEE Transactions on Antennas and Propagation, 978–986 (2007)
6. Zhiming, C., Zhang, Y.P.: Bit-error-rate analysis of UWB radio using BPSK modulation over inter-chip radio channels for wireless chip area networks. IEEE Transactions on Antennas and Propagation, 2379–2387 (2009)
7. Zigangirov, K.S.: Theory of Code Division Multiple Access Communication. IEEE Press (2004)
8. Robert, C.Q., Huaping, L., Xuemin, S.: Ultra-Wideband for multiple access communications multiple access technologies for B3G wireless communication. IEEE Communications Magazine (February 2005)
9. Benvenuto, N., Cherubini, G.: Algorithms for Communications Systems and their Applications. John Wiley & Sons Ltd. (2002)
10. Mengali, U., Carbonelli, C.: Synchronization Algorithms for UWB Signals. IEEE Transaction on Communication 54(2) (February 2006)
11. Nekoogar, F., Dowla, F., Spiridon, A.: Rapid Synchronization of Ultra-Wideband Transmitted-Reference Receivers. Wireless 2004 Calgary (2004)
12. Win, M., Scholtz, R.: Ultra-Wide Bandwidth Time-Hopping Spread-Spectrum Impulse Radio for Wireless Multiple-Access Communications. IEEE Transaction on Communication 48(4) (April 2000)

Author Index